P9-CFT-971

D0015216

GUANT

AND THE ABUSE OF

ÁNAMO

PRESIDENTIAL POWER

Joseph Margulies

SIMON & SCHUSTER

NEW YORK • LONDON • TORONTO • SYDNEY

SIMON & SCHUSTER
Rockefeller Center
1230 Avenue of the Americas
New York, NY 10020

SIMON & SCHUSTER and colophon are registered trademarks
of Simon & Schuster, Inc.

For information about special discounts for bulk purchases,
please contact Simon & Schuster Special Sales at
1-800-456-6798 or business@simonandschuster.com

Designed by Dana Sloan

Manufactured in the United States of America

10 9 8 7 6 5 4 3 2 1

Library of Congress Cataloging-in-Publication Data
Margulies, Joseph.
   Guantánamo and the abuse of presidential power / Joseph Margulies.
      p.   cm.
   Includes bibliographical references and index.
   1. War and emergency powers—United States.   2. Prisoners—Civil rights—United
States   3. Due process of law—United States.   4. War on Terrorism, 2001—Law and
legislation—United States.   5. Prisoners of war—Legal status, laws, etc.   6. Guantánamo
Bay Naval Base (Cuba)   7. United States. Marine Corps—Prisons.   I. Title.
KF5060.M373 2006
342.73'062—dc22   2006045633
ISBN-13: 978-0-7432-8685-5
ISBN-10: 0-7432-8685-5

To SLB and DRM

In questions of power, then, let no more be said of confidence in man, but bind him down from mischief by the chains of the Constitution.

—Thomas Jefferson, Kentucky Resolutions of 1798

All men of military genius are fond of centralization, which increases their strength; and all men of centralizing genius are fond of war, which compels nations to combine all their powers in the hands of the government.

—Alexis de Tocqueville, *Democracy in America*

CONTENTS

GUANTÁNAMO
AND THE ABUSE OF
PRESIDENTIAL POWER

PREFACE

We sat at a steel table in one of the small concrete boxes that pass for prison cells at the U.S. naval base at Guantánamo Bay, Cuba. Across from me was my client Mamdouh Habib, an Australian. By order of the U.S. military, Mamdouh sat with his back to the door, forbidden to face the natural light. His feet were shackled together. The shackles were bolted to the floor. At my request, the guards had unshackled his hands. I had spent all day with Mamdouh, and the day before as well. As I got up to leave, Mamdouh took my arm. "I'm dying here, Joe. I'm going to die here. They'll never let me go home." It was the Saturday before Thanksgiving, 2004. He had been a prisoner at Guantánamo since early May 2002.

I sat back down. I had represented Mamdouh almost since he had arrived at the base, even though for most of that time he did not know he had a lawyer. He was part of a lawsuit my colleagues and I filed in 2002 on behalf of four prisoners at Guantánamo. I was lead counsel in that case—*Rasul and others v. George W. Bush*, named for Shafiq Rasul, a British prisoner.* Mamdouh, like the rest of the prisoners at the base, hadn't even known the case was pending. Now, four months after the Supreme Court had ruled in our favor in *Rasul*, he was still at the base. And he had given up hope. He had a wife in Australia, a daughter so young she barely remembered him, and

---

* I would be remiss if I did not immediately recognize my co-counsel: Michael Ratner, Steven Watt, and Barbara Olshansky, of the Center for Constitutional Rights in New York, and Clive Stafford Smith, then in New Orleans. Our case was consolidated with a similar case brought by the law firm of Shearman & Sterling, under the leadership of Tom Wilner, Neil Koslowe, and Kristine Huskey. Together, these two cases would go to the Supreme Court.

three older children who wondered if they'd ever see their father again. "You don't have the luxury of giving up hope," I told him.

On January 28, 2005, Mamdouh stepped carefully down the steel stairs of a Gulfstream jet at Sydney Airport. Stooped and weather-beaten, he looked old for his forty-nine years. As he squinted in the stark Australian sun, he gazed around uneasily, unsure of his bearings. He was home. I had flown with him from Guantánamo in a plane chartered by the Australian government, west from Cuba and across the Pacific Ocean, careful not to cross over into U.S. airspace. I am the only lawyer allowed by the U.S. government to accompany a prisoner home from the base, a courtesy I cannot explain.

An Australian official ushered us toward another plane—a six-seat prop plane idling nearby. Unbeknownst to me, our local counsel in Australia, Stephen Hopper, had arranged to fly us to a small airfield nearby in order to avoid the media scrum in Sydney. As soon as we descended the steps of one plane we were hurried up the steep steps of another. As Mamdouh stepped into the tiny six-seater, he noticed a woman sitting quietly in the rear of the plane, dressed in black pants and a plain white top, her hands nervously folded in her lap. It was his wife, Maha. He had not seen her for more than three years and, for a brief moment, he paused as if stunned by the sight. At Guantánamo, American interrogators had told him his wife was dead, and though he had spoken with her briefly since that lie, the simple sight of his wife shook him deeply. He collapsed in her arms, weeping, as the plane taxied unsteadily down the runway and then rose quickly into the crystalline sky.

I have been a lawyer for many years but few moments in my legal career have been as gratifying as the sight of Mamdouh Habib reunited with his wife. He spent more than three years in prison: six months in a prison outside Cairo (having been delivered by the Americans and tortured by the Egyptians), and more than two years at Guantánamo. He was never charged with any wrongdoing and the government has never defended his detention in open court. As I write this, in the spring of 2006, nearly five hundred prisoners remain at Guantánamo. Hundreds of others are held at facilities all over the world. They, like Mamdouh, are prisoners of the Bush Administration's post-9/11 detention policy. This book is about that policy.

INTRODUCTION

I

Not long after the attacks of September 11, 2001, President George W. Bush warned that the war on terror would be different from other wars that had come before it. "Our war on terror begins with al-Qaeda," he said, "but it does not end there. It will not end until every terrorist group of global reach has been found, stopped and defeated.... Americans should not expect one battle, but a lengthy campaign, unlike any other we have ever seen."[1] The defining, and most controversial, characteristic of the Bush Administration's response to 9/11 has been its policy toward captured prisoners. In that regard, the Administration is certainly correct: the detention policy developed after 9/11 is "unlike any other we have ever seen."

In a speech to the nation on the evening of September 11, 2001, President Bush vowed to "make no distinction between the terrorists who committed these acts and those who harbor them."[2] On October 7, as the ruins of the World Trade Center still smoldered, the United States attacked Afghanistan with the aim of ousting the fundamentalist Taliban regime and destroying the al-Qaeda terrorist network. The campaign in Afghanistan was the center of our immediate response to 9/11, but the war on terror has been a much broader conflict, in a much wider theater.

The Bush Administration maintains that people seized in this conflict may be taken—kidnapped if necessary—from any location in the world, even thousands of miles from any battlefield, without the knowledge or participation of the host government and without any judicial process. They may be shipped to an offshore prison on nothing more than the judgment of a single, anonymous field commander. They may be held for the rest of their lives, based solely on the president's self-asserted authority. At the prison, they can be subjected to any conditions the military devises. And throughout their imprisonment, they may be held incommunicado and in solitary confinement, without access to courts or counsel, without charges of any kind, unknown to the world, and without the benefit of the Geneva Conventions, an international treaty signed and ratified by the United States and designed to protect people seized during armed conflict. The Bush Administration has incarcerated thousands of people in far-flung prisons around the world. Several dozen are being held by the CIA in secret locations unknown to all but a select few. Approximately two hundred others have been rendered to countries with a long history of torturing prisoners.

The most visible—but by no means the only—embodiment of this detention policy is found at the Guantánamo Bay Naval Station, a U.S. military base in Cuba.* Prisoners began to arrive at the base in January 2002. They were initially housed in outdoor cages at a makeshift facility called Camp X-Ray. My clients, David Hicks and Mamdouh Habib of Australia and Shafiq Rasul and Asif Iqbal of England, were among the first to arrive. In April, the prisoners were moved to a new facility, Camp Delta. Modeled on maximum-security prisons in the United States, this facility has a capacity of more than one thousand prisoners.[3]

The prison at Guantánamo was originally intended to serve several purposes. First, it was a prison camp—a place to hold people captured during the conflict. Second, because the Administration originally expected to charge the prisoners with war crimes, the prison was meant to serve as the site where these tribunals would take place. But the third, and by far the most important purpose of the prison, was as an interrogation chamber. Virtually everything about the facility—its location, its design, its day-to-day operation—was intended to serve this last goal.[4]

The detention policy that produced Camp Delta has created a human rights debacle that will eventually take its place alongside other wartime misadventures, including the internment of Japanese-Americans during World War II, the prosecutions under the Espionage and Sedition Acts dur-

---

* Throughout this book I have followed the convention of spelling "Guantánamo" with an accent over the second *a,* except where I quoted a document that spells the word without the accent.

ing World War I, and the suspension of the writ of habeas corpus during the Civil War. The import of this policy was captured by a letter from T. J. Harrington, the deputy assistant director of the FBI Counterterrorism Division, to Major General Donald Ryder of the Army's Criminal Investigation Command. On July 14, 2004, Harrington wrote to advise Ryder of several "situations" observed by FBI agents involving "highly aggressive interrogation techniques being used against detainees in Guantánamo."

Some of the interrogation rooms at Guantánamo have a two-way mirror that allows observers in another room to monitor the interrogation. On one occasion, the interrogator—one Sergeant Lacey—walked into the observation room and ordered a Marine to cover the two-way mirror. The FBI agent present in the observation room immediately suspected this was "an attempt to prohibit those in the observation room from witnessing her [Lacey's] interaction with the detainee." The agent then tried to watch the interrogation through a surveillance camera. Lacey anticipated this as well, and positioned herself between the camera and the prisoner. Harrington recounts what the FBI agent could see of Lacey's "interrogation":

> The detainee was shackled and his hands were cuffed to his waist. S[pecial] A[gent] Clemente [the FBI agent] observed Sgt. Lacey apparently whispering in the detainee's ear, and caressing and applying lotion to his arms (this was during Ramadan when physical contact with a woman would have been particularly offensive to a Moslem male). On more than one occasion the detainee appeared to be grimacing in pain, and Sgt. Lacey's hands appeared to be making some contact with the detainee. Although SA Clemente could not see her hands at all times, he saw them moving towards the detainee's lap. He also observed the detainee pulling away and against the restraints. Subsequently, the marine who had previously taped the curtain [in the observation room] and had been in the interrogation room with Sgt. Lacey during the interrogation re-entered the observation room. SA Clemente asked what had happened to cause the detainee to grimace in pain. The marine said Sgt. Lacey had grabbed the detainee's thumbs and bent them backwards and indicated that she also grabbed his genitals. The marine also implied that her treatment of that detainee was less harsh than her treat-

ment of others by indicating that he had seen her treatment of other detainees result in detainees curling into a fetal position on the floor and crying in pain.[5]

Sergeant Lacey's "interrogation," while disturbing, was not unusual.

Camp Delta has held nearly eight hundred prisoners from more than forty countries, some for the entire four years of its existence. A number of children have been held at the base, including three who were ten, twelve, and thirteen years old at the time of their capture.[6] Nearly five hundred prisoners remain at the facility. What has life in this prison come to mean for them? An answer is suggested by another "situation" described in Harrington's letter.

> In September or October of 2002 FBI agents observed that a canine was used in an aggressive manner to intimidate detainee #63 and, in November 2002, FBI agents observed detainee #63 after he had been subjected to intense isolation for over three months. During that time period, #63 was totally isolated (with the exception of occasional interrogations) in a cell that was always flooded with light. By late November, the detainee was evidencing behavior consistent with extreme psychological trauma (talking to non-existent people, reporting hearing voices, crouching in a corner of the cell covered with a sheet for hours on end).[7]

This was the prison—and these the conditions—my colleagues and I challenged in *Rasul v. Bush*. On June 28, 2004, the United States Supreme Court struck down these lawless detentions, rejecting the Administration's core contention that the prison at Guantánamo was beyond the reach of the law. After *Rasul*, a prisoner at Guantánamo who invokes the authority of the federal court must be released unless the government establishes the lawfulness of his incarceration by a fair process. No person may be imprisoned at Guantánamo without proof, presented before a neutral tribunal, that the incarceration is justified.[8] At least, that's what the decision said. Enforcing this decision is another matter.

· · ·

Since *Rasul,* I have often been asked how I became involved in the case. People seemed perplexed that lead counsel was a lawyer from Minneapolis, rather than, I suppose, someone from either of the two coasts. Perhaps appropriately, then, the best place to start is the Walker Art Center, an acclaimed museum of contemporary art on the western edge of downtown Minneapolis. It stands adjacent to the Minneapolis Sculpture Garden, home of Claes Oldenburg and Coosje van Bruggen's whimsical installation *Spoonbridge and Cherry,* a colorful, quirky, and beloved symbol of the Twin Cities. On November 12, 2001, the Walker, along with the University of Minnesota, sponsored a community forum entitled "Understanding September 11th."

Because of my work as a civil liberties lawyer, I was asked to speak on a panel that examined whether the Bush Administration's response to 9/11 represented a threat to civil liberties. Then, as now, people were concerned with various provisions of the USA-PATRIOT Act, which raced through the House and Senate despite widespread criticism from civil libertarians. Observers were also deeply troubled that the Administration had seized and detained hundreds of Muslims after September 11, but had refused to disclose their names and had closed their immigration proceedings to the public and the press. The event at the Walker was well attended. Several hundred people filled the auditorium; many were deeply skeptical about these and other developments in the newly minted "war on terror."

Despite this, and perhaps to the surprise of the conference organizers, I struck a cautiously optimistic tone. While the PATRIOT Act contained a number of worrisome provisions, nothing in it compared to the Espionage and Sedition Acts, which made it a crime to speak against World War I. Likewise, while the post-9/11 immigration detentions were alarming, at least the detained men and women were represented by counsel, and their cases were proceeding in established federal courts. So far, the Administration had not proposed anything like the debacle of Japanese internment. Perhaps—I hoped—we had learned from our mistakes.

The next day, President Bush announced the plan to try suspected terrorists in military tribunals. As originally contemplated, these trials would use an ad hoc set of rules that bore only a passing resemblance to the procedures used in traditional criminal or military prosecutions. If convicted, defendants would be sentenced to death, with no right to appeal and no review of their conviction or sentence in federal court. The next month, Defense Secretary Donald Rumsfeld announced that the trials would take place at the U.S. naval base at Guantánamo Bay, Cuba. Soon after, Rumsfeld said that prisoners at the base would not be protected by the Geneva Conventions.[9]

I have been a lawyer for nearly twenty years. In that time, I have represented men and women on death row; I have defended people accused of the most serious crimes; I have represented people mistreated or beaten by police officers and prison staff. This meandering career has taken me to courtrooms, prisons, and jails all over the country. But the river that connects the past to the present has been an unwavering belief that in matters of personal liberty, the most important question is not whether the government has the power to incarcerate a person—almost invariably, it does. The proper question is whether that power has been exercised lawfully.

The most important time to ask this question is precisely when the allegations against a person are the most serious, since that is when an aggrieved society feels, quite naturally, the most powerful impulse to suspend the requirements of the law. This creates two problems, one more obvious and tangible than the other. The obvious one is that, in our zeal to see that justice is done, we will deprive an innocent person of his liberty or his life. Since 1973, for instance, 121 people nationwide have been released from death row based on evidence of innocence. In Illinois, where I now live, as many death row inmates in the modern era have been exonerated as have been executed. By any measure, these are not comforting statistics.

But for me, the risk of error in the outcome is not the only evil to be avoided. It is not even the greatest evil. Respect for the rule of law is a virtue in its own right, a virtue that becomes *more* important, rather than less, as the stakes increase. But like other civic virtues, the benefits of the law may not be immediately obvious. In fact, in times of public excitement, strict adherence to the law is often mocked as a frivolous luxury, standing in the way of what is widely perceived as the "just" outcome. Those who call for compliance with the law are often met with scorn and derision, or worse. I have always viewed these criticisms as misguided. The necessity of the cause was stated elegantly and emphatically by Justice Brandeis almost eight decades ago:

In a government of laws, existence of the government will be imperiled if it fails to observe the law scrupulously. Our government is the potent, the omnipresent teacher. For good or for ill, it teaches the whole people by its example. Crime is contagious. If the government becomes a law-breaker, it breeds contempt for law; it invites every man to become a law unto himself; it invites anarchy. To declare that in the administration of the criminal law the end justifies the means—to declare that the government may commit crimes in order to secure the conviction of a private criminal—would bring terrible retribution. Against that pernicious doctrine this court should resolutely set its face.[10]

This is the spirit that has animated the litigation in *Rasul*. The question is not whether the United States has the power to imprison people seized in connection with the war on terror; without doubt the government has such power. The question is, and has always been, whether the exercise of this power would be restrained by the rule of law.

One of the leading authorities on international law and the death penalty is a Minneapolis lawyer named Sandra Babcock.* Her career has followed a trajectory similar to my own, and she had the same reaction as I did to the president's announcement of November 13. She and I immediately arranged a conference call with colleagues around the country who, collectively, had the relevant expertise to challenge these developments, including experts in the laws of war, the death penalty, civil rights, and international human rights. One of the first people we contacted was Michael Ratner, president of the New York–based Center for Constitutional Rights and one of the country's foremost human rights advocates.

The prisoners in Cuba were eventually allowed to send a single-page letter to their families, censored by the United States and delivered by the International Red Cross. Australian David Hicks wrote to his father, Terry. He in turn contacted Adelaide lawyer Stephen Kenny, who then contacted us. In late January 2002, at the Center for Constitutional Rights in New York, we met to plan the litigation. Sandra and I were there, along with Michael Ratner and other lawyers from the Center. Stephen Kenny called in from

---

* Disclosure: Sandra is also my wife.

Australia. Clive Stafford Smith, a death penalty lawyer and another early ally in the litigation, joined the call from his office in New Orleans.

During that call, Kenny pressed us to challenge the detentions as quickly as possible. When he first learned that David Hicks had been brought to Guantánamo, Kenny asked the U.S. government for word about his welfare, and for an immediate statement of the allegations against Hicks that justified his imprisonment, but to no avail. The United States did not even officially acknowledge that Hicks was being held at the base, let alone permit him any contact with the outside world. (Kenny knew his client was in Cuba only because the Australian Government received confirmation from the United States.) This legal limbo could not be allowed to persist, Kenny said, and had to be challenged in court.

But Hicks had not yet been brought before a military tribunal. I remember wondering at this meeting whether we needed to wait until the government started the military trials before we could bring a legal challenge. Kenny was indignant. "They'll never start the tribunals if they don't have to," he said. And indeed, the rules governing the tribunals were still a work in progress, months, if not years, from completion. Should we do nothing until the trials began? What incentive did the United States have to start costly and potentially embarrassing military trials if they could hold the prisoners as long as they saw fit, with no legal process and no means by which a prisoner could demand that the military defend the detention? In short, what did they lose simply by maintaining the status quo?

In the meantime, senior members of both political parties were suggesting that the war on terror might require that we overcome our historic squeamishness against the use of torture. In an interview on *Meet the Press*, Vice President Dick Cheney said that the war might require that the government go "to the dark side" in its dealings with prisoners. Regrettably, responsible public figures went even further. Just a few days before my talk at the Walker, for instance, Harvard University law professor Alan Dershowitz published a controversial piece in the *Los Angeles Times* advocating the use of "torture warrant[s]" against suspected terrorists. He later suggested that, in the so-called ticking time bomb scenario, interrogators should be allowed to insert a sterilized needle under a prisoner's fingernails.[11] And the Administration had already said the prisoners at the base would not be protected by the Geneva Conventions. In this climate, Kenny argued that the immediate legal challenge was not to some tribunal that loomed in the uncertain future, but to Hicks's present, indefinite detention without legal process.

He was right, and the first challenge to the Administration's post-9/11 detention policy was beginning.

II

Much of the current controversy about Guantánamo Bay has focused on the Administration's *legal* position—the remarkable claim that the prisoners have no rights because they are foreign nationals detained outside the sovereign territory of the United States. But this focus suggests that the prisoners' treatment was the consequence of a carefully reasoned legal judgment—as if the Administration had objectively determined it could hold them in strict isolation, without access to court or counsel, without charges and without the protections of the Geneva Conventions, and subject them to repeated interrogations under excruciating conditions because the prisoners have no legal right to anything else.

In fact, the reverse is true. As can often be the case in times of conflict, the Administration constructed its legal position to serve its policy preference. Unlike prior conflicts, however, the policy preference of the Bush Administration in the war on terror has been to deprive prisoners of all conceivable protections. As we shall see, the detentions at Guantánamo and elsewhere were deliberately fashioned to maximize secrecy, isolation, and control. These characteristics were considered essential to the interrogations that would take place. This produced an elaborate, and ultimately unsuccessful, legal argument—the argument rejected by the Supreme Court in *Rasul.* But the policy drove the legal analysis, and not, as is sometimes suggested, the other way around. To understand the detentions at Guantánamo, therefore, we must understand this policy preference.

On September 14, 2001, Congress authorized the president to use military force in the fight against al-Qaeda. Since that time, the president has treated the war on terror as an armed conflict and has invoked his constitutional power as commander in chief. The precise scope of the president's war power is notoriously ill defined and the subject of endless constitutional debate. It is indisputably true, however, at least as a historical matter, that the president is given substantially more latitude by the other branches of government during wartime than during peace. As Supreme Court Justice Frank Murphy once observed, the war power gives the president "authority to exercise measures of control over persons and property which would not in all cases be permissible in normal times." [12]

But while Congress has authorized the use of force and the president has sent troops into battle, this conflict is very different from others that came before it. Unlike prior conflicts, the Administration argues, this one is not confined to a particular theater of operations. Al-Qaeda is a global threat and, for this reason, the Administration demands the authority to take the battle anywhere in the world. In addition, al-Qaeda's adherents may be citizens of any nation in the world—including America. According to the Administration, therefore, the familiar concepts of enemy and ally have lost their traditional meaning. In the war on terror, anyone may be designated the enemy. The president claims that only he may make this designation, and that his designation is conclusive and may not be reviewed by any court.

Furthermore, support for al-Qaeda may take countless forms. While it certainly includes taking up arms against the United States and its allies, it also includes plotting the next terrorist attack. Or it may include raising money for its unlawful operations. Or laundering money in legitimate operations. It may even include doing nothing except waiting for a call to action. To meet this many-headed Hydra, the president claims he—and he alone—must have the flexibility to define the enemy as he sees fit, and to act against it no matter what form it takes.

Finally, and for all of these reasons, the Administration is hard pressed to say when the war will end. Because we are accustomed to think of war as a contest between nations, we understand at a practical level that the war is over when the enemy can no longer maintain an army in the field, or when it sues for peace or surrenders. But the war on terror pits us against an ideology. Secretary of Defense Rumsfeld has described our effort as a "global struggle against the enemies of freedom, the enemies of civilization." [13] How do we know when we have defeated "the enemies of freedom"? A conflict so nebulous is unlikely to end with either a single, recognizable event or within a foreseeable period. At least in these respects, the war on terror is more metaphorical than literal, like our own Sisyphean wars on drugs and poverty.

These differences do not merely distinguish this conflict from its predecessors. As we shall see, they also provide the occasion for a claim by the president to an unprecedented expansion of executive power. Consider what these differences imply. Because al-Qaeda knows no boundaries, the power invoked by the president extends over the entire globe. Because anyone may be a follower of al-Qaeda, and because support for al-Qaeda may take almost any form, the president claims he must enjoy the power to designate anyone as the enemy, and act against him by taking him into custody wherever he may be located. Because, the Administration maintains, the prisoners have no rights, they can be subjected to any conditions the executive may create and interrogated using any methods the military may devise. Finally, because the war has no definite end, neither does the president's power. This combination of endless conflict with unbounded executive power creates a claim to unlimited presidential authority.

More than fifty years ago, when President Harry Truman invoked the war power to justify his seizure of the steel mills, Supreme Court Justice Robert Jackson warned that "[n]o penance would ever expiate the sin against free government of holding that a President can escape control of executive powers by law through assuming his military role." [14] But the concern that animated Justice Jackson's warning did not suddenly spring forth in 1952. As the Court wrote in an 1866 case involving unlawful imprisonment during the Civil War, the drafters of the Constitution "knew—the history of the world told them—the nation they were founding, be its existence short or long, would be involved in war; how often or how long continued, human foresight could not tell; and that unlimited power, wherever lodged at such a time, was especially hazardous to freemen." [15] For that reason, the Constitution has always been understood to restrain presidential power, even—and perhaps especially—during what the Court has euphemistically called "troublous times." While the power to wage war is awesome indeed, "[e]ven the war power does not remove constitutional limitations safeguarding essential liberties." [16]

But it is precisely this historic balance between power asserted and power restrained that has been upset in the war on terror. As we will see, the Administration claims all the authority that could conceivably flow to the executive branch during a time of armed conflict, but accepts none of the restrictions. The result is unchecked, almost imperial power: the power to define the enemy, to act against this enemy anywhere in the world, to imprison him indefinitely without legal process and under any conditions, and to prevent review of any of these discretionary actions by the courts. All of this power is limited only by the president's promise to exercise it wisely. Nowhere is this power, and its abuse, more evident than at Guantánamo Bay.

In the end, the detentions at Guantánamo are important not simply—and perhaps not even principally—because of the unpardonable treatment the men and boys at the prison have been forced to endure, and not simply because of the unprecedented legal position the Administration has taken to defend this state of affairs. Guantánamo is important, as well, because of what it reveals about the Administration's vision of presidential power, and the lengths to which it will go to defend this radical vision. Lives have been, and will continue to be, ruined by the Administration's detention policy, but in time, the policy—like earlier wartime misadventures—will fade into the distant past. But when we look back at the crumbling shell of Camp Delta, we will be forced to confront its lasting damage—to the Constitution, to the country, and to the rule of law. For centuries we have understood that "[t]he accumulation of all powers legislative, executive, and judiciary in the same hands . . . may justly be pronounced the very definition of tyranny." [17] The president himself captured what is at stake with these detentions: "We are in a fight for our principles, and our first responsibility is to live by them." [18]

Part One

★

UNDERSTANDING
CAMP DELTA

"AN ATMOSPHERE OF DEPENDENCY AND TRUST"

I

In the Introduction, we saw for the first time—and apparently in spite of her best efforts—the methods of Sergeant Lacey, who, according to an FBI agent on the scene, grabbed a prisoner's genitals in the course of an interrogation. We also learned about "detainee #63," who "had been subjected to intense isolation for over three months," after which time he was seen "evidencing behavior consistent with extreme psychological trauma (talking to non-existent people, reporting hearing voices, crouching in a corner of the cell covered with a sheet for hours on end)." As we will see, Sergeant Lacey's conduct is by no means an aberration. A Pentagon investigation confirmed "numerous instances" in which female interrogators, using dye, pretended to flick or spread menstrual blood on prisoners.[1] The technique was intended to interfere with the prisoners' prayer; a Pentagon official familiar with the investigation said, "If a woman touches him prior to prayer, then he's dirty and can't pray."[2] Nor is this confined to Guantánamo. Since 9/11, the United States has opened approximately six hundred investigations into prisoner abuse. As of February 2006, ninety-eight prisoners had died in U.S. custody, and thirty-four of these deaths are being investigated by the military as suspected or confirmed homicides.[3]

These events naturally lead us to ask why the Administration created Camp Delta and the other prisons in the war on terror. One answer is that the Administration needed a place to hold captured prisoners, just as in any war. But these are not like the prisons we built for captives in World War II, or Korea, or Vietnam. To understand these prisons, we must return—however painful it may be—to that Tuesday morning, September 11, 2001. I was living in Minneapolis at the time and was driving to my office when I heard the news on the radio that the first World Trade Center tower had been hit by a plane. No one seemed to understand what had taken place, and there was some thought it may have been an accident. Inside, my colleagues and I watched the scene unfold on television. My wife was in Mexico City on business at the time and I reached her in her hotel. The telephone was our only connection, but we clung to it like a lifeline as the second plane crashed into the south tower. Soon we learned about the plane at the Pentagon, and not long after about the plane downed in Pennsylvania. This was not an accident.

For a time, all was chaos. Speculation flew and confusion reigned. There was a rumor that a plane was unaccounted for, somewhere near Seattle. Before long, all planes were grounded, leaving my wife stranded in Mexico. Like so many others, and though thousands of miles apart, we watched together on television as the stricken towers fell. We spent anxious hours trying to reach our friends in New York, many of whom lived and worked in the shadow of what came to be known as Ground Zero. But our efforts were in vain; lines were down and circuits were jammed. For the next several days, I shook my head in silent disbelief and could not help but cry at the tragic stories of family members wandering the streets of New York, checking hospitals and morgues, looking for the loved ones they had so casually kissed goodbye that Tuesday morning. We cannot escape these memories, nor should we try. And we cannot fairly evaluate what took place in the days, months, and even years that followed unless we are willing to keep these memories in mind.

The Bush Administration has not provided a complete explanation for its detention policy. (Part of the motivation for this book is that no one else has either.) But that explanation emerges clearly enough if we examine things from the Administration's perspective, beginning with 9/11. On that day, al-Qaeda carried out the most destructive foreign attack on U.S. soil in this country's history. Thousands died, and the lives of thousands of others were shattered forever. The damage to the economy quickly raced into the billions of dollars. More importantly, the nation emerged from that morning different from the night before, and not simply for the rage and confusion that followed in the wake of the attack.

And while September 11 was successful beyond the maddest dreams of its planners, it should not have been a complete surprise. As the 9/11 Commission and others have rightly pointed out, the threat of Islamic terrorism had been present for years:

- **1993:** A group led by Ramzi Yousef detonated a bomb at the base of the World Trade Center. The police also uncovered a plot by Sheik Omar Abdel Rahman to blow up a number of New York landmarks, including the Holland and Lincoln tunnels.
- **1995:** Police in Manila uncovered a plot by Yousef to blow up a dozen U.S. airliners over the Pacific.
- **1996:** A truck bomb in Dhahran, Saudi Arabia, exploded at the base of the Khobar Towers, killing nineteen U.S. servicemen and wounding hundreds of others.
- **1998:** Osama bin Laden issued his now infamous fatwa claiming it was God's decree that Muslims kill Americans. Al-Qaeda operatives carried out nearly simultaneous truck bomb attacks on the U.S. embassies in Nairobi, Kenya, and Dar es Salaam, Tanzania, killing 224 and wounding thousands.
- **1999:** A U.S. Customs agent arrested Ahmed Ressam at the U.S.-Canadian border as he was smuggling explosives into the country. His target was Los Angeles International Airport.
- **2000:** Al-Qaeda operatives in Aden, Yemen, used a motorboat filled with explosives to blow a hole in the side of the USS *Cole*, killing seventeen servicemen.[4]

Though bin Laden was certainly a grave and growing threat, his success that morning in 2001 demonstrated just how little we knew about al-Qaeda, including the extent to which the terror network had penetrated American society and its plans for the future. Even if various intelligence agencies knew scattered pieces, in the years before 9/11 "there was no comprehensive review of what the intelligence community knew" about the organization.[5] Whatever else 9/11 may signify, therefore, it surely represented a failure (and perhaps an indictment[6]) of the intelligence community. Three days after the attacks, Congress authorized the president to use "all necessary force" against those responsible.[7] On September 20, the president vowed to meet this threat by using "every resource at our command," including "every necessary weapon of war."[8]

Once the Administration decided to mount a military response, it was inevitable that the military (and, we will see, the CIA) would capture a substantial number of people. The Administration no doubt hoped at least some fraction of these prisoners would be members of al-Qaeda. But at the same time, the Administration must have considered that the number of prisoners with useful intelligence was potentially quite small. Military planners estimate that during counterinsurgency operations, the enemy "capture rate" "may be very low," in part because the "failure of the enemy to wear a uniform or other recognizable insignia results in an identification problem. As a result, large numbers of civilian suspects may also be detained during operations."[9] In Vietnam, for example, the military reported that only one of every six detainees taken into custody was actually a prisoner of war.[10] But having these prisoners in custody provided the Administration with an opportunity to shed light on a dark and shadowy enemy—assuming it could identify the few prisoners with useful information, and extract it during interrogations.

The Bush Administration also might have expected this would be no easy task. Al-Qaeda, like a number of clandestine military organizations, is obsessed with secrecy. During the search of an alleged al-Qaeda member's home in Manchester, England, police found a training manual that showed just how carefully the organization guards its internal structure. The manual cautioned members to establish widely dispersed cells "whose members do not know one another, so that if a cell member is caught the other cells would not be affected, and work would proceed normally."[11] The manual also advised members to employ a variety of deceptions and subterfuges to disguise their identity and objectives. All of this makes the task of extracting intelligence from al-Qaeda agents that much more difficult. Yet, as we will see, U.S. military regulations explicitly prohibit torture and all forms of coercive interrogations. These regulations were written to comply with the Geneva Conventions, which were drafted to ensure that people captured during armed conflict are treated humanely.* If we followed the law, would we miss the chance to acquire valuable intelligence?

Finally, though 9/11 was undoubtedly a monstrous crime, the Bush Administration could have concluded that interrogations in the war on terror were fundamentally different from interrogations in a criminal case. A police interrogator typically wants to know whether a suspect committed a crime that took place sometime in the past. But a military interrogator typically wants to know the nature and character of the enemy, including its structure and future plans. Learning about a particular event that took place in the past may be only incidental to this purpose. The difference between police and military interrogations, therefore, is frequently (but not always) the difference between gathering evidence to be used in the prosecution of an event that has already taken place and gathering intelligence to be used for a military campaign that will take place in the future. And since 9/11 was principally an intelligence failure, the Administration could have believed the interrogations should look more like the latter than the former.[12]

II

The Administration's vision of military intelligence-gathering is based on the "mosaic theory," which maintains that intelligence—particularly human intelligence (labeled HUMINT and referring to intelligence extracted from people)—about an unconventional enemy is not likely to come from a single, all-important interrogation with one captured prisoner. By design, each prisoner knows only a small piece relating to his own involvement, and in some cases may not even understand the significance of that piece, which emerges only when combined with other, seemingly innocent, pieces of information culled from interrogations with every other prisoner. And with each new prisoner, analysts need to retrace their steps, cross-checking the new information against the old. This may require that prisoners be interviewed over and over again, even if they had been questioned at length only days or weeks earlier. Only through this painstaking

---

* The Geneva Conventions are discussed in greater detail in Chapter 3.

process will a mosaic finally emerge that captures the complete picture of the enemy and its plans, or so the Administration maintains.

The Bush Administration first articulated this theory within days of 9/11, when it began to detain hundreds of people, most of whom were Muslim men, for alleged violations of their immigration status. These immigration detentions are not the focus of this book, since they took place within a preexisting legal framework.[13] But these detentions are nonetheless important to our inquiry, because the Administration altered that framework in important ways that shed light on the eventual detentions at Guantánamo and elsewhere.

Prior to 9/11, people arrested for immigration violations were typically released on bond while their cases worked their way through the courts. For the immigration detentions after 9/11, however, the Administration adopted a wholesale policy of preventive detention—the controversial practice of incarcerating people while the government determines whether they did anything wrong.[14] In scores of proceedings, the Administration defended this practice by submitting the same affidavit from FBI Agent Michael Rolince, who explained that "the business of counterterrorism intelligence gathering in the United States is akin to the construction of a mosaic."[15] According to Rolince:

> At this stage of the investigation, the FBI is gathering and processing thousands of bits and pieces of information that may seem innocuous at first glance. We must analyze all that information, however, to see if it can be fit into a picture that will reveal how the unseen whole operates. . . . What may seem trivial to some may appear of great moment to those within the FBI or the intelligence community who have a broader context within which to consider a questioned item or isolated piece of information. At the present stage of this vast investigation, the FBI is gathering and culling information that may corroborate or diminish our current suspicions of the individuals who have been detained. . . . In the meantime, the FBI has been unable to rule out the possibility that respondent is somehow linked to, or possesses knowledge of, the terrorist attacks on the World Trade Center and the Pentagon. To protect the public the FBI must exhaust all avenues of investigation while ensuring that critical information does not evaporate pending further investigation.[16]

At the same time, the Administration wanted to construct this "mosaic" in secret. It refused to disclose "the number of people arrested, their names, their lawyers, the reasons for their detention, and other information related to their whereabouts and circumstances."[17] It also ordered that the press be excluded from all immigration proceedings involving these detainees, and that the cases not be listed on the public docket. But secret arrests and closed courts are virtually unheard of in this country. The government had never before tried to close an entire set of cases based on a blanket, undifferentiated claim that closure was a good idea, rather than on a case-by-case demonstration of need. A number of organizations filed requests under the Freedom of Information Act seeking, among other things, the names of the prisoners and their attorneys, the location of their arrest, and the location of their incarceration.[18]

The Administration refused to budge, arguing that even the most modest disclosures would threaten national security. The organizations sued in federal court in Washington, D.C., and the Administration defended its claim to secrecy in a declaration by James Reynolds, chief of the Terrorism and Violent Crime Section in the Criminal Division of the Justice Department. In his declaration, Reynolds warned that "as long as these investigations remain open and active, disclosing the information in question could result in significant harm to the interests of the United States. . . ."[19]

> [R]eleasing the names of the detainees who may be associated with terrorism and their place and date of arrest would reveal the direction and progress of the investigations by identifying where DOJ [Justice] is focusing its efforts. In effect, it would allow terrorist organizations to map the progress of the investigation and thereby develop the means to impede them. Even disclosing the identities of those detainees who have been released may reveal details about the focus and scope of the investigation and thereby allow terrorists to counteract it. . . . The rationale that underlies the withholding of the names of the detainees similarly supports the nondisclosure of their lawyers' identities. . . . Release of such a list may facilitate the identification of the detainees themselves and the harms described above could ensue.[20]

Several things emerge from these events, and from the Rolince and Reynolds declarations in particular. First, the "mosaic theory" contemplates the prospect of prolonged detention. The process of "gathering and culling" "thousands of bits and pieces of information that may seem innocuous at first glance" could take months, if not years. This would be particularly true if the Administration were determined to "exhaust all avenues of investigation" before deciding that a particular prisoner was not "somehow linked to, or possess[ing] knowledge of," the 9/11 attacks. In theory, constructing this "mosaic" authorizes indefinite detentions, since it depends on both retrospective and prospective approaches to intelligence. One can never know in advance just how much time a particular investigation will require.

Second, Reynolds's declaration reveals a decided preference for conducting these investigations with as much secrecy as possible. In the immigration hearings that were the subject of his declaration, the prisoners had the right to hire a lawyer. But it is clear from his affidavit that, if the Administration could have excluded counsel, it would have. And finally, the immigration violations that provided the ostensible basis for the detentions were admittedly pretextual. That is, they simply provided a basis to hold the prisoners while the FBI completed its investigation. In that respect, the detentions were never meant to produce criminal charges. Any given interrogation may have produced evidence of a crime (in point of fact, no person arrested under this program was charged in connection with 9/11),[21] but that was not their primary purpose. The detentions were preventive. As a result, the great majority of prisoners were held for months but never charged with any wrongdoing. They were simply held until the investigation was over.

In short, the immigration detentions in the immediate wake of September 11 were prolonged, secret, preventive detentions, the true purpose of which was to allow the FBI to investigate whether the prisoner posed any threat to security. All of these elements would eventually become part of the detentions in the war on terror. But the immigration detentions only begin to explain the Administration's detention policy. In particular, the immigration detentions were under the control of the Justice Department, whereas virtually all of the prisoners held in connection with the war on terror, at Guantánamo and elsewhere, are in the custody of the Defense Department and the CIA. How do the military and the CIA gather "human intelligence"? What conditions are necessary to make these interrogations a success? To understand this part of the detention policy, we must look elsewhere.

III

The overwhelming majority of people imprisoned by the Administration in the war on terror have been foreign nationals, and the majority of these have been imprisoned under the detention policy described in the last chapter: potentially indefinite, virtually incommunicado incarceration, without charges, without recourse to courts or counsel, and without the benefit of the Geneva Conventions. But a number of U.S. citizens have also been swept up in this policy, and two that we know of were detained in this country: Yaser Hamdi and José Padilla.* Hamdi was seized in Afghanistan and transported to Guantánamo Bay. When it was discovered he was an American citizen, he was transferred to a naval brig in Norfolk, Virginia. Later he was moved to a brig in Charleston, South Carolina, where he was held in solitary confinement. José Padilla was seized at O'Hare Airport in Chicago and transferred to New York. Initially, he was held in the custody of the Justice Department then later handed over to the Defense Department, which moved him to the same Charleston brig that held Hamdi.[22]

Lawyers for Hamdi and Padilla challenged the detentions, arguing that U.S. citizens held thousands of miles from any battlefield had to be charged with a crime or released. I discuss these cases in detail later in the book. For now, however, we are concerned with events that took place shortly after their seizure, when the lawyers for Hamdi and Padilla did what any lawyer would do, and what lawyers had always been allowed to do in this country: they tried to meet with their clients. The Defense Department, however, refused to permit it. The attorneys protested in court, and the Administration

---

* We do not know the number of U.S. citizens detained overseas. As of the summer of 2005, at least five were in custody in Iraq alone. See "Five American Detainees Held By U.S. Military In Iraq," Reuters, July 6, 2005. At least one of these five has since been released without charges, but we do not know whether others have been captured since then, nor do we know whether any Americans are in custody outside Iraq.

defended its unprecedented position by submitting statements from senior military officials.[23]

In Hamdi's case, the Administration relied on a declaration from Colonel Donald Woolfolk, at that time the acting commander of the detention facility at Guantánamo Bay. In Padilla's case, they relied on a similar declaration from Vice Admiral Lowell Jacoby, director of the Defense Intelligence Agency. The Woolfolk and Jacoby declarations go a long way toward explaining the uncompromising logic of the Administration's detention policy. Both officials began with the warning that the nation's security depends almost entirely on the ability to successfully interrogate prisoners captured in connection with the war on terror. Colonel Woolfolk, for instance, said that "interrogation provides information that likely could not be gleaned from any other source," and warned that "[l]oss of this tool, *in any respect,* would undermine our nation's intelligence gathering efforts, thus crippling the national security of the United States."[24] He insisted that attacks like that of September 11 could become "tragically common" if the court failed to heed his admonitions.[25] Admiral Jacoby was less alarmist but equally stern, cautioning that "[t]he security of this Nation . . . is dependent upon the United States Government's ability to gather, analyze, and disseminate timely and effective intelligence."[26]

Jacoby and Woolfolk then described the essential elements of a successful interrogation. Foremost, success depends on the ability to create and maintain "an atmosphere of dependency and trust between the subject and the interrogator."[27] The prisoner must come to believe that his welfare is completely dependent on his interrogator, and to trust that his only hope is to cooperate completely. Developing this relationship takes time, potentially "months, or even years."[28] Even after the trust relationship is formed, according to Jacoby's declaration, the nature of the interrogation process must be ongoing: as the military learns information from one prisoner, it must renew and repeat its interrogation of prisoners captured earlier.[29] This, of course, makes it impossible to say how long a particular prisoner may be of use to the United States, since his value conceivably depends on what the military learns from people who may be captured in the future.

To maintain this delicate "atmosphere," the military must hold the prisoner in a "secure," "tightly controlled environment."[30] *Any* interruption, however brief and for whatever reason, would "sever" the carefully crafted relationship between the interrogator and his prisoner, which in turn would imperil national security.[31] It follows, therefore, that the prisoner cannot, under any circumstances, be allowed access to counsel until the interrogation is complete. "Any insertion of counsel into the subject-interrogator relationship—even if only for a limited duration or for a specific purpose—can undo months of work and may permanently shut down the interrogation process."[32] Counsel instills in the prisoner the dangerous and misguided belief that he may secure relief "through an adversarial civil litigation process"—that is, the courts. This would be disastrous to the "sense of dependency and trust that the interrogators are attempting to create." The prisoner must realize that his welfare is wholly in the hands of his interrogators, and "that help is not on the way."[33] In short, the interrogator's battle is won only when the prisoner believes that all is lost, for only then will he abandon his resistance.

Taken together, the declarations from Jacoby, Woolfolk, Rolince, and Reynolds lay the groundwork for much of the Bush Administration's detention policy. We see a model that contemplates prolonged, potentially permanent incarcerations, characterized by isolation (meaning the prisoners will be held with limited or no access to the outside world), secrecy (meaning their identity will be known only to the Administration), and control (meaning the prisoners' conditions will be controlled solely by their captors, in order to impress upon them that "help is not on the way"). Furthermore, the policy adopts what could be thought of as a default position in favor of continued incarceration.[34] While it may seem to the uninitiated that the prisoner knows only "innocuous" facts, the true import of his information may become known only once the military has the opportunity to reinterrogate him based on information learned from other prisoners, *including prisoners who have not yet been captured.* Only by this painstaking process can the government exclude "the possibility"—however remote—that the prisoner "is somehow linked to, or possesses knowledge of, the terrorist attacks." In any given case, therefore, the most critical decision is the first one; once a detention begins, the institutional mind-set virtually guarantees that it is unlikely to end anytime soon.[35] It also means, inevitably, that some number of innocent people will be detained. The only question is how long they will be held before they are cleared of any wrongdoing and released. In the immigration detentions, the average length of time between arrest and clearance by the FBI was eighty days. More than a quarter of the clearances took longer than three months.[36]

Yet these declarations still are not enough to explain the whole of the detention policy. Just what does it mean to create an "atmosphere of dependency and trust"? What does the prisoner's "secure" and "tightly controlled environment" look like? Precisely how does the military convince a prisoner that "help is not on the way"? In his declaration, Colonel Woolfolk promised—falsely, it would turn out—that the military does not use "corporal" forms of persuasion, and that its interrogation methods were "humane." What does that mean? Perhaps not surprisingly, Admiral Jacoby and Colonel Woolfolk were deliberately vague about all of this.

TWO

"DEBILITY, DEPENDENCE, AND DREAD"

I

Military interrogation presents an elemental challenge: the interrogator wants to learn what the prisoner wants to withhold. The very nature of the enterprise invites abuse, since the obvious temptation is to extract the information by any means necessary. And the temptation to use brute force rises with the perceived cost of failure. The more significance we attach to the information sought, the greater the risk that the interrogator will resort to violence in order to get it. This, of course, presents two concerns. The first is the need to avoid false confessions. The military obviously has no legitimate interest in obtaining unreliable intelligence, and the most compelling practical objection to the use of torture is the likelihood that it will produce just that. The second concern should be no less obvious: torture is abhorrent. Among civilized nations, few principles are more firmly established than the absolute prohibition on torture. But even this moral imperative has a pragmatic dimension. The use of torture by one side in an armed conflict will almost inevitably produce reprisals by the other. Eventually, the conflict degenerates into escalating acts of barbarity. One important reason why modern armies take care not to mistreat prisoners, therefore, is a concern for the welfare of their own soldiers.

The U.S. Army has lived by these principles for nearly 150 years. Army Field Manual 34-52, *Intelligence Interrogation* (FM 34-52), which represents the military's "capstone doctrine for the conduct of interrogation operations,"[1] instructs interrogators in a series of techniques designed to over-

29

come a prisoner's reluctance without resorting to torture or unlawful coercion. And the touchstone for maintaining this balance is restraint:

> Experience indicates that the use of prohibited techniques is not necessary to gain the cooperation of interrogation sources. Use of torture and other illegal methods is a poor technique that yields unreliable results, may damage subsequent collection efforts, and can induce the source to say what he thinks the interrogator wants to hear.[2]

Abusive interrogations are not merely counterproductive. As the Army recognizes, "[r]evelations of [the] use of torture by US personnel will bring discredit upon the US and its armed forces while undermining domestic and international support for the war effort. It may also place US and allied personnel in enemy hands at a greater risk of abuse by their captors."[3] For that reason, FM 34-52 emphasizes repeatedly that "[e]verything the interrogator says and does must be within the limits" of the Geneva Conventions, which expressly prohibit torture and coercive interrogations.* The Field Manual also prohibits retaliation: "knowing the enemy has abused US and allied PWs [prisoners of war] does not justify using methods of interrogation specifically prohibited by the [Geneva Conventions] and US policy."[4]

For the great majority of prisoners, maintaining this balance sounds more difficult than it is. Most people cannot tolerate high levels of anxiety for very long. Yet few events in an armed conflict produce higher levels of anxiety than becoming a prisoner. "The circumstances of capture are traumatic for most sources. Capture thrusts them into a foreign environment over which they have no control." For most prisoners, this creates an almost irresistible desire to cooperate with their questioners. With these prisoners, interrogators need not use anything more aggressive than direct questioning. "The interrogator asks questions directly related to information sought, making no effort to conceal the interrogator's purpose. The direct approach, always the first to be used, . . . is the most effective. Statistics show in World War II, it was 90 percent effective. In Vietnam and Operations Urgent Fury, Just Cause, and Desert Storm, it was 95 percent effective."[5]

---

* The Geneva Conventions are discussed in more detail in Chapter 3.

Yet the direct approach will not always work, and for "hesitant or unco-operative sources," the Field Manual encourages interrogators to employ a host of "psychological ploys" and "verbal trickery" that may be used to extract information from resistant sources. Some of these ruses are not particularly sophisticated. The "incentive approach," for instance, simply involves "the application of inferred discomfort"—the promise or threat of better or worse treatment in exchange for cooperation. The "file and dossier" approach calls for the creation of an overstuffed file, suitably marked to look as though it contains the prisoner's entire life history. The sheer volume of material, selectively disclosed to a confined captive, convinces him that all is lost and that "it would be useless to resist." But other techniques are considerably more ominous. The "fear-up" approach, for instance, "is the exploitation of a source's preexisting fear during the period of capture and interrogation." The objective "is to convince the source he does indeed have something to fear; that he has no option but to cooperate." Another approach involves "attacking the source's sense of personal worth." This technique, known as "pride and ego-down," calls for the interrogator "to pounce on the source's sense of pride." [6]

All of these "psychological techniques" share a common goal: to expose "weaknesses which, if recognized by the interrogators, can be exploited" during an interrogation.[7] Though no two interrogations are alike, in every case the interrogator must "[e]stablish and maintain control over the source and interrogation," and "[m]anipulate the source's emotions and weaknesses to gain his willing cooperation."[8] In this context, "willing" does not mean voluntary. Instead, it "refers to the source's answering the interrogator's questions, not necessarily his cooperation."[9] Furthermore, a prisoner is most apt to be "willing" to cooperate "immediately after undergoing a significant traumatic experience."[10] That is why capture opens a window of opportunity for productive questioning. This initial "vulnerability," however, "passes quickly. An individual's established values begin to assert themselves within a day or two. When this happens, much of an individual's susceptibility to interrogation is gone."[11] Since a prisoner can be captured only once, the interrogator who was not present when the prisoner was taken into custody cannot take advantage of this momentary vulnerability—unless, that is, she subjects the prisoner to a new "significant traumatic experience."

The Army knows that many of the psychological manipulations described in FM 34-52 can be abused. For example, the "fear-up" approach
"has the greatest potential to violate the laws of war" because the prisoner
may believe he will be punished or injured if he does not cooperate, a threat
which violates the Geneva Conventions. "The pride and ego-down approach is also a dead end in that, if unsuccessful, it is difficult for the interrogator to recover and move to another approach . . . without losing all
credibility." And great care must be used when employing the "incentive
approach" because the prisoner "might be tempted to provide false or inac-
curate information to gain the desired luxury item or to stop the interrogation." [12] In fact, because an overzealous interrogator may be tempted to
contrive techniques that, in the words of the Field Manual, "approach the
line" between lawful and unlawful methods, the military cautions interrogators to "consider these two tests" before using any controversial approach:

> Given all the surrounding facts and circumstances, would a reasonable
> person in the place of the person being interrogated believe that his
> rights, as guaranteed under both international and US law, are being
> violated or withheld, or will be violated or withheld if he fails to coop-
> erate.

> If your contemplated actions were perpetrated by the enemy against US
> PWs [prisoners of war], you would believe such actions violate interna-
> tional or US law.

If the interrogator answers either of these questions in the affirmative, he is
trained not to go forward with the proposed technique. [13]

But this description is still incomplete. Because FM 34-52 was always intended to be a public document, the reader is left to imagine how the military "establishes and maintains control" or what it takes to make a prisoner
"susceptible" to interrogation, or "willing" to cooperate. More importantly,
the techniques described in FM 34-52 are constrained by the Geneva Conventions. As noted earlier, the Conventions prohibit all forms of coercive
interrogations. For that reason, FM 34-52 does not tell us what an inter-

rogator would do if she were *not* subject to the Conventions. As we will see in the next chapter, in February 2002, President Bush issued his fateful order that the prisoners captured during the war on terror would not be protected by the Conventions. In the months that followed, the Administration devised a set of coercive interrogation techniques that went far beyond those described in FM 34-52—in fact, far beyond anything military interrogators had ever been authorized to use before. To take the last step toward understanding Camp Delta, therefore, we need to consult what one experienced observer has called "the most comprehensive and detailed explanation in print of coercive methods of questioning"—the KUBARK manual, the infamous CIA Cold War handbook on interrogation theory and practice.[14] As reporter Mark Bowden has said, "If there is a bible of interrogation, it is the Kubark Manual."[15]

II

The KUBARK manual is an extraordinary document. Drafted in 1963, it draws on postwar research into the psychology of human behavior and on the CIA and military intelligence doctrine of the time. The result is a comprehensive theory of interrogation distilled into practical lessons to be used by CIA interrogators. Betraying its Cold War origins, KUBARK operates on the assumption that most interrogations will be directed at "foreign intelligence and security services or Communist organizations."[16] The CIA removed this focus twenty years later, however, when it drafted the *Human Resource Exploitation Training Manual* to meet its needs in Latin America. This version relies on the same theory and encourages many of the same practices as the original. Both became public in 1997 after a protracted legal battle waged by reporters from the *Baltimore Sun,* who obtained the documents under the Freedom of Information Act.

KUBARK and Army Field Manual 34-52 endorse the same basic approach to intelligence-gathering and rely on many of the same manipulative techniques. But the KUBARK manual goes far beyond the Field Manual in two significant respects. First, the KUBARK manual was never intended to be a public document. It was meant to describe interrogation techniques that would be used only in covert CIA operations. Since psychological ploys lose their effectiveness if the subject knows what is afoot, the CIA had an obvious interest in keeping this manual secret.[17] But this promise of secrecy is precisely what makes the manual so valuable to us, because secrecy induced the unknown author of the KUBARK manual to write with refreshing—some would say alarming—candor. And second, unlike the Army Field Manual, the KUBARK manual describes interrogation techniques that are not constrained by the Geneva Conventions. It therefore allows us to see what an unrestrained counterintelligence interrogation might look like.

The KUBARK manual operates on the premise that a prisoner will divulge what he knows only when he realizes that resistance is pointless. To that end, the prisoner must come to believe his captors are "all-powerful," and that he is helpless and alone, completely dependent on his captors. Confusion, fear, and isolation are the interrogator's stock in trade, for they "create and amplify an effect of omniscience." "The interrogator can and does make the subject's world not only unlike the world to which he had been accustomed but also strange in itself—a world in which time, space, and sensory perception are overthrown." The objective "is to generate maximum pressure . . . inside the interrogatee [until h]is resistance is sapped." Everything the interrogator says and does is designed to bring the prisoner to this point of surrender.[18]

Like the Army Field Manual, the KUBARK manual recognizes that the "manner and timing of arrest" can prove deeply traumatic. Because the goal is to produce *"the maximum amount of mental discomfort"* [emphasis in original], the prisoner should be arrested when he least expects it. Early morning raids are best, both because "surprise is achieved then, and because a person's resistance . . . is at its lowest." But this sense of disorientation must not be allowed to lapse. "Little is gained if confinement merely replaces one routine with another." For that reason, the prisoner's environment should "enhance" his sense of "being cut off from the known and . . . being plunged into the strange." Detention also allows the interrogator to control the prisoner's environment. "Manipulating these into irregularities, so that the subject becomes disoriented, is very likely to create feelings of fear and helplessness." [19]

In the orchestrated effort to break down a prisoner's resistance, nothing is left to chance and no detail is overlooked. The interrogation room "should be free of distractions. The colors of walls, ceiling, rugs, and furniture should not be startling. Pictures should be missing or dull." There should be no telephone in the room, since a phone "is a visible link to the outside; its presence makes a subject feel less cut-off, better able to resist." The interrogations themselves "should not be held on an unvarying schedule" because "[t]he capacity for resistance is diminished by disorientation. The subject may be left alone for days; and he may be returned to his cell, allowed to sleep for five minutes and brought to an interrogation which is conducted as though eight hours had intervened. The principle is that sessions should be so planned as to disrupt the source's sense of chronological order." [20] Virtually every aspect of the Administration's detention policy, and everything it has done at Guantánamo, has been shaped by this uncompromising vision of intelligence gathering.

Shafiq Rasul and Asif Iqbal were boyhood friends. They grew up together in Tipton, a small town in Britain's west Midlands. They are Muslim, but not especially devout and certainly not fundamentalist. They are clean-shaven, for instance, and have a number of non-Muslim friends. In early September 2001, they traveled to Pakistan. Asif's parents had arranged for him to marry a woman in Faisalabad. Shafiq planned to stay on after the wedding to take computer courses, because the fees were lower than in England. They traveled with a third Tipton friend, Rhuhel Ahmed, who was to be Asif's best man. Asif and Rhuhel were twenty; Shafiq was twenty-four. [21]

Like many young men, the "Tipton Three," as they came to be known, had an impetuous streak. In fact, looking back, it is fair to say they were foolish. In early October 2001, they traveled from Pakistan to Afghanistan, hoping to provide humanitarian aid in what everyone knew would soon become a country ravaged by war. They planned to use the money they had saved for their trip. But as the bombing began and the ground war heated up, the three young men realized how foolhardy their plan had been. They tried to flee and eventually joined a group of refugees streaming out of Kunduz, in northeastern Afghanistan. Soon they were surrounded by troops loyal to the Afghan warlord Rashid Dostum. Dostum's men bombed the convoy. The young Brits, along with hundreds of others, surrendered. Eventually they were jammed into closed metal containers and trucked to Dostum's prison at Shebargan. Scores of prisoners suffocated during the trip. After a little more than a week in Shebargan, the three were visited by representatives of the International Red Cross, who promised to alert the British government. In late December, however, after about a month in Dostum's prison, they were handed over to the Americans. They were hooded, taken to the airport, shackled together, and flown to the U.S. military base in Kandahar, in southwest Afghanistan, where they were subjected to a series of violent interrogations, always at gunpoint.[22] In January 2002, they were brought to Guantánamo.

Rasul has described some of the KUBARK methods used against him at the base:

> If it hadn't been for the Arabs knowing by the position of the sun when to pray, we wouldn't have known even that. We didn't know the time. We know the dates we know because we counted for ourselves and some soldiers would tell us enough to let us slightly keep track, otherwise there was no way and there was never meant to be any way. Sometimes the prayer call would be played five times a day, but then it would be stopped again.[23]

The combined effect of these physical, environmental, and emotional manipulations is to "enhance" the "unsettling effect" of the tricks and ruses described in the KUBARK manual. The interrogator manipulates the prisoner's reality, creating an ominous, threatening, and bizarre world that "disrupt[s] radically the familiar emotional and psychological associations of the subject. When this aim is achieved, resistance is seriously impaired." At that critical moment, the prisoner enters "a kind of psychological shock or paralysis" caused by "a traumatic or sub-traumatic experience." This experience shatters the "world that is familiar to the subject as well as his image of himself within that world." When this occurs, "the source is far more open to suggestion [and] far likelier to comply."[24]

But the KUBARK manual recognizes that even these "radical" disruptions may not be enough to overcome the resistance of some sources. For these prisoners, the manual reserves its most aggressive, coercive approaches. In this context, "coercive" refers to the application of *external* pressures that destroy a prisoner's capacity to function as a "civilized man." The goal is to produce a "regression of the personality to whatever earlier and weaker level is required for the dissolution of resistance and the inculcation of dependence." Research has shown this usually doesn't take much. "Relatively small degrees of homeostatic derangement, fatigue, pain, sleep loss, or anxiety" are generally sufficient. The manual discusses a number of coercive techniques, the goal of which is to instill a sense of "debility, dependence, and dread."[25]

> I was suddenly collected and taken to one of the three isolation blocks, "November." I asked the Sergeant why I was being moved and he said, "We don't know. The order is from the interrogators." I was placed in a metal cell painted green inside. . . . It was extremely hot, hotter than the other cells I'd been in previously. . . . There was a glass panel at the hatch at the front of the cell so they could keep an eye on us. . . . For the first week I had no idea what was going on.
>
> Shafiq Rasul[26]

Another effective weapon in the interrogator's arsenal of coercive techniques is isolation. By depriving a prisoner of "stimuli," the interrogator intensifies the sense of anxiety, "depriving the subject's mind of contact with an outer world and thus forcing it upon itself."[27]

> If you were already depressed it [isolation] makes you more depressed because you keep thinking negatively about the same thing and there's no one there to comfort you or distract you. Sometimes you welcome interrogation when you've been in isolation because there is someone to talk to and it's a release and no doubt that's what interrogators are counting on when they keep you there.
>
> Asif Iqbal[28]

> I was returned to my cell with no explanation as to why I had been brought to interrogation and I was then left in the isolation cell for a further week. Again, nobody would explain to me what was going on and I felt I was going crazy inside my head.
>
> Shafiq Rasul[29]

Finally, the KUBARK manual recognizes that the threat of coercion is often more effective than coercion itself. "The threat to inflict pain, for example, can trigger fears more damaging than the immediate sensation of pain." In the same way, the threat of debility, "for example, a brief deprivation of food—may induce much more anxiety than prolonged hunger." For that reason, KUBARK recommends creating a menacing environment in which the prisoner lives with the dread that what little comfort exists in his world will be taken away. Notably, because the fear creates a more pronounced sense of mental discomfort than the reality, the manual recommends against the sustained use of pain and debility—not because of any moral objections, but because "it appears probable that the techniques of inducing debility become counter-productive at an early stage." [30]

> During the whole time that we were in Guantanamo, we were at a high level of fear. When we first got there the level was sky-high. At the beginning we were terrified that we might be killed at any minute. The guards would say to us, "We could kill you at any time." They would say, "The world doesn't know you're here, nobody knows you're here, all they know is that you're missing and we could kill you and no one would know." . . . All the time we thought that we would never get out. Most especially, if we were in isolation there would be a constant fear of what was happening and what was going to happen.
>
> Shafiq Rasul [31]

The CIA brought KUBARK out of the Cold War in 1983 when it wrote the *Human Resource Exploitation Training Manual.* This manual instructs interrogators in the use of many of the same approaches as KUBARK, including debilitating techniques like prolonged constraint or exertion, exposure to "extremes of heat, cold or moisture," and "manipulation of the subject's environment." Like the KUBARK manual, the *Exploitation Training Manual* also counsels interrogators to consider "deprivation of sensory stimuli" since this "induces stress and anxiety. The more complete the deprivation, the more rapidly and deeply the subject is affected." Interrogators may also find it helpful to use, or threaten to use, "pain" in the course of their efforts. [32]

According to the former deputy director of operations at the CIA, Honduran military intelligence officers were trained by the CIA in the use of the techniques described in the *Exploitation Manual*. Accounts provided by some of these officers, and by survivors of their torture, give us some insight into how the classroom lessons were implemented in the field. For instance, the *Exploitation Manual* suggests the interrogator may want to show the prisoner "carefully selected letters from home" to imply "that [the prisoner's] relatives are under duress or suffering." A former Honduran intelligence officer later recounted what this particular instruction produced in practice: "We would show [the prisoners] photos of their family. We would say, 'We're going to get your mother and rape her in front of you.' Then we would make it seem like we went to get the mother." * [33] Another Honduran intelligence officer recalled that the CIA instructors taught them to use "aversions." "If a person did not like cockroaches, then that person might be more cooperative if there were cockroaches running around the room."† The *Exploitation Manual* includes the chilling reminder that "[t]hroughout his detention, subject must be convinced that his 'questioner' controls his ultimate destiny, and that his absolute cooperation is essential to survival." [34]

III

We begin to see what the Administration had in mind when it created Camp Delta: the ideal interrogation chamber. In this world, interrogators are allowed—indeed, they are encouraged—to disorient, confuse, shame, embarrass, and exhaust the prisoners, and to keep them in this condition as long as the interrogators believe necessary. They are permitted to traumatize the prisoners, for traumatic experiences open the greatest window of psychological vulnerability. They are expected to maintain total control over the prisoners, who are held *incommunicado* to maximize their sense of

---

* In December 2002, interrogators at Guantánamo sought and received approval to manufacture "scenarios designed to convince the detainee that death or serious painful consequences are imminent for him and/or his family." At least in Cuba, this technique can no longer be used without approval by the Secretary of Defense. See Chapter 5.

† In late 2002, the military sought and received approval to use "individual phobias (such as fear of dogs) to induce stress" during interrogations. See Chapter 5. This practice was employed at Camp Delta, and later became widespread at Abu Ghraib prison in Iraq.

"debility, dependence, and dread." In this environment, prisoners will real-ize, at the most primal level, that their lives depend on nothing less than a complete surrender to their interrogator. They are deprived of virtually all contact with the outside world. At a prison like this, judges will not be allowed to oversee interrogations and attorneys will not be allowed to inter-fere. At a prison like this, interrogators operate unrestrained by the quaint niceties of the law. To the greatest extent possible, a prison like this is law-less.

Two aspects of the Administration's detention policy merit immediate comment. First, the interrogation techniques described in the KUBARK manual and FM 34-52 *assume* the person being interrogated belongs in cus-tody. The interrogator operates on the assumption that the person has been properly classified as a hostile or enemy "source," which means that a pris-oner's protestations of innocence are automatically met with disbelief; the more the prisoner protests his innocence, the more apparent it becomes that he is being uncooperative. In order to break down this "resistance," the prisoner will be subjected to increasingly coercive interrogation techniques. In that way, innocent prisoners may end up enduring the worst treatment.

Shafiq Rasul, one of my clients, has described how this unfolded in his case. At one point during his incarceration at Guantánamo, he was brought to an interrogation room and shown photographs. One photo was a still taken from a video. In the photo, three people were sitting together with an-other person sitting behind them. Interrogators had labeled the picture. The three people in front had been labeled as Shafiq, Asif Iqbal, and Rhuhel Ahmed, another British citizen at the base; the person behind them had been labeled Mohammed Atta, one of the organizers of the 9/11 hijackings. Shafiq recounts the interrogation that followed:

> [The interrogator] started basically accusing me of being present at the meeting, of being the person in the picture and of being involved with Al-Qaeda and with [the] September 11 hijackings. I was denying it but he wouldn't believe me. When I saw the photographs I could see that they were purportedly from 2000 and I knew that I was in England dur-ing that time, which I told him. After the first interrogation I was brought back to my cell and then a few days later brought out again.

This time I was short shackled.* I was left squatting for about an hour and then [the interrogator] came back again . . . trying to get me to admit that I was in the photographs. I was telling him if you check you will find out that I was in England during this time. After a while he left the room and I was left again in the short shackle position for several hours. . . .

Eventually, Shafiq was taken back to his cell. Every four or five days, he was brought back to the interrogation room. Sometimes he was interrogated. Other times he "was short shackled and left for hours at a time and not interrogated at all."

This happened about 5 or 6 times. On a couple of occasions when I was left in the short shackle position they would play extremely loud rock or heavy metal music which was deafening. Probably the longest period of time I was left in the short shackle position was 7 or 8 hours. . . .

As the interrogations dragged on, Shafiq remained adamant that he was not the person depicted in the photo. "[B]ut the Americans had made up their mind," he said, "and refused to accept my account."

I told them in detail that at the time the video was supposed to have been taken I was working in Curry's [an electronics store] in England and going to college. When I said this, they would turn it around and say that I knew I was going to Afghanistan at the relevant time and therefore I had laid a false alibi before I left. . . .

---

* Short shackling occurs when a prisoner's hands and feet are shackled together, with the shackles bolted to the floor and the prisoner unable to stand. In Shafiq's case, he was forced to squat on his haunches, unable to sit, stand, or roll onto his back or sides. See Shafiq Rasul et al., "Composite Statement: Detention in Afghanistan and Guantánamo Bay," July 26, 2004, 66, available at http://www.cct-n4.org/UZ/reports/report.org? 06;ID=46UT8M231*Content=424. According to military officials familiar with the practice, short shackling was routinely employed at Camp Delta. See Neil A. Lewis, "Broad Use Cited of Harsh Tactics at Base in Cuba," *New York Times,* Oct. 17, 2004.

Interrogators then ordered that Shafiq be placed in solitary confinement and left alone for what he estimates was more than a month. Eventually, the interrogations resumed. This time he was shown the video from which the still was taken. It was a rally in Afghanistan, and included a speech by Osama bin Laden. A different interrogator told Shafiq to admit he was in the video.

> I said it wasn't me but she kept pressing that I should admit it. She was very adamant. She said to me, "I've put detainees here in isolation for 12 months and eventually they've broken. You might as well admit it now so that you don't have to stay in isolation." Every time I tried to answer a question she insisted I was lying. She kept going on and on at me, pressuring me, telling me that I was lying, telling me that I should admit it. Eventually, I just gave in and said, "Okay, it's me." The reason I did this was because of the previous five or six weeks of being held in isolation and being taken to interrogation for hours on end, short shackled and being treated in that way. I was going out of my mind and didn't know what was going on. I was desperate for it to end.[35]

British intelligence later confirmed that Shafiq, Asif, and Rhuhel had been in England when the video was made, precisely as Shafiq had repeatedly told his interrogators.[36] All three have been released. But for the fortuitous intervention of the British authorities, all three men might still be in Cuba as "confessed" terrorists.

A second aspect of the Administration's detention policy also deserves special mention at this point. As we have seen, the Administration's approach to coercive interrogations is an echo of the approach described in the KUBARK manual. But this manual was intended to provide training for clandestine, counterintelligence interrogations conducted by the CIA. By their very nature, CIA operations of this sort are conducted in secret, with comparatively little oversight.[37] While the secrecy and independence of CIA operations undoubtedly provides it with greater operational flexibility, the same independence creates a risk of abuse, as the history of covert CIA operations repeatedly demonstrates.[38] Precisely because the CIA enjoys powers that are, as a practical matter, largely unregulated, its sphere of operations should be narrow. Clandestine CIA operations do not and should not replace traditional military or law enforcement operations.

Compared to the CIA, military operations undertaken by the Defense Department and the various branches of the armed forces are vast and far-flung. They may capture prisoners by the thousands all over the world, and imprison them for years. Unlike the CIA, the modern Army has always understood that its operations are subject to, and constrained by, the laws of war. In particular, the U.S. military has always understood that the detention and interrogation of captured prisoners is governed and restrained by the Geneva Conventions and the regulations of the U.S. Army.

The Bush Administration's post-9/11 detention policy upsets this balance, merging the broad scope of military operations with the unchecked power of clandestine interrogations.[39] We should take special note of this phenomenon, for we will see it again: throughout the war on terror, the Administration has appropriated power from particular sources while rejecting the corresponding limits. The result is an Administration that exercises substantially more power in the conduct of military operations, with fewer restraints, than ever before.

THREE

"THE SYSTEM THAT HAS BEEN DEVELOPED"

To deny the protection of the [POW] convention to all captured military personnel on the basis of a unilateral assertion that they are all war criminals is to make a mockery of both the convention and the customary law upon which it rests.

—George Aldrich, deputy legal advisor, Department of State, April 13, 1973[1]

We conclude... the president could reasonably interpret [the POW convention] in such a manner that none of the Taliban forces fall within the legal definition of POWs... A presidential determination of this nature would eliminate any legal "doubt" as to the prisoners' status, as a matter of domestic law, and would therefore obviate the need for [case by case determinations].

—Jay Bybee, assistant attorney general, Department of Justice, February 7, 2002[2]

I

The litigation in *Rasul* raised a deceptively simple question: what is the role of the judiciary in the war on terror? It is customary to think of war as a no-holds-barred affair. This, of course, is the import of the oft-quoted Latin expression, *Inter arma silent legis*—"In time of war, laws are silent." But though it sometimes must struggle to be heard, the law in this country retains its voice during wartime in two significant respects: first, our constitutional structure ensures that the exercise of military discretion will be kept within its proper sphere; second, the laws of war guarantee that, even within this sphere, armed conflict will not descend into lawless anarchy. The law is not always successful in this regard and its failures have had disastrous results, but it is certainly incorrect to say that war is lawless. Twin legal systems—the separation of powers and the laws of war—limit war's reach and regulate its conduct. Together, they are indispensable if a constitutional democracy, tested by the strain of war, is to remain "a government of laws, and not of men."

On December 27, 2001, Defense Secretary Donald Rumsfeld announced the Administration's plans to send al-Qaeda and Taliban prisoners to the naval base at Guantánamo Bay. At that time, the United States had forty-five prisoners in custody, thirty-seven of whom were in custody at the Kandahar airport in Afghanistan. The other eight, including American citizen John Walker Lindh, were aboard the amphibious assault ship USS *Peleliu,* in the northern Arabian Sea. More than three thousand prisoners were already being held elsewhere in Afghanistan by anti-Taliban forces, including the Northern Alliance and various Afghan warlords.[3]

Recall the Administration's unusual demands for these prisoners: it wanted to detain and question prisoners for as long as the president saw fit, under any conditions the interrogators might create, without the risk of interference by courts and counsel into the delicate "relationship" between interrogators and prisoners. To meet these demands, the Administration turned to a small cadre of lawyers drawn principally from the Office of Legal Counsel in the Justice Department, the Office of the White House Counsel, and the Office of the Vice President.[4] The public was afforded a rare window into their thinking when a series of classified memos was leaked to the press and public in May and June 2004. Drafted in the first frantic months after September 11, these memos are a blueprint for the creation of a prison beyond the law.

One of the earliest memos, dated December 28, 2001, was written by John Yoo and Patrick Philbin, then with the Office of Legal Counsel. It examined "whether a federal district court would properly have jurisdiction to entertain a petition for a writ of habeas corpus, filed on behalf of an alien detained at the U.S. naval base at Guantánamo Bay, Cuba."[5] Habeas corpus—Latin for "you have the body"—is "the fundamental instrument for safeguarding individual freedom against arbitrary and lawless state action."[6] It acts as a check on executive detention by forcing the government to defend a prisoner's incarceration in court. The genius of the writ is "its capacity to reach all manner of illegal detention—its ability to cut through barriers of form and procedural mazes."[7] For centuries it has protected foreign nationals as well as U.S. citizens. When confronted with a prisoner's application for the writ, the government must justify the prisoner's detention. If the government cannot or will not make this showing, the court must order the prisoner released.

The Supreme Court once described habeas as "the precious safeguard of personal liberty."[8] Sometimes called the Great Writ, habeas has been part of our legal tradition since before the nation's founding. Though the writ traces its origin to English common law, today it is guaranteed by federal statute and the U.S. Constitution. Under one part of the habeas statute, the government must establish that a prisoner's custody does not violate the "Constitution or laws or treaties of the United States." Under another part of the statute, which allows a court to order the release of any person held "under or by color of the authority of the United States," the government must establish the factual and legal basis for the prisoner's detention. Here the questions are whether the government has a legal right to hold the prisoner, and if so, whether they're holding the right person.[9]*

Yet for all its importance habeas is subject to a critical limitation: if the court does not have jurisdiction over the lawsuit, the government cannot be made to account for the detention—even if the detention is illegal. The

---

* We should distinguish here between two different kinds of habeas. Today the most common form of habeas involves review by a federal court of a state prisoner's criminal conviction. This federal postconviction review, however, is a relatively recent addition to the law. "[T]he classical function of habeas corpus was to assure the liberty of subjects against detention by the executive or the military without any court process at all." See Paul Bator, "Finality in Criminal Laws and Federal Habeas Corpus for State Prisoners," 76 *Harvard Law Review* 441, 475 (1963); *I.N.S. St. Cyr*, 533 U.S. 289, 301 (2001). Because the prisoners at Guantánamo had not received "any court process at all," *Rasul* involved habeas in its "classical" form.

memo written by Yoo and Philbin, therefore, did not ask whether the proposed detentions at Guantánamo would be legal, but whether a federal court would even have the authority to ask the question.

It is apparent from the jurisdiction memo that the preferred outcome for the Bush Administration was a determination that the prisoners were beyond the jurisdiction of a federal court. In fact, the memo cautions that a contrary result could "interfere with . . . the system that has been developed" by allowing a federal court to review, among other things, the lawfulness of a prisoner's detention.[10] That was why the Administration rejected an earlier proposal to hold prisoners at the military bases at Midway and Wake islands, since those facilities are indisputably within the jurisdiction of a federal court.[11] Driven by its approach to intelligence gathering, from the earliest days of the war on terror the Administration wanted to place these prisoners, and the lawfulness of executive conduct, beyond the scrutiny of a federal court. In addition, the assumption underlying the jurisdiction memo is that the prisoners would not be charged with violations of the criminal law and prosecuted in federal court; there is a jurisdiction question only if these are meant to be offshore military detentions, and not domestic criminal prosecutions, in which federal jurisdiction would be guaranteed.

To reach the desired result, Yoo and Philbin relied principally on *Johnson v. Eisentrager*, a Supreme Court case from 1950 involving German nationals captured in China in the closing weeks of World War II. After Germany surrendered but while Japan fought on, the United States captured twenty-seven Germans in China and accused them of assisting the Japanese, in violation of the terms of Germany's unconditional surrender. After getting permission from the Chinese government, the United States charged the twenty-seven with war crimes and tried them before a U.S. military commission sitting in Shanghai. These commissions had been authorized by Congress and approved by the Supreme Court in earlier cases.[12]

Throughout the proceedings, the defendants in *Eisentrager* enjoyed many of the rights we typically associate with a criminal trial. They had the right to counsel, and could either hire their own lawyers or rely on attorneys appointed by the commission, who would defend them without charge. Through counsel, the defendants could examine the evidence against them prior to trial, prepare their defense, call defense witnesses, cross-examine prosecution witnesses, introduce evidence in their favor, challenge the admissibility of the government's evidence, and make opening statements and closing arguments. Their trial, which began in the fall of 1946, did not conclude until early 1947. In the end, six of the prisoners were acquitted and released, and twenty-one were convicted and sentenced to various terms, ranging from five years to life imprisonment. After trial, the prisoners were repatriated to Germany, where they were held in an Allied prison. From there they filed a petition for a writ of habeas corpus in federal court in Washington, D.C., raising various challenges to their trial. The case eventually made its way to the Supreme Court, which held that their trial had been fair and that they had no right to habeas.[13]

At first blush, it is hard to see how Yoo and Philbin could have thought *Eisentrager* would help the Administration. Unlike the prisoners in *Eisentrager,* the great majority of the prisoners at Guantánamo were not expected to have any legal process at all. That was the whole point—the Administration wanted to detain and interrogate them without interference from any legal machinery. It is one thing to hold, as the Court did in *Eisentrager,* that war criminals who had been tried, convicted, and sentenced by a lawful military commission, and who had an opportunity to challenge the allegations against them, could not secure another review in a civilian court. But it is quite another to extend that holding to people who have never been charged, let alone tried and convicted.

But Yoo and Philbin relied on other language in *Eisentrager* to support their argument. In its opinion, the Supreme Court described postwar China (where the crime and trial took place) as an area subject to martial law, and Germany (where the defendants were eventually imprisoned) as enemy-occupied territory. Collectively, the Court said these areas were outside our "territory," beyond the "territorial jurisdiction" of the federal courts, and outside our "sovereignty." The Court also considered it significant that the prisoners were "enemy aliens," meaning they were citizens of a country at war with the United States. And it pointed out that the prisoners had been tried, convicted, and sentenced by a lawful military commission. Unfortunately, however, Justice Jackson, writing for the six-person majority, did not elaborate on the significance of these various facts. Instead he simply concluded that the sum of these circumstances placed the prisoners beyond the reach of a federal court.[14]

This ambiguity gave Yoo and Philbin all the room they needed. In their memo, they noted that the United States leases Guantánamo from Cuba, and that while the United States enjoys "complete jurisdiction and control" over the base, Cuba retains "ultimate sovereignty." These terms are not defined in the lease and to this day, no one is quite sure what "ultimate sovereignty" means.[15] Still, Yoo and Philbin relied on this language to argue that Guantánamo is legally equivalent to Germany and China, since all three could theoretically be described as beyond the sovereign territory of the United States. The fact that Germany was enemy territory that we occupied as a temporary incident of war, and that China was an active theater of military operations subject to martial law, was considered irrelevant. The fact that Guantánamo is seven thousand miles from the battlefield was irrelevant, too. The fact that the prisoners in *Eisentrager* were citizens of a country at war with the United States who had received a fair process to challenge the lawfulness of their continued detention—that didn't matter either. The fact that a hundred-year-old lease gave Cuba some undefined and indiscernible quantum of "sovereignty" over the base, was, for Philbin and Yoo, conclusive.

This became the core of the Administration's argument in *Rasul* and it is worth examining it in more historical detail. In 1901, after the Spanish-American War, the United States occupied Cuba. We offered to end the occupation, but only if Cuba included in its constitution a number of clauses drafted by the United States.[16] Known as the Platt Amendment, these provisions forced Cuba to agree "that the United States may exercise the right to intervene" in Cuba and its affairs, and that Cuba would "embody the foregoing provisions in a permanent treaty with the United States." In order to end the U.S. occupation, Cuba reluctantly added the provisions, verbatim, as an appendix to its constitution on June 12, 1901.[17]

One provision of the Platt Amendment (and therefore of the original Cuban constitution) required that Cuba "sell or lease to the United States the lands necessary for coaling or naval stations." Two years later, in 1903, Cuba leased Guantánamo Bay to the United States. Article 3 of the lease included the curious language identified by Yoo and Philbin:

> While on the one hand the United States recognizes the continuance of
> the ultimate sovereignty of the Republic of Cuba over the above de-

scribed areas of land and water, on the other hand the Republic of Cuba consents that during the period of occupation by the United States of said areas under the terms of this agreement the United States shall exercise complete jurisdiction and control over and within said areas . . . [18]

The lease is indefinite and cannot be terminated without the consent of the United States, which has repeatedly declared its intention to remain as long as it sees fit.[19] Guantánamo is the only U.S. military base in the world where the United States exercises complete and exclusive jurisdiction and control in perpetuity, indifferent to the view or consent of the host nation.[20]

In light of this history, it is not surprising that the United States has long considered Guantánamo "practically . . . a part of the Government of the United States."[21] President Theodore Roosevelt said the base was "ours." Former Solicitor General Theodore Olson, who would eventually represent the United States before the Supreme Court in *Rasul,* once described the base as part of our "territorial jurisdiction" and "under exclusive United States jurisdiction."[22] Congress has often extended federal statutes to Guantánamo, and federal courts routinely take jurisdiction over disputes that arise from the base.[23] U.S. law governs the conduct of all who are present on the base, and crimes committed on the base are prosecuted on the mainland in the government's name.[24] Equally important, Cuba's laws are wholly ineffectual at Guantánamo. The Castro government has long characterized the U.S. presence as illegal, has ordered the United States to leave, and has refused to cash the annual rent payment of $4,085 the United States has tendered pursuant to the lease.[25] "Ultimate sovereignty" apparently does not imply any actual authority, as the United States has ignored Cuba's complaints.* As one scholar has aptly observed, "[a]t Guantánamo, the United States is accountable only to itself."[26]

The United States is required under the lease to maintain fences around

---

* Underscoring the difference between Guantánamo and other military bases used by the United States in the war on terror, the government of Uzbekistan has recently evicted the U.S. from that country because we had criticized Uzbekistan's treatment of refugees. The U.S. acknowledges that, unless Uzbekistan changes its mind, the U.S. must comply with this demand and abandon its military base, notwithstanding the strategic importance of the base to U.S. operations in Afghanistan. See Steven R. Weisman and Thom Shanker, "Uzbeks Order U.S. from Base in Refugee Rift," *New York Times,* July 31, 2005, A1.

the perimeter of the base. But inside these fences, the occupants of the base enjoy all the trappings of a small American city. It is "entirely self-sufficient, with its own water plant, schools, transportation, and entertainment facilities."[27] It has a number of commercial centers, with a McDonald's, a movie theater, and a Starbucks. With a total area of over forty-five square miles in the southeastern corner of Cuba, the base is larger than the island of Manhattan and nearly half the size of the District of Columbia.[28] During the *Rasul* litigation, I came to refer to the suggestion that Guantánamo was—in spite of all appearance to the contrary—no different from wartime China or Germany as "the Guantánamo fiction."

For perfectly sound reasons, the president, as commander in chief, enjoys broad discretion in the conduct of military affairs. Whether troops should proceed against this or that target is generally not a question for a congressional committee or a federal court. By their very nature, military judgments in the field, which may call for prompt and decisive action, do not lend themselves to Congress's ponderous, and partisan, deliberative process. Similarly, judges typically do not have, and cannot reliably acquire, the information needed to make military decisions. Even if they could learn what they needed to know, the nature of the judicial process means judges could not possibly act quickly enough; even if they were able to act with necessary dispatch, the issue they would be called to resolve is not likely to be a legal question. So the Constitution sensibly vests the conduct of military affairs in a single person: the commander in chief.

On the other hand, precisely because the president is given such broad latitude to conduct military affairs, the outer bounds of what constitutes a military matter have always been carefully policed. The obvious risk, borne out by the lesson of history, is that military judgments will migrate beyond the battlefield and encroach upon the other branches of government. Questions properly reserved for the legislature will become the subject of pressing military concern; judicial questions will masquerade as matters of urgent military necessity.[29] By supplanting the rest of government, the wartime president threatens to become commander in chief of the entire country, and not simply, as the Constitution would have it, "of the Army and Navy of the United States."[30]

For this reason, the executive cannot be left to decide when and whether it has crossed the line. During a war, we entrust the executive branch with the responsibility to provide for national security. But this responsibility weighs heavily on any wartime Administration, leaving it ill disposed to any suggestion that it has overstated the nation's security needs. In recognition of this, the law has developed with unmistakable clarity: "What are the allowable limits of military discretion, and whether or not they have been overstepped in a particular case, are *judicial questions.*" Or, as former Chief Justice Harlan Stone put it somewhat more recently, military action is not "proof of its own necessity."[31] Since almost the dawn of the Republic, the Supreme Court has regularly reviewed the president's actions as commander in chief, and has not infrequently struck them down as unconstitutional.[32]

The jurisdiction memo reflects a deliberate attempt to prevent the federal courts from fulfilling their constitutional role of ascertaining whether, by incarcerating prisoners at Guantánamo, "the limits of military discretion" have been "overstepped." Incarcerated thousands of miles from an active theater of operations in an area subject to our complete and exclusive jurisdiction and control, and long removed from the exigencies of any field command, these prisoners would be seeking habeas in its "classical" form— judicial review of a prisoner's military detention that was unsupported by "any court process at all."[33] Yet we are to understand from this memo that the Administration's decision to transport them to an offshore prison ninety miles from Miami would make all the difference.

II

Perhaps we are being unfair. While the legal analysis in the jurisdiction memo may be facile, is its premise nonetheless sound? Should prisoners in the war on terror become litigants in federal court? To answer these questions, we must first turn our attention to the laws of war, and then to a second Justice Department memo, this one written by John Yoo and Special Counsel Robert Delahunty. Dated January 9, 2002, this memo asked whether prisoners captured in connection with the conflict in Afghanistan were protected by the laws of war, including the Geneva Conventions. If the jurisdiction memo placed the prisoners beyond the protection of the federal courts, the "Geneva memo" placed them beyond the law.[34]

• • •

For centuries, the conduct of war has been regulated by written and unwritten constraints on participants' behavior. These constraints were intended to ameliorate the predictable excesses of armed conflict. Collectively, they are known as the laws of war.* If we think of these laws as a tree, the trunk quickly splits into two main branches. One branch governs the right to engage in war (usually called *jus ad bellum*), and another governs the proper conduct of war (called *jus in bello*). Our interest is with the second branch, *jus in bello,* which also splits in two. One part of *jus in bello* describes the means and methods of allowable warfare, known as "Hague law," while another describes the proper treatment of people captured during armed conflict, known as "Geneva law." Hague law is named for a series of conventions originally drafted in The Hague, Netherlands, in 1899 and 1907, while Geneva law is named for the several conventions drafted in Geneva, Switzerland, first in 1864 and most recently in 1949. In addition to these formal, written constraints, the conduct of war is also regulated by unwritten practices universally recognized and accepted by civilized nations. These unwritten codes, called the customary international laws of war, include those principles that have achieved such universal acceptance among the nations of the world as to have the force of law.[35] In many respects, this "common law of war" overlaps with the provisions of formal treaties.[36]

Writers, as well as senior members of this Administration, sometimes refer confusingly to the "Geneva Convention," as though there were only one. In fact, however, there are four conventions, each of which provides a detailed set of rules governing a different class of protected persons: Geneva I protects the wounded and sick on land; Geneva II protects the wounded, sick, and shipwrecked at sea; Geneva III protects prisoners of war (and for that reason is often called the Prisoner of War, or POW Convention); and Geneva IV protects civilians (and is often called the Civilian Convention). Today, nearly every country in the world has pledged to abide by the Geneva Conventions. One hundred ninety-one countries, including the United States and Afghanistan, have ratified the Conventions, making it one of the most widely endorsed international treaties the world has ever known.[37]

---

* The laws of war are sometimes also referred to as the law of armed conflict, or international humanitarian law.

Like many legal codes, the laws of war both grant and limit power. They give countries broad power to conduct military affairs, but also restrain them in the use of that power. The Geneva Conventions allow countries to detain combatants for the duration of hostilities.[38] In a conflict that takes place in a defined theater of operations, this is a sensible precaution meant to prevent captured prisoners from returning to the battlefield. In addition, with some exceptions, the laws of war allow countries to hold combatants apart from the civilian judicial system. Being a soldier is not a crime, and detention as a prisoner of war is not a punishment; it merely prevents the prisoner from returning to hostilities. For that reason, a person held under the laws of war ordinarily has no right to insist he be charged with an offense or brought before a judge. He is a military prisoner, not a criminal defendant.[39]

On the other hand, while the laws of war give countries great power over prisoners, it would be a mistake to conclude that captured combatants have no rights. The unmistakable purpose of the Geneva Conventions is to prevent the military from mistreating people in their custody. Geneva III (the POW Convention) protects people who meet the criteria for designation as a POW, meaning they carry arms openly, follow an organized command structure, wear a fixed badge or insignia, and comply with the laws of war.[40] These so-called lawful combatants cannot be punished for their acts as soldiers.* If captured, they "must at all times be humanely treated" and cannot be subjected to "acts of violence or intimidation."[41] While POWs may be interrogated, "[n]o physical or mental torture, nor any other form of coercion, may be inflicted." And POWs who refuse to answer questions "may not be threatened, insulted, or exposed to unpleasant or disadvantageous treatment of any kind."[42]

But what if the prisoner does not qualify as a POW? One mistake commonly made is to assume that, if the combatant does not qualify as a POW, then he has no rights under the Geneva Conventions. This is clearly not correct. Geneva IV (the Civilian Convention) applies broadly to all people "who, at a given moment and *in any manner whatsoever*, find themselves" in enemy hands. The Civilian Convention protects these people—even if they

---

* POWs are sometimes also called "privileged combatants," to reflect the fact that their lawful use of force is privileged, and cannot be punished.

have violated the laws of war and are therefore "unlawful combatants" *—from "acts of violence or threats thereof." [43] ("Civilian" is a term of art in the Convention, and is not limited to those people who were not engaged in hostilities.) They too may be interrogated, but cannot be subjected to "physical or moral coercion . . . to obtain information from them or from third parties," nor can they be subjected to torture, corporal punishment, or physical suffering. [44] There is no gap between Conventions III and IV, no fissure into which prisoners may fall, unprotected by the law. According to the authoritative commentary on the Conventions prepared by the International Committee of the Red Cross,

> Every person in enemy hands must have some status under international law: he is either a prisoner of war and, as such, covered by the Third Convention, [or] a civilian covered by the Fourth Convention. . . . There is no intermediate status; nobody in enemy hands can fall outside the law. [45]

This is also the approach that has long been taken by the U.S. Army, whose regulations provide that prisoners who do not qualify for protection as POWs are still protected under the Civilian Convention, regardless of the label attached to their status. [46]

In addition, all people detained during an armed conflict are protected by Common Article 3 (so called because it is the same in all four Conventions). This article unambiguously bans all "violence to life and person," "cruel treatment and torture," "outrages upon personal dignity," and "humiliating and degrading treatment." [47] The United States has long accepted the view, shared by the international community, that Common Article 3 is part of customary international law, which means it articulates universally accepted norms of civilized behavior and therefore binds the military in all circumstances. [48]

Finally, the Geneva Conventions explicitly account for the possibility that the military may capture a person whose status is not immediately clear

---

* Unlawful combatants are also sometimes referred to as "unprivileged combatants," or "unprivileged belligerents," meaning they did not comply with the laws of war.

and who may in fact be innocent. In that event, Article 5 of the POW Convention requires that "any doubt" regarding the person's status be resolved by a "competent tribunal," and that all detainees enjoy POW status until a tribunal determines otherwise. The U.S. military has adopted a comprehensive set of regulations that implement Article 5. As we will see in the next chapter, these regulations trace their origin to the Vietnam War, the first time the military regularly captured people whose status under the Conventions was uncertain. Rather than allow innocent detainees to languish in custody, the military created "Article 5" tribunals to resolve all doubtful cases. Any prisoner who asserted a right to POW status was entitled to a hearing. At these proceedings, prisoners enjoyed the "fundamental rights considered to be essential to a fair hearing," including the right to notice and an opportunity to be heard. Today, these regulations are binding on all branches of the armed forces, and Article 5 hearings have become a settled part of military practice. If an Article 5 tribunal determines the detainee is innocent, he must be immediately returned to the point of capture and released.[49]

In short, war is not, by any account, a license to exercise unlimited power. While the laws of war invest countries with broad authority to capture and detain combatants, they also demand compliance with a corresponding set of restraints. Among other things, these restraints provide important protections against abusive treatment, coercive interrogations, and wrongful imprisonment. Yet on January 9, 2002, two days before the first prisoners arrived at the Guantánamo base, Yoo and Delahunty argued that while the president, as commander in chief, was subject to none of the restraints imposed by the laws of war, he could claim all of their power.

In their memo, Yoo and Delahunty constructed an elaborate argument purporting to exclude the prisoners at Guantánamo from the Geneva Conventions. They pointed out that the treaty is an agreement between nations, or "High Contracting Parties." Since al-Qaeda is not a country, its members cannot claim protection under the Conventions. They also said that, even if the Conventions applied to al-Qaeda and the Taliban, the president could conclude, unilaterally and without the need for individual Article 5 hearings, that members of both groups had no right to be treated as POWs because they did not always carry arms openly, follow an organized command structure, wear a fixed badge or insignia, or comply with the laws of war—the criteria for POW status under Geneva III. They dispensed with the minimum humanitarian principles of Common Article 3 by pointing out that customary international law is not enforceable in federal court.[50] And finally, Yoo and Delahunty argued that while the prisoners did not enjoy any *protections* under the laws of war, they could be subjected to the *disabilities,* including indefinite detention without legal process. While they acknowledged that this result could seem "counter-intuitive," they defended it as "a product of the President's Commander in Chief and Chief Executive powers to prosecute the war effectively."[51]

The Geneva memo has been roundly criticized, and rightly so. For one thing, it suffers from an obvious logical gap. Yoo and Delahunty argue that prisoners at Guantánamo have no rights because Taliban and al-Qaeda fighters, for a variety of reasons, supposedly do not enjoy the protections of either the Geneva Conventions or customary international law. But this argument collapses if the prisoners are not associated with these groups. In other words, the argument assumes the military has seized the right people. But that is precisely what Article 5 hearings are meant to determine. The suggestion that the president, by unilateral fiat, can dispense with Article 5 hearings simply by declaring that there is no doubt about the status of any prisoner, is ludicrous. Worse, it is sadly reminiscent of the position taken by the North Vietnamese, who claimed the authority to declare, unilaterally, that American and South Vietnamese prisoners were ineligible for the protection of the Geneva Conventions because they did not comply with the laws of war. Quite properly, the United States scoffed at this interpretation, as indicated by the quote at the start of this chapter. To differentiate us from the North's obvious perversion of the Geneva Conventions, the military developed Article 5 hearings, which require a determination by a "competent tribunal" on a case-by-case basis. The president may be many things, but he is not a tribunal.

Second, even if a prisoner is not entitled to POW status, and even if that fact were lawfully established by an Article 5 hearing, that prisoner is surely entitled to protection under Geneva IV (the Civilian Convention), which applies to all persons "who, at a given moment and in any manner whatsoever, find themselves, in case of conflict or occupation," in enemy hands.[52] This is precisely the approach taken by the U.S. Army, which provides that a person excluded from POW status by a valid Article 5 hearing is nonetheless a "protected person" under the Civilian Convention.[53] Yoo and Delahunty do not discuss the Civilian Convention or the Army regulations in the Geneva memo.

Third, even if the prisoners were not covered by either the Civilian Convention or the POW Convention, they would still be entitled to the minimum, irreducible humanitarian principles of Common Article 3, which prohibit "violence to life and person," "cruel treatment and torture," "outrages upon personal dignity," and "humiliating and degrading treatment."[54] As noted, the United States has long agreed that Common Article 3 reflects customary international law. At the same time, the U.S. government has insisted for years that such customary international law binds other governments in their treatment of U.S. citizens. In August 2001, for instance, the Taliban arrested twenty-four missionaries, including two U.S. citizens, and charged them with preaching Christianity, which was a capital crime under the Taliban regime. The State Department demanded that U.S. consular officials be given immediate access to our citizens. Afghanistan, however, was not a party to the Vienna Convention on Consular Relations, the international treaty governing consular access. No matter, the State Department said. Consular access was guaranteed by customary international law, which meant that Afghanistan had a binding "obligation . . . to permit consular visits." The prisoners were freed in November 2001.[55] For Yoo and Delahunty to suggest that the United States may ignore customary international law at its pleasure is simply mistaken.

Finally, and perhaps most importantly, the argument that the president, merely by assuming the mantle of commander in chief, may pick and choose from among the laws of war, applying them selectively to restrain others but not himself, is simply breathtaking. It amounts to a frank declaration that in war, the law really is silent. It says, in just so many words, that the law applies to others but not to the president.

It is important to understand the combined effect of these memos. Both take as their starting point a conclusion that these would be military prisoners, not criminal defendants. By invoking the laws of war, the Administration attempted to bypass the checks and balances of a criminal courtroom.

The Geneva memo ensured that the prisoners would not receive the benefit of the rights guaranteed them as captives in an armed conflict, and the jurisdiction memo ensured that no other protections would take their place. The litigation in *Rasul* was an attempt to restore the balance between power asserted and power restrained by bringing Camp Delta within the authority of the federal courts.

Part Two

☆

UNLIKE ANY OTHER
WE HAVE EVER SEEN

FOUR

"YOU ARE NOW THE PROPERTY OF THE U.S. MARINE CORPS"

I

In early 2002, the naval base at Guantánamo was a blur of activity. On January 6, Brigadier General Michael Lehnert received an urgent order from his boss, Defense Secretary Donald Rumsfeld. He was told to build a prison. He had ninety-six hours. At the time, Lehnert was the commanding officer at Naval Station Guantánamo Bay. The result was Camp X-Ray: row after row of narrow, open-air cells made of chain-link fencing secured in hastily poured concrete slabs, and then topped with coils of razor wire. One reporter who saw it thought it looked like "a high security kennel."[1] James Yee, Muslim chaplain at the base in 2002–2003, compared it to "an outdoor cattle stable."[2] Lehnert finished the job with nine hours to spare.

On January 11, the first planeload of twenty prisoners arrived at the base. Heavily armed Marines surrounded the plane as it touched down from Afghanistan. A Navy helicopter hovered overhead with a gunner hanging off the side.[3] Prisoners stepped uneasily from the plane, shackled at the wrists and ankles. Their shackles were joined together by a third chain that looped around their waists. An official described them as "wobbly and disoriented."[4] Dressed in orange jumpsuits and wearing blacked-out goggles and heavy earmuffs, they were made to kneel on the gravel for hours as they were processed, while Marines patrolled nearby.

The Tipton Three—Shafiq Rasul, Asif Iqbal, and Rhuhel Ahmed—were shipped to Guantánamo on January 14, as part of the second group brought to the base.*

> I was told to bend over and then I felt something shoved up my anus. I don't know what it was but it was very painful. I was then taken to another part of the tent . . . and photographs were taken of me. . . . After the photos I was given an orange uniform. . . . Then black thermal mittens were placed on my hands and taped on around the wrist. Goggles were placed on my eyes. These were rather like ski goggles but with the eye pieces painted out. Then ear muffs were put on like builders' ear muffs. A face mask, which was rather like a surgical mask, was put round my nose and mouth. I was then taken outside. I could barely hear or see a thing and was made to sit down on the gravel ground. [After the flight to Cuba] we were taken off the plane and made to sit on the ground outside. I was still goggled and masked. . . . We were then led onto a bus. . . . The bus then went onto a ferry which went over to the camp. On our arrival at the camp somebody lifted the ear muffs I was wearing and shouted into my ear, "You are now the property of the U.S. Marine Corps." We were told this was our final destination.
>
> Shafiq Rasul[5]

Lehnert had been told to make Camp X-Ray humane but not comfortable. Confined in separate cells, each prisoner was provided the bare essentials: a bucket in which to relieve himself; a mat to sleep on; two towels (one to use as a prayer mat, another to wash with); no blanket.[6] Guards patrolled the outdoor cages constantly. The lights overhead stayed on all night long. Prisoners were confined to their cells twenty-four hours per day, except for fifteen-minute breaks, twice a week, when they were led, shackled, to a small

---

* We also represented Mamdouh Habib and David Hicks, two Australians. Mamdouh's case is discussed in detail in Chapter 10. Hicks was living in Afghanistan when the war started. He was captured by the Northern Alliance, which transferred him to U.S. custody. Hicks's father believed his son may at one time have joined the Taliban, although it is not clear in what capacity. Hicks is one of a handful of prisoners at the base who have been charged with violations of the laws of war. As of this writing, he has not yet been tried and his case has been stayed pending the result of a challenge to the military commissions, now before the U.S. Supreme Court.

pen—one at a time—to exercise.[7] For many prisoners, the color of the uniforms was an added source of psychological stress. In a number of Arab countries, orange uniforms are for condemned prisoners, and many of the inmates at Camp X-Ray believed they were going to be executed. Military officials debated whether to tell them the truth. In the end, they decided to wait until after the first round of interrogations.[8]

Senior Administration officials promptly described the prisoners as "among the most dangerous, best trained, vicious killers on the face of the earth." They were "the worst of a very bad lot," "very dangerous people who would gnaw hydraulic lines in the back of a C-17 to bring it down."[9] Defense Secretary Rumsfeld declared them "unlawful combatants" who "do not have any rights under the Geneva Convention," apparently a reference to the POW Convention. He added, however, that the United States, as a gesture of goodwill, would "for the most part, treat them in a manner that is reasonably consistent with the Geneva Conventions, to the extent they are appropriate."[10]

But almost as soon as the base opened, doubts began to emerge about the Administration's untested hyperbole. On January 27, Secretary Rumsfeld, in unscripted remarks to reporters, asked rhetorically about the newly arrived prisoners: "Were their actions not really egregious? Were they picked up inaccurately or improperly or not improperly or inaccurately—unintentionally? Sometimes when you capture a big, large group there will be someone who just happened to be in there that didn't belong in there."[11] Major General Michael Dunlavey arrived the next month to supervise interrogations and quickly learned that as many as half the prisoners at the base had little or no intelligence value.[12] The Administration said there was an elaborate screening process in Afghanistan to separate the wheat from the chaff. Yet hundreds of prisoners were sent to the base before the screening criteria discussed the threat they might represent. In March, Lieutenant Colonel Bill Cline, deputy camp commander at the time, reported that an unknown number of prisoners were innocent "victims of circumstance," caught up in the wrong place at the wrong time.[13] The following month, Dunlavey traveled to Afghanistan to complain that too many "Mickey Mouse" prisoners were being sent to the base.[14] Commanders in Afghanistan acknowledged the problems but said they had no other place to send suspects who might, conceivably, have some intelligence value. "Basically," one senior officer reported, Dunlavey was told "General, please shut up and go home."[15]

Dozens of prisoners described in classified intelligence reports as farmers, cab drivers, cobblers, and laborers were shipped to the prison, even though intelligence officers at Bagram and Kandahar air bases had concluded after repeated interrogations that they should be released. An Arab prisoner who allegedly fought for the Taliban was among the first to arrive at Guantánamo. He had a severe head wound that left him virtually unable to communicate. Interrogators in Afghanistan had repeatedly recommended against his transfer to Cuba. "He had basically had a combat lobotomy," one official said. At Guantánamo, he was nicknamed "half-head Bob."[16] Another prisoner brought to the base in 2002 ate his feces and drank his urine. Psychiatrists concluded he was insane. Interrogators called him "Wild Bill" and released him in April.[17] In January 2002, then–White House counsel Alberto Gonzales asked the Pentagon to fill out a one-page form for each prisoner describing his alleged involvement with terrorism so military prosecutors could decide who would be tried for war crimes. Intelligence officers quickly reported back that they did not even have enough evidence on most prisoners to complete the forms.[18]

In late February 2002, the military broke ground on Camp Delta, a more permanent facility that replaced Camp X-Ray, and completed the transfer from X-Ray to Delta in late April. Within Delta, prisoners are currently held in one of four camps.[19] Camps One, Two, and Three (numbered for the first three camps that were built) are maximum-security facilities divided into nineteen cellblocks. Each cellblock contains forty-eight cells, with two rows of twenty-four cells running down opposite sides of a long corridor. Cell doors and walls are made of a tight wire mesh.[20] Each prisoner lives in a six-foot-eight-inch by eight-foot cell twenty-four hours per day, except for twenty to thirty minutes' individual exercise five days a week (up from two), followed by a five-minute shower. Shackled whenever they leave their cells, the prisoners exercise in a twenty-five by thirty-foot cage set on a concrete slab.[21] Bright lights shine in the cells around the clock. Guards constantly patrol the rows, with each cell observed by a guard at least once every thirty seconds.[22]

Each cell is furnished with a toilet made from a hole in the ground and a sink positioned low enough to allow prisoners to wash their feet for prayers.

The water, like all the water at the base, is a pale shade of yellow. On the floor of every cell is a spray-painted arrow pointing to Mecca. Prisoners sleep on a shelf-bunk with a mattress.[23] Each prisoner is given a T-shirt and boxer shorts, as well as a number of "comfort items," including a toothbrush, toothpaste, soap, washcloth, prayer cap, two blankets, one sheet, and a copy of the Koran. "Comfort items" can be taken from the prisoner as discipline, though the military says it no longer confiscates the Koran for disciplinary infractions. There is no air-conditioning in Delta. According to the Pentagon, the average summer temperatures at the base "are between 90°F and 100°F with a heat index of over 100°F." In winter, the base cools to "a heat index of over 90°F." The Pentagon says the cells "are air-cooled by a strong ocean breeze circulating through windows and walls."[24]

In March 2003, the military opened Camp Four, now reserved for the most "cooperative" prisoners. Prisoners sleep in dormitories, and are allowed to eat and exercise together. They also wear white, rather than orange, uniforms. Camp Four has a maximum capacity of approximately 160. The prison in Cuba has also been home to some number of juveniles. According to the Pentagon, three children were released in January 2004. They were apparently ten, twelve, and thirteen at the time of their capture.[25] Major General Geoffrey Miller, base commander from late 2002 until May 2004, said at least two of these boys had been kidnapped and forced to join the Taliban. These children were held at Camp Iguana, a separate facility. By all accounts, conditions for the children at Iguana were dramatically better than for the prisoners at Delta. The boys were allowed extended exercise, for instance, and daily showers. They were given religious instruction and basic education in reading, writing, and mathematics. Still, not all juveniles at the base are held at Iguana. In January 2004, the military acknowledged "a small number" of children remain in custody. The exact number is unknown, both because the Administration refuses to provide the information, and because once a prisoner turns sixteen, the Pentagon no longer counts him as a juvenile.[26] According to one report, as of June 15, 2005, there were nine prisoners at the base under the age of eighteen, none of whom was being held at Iguana.[27]

By August 2002, intelligence officials were dismayed to discover there were "no big fish" among the nearly six hundred prisoners at the base.[28] The same month, at the request of the National Security Council, the CIA sent a senior Arab-speaking intelligence analyst to the base. After assessing conditions and meeting with interrogators, he concluded in a classified report that many of the prisoners had no meaningful ties to terrorism. Yet he found the prisoners were held under harsh conditions that, at least for some, included extended isolation. He warned that these conditions could quickly become counterproductive.[29] This was before the most aggressive interrogation techniques were put in place.

In late October 2002, the Defense Department quietly released four prisoners. One of the four, Faiz Muhammed from Afghanistan, said he was 105. "Babbling at times like a child, the partially deaf, shriveled old man was unable to answer simple questions. He struggled to complete sentences and strained to hear words that were shouted at him. His faded mind kept failing him." Interrogators called him "Al-Qaeda Claus." A second released prisoner "walked with a cane and claimed to be 90."[30] General Dunlavey later said some of the prisoners at the base were "older than dirt."[31] At the same time, the Administration continued to insist the inmates were all "the worst of the worst." Two days later, thirty-four prisoners were added, and the prison population reached approximately 625.[32]

In retrospect, mistakes were inevitable. To begin with, the military had no choice but to rely on local intelligence. But this can be a tricky business in Afghanistan, a country riven by bitter internecine rivalries. The Taliban's rise to power had been marked by a "bloody drama of betrayals, counter-betrayals and inter-ethnic bloodshed."[33] Regional warlords, drug dealers, tribal factions, and even members of the Northern Alliance (the group fighting against the Taliban from its bases in northern Afghanistan) all had an interest in leading the United States astray. Tossed into an unfamiliar setting, the military struggled to decipher these shifting alliances. Progress was inevitably slow. One intelligence officer complained that tribal structure in Afghanistan has "a level of complexity that is almost unfathomable." As a result, he said, "we haven't managed in the least to understand the country."[34] Long-standing feuds led to worthless intelligence; reliable information was almost unheard of. Often, the tips the Army received were nothing more than attempts by one clan to retaliate against another. As one Special Forces commander put it, "for every report saying this guy's Al Qaeda, there's another saying this guy's a saint."[35] Even interpreters were a problem: "We can't tell if they're loyal."[36]

The lack of reliable intelligence was exacerbated by the nature of the conflict. Very few of the prisoners at Guantánamo were captured during conventional battles with the U.S. military.[37] In fact, only 5 percent of the prisoners at the base were even captured by the United States. The great majority were captured either by the Northern Alliance, tribal warlords, or Pakistani intelligence officers during raids on villages, mosques, and houses, where supposed combatants were indistinguishable from innocent civilians.[38] But the obvious risk under these circumstances is that the person blending in with the civilian population is, in fact, a civilian.

Certain tactics by the United States made matters even worse. Shortly after the ground war began, the military littered Afghanistan with leaflets offering to pay cash bounties, reportedly as high as $5,000 for each member of the Taliban and $20,000 for each member of al-Qaeda. In a press briefing in November 2001, Secretary Rumsfeld said these leaflets were "dropping like snowflakes in December in Chicago."[39] The flyers offered "wealth and power beyond your dreams." One promised "millions of dollars for helping the Anti-Taliban force catch Al-Qaida and Taliban murderers. This is enough money to take care of your family, your village, your tribe for the rest of your life."[40] But experienced intelligence officers know that bribes cannot build trust. Establishing the relationships that will ensure a steady flow of reliable intelligence is a question of time, not money. In an impoverished country beset by factionalism, the Pentagon's ill-advised bounty program produced predictable results: a steady flow of miserable prisoners trussed up and tossed into the back of pickup trucks, delivered by villagers with their hands outstretched. A number of these prisoners were later shipped to Camp Delta.*[41]

---

* The military seems not to have learned its lesson from this leafleting. In May 2004, the military began to distribute leaflets in Afghanistan that made humanitarian aid contingent on whether Afghans provided information about al-Qaeda and the Taliban. The move outraged aid organizations whose work is independent of the military. Médecins Sans Frontières, the international medical organization, said the threat endangered aid workers. After being alerted to the leaflets by the British newspaper *The Guardian,* the Pentagon said it was a mistake and promised to discontinue the practice. See Ewen MacAskill, "Pentagon Forced to Withdraw Leaflet Linking Aid to Information on Taliban," *The Guardian,* May 6, 2004.

Even when the military managed to capture a "member" of the Taliban, that was no guarantee the prisoner was in fact hostile to the United States or that he had committed a belligerent act. The Taliban, like many militia forces with imperfect control over its territory, often resorted to forced conscriptions—kidnappings—to fill its ranks.[42] In time, the cash-strapped militia allowed conscripts to buy their way out of service, but only if they could pay what amounted to six months' wages, an amount far beyond the means of most Afghans.[43] In addition, the Taliban achieved many of its military successes by bribing warlords and drug dealers, who handed over the fighters under their control in exchange for substantial cash payments.[44] As a result, the Taliban often included troops whose commitment to the cause was lukewarm at best. That may explain why, in the words of Lieutenant Colonel Thomas Berg, who was part of the original team set up by the Pentagon to work on military prosecutions at Guantánamo, "in many cases, we had simply gotten the slowest guys on the battlefield. We literally found guys who had been shot in the butt."[45]

At the Pentagon, frustration mounted as the months passed and the prison still failed to yield the cache of intelligence about al-Qaeda that the Administration had expected. "We thought the detainees were all masterminds," one intelligence officer later acknowledged. "It wasn't the case. Most of them were just dirt farmers in Afghanistan."[46] According to one military official, under the normal rules of engagement, many of the prisoners at the base "would not have been detained."[47] But the "normal rules" did not apply at Camp Delta, and the same mind-set that brought so many innocent or harmless prisoners to the base made it nearly impossible to release them: no one wanted to accept the risk of releasing a prisoner, who, despite all evidence to the contrary, was dangerous. As a consequence, just as with the immigration detentions in the United States shortly after 9/11, a default position developed in favor of continued detention. The Defense Department promised to spell out new criteria that would improve the screening of prisoners sent to the base, but the changes were repeatedly delayed.[48] By June 2003, the military had released only nine prisoners, four of whom were transferred to the custody of Saudi Arabia.[49]

Acting on instructions from our clients' families, we filed the lawsuit in *Rasul (Shafiq Rasul and others v. George W. Bush and others)* on February 19,

2002, in federal district court in Washington, D.C.[50] The issue in the litigation was not whether the president had a right to detain prisoners who committed a belligerent act against the United States or its coalition partners during the war in Afghanistan. Instead, the issue was whether they could be held without legal process. By the Administration's own account, the war on terror had no foreseeable end, which meant that prisoners captured by the United States might be held for the rest of their lives. At the same time, the Administration had turned its back on the Geneva Conventions, which meant the prisoners could be held under uniquely severe conditions. Yet the very nature of the conflict produced an intolerably high risk that an innocent person would be captured and sent to Cuba. The likelihood that an innocent man would be subject to lifelong detention under oppressive conditions meant the government had to provide some lawful way to separate combatant from civilian, which included notice of what they had supposedly done to justify their detention and a fair opportunity to confront the allegations against them. In short, *Rasul* did not ask whether the president had the power to detain, but whether his power would be restrained by the rule of law.

The Administration's immediate reaction to our lawsuit was to prevent our clients from learning of its existence. The Administration's lawyers did not merely ask the court to dismiss the case: they took the position that our clients should not be allowed to know the litigation had started. We were not allowed to speak or meet with our clients. We could not even send them a copy of the lawsuit. (We could mail them anything we wanted, but the military would not deliver it to them.) *Rasul* is apparently the first case in more than 150 years in which the subjects of the litigation did not know that a case was under way on their behalf.*

II

The Administration's decision to jettison the Geneva Conventions sparked an immediate firestorm in the Pentagon and the State Department. Secre-

---

* I exclude cases involving litigants whose mental incompetence made them incapable of grasping the fact of the litigation. Our clients *could have* known about the litigation, but were prevented from doing so by the Administration.

tary of State Colin Powell urged the president to reconsider. Powell, a career military man and former chairman of the Joint Chiefs of Staff, warned that the United States had *never* denied the applicability of the 1949 Conventions, even though several prior conflicts did not present the prototypical conflict for which the Conventions were intended. He cautioned that the president's decision would deprive the United States of the right to invoke the Conventions to protect U.S. or coalition forces; provoke "widespread condemnation" among our allies; interfere with the war on terror by discouraging international cooperation with the United States; "undermine U.S. military culture" by introducing "an element of uncertainty in the status of adversaries"; and encourage other countries to avoid compliance with the Geneva Conventions by looking for "technical 'loopholes.' " And with some prescience, Powell added that the president's decision "deprives us of a winning argument to oppose habeas corpus actions in U.S. courts." Any exclusion from the Conventions, Powell said, should be made on a "case-by-case basis following individual [Article 5] hearings."[51]

Powell had powerful backers within the Administration. William Howard Taft IV, the legal advisor to the State Department, warned that the president's position broke with settled U.S. military practice, deprived U.S. troops of "any claim to the protections of the [POW] Convention," and weakened the protections our troops could expect in future conflicts. Other State Department lawyers stressed that by applying the Conventions, the United States sent an unmistakable signal to the international community that its conduct was based "on its international treaty obligations and the rule of law, not just on its policy preferences."[52] Military lawyers with the Joint Chiefs of Staff also objected to the president's position. The Joint Chiefs believed the president should "treat all detainees as if the [POW] Convention applied."[53]

The position taken by the State Department and the Joint Chiefs should come as no surprise. The United States has long been at the forefront of international efforts to mitigate the cruelty of armed conflict by safeguarding the welfare of captured combatants. In 1785, even before the Constitution was ratified, the United States completed negotiations with Prussia on one of the first treaties by countries at peace to provide for the protection of prisoners in the event of war.[54] To prevent "the destruction of prisoners of war," the two countries "solemnly pledge[d] themselves to each other, and to the world" that prisoners would not be mistreated. They would not "be put into irons, nor bound, nor otherwise restrained in the use of their limbs." Wisely, the drafters took a dim view of the suggestion that military necessity could ever justify departing from this solemn pledge. "[O]n the contrary, . . . the state of war is precisely that for which [the protections] are provided, and during which they are to be as sacredly observed as the most acknowledged articles in the law of nature or nations." [55]

During the Civil War, Francis Lieber of Columbia University drafted General Order 100, *Instructions for the Government of Armies of the United States in the Field,* for the use of the Union Army. This document, now known universally as the Lieber Code, was the first comprehensive attempt to codify the rules of land warfare, and included strict rules governing the treatment of captured prisoners.[56] While prisoners of war could be subjected to the "inconveniences" that arise from their capture, including detention for the duration of hostilities, they were also "entitled to the privileges" of their condition. Lieber embraced the principle that continues to define the modern laws of war: being a soldier is not a crime, and for that reason, captured combatants must be spared "intentional suffering or indignity," "cruel imprisonment, want of food[,] mutilation, death, or any other barbarity." While they may be interrogated, "the modern law of war permits no longer the use of any violence against prisoners in order to extort the desired information, or to punish them for having given false information." Nor does this rule diminish with the exigencies of war. "Military necessity does not admit of cruelty . . . nor of torture to extort confessions." Throughout the conflict, prisoner and captor alike remain "moral beings, responsible to one another and to God." [57]

The Lieber Code remained in force until well into the twentieth century. In 1900, during the war in the Philippines, Major Edwin F. Glenn decided to use the "water cure"—forcing prisoners to ingest huge amounts of water—as an interrogation technique against the local insurgency:

> A man is thrown down on his back and three or four men sit or stand on his arms and legs and hold him down; . . . a carbine barrel or a stick as big as a belaying pin . . . is simply thrust into his jaws and his jaws are thrust back, and, if possible, a wooden log or stone is put under his head or neck, so he can be held more firmly. In the case of very old men I have

seen their teeth fall out. . . . He is simply held down and then water is poured onto his face down his throat and nose from a jar; and that is kept up until the man gives some sign or becomes unconscious. And then . . . he is simply . . . rolled aside rudely, so that water is expelled. A man suffers tremendously, there is no doubt about it.[58]

Glenn defended his unorthodox approach by insisting it was a matter of urgent military necessity, and that desperate times called for desperate measures. The insurgents did not comply with the laws of war, he said, and the United States could ill afford to be hamstrung by such antiquated notions. The judge advocate general at Glenn's court-martial was not impressed. The U.S. Army banned the use of torture to "extort confessions," he concluded, and "the [necessity] defense fails completely, inasmuch as it is attempted to establish the principle that a belligerent who is at war with a savage or semi-civilized enemy may conduct his operations in violation of the rules of civilized war. This no modern State will admit for an instant . . ."*[59]

Throughout the twentieth century, the United States military continued to define itself by the humanitarian conviction that war—despite its inevitable horrors—should not be a senseless descent into anarchy. After World War I, the United States participated actively in the international conference that produced the predecessor to the current Geneva Conventions, the 1929 Geneva Convention Relative to the Treatment of Prisoners of War. Early in World War II, the United States announced that it would comply with the 1929 Convention and frequently invoked that compliance to distinguish the nobility of our actions from the enemy's unprincipled rapacity.

In the course of World War II, more than four hundred thousand German, Italian, and Japanese POWs were held in prisoner of war camps around the United States, and the U.S. treated these prisoners with an almost compulsive regard for the Conventions, regularly going well beyond what was required by the treaty.[60] The Conventions, for instance, required that prisoners be provided the same living conditions as the soldiers who

---

* In 2002, one hundred years after Major Glenn's court-martial, the Administration authorized the CIA and the U.S. military to use the descendant of the water cure—waterboarding—as an interrogation technique in the war on terror. See Chapter 5.

guarded them. But at camps around the country, POWs were arriving before their barracks were finished, which meant the prisoners had to sleep in tents. In order to comply with the Conventions, camp commanders actually ordered American soldiers to sleep in similar tents until the prisoners' barracks were completed.[61] We had signed and ratified the Conventions and we intended to honor that commitment.

Our policy in this regard was partly a matter of enlightened self-interest. In the course of the war, more than ninety thousand American soldiers would become prisoners of the Third Reich.[62] Public officials at all levels of government knew that Germany would never accept the mistreatment of its prisoners without exacting a reciprocal toll on American POWs. This threatened to produce a spiral of retaliatory reprisals, until the war degenerated into precisely the unmitigated horror the United States had labored so assiduously to prevent.

But it was not only self-interest. Even after liberated American prisoners reported that they had not been treated nearly as well as German POWs in this country, President Franklin Roosevelt's War Department tersely rejected any suggestion that this should prompt a change in U.S. policy. Testifying before Congress, the assistant provost marshal explained that "for us to treat with undue harshness the Germans in our hands would be to adopt the Nazi principle of hostages. The particular men held by us are not necessarily the ones who ill-treated our men in German prison camps. To punish one man for what another has done is not an American principle."[63]

But the most compelling evidence that America's position did not depend on the position taken by its enemy comes from our treatment of Japanese POWs. The United States extended the benefit of the Geneva Conventions to the Japanese, as it did to all enemy prisoners, even though Japan had not ratified the Conventions and refused to be bound by them. In April 1942, American aviators under the command of Major General James Doolittle bombed Tokyo and other Japanese cities. The Japanese captured the crews of two bombers. The downed airmen were tried by the Japanese and convicted as war criminals, the allegation being that they had deliberately bombed civilian targets. Several were beheaded. In a message to the nation, President Roosevelt, "with a feeling of deepest horror," announced the "barbarous execution" and vowed that the people "personally and officially responsible for these diabolical crimes" would be brought to justice.[64]

The Japanese fired back a defense, claiming the airmen were war criminals. They had confessed to bombing nonmilitary installations and to deliberately firing on civilians—conduct that meant they were not entitled to the protection of the Geneva Conventions. The State Department scoffed at these "confessions":

> With regard to the allegation of the Japanese Government that the American aviators admitted the acts of which the Japanese Government accuses them, there are numerous known instances in which Japanese official agencies have employed brutal and bestial methods in extorting alleged confessions from persons in their power. It is customary for those agencies to use statements obtained under torture, or alleged statements, in proceedings against the victims. If the admissions alleged by the Japanese Government to have been made by the American aviators were in fact made, they could only have been extorted fabrications.[65]

This was only one in a long series of outrages perpetrated by the Japanese against American POWs. Nearly 40 percent of the U.S. soldiers taken prisoner by Japan did not come home.[66]

Japan's mistreatment of American POWs presented the United States with a choice: either we could use it as a license to abuse Japanese prisoners, or we could give force and weight to our protests against these atrocities by refusing to commit any of our own. The Army Field Manual in use at the time left no doubt which path the United States would choose:

> In accordance with the Geneva Convention of 1929, no coercion may be used on prisoners or other personnel to obtain information relative to the state of their army or country; and prisoners or others who refuse to answer may not be threatened, insulted, or exposed to unpleasant or disadvantageous treatment of any kind.[67]

World War II revealed deficiencies in the 1929 Geneva Conventions, and in 1949 the international community gathered in Geneva to fix the problems. The American delegation to the 1949 conference played "a major role both in the preparatory steps and in the conference proceedings."[68] Yet when

the Korean War started in 1950, neither the United States nor Korea had ratified the 1949 Conventions. In the North, American prisoners were treated
with a barbarism that defies description and the death rate of American
POWs in Korea was staggering.* Still, the United States, precisely in order to
distinguish us from the savagery of our enemy, was meticulous in its commitment to the Conventions. General Douglas MacArthur, commanding
the U.N. troops in Korea, "directed the forces under [his] command to abide
by the detailed provisions of the prisoner of war convention," including "the
humanitarian principles" of Common Article 3.[69]

In 1955, with the memories of Korean atrocities still fresh, the Senate
debated whether to ratify the 1949 Conventions. The Eisenhower Administration urged ratification both to maintain America's moral leadership in
the international community, and to help ensure that U.S. troops would not
be mistreated in future conflicts. Secretary of State John Foster Dulles told
the Senate that ratification would set the "authority of the United States" on
the side of the humane treatment of prisoners, "which would influence favorably future behavior toward prisoners of war." At the same time, he
stressed that American "participation is needed to . . . enable us to invoke
[the Conventions] for the protection of our nationals."[70]

Senator Mike Mansfield echoed Dulles. "[I]t is to the interest of the
United States that the principles of these conventions be accepted universally by all nations." "The conventions point the way to other governments,"
Mansfield said. "Without any real cost to us, acceptance of the standards
provided for prisoners of war, civilians, and wounded and sick will insure
improvement of the condition of our own people as compared with what
had been their previous treatment."[71] Senator Alexander Smith was equally
clear: "I cannot emphasize too strongly that the one nation which stands to
benefit the most from these four conventions is our own United States. . . .
To the extent that we can obtain a worldwide acceptance of the high standards in the conventions, to that extent will we have assured our own people
of greater protection and more civilized treatment."[72] The Senate ratified
the 1949 Geneva Conventions in July 1955.

During the Vietnam War, Hanoi refused to extend the protections of the
Geneva Conventions to captured American pilots, claiming they were ille-

---

* Korean interrogations are discussed in more detail in Chapter 6.

gal combatants—"pirates"—engaged in an unlawful war.[73] Though Hanoi promised to treat American prisoners humanely, its promise could not protect the prisoners, particularly in the early stages of the war. Hundreds of U.S. prisoners were tortured and mistreated. A number were killed and their bodies mutilated. Yet the United States decided early in the war to apply the Conventions to the North Vietnamese, and never wavered from this position. In fact, the United States successfully prevailed upon the South Vietnamese to comply with the Conventions, a move the South Vietnamese had resisted out of fear that it would legitimize the government in the North.[74]

Vietnam was in many respects an unconventional conflict. Many of the combatants—particularly the irregular units of the Viet Cong—did not wear uniforms or carry their arms openly, as required by the POW Convention. In fact, the Viet Cong often made a concerted effort to appear indistinguishable from innocent civilians, roaming across the country and passing behind enemy lines. The Viet Cong also terrorized civilians, kidnapping and assassinating public officials miles from any battlefield. Indeed, the very concept of a "battlefield" often had no meaning in Vietnam. Fighting frequently spilled into neighboring countries as combatants passed across porous, poorly patrolled borders. Despite these complications, the United States applied the Conventions to any person captured during military operations, regardless of where they were seized, what they were wearing at the time of their capture, or whether they were part of a regular army.[75]

Almost from the moment of their arrival, American troops in Vietnam received training in the Geneva Conventions. As part of this training, every soldier in Vietnam was given a small card shortly after his arrival. Titled "The Enemy in Your Hands," the card included these admonitions:

AS A MEMBER OF THE US MILITARY FORCES, YOU WILL COMPLY WITH THE GENEVA PRISONER OF WAR CONVENTIONS OF 1949 TO WHICH YOUR COUNTRY ADHERES.

YOU CANNOT AND MUST NOT
MISTREAT YOUR PRISONER
HUMILIATE OR DEGRADE HIM
TAKE ANY OF HIS PERSONAL EFFECTS WHICH DO
NOT HAVE SIGNIFICANT MILITARY VALUE

REFUSE HIM MEDICAL TREATMENT IF REQUIRED
AND AVAILABLE
ALWAYS TREAT YOUR PRISONER HUMANELY

On the back of the card, there was a quote from President Lyndon Johnson:

THE COURAGE AND SKILL OF OUR MEN IN BATTLE WILL BE MATCHED
BY THEIR MAGNANIMITY WHEN THE BATTLE ENDS.[76]

Because the Viet Cong deliberately tried to disguise themselves as civilians, mistakes in the field were inevitable. One possibility was that soldiers would mistake combatants for innocent civilians. In war, the price of this particular mistake, exacted the moment a soldier turns his back, is exceedingly high. For that reason, military planners in Vietnam recognized that the more likely mistake would be the reverse: soldiers were likely to err on the side of caution and take a number of innocent civilians into custody, despite prisoners' protestations of innocence. In other words, the very nature of the conflict in Vietnam created a serious risk that the military would capture some unknown number of innocent people. And in fact, this is precisely what happened: the military estimates that in Vietnam, only one in six people taken into custody was a POW.[77]

In one of the most important innovations of the entire conflict, the United States responded to this reality by drafting regulations that created tribunals to resolve all doubtful cases. At these tribunals, the first of their kind in the world, prisoners enjoyed the "fundamental rights considered to be essential to a fair hearing," including the right to notice of the charges and an opportunity to be heard.[78] If the tribunal determined the detainee was innocent, he was immediately taken back to where he had been captured and was set free. If the tribunal determined he was a combatant, he was held as a prisoner of war, with the full protections of the Geneva Conventions. And if the tribunal determined he was a spy, saboteur, criminal, or terrorist, he was turned over to the South Vietnamese for criminal prosecution. No person was held without some legal status, and every detainee enjoyed POW status unless and until the tribunal determined otherwise. And even if the military determined the prisoner was not entitled to POW status, he was still given the protections of Common Article 3. These regulations are now binding on all branches of the armed forces, and the hearings have become a settled part of military practice.[79]

The determination by the Viet Cong to blend in with the civilian population, and to carry out terrorist attacks on civilian and military targets, also created an urgent need for timely, reliable military intelligence. For that reason, the interrogation of captured prisoners became an essential part of the war effort. But the demand for intelligence was not allowed to diminish the official commitment to the Geneva Conventions. The military drafted regulations warning that "all interrogations will be conducted according to the Geneva Conventions . . . with particular regard to the prohibitions against maltreatment" of prisoners. Interrogators were reminded that these prohibitions "apply equally" to *all detainees* in U.S. custody, whether or not they were eventually classified as prisoners of war. Interrogations were expected to be completed within days of a person's capture, and any detention for questioning that lasted more than four months required special authorization.[80] In addition, military doctrine at this time began to acknowledge the reciprocal benefit of restraint during interrogations:

> [F]orce is neither an acceptable nor effective method of obtaining accurate information. Observation of the Geneva Conventions by the interrogator is not only mandatory but advantageous because there is a chance that our own personnel, when captured, will receive better treatment, and enemy personnel will be more likely to surrender if the word goes out that our treatment of P[risoners of] W[ar] is humane and just.[81]

In short, the U.S. detention policy in Vietnam was based on an unwavering commitment to the letter and spirit of the Geneva Conventions. To implement this policy, the military constructed a novel legal framework, drafting regulations that adapted and applied the Conventions to an unconventional conflict. But the legal framework was intended to serve the policy preference—a policy that made the humane treatment of prisoners its highest priority. And though the government in the North never recognized the application of the Conventions, the highly visible and widely praised determination by the United States to apply the Conventions led directly to improvements in the treatment of American prisoners. One of those prisoners was Senator John McCain. Speaking in 1999, on the fiftieth anniversary of the current Conventions, McCain had this to say about his ordeal:

> The Geneva Conventions and the Red Cross were created in response to the stark recognition of the true horrors of unbounded war. And I thank God for that. I am thankful for those of us whose dignity, health and lives have been protected by the Conventions. And I am thankful for all the many thousands of fine young men and women who will someday find themselves in the same situation. . . . I am certain we all would have been a lot worse off if there had not been the Geneva Conventions around which an international consensus formed about some very basic standards of decency that should apply even amid the cruel excesses of war.[82]

The U.S. policy in Vietnam did not go unnoticed. In Saigon, the delegate for the International Committee of the Red Cross (ICRC), which monitors compliance with the Geneva Conventions, congratulated the United States for its expansive reading of the Conventions, and for embracing the spirit of the POW Convention even when the realities of the conflict would have tempted a weaker country to adopt a more narrow construction. "The dreams of today are the realities of tomorrow," he said, and in time, perhaps other countries would follow America's enlightened example. That day "will be a great one for man [sic] concerned about the protection of men who cannot protect themselves. . . . May it then be remembered that this light first shone in the darkness of this tragic war in Vietnam."[83]

Examples like these can be readily multiplied for the simple reason that the United States military has *always* considered itself bound by the Geneva Conventions. Throughout the modern era—in Grenada, Haiti, Panama—wherever and whenever the United States has deployed its armed forces, even as conflicts became increasingly asymmetrical and no longer pitted army against army on fixed fields of battle, the military has consistently taken the position that it would adhere to the Geneva Conventions.[84] In the first Gulf War, the United States followed the Geneva Conventions and conducted nearly twelve hundred Article 5 hearings, finding that 310 detainees were POWs; the rest were refugees. The military has continued to conduct these hearings during the present conflict in Iraq.[85] At the same time, at least since the Lieber Code, U.S. military regulations have always prohibited the use of coercive interrogation techniques. Since 1929, military interrogation doctrine has complied with the Geneva Conventions and *every* military interrogation field manual published since World War II, without exception, has warned interrogators that they may not use force during their interrogations.[86]

A word of caution is in order here. As Mr. Dooley has rightly observed, "Th' further ye get fr'm anny peeryod, th' better ye can write about it. Ye are not subject to interruptions by people that were there."[87] There are still many people who were in Vietnam, and they will say that American soldiers sometimes brutally tortured captured Viet Cong fighters to get intelligence, notwithstanding the card in their pocket.[88] And the covert CIA program in Vietnam, code-named PHOENIX, provided financial and military assistance to South Vietnamese intelligence officers who tortured and killed thousands of prisoners.[89] Indeed, the iconic picture from Abu Ghraib prison of a hooded prisoner standing on a box with his arms outstretched and electrical wires clipped to his genitals is a technique sometimes called "the Vietnam."[90] In light of this history, the intimation that torture has never before sullied the military's name has been ridiculed as "the myth of original sinlessness."[91]

Some may argue that the lesson of this history is that torture is simply an ugly fact of war, and that the Bush Administration's official position on the Geneva Conventions matters not one whit to soldiers in the field. There is something to be said for this argument, but in the end I do not accept it. There are important differences between Vietnam and the war on terror that should not be overlooked. For the first time, coercive interrogations now enjoy official sanction. Today, when the military orders a prisoner to be held in solitary confinement for thirty days with no human contact apart from his interrogators, or when a CIA agent subjects a prisoner to waterboarding, their actions are cloaked with the authority of the United States government. In Vietnam, those who tortured enemy prisoners acted alone. There is a difference between what happens *because of* official policy, and what happens *in spite of* it. One indicator of this difference is in the reaction of the International Committee of the Red Cross. In Vietnam, the ICRC was effusive in its praise for our commitment to the Conventions, though it was certainly aware of the abuses. Today, the ICRC has criticized the treatment of prisoners at Camp Delta as "tantamount to torture." [92]

More importantly, by blurring the line between lawful and unlawful interrogations, the Administration makes it virtually impossible to hold wrongdoers accountable. When abusive or coercive interrogations are condemned as out of bounds, its practitioners are by definition acting wrongfully, even if they enjoy a wink and a nod from their superiors. And when such practices are uncovered, there is still hope that the perpetrators will be held accountable and that policies will change. When the abuses of the PHOENIX program came to light, for instance, the CIA discontinued its operation and ordered its agents to follow the same guidelines as the military. [93] But when torture is institutionalized, it becomes almost impossible to rein in. Instead, we see quibbling and dissembling about whether the actions that took place in a particular case fall on this or that side of an increasingly indistinct line, and whether, just in this one instance, the behavior was justified by the ineffable demands of "urgent military necessity." In the end, the line disappears and we are left with only the president's promise that he knows where it is.

III

Consistent with this country's uninterrupted respect for the laws of war, on October 17, 2001, General Tommy Franks, commander of all coalition forces in Afghanistan, ordered his troops to comply with the Geneva Conventions and existing military regulations, including the due process protections of Article 5. [94] The first prisoners were captured in Afghanistan the following month. In January 2002, as the first prisoners began to arrive at Camp X-Ray, Lieutenant Colonel T. L. Miller, a military lawyer, drafted a memorandum outlining how Article 5 hearings would be conducted at the base. Because Article 5 hearings are ordinarily conducted in the field, the memo raised logistical concerns: How would the tribunal work at Guantánamo? If a prisoner were found to be a POW, how should his conditions of confinement be changed? Given the number of prisoners arriving, should the military convene more than one panel? The memo seems to take it as a given that the military would conduct Article 5 hearings. [95]

On January 19, 2002, Secretary Rumsfeld rescinded Franks's order. In a memo to the chairman of the Joint Chiefs of Staff, he repeated his earlier public announcement that members of al-Qaeda and the Taliban would not be protected by the Geneva Conventions, though they should be treated "humanely, and, to the extent appropriate and consistent with military necessity, in a manner consistent with the principles of the Geneva Conventions of 1949."[96] On February 7, 2002, Assistant Attorney General Jay Bybee completed a legal memo that purported to authorize the president, as commander in chief, to dispense with Article 5 hearings based on his unilateral judgment that the prisoners were all war criminals.

That same day, the president issued an executive order that said the war on terror "ushers in a new paradigm" that required "new thinking in the law of war." This "new thinking" led him to conclude that the Geneva Conventions would not apply to the conflict with al-Qaeda because it is not a "High Contracting Party" to the Conventions. As for the Taliban, the president decided the POW Convention would apply to them, but that they were all "unlawful combatants" who did not qualify as prisoners of war, without the need for individual Article 5 hearings. Finally, he decided that the minimum humanitarian requirements of Common Article 3 did not apply to any prisoner.[97]

The next month, the Administration began to refer to the prisoners at Guantánamo as "enemy combatants," a term previously unknown in the Geneva Conventions and U.S. military regulations. According to the Administration, "enemy combatants" could be held under the laws of war for the duration of hostilities (appropriating the power that comes from war), but without any rights or protections that ordinarily protect people held during armed conflict (rejecting all limitations on the use of that power). Throughout modern U.S. military history, it would have been inconceivable for a commander in chief to take the position that treatment of prisoners was not constrained by the laws of war. In fact, imprisonment beyond the law has always been the very antithesis of this country's wartime experience.

FIVE

DEBATING TORTURE

*The greatest dangers to liberty lurk in insidious encroachments
by men of zeal, well-meaning, but without understanding.*

—Justice Louis Brandeis,
Olmstead v. United States (1928)

I

The Administration has settled on the trilogy "safe, humane, and professional" to describe the interrogation operations at Guantánamo. Inasmuch as these interrogations are part of the struggle against what Secretary Rumsfeld called "the enemies of civilization," it is fair to ask what this means. The answer came on an otherwise uneventful Sunday, June 12, 2005. The Senate Judiciary Committee had scheduled its first hearings on the Administration's detention policy for the following Wednesday, June 15—a move that prompted the *Washington Post* to write an editorial with the sarcastic headline "Congress Awakens"—and had invited me to testify.* I was working on my remarks when Eric Freedman, a professor of constitutional law at Hofstra Law School and longtime friend and colleague, forwarded me a link to the Web site for *Time* magazine. *Time* had somehow obtained classified logs from the interrogation of a so-called high value prisoner at Guantánamo named Mohammed al Qahtani.

Al Qahtani is detainee 063. As the reader may recall from the Introduc-

---

* See Chapter 12.

tion, by the fall of 2002, after more than three months of "intense isolation," al Qahtani "was evidencing behavior consistent with extreme psychological trauma (talking to non-existent people, reporting hearing voices, crouching in a cell covered with a sheet for hours on end)." Despite his condition, the most coercive phase of his interrogation had not yet begun. The logs obtained by *Time* span a fifty-day period from late November 2002 until January 2003.

If there were any doubt that the coercive interrogations at Guantánamo trace their origin to the techniques described in the KUBARK manual, that doubt was dispelled by al Qahtani's interrogation logs, which could have been lifted straight from KUBARK. Al Qahtani was kept to a grueling schedule. Interrogations typically began at 4:00 A.M. and lasted until midnight (and this for a prisoner who was already, according to the FBI, suffering "extreme psychological trauma" and hallucinating). According to the military, in forty-eight of the fifty-four days from November 23, 2002, to January 16, 2003, al Qahtani was interrogated eighteen to twenty hours per day.[1] If he fell asleep during a session, he was doused with water. Sometimes, if he did not cooperate, he was made to stand at attention or sit immobile for hours at a time on a metal chair. On rare occasions, al Qahtani was given extra time to sleep, but then interrogated at irregular intervals. This not only left him disoriented, it impressed upon him that he had no control over his environment and routine. His time, his body, and his mind belonged to his captors.[2]

The logs themselves are stubbornly impersonal, with an almost clinical tone. Al Qahtani is never identified by name—he is only "detainee." His questioners are equally anonymous—identified as "interrogator," "interrogators," or "Sgt. A." At no time do the interrogators acknowledge they are dealing with a human being. In the same way, the interrogations were obviously meant to convince al Qahtani that he occupied a place in the world somewhere beneath that of an animal. On December 11, 2002, for instance, "[d]etainee was reminded that no one loved, cared, or remembered him. He was reminded that he was less than human and that animals had more freedom and love than he does." After this "reminder," the log continues:

He was taken outside to see a family of banana rats. The banana rats were moving around freely, playing, eating, showing concern for one another. Detainee was compared to the family of banana rats and reinforced that they had more love, freedom, and concern than he had. Detainee began to cry during this comparison.

Five days later, "[d]etainee was instructed to clean room. Interrogator told detainee that he will not be allowed to leave trash all around and live like the pig that he is. He picked up all the trash from the floor while hands were still cuffed in front of him. . . ." After another four days, al Qahtani refused to take water from an interrogator. This was interpreted as a sign of disrespect. The unnamed interrogator then decided to teach al Qahtani some "lessons in respect":

Told detainee that a dog is held in higher esteem because dogs know right from wrong and know to protect innocent people from bad people. Began teaching the detainee lessons such as stay, come, and bark to elevate his social status up to that of a dog. Detainee became very agitated.

All the while, the interrogators worked to induce feelings of humiliation, fear, and despair. On a number of occasions, military dogs were used "in an aggressive manner" to frighten and intimidate him.[3] Al Qahtani was strip-searched and made to stand nude in the presence of his interrogators, including women. He was forced "to bark like a dog and growl at pictures of terrorists." During one session, an interrogator tied a leash to his neck, led him around the room, and forced him to perform a series of dog tricks. Interrogators hung pictures of "scantily clad women around his neck" and taped a picture of a 9/11 victim to his pants. He was taken to a booth decorated with American flags. He was forced to stand for the playing of the U.S. national anthem. His head and beard were shaved. He was repeatedly subjected to "the close physical presence of a woman." On two occasions a female interrogator straddled him while military police held him down. Another time he was forced to wear a woman's bra and had a thong placed on his head during an interrogation. He was told that his mother and sister were whores, that he was a homosexual, and that his sexual orientation was known to other prisoners. On one occasion, he was forced to dance with a male interrogator.[4]

When al Qahtani could no longer endure this treatment, he told his captors he wanted to commit suicide, and again refused food and water. He became seriously dehydrated and officials forcibly administered an enema.[5] Yet even when he was placed under a doctor's care, loud music was played in his room to "prevent detainee from sleeping." At one point, al Qahtani's heartbeat slowed to thirty-five beats per minute. During this period, medics forcibly administered fluids by an IV drip, giving al Qahtani three and a half bags of fluid during a single interrogation. Al Qahtani asked that he be allowed to go to the bathroom. His request was denied and the interrogation continued. Soon, al Qahtani asked again, and was told he would be allowed to go if he answered more questions. Eventually, al Qahtani asked a third time to go to the bathroom, but was told to urinate in his pants, which he did. The log then notes, "[h]e is beginning to understand the futility of his situation. . . . He is much closer to compliance and cooperation than at the beginning of the operation."[6]

But apparently, even this was not satisfactory. Later in 2003, officials gave al Qahtani a tranquilizer, put him in sensory deprivation clothing with blackened goggles, and told him he was being sent to the Middle East. After he boarded a plane that flew for several hours, the plane returned to Guantánamo, where he was put in an isolation cell and subjected to further rounds of aggressive interrogations at the hands of interrogators impersonating Egyptian security operatives. To facilitate this subterfuge, al Qahtani was kept isolated from the representatives of the International Red Cross for a period of several months.[7]

When the *Time* story broke, the Pentagon defended the professionalism of al Qahtani's interrogators.[8] The Pentagon said that during the period covered by these logs, al Qahtani confessed to being the so-called twentieth 9/11 hijacker. Other officials familiar with his interrogation, however, said that the military's aggressive interrogation techniques "were largely unsuccessful" and that he was most forthcoming under conventional questioning.[9] According to the Pentagon, he was supposed to have been the fifth hijacker aboard the plane downed in Pennsylvania, the only plane with four hijackers. Al Qahtani later recanted this confession.[10] To date, no evidence has been presented in open court to substantiate the Pentagon's claims. Al Qahtani remains at the base, along with thirty other prisoners he implicated during his interrogations.[11]

II

Al Qahtani's interrogation was the product of a gradual devolution that began not long after the first prisoners arrived in Cuba. In the late spring or early summer of 2002 (the precise date is unknown), former White House Counsel (and now Attorney General) Alberto Gonzales posed a new question to John Yoo and his colleague Jay Bybee at the Office of Legal Counsel in the Justice Department. Gonzales asked whether U.S. agents were constrained by the federal anti-torture statute, which makes it a crime for American officials to torture people outside the country. Congress passed the statute in 1994 as part of our obligations under the U.N. Convention Against Torture and Other Cruel, Inhuman or Degrading Treatment or Punishment, usually known as the Convention Against Torture, or the CAT.[12]

The question arose because the CIA had custody of a number of senior al-Qaeda operatives in detention centers outside the United States, and wanted to know whether their agents risked prosecution under this statute if they employed particularly aggressive interrogation techniques.[13] For the first time in U.S. history (at least so far as we know), an Administration wanted to answer this question: how far can interrogators go in their coercion without being prosecuted as torturers? And while the question as originally posed was meant to apply to the relatively few prisoners in CIA custody (currently two or three dozen by most accounts, although approximately three thousand have reportedly passed through CIA custody since 9/11[14]), within months the guidance provided by Yoo and Bybee would govern all interrogations in the war on terror.

On August 1, 2002, Bybee and Yoo answered Gonzales's question in their now infamous "torture memo."[15] Like the earlier Office of Legal Counsel memos on federal jurisdiction and the Geneva Conventions, the torture memo is sharply partisan and deeply flawed—with the former aspect substantially responsible for the latter. To begin with, the authors used a definition of torture that made the anti-torture statute all but toothless. The statute defines torture as "severe physical or mental pain or suffering." Not content with this language, Bybee and Yoo said that torture requires pain that is "excruciating and agonizing." "Physical pain amounting to torture must be equivalent in intensity to the pain accompanying serious physical injury, such as organ failure, impairment of bodily function, or even death. For purely mental pain or suffering to amount to torture . . . it must result in significant psychological harm of significant duration, *e.g.,* lasting for months or even years." [16] Bybee and Yoo identified only seven interrogation techniques that constituted torture under this definition:

(1) severe beatings using instruments such as iron barks, truncheons and clubs; (2) threats of imminent death, such as mock executions; (3) threats of removing extremities; (4) burning, especially burning with cigarettes; (5) electric shocks to genitalia or threats to do so; (6) rape or sexual assault, or injury to an individual's sexual organs, or threatening to do any of these sorts of acts; and (7) forcing the prisoner to watch the torture of others. [17]

Other interrogation techniques, they said, "would have to be similar to these" before they amounted to torture. [18]

Even if a particular act constituted torture, Bybee and Yoo said, because the statute is a specific-intent crime a criminal defendant would be guilty only if torture had been his "precise objective." [19] Though the defendant might know his actions would produce severe pain, "if causing such harm is not his objective, he lacks the requisite specific intent even though the defendant did not act in good faith." According to Bybee and Yoo, "a defendant is guilty of torture only if he acts with the *express purpose* of inflicting severe pain or suffering." [20]

Finally, Bybee and Yoo argued that, even if a defendant committed an act constituting torture under their narrow definition, and even if he acted with the "express purpose" of violating the law, he would still be immune from prosecution if his actions were directed by the president. As commander in chief, the president had the unilateral and inherent authority to order *any* interrogation technique that he, in his sole discretion, believed was necessary. Once the president issued such an order, any attempt by Congress to interfere with this command—for example, by prosecuting interrogators for violating the anti-torture statute—would be unconstitutional. [21]

The torture memo became public in June 2004, precisely when the

Supreme Court was preparing its opinion in *Rasul*. Since its appearance, the condemnation has been nearly unanimous. Harold Koh, dean of the law school at Yale University, called the memo "perhaps the most clearly erroneous legal opinion I have ever read." Columbia University law professor Jeremy Waldron considered it "a disgrace," and Georgetown University law professor David Luban said it "falls far below the minimum standards of professional competence." Even conservative scholars, otherwise supportive of the Administration's post-9/11 detention policy, have balked at the torture memo. Ruth Wedgwood, an outspoken supporter of the Administration's detention policy in its earliest days, described the memo's legal position as a throwback to "the 14th century, when an outlaw was treated like a wild beast." Other commentators have been even less charitable.[22]

The torture memo richly deserves these attacks. To begin with, the legal analysis is flawed in several respects, starting with its indefensibly narrow definition of torture. As noted, the anti-torture statute defines torture as simply "severe physical or mental pain or suffering," which tracks similar language in the Convention Against Torture. It says nothing to indicate the pain must be "equivalent in intensity to the pain accompanying serious physical injury, such as organ failure, impairment of bodily function, or even death." The authors import this language from a different statute, a 2000 law on the availability of public health benefits to cover emergency medical conditions. It is simply bizarre that Bybee and Yoo would try to define "severe pain" without reference to the context in which these words were used—a statute intended to fulfill our obligations under an international treaty meant to prevent torture—and it is even more strange that they should believe the words would have the same meaning in the torture statute as they do in a statute intended to address the problem of scarce medical resources.

But in fact, the medical benefits statute does not even define "severe pain." It says that people cannot receive emergency benefits unless they suffer from a condition that causes "acute symptoms of sufficient severity (including severe pain)" such that the failure to provide emergency treatment might produce organ failure, death, or impairment of a bodily function. In other words, the statute recognizes that a person experiencing severe pain might be suffering from a serious condition (such as organ failure) that would make him eligible for medical benefits. Bybee and Yoo confuse an illustration with a definition. Running a marathon may exhaust me, but that does not mean that exhaustion requires that I run a marathon, or that the effort required by the run is the definition of exhaustion.[23]

Bybee and Yoo compound their first mistake with a second: though they are correct that the torture statute requires that the defendant act with "specific intent," their analysis is misleading. When lawyers say a defendant acted "knowingly," they mean with an awareness that her actions would produce a particular result. But when they say she acted with "specific intent," they mean *in order to achieve* a particular result—the result was the purpose of her actions. A surgeon knows her patient will awake in a great deal of pain, but pain is not the purpose of her actions and she is no torturer. She knowingly inflicts pain, but not with the specific intent to do so. In that context, there is a meaningful difference between knowledge and intent. But during an interrogation, the difference between knowledge and intent disappears. As David Luban has pointed out, "[i]n interrogation, if you knowingly inflict pain, it's because you are trying to inflict pain. This is one context where specific intent and knowledge empirically coincide."[24] By stressing over and over again that an interrogator may knowingly inflict pain without running afoul of the law, Bybee and Yoo rely on a theoretical gap between knowledge and intent that, in this context, does not exist. In doing so, they communicate unmistakably that, so long as the interrogator can credibly profess honorable intentions, she will not be of guilty mind.

But perhaps the most worrisome part of the torture memo is its attempt to transform the commander in chief power into the ultimate constitutional trump card, no matter what Congress may have said. Or, as Yoo later put the matter to a reporter with the *New Yorker,* Congress cannot "tie the president's hands in regard to torture as an interrogation technique. . . . It's the core of the commander-in-chief function. They can't prevent the president from ordering torture."[25]

In 1952, President Truman attempted to seize the steel mills in this country, ostensibly to prevent a work stoppage and ensure an uninterrupted flow of weapons to the troops in Korea. Truman expressly grounded his actions in his constitutional obligation as commander in chief to wage war effectively. A work stoppage, he said, "would immediately jeopardize and imperil our national defense . . . and would add to the continuing danger of our soldiers, sailors, and airmen engaged in combat in the field."[26] The steel companies immediately challenged the seizure and the case quickly made its way to the Supreme Court. The Truman Administration defended its actions by making much the same claim to the plenary power of the president as Bybee and Yoo have made. During a time of armed conflict, Truman's lawyers said, the president, as commander in chief, must be permitted to define the need and provide the solution, without interference by other branches of government.[27]

The Supreme Court disagreed. In *Youngstown Sheet & Tube Co. v. Sawyer,* the Court ruled that the seizure had been illegal because it was inconsistent with the Taft-Hartley Act, a federal labor statute.[28] The majority opinion was written by Justice Hugo Black. But the most important opinion was written by Justice Robert Jackson, who concurred with the majority but wrote separately to describe the role of the commander in chief in our constitutional democracy. Justice Jackson's concurrence in *Youngstown* is rightly regarded as one of the most famous, and most important, opinions in Supreme Court history. The torture memo does not so much as mention it.

In his opinion, Jackson described a useful, if admittedly oversimplified, matrix to help understand the relationship between the commander in chief power and the Congress. When the president acts as commander in chief, his actions fall into one of three categories: if he acts consistent with the express or implied intent of Congress his power "is at its maximum"; if Congress has not spoken, or when the will of Congress cannot be divined, "there is a zone of twilight," and the scope of presidential power is uncertain; and if his actions are inconsistent with the express or implied will of Congress, his power "is at its lowest ebb." In this third category, Jackson said, the Court cannot uphold the president's power unless it is prepared to say that Congress has acted beyond its constitutional authority.[29] Truman's actions fell into Category III: the Taft-Hartley Act established the proper procedure to be followed, which Truman had ignored. Because Congress was clearly within its rights to pass the Taft-Hartley Act, the president's seizure was illegal.

But Congress just as clearly had the constitutional authority to enact the anti-torture statute in 1994. Article I of the Constitution defines the power given to Congress, and three separate clauses in Article I give Congress the power to enact legislation like the anti-torture statute. Congress has the power to "define and punish . . . offences against the law of nations"; to "make rules concerning captures on land and water"; and "to make rules for the government and regulation of the land and naval forces." Bybee and Yoo never explain why these passages of the Constitution do not empower Congress to outlaw torture. They simply ignore them, ignore *Youngstown*, and assert that the anti-torture statute cannot impinge on the president's inherent power "to wage war effectively."

It is important to understand the implications of the Bush Administration's argument, since they go far beyond the torture memo. In this view, once the president invokes his authority as commander in chief, his actions are unassailable, even if they are contrary to the express will of Congress. So long as the president can trace a plausible connection between a proposed course of conduct and the war effort, then the action is not only lawful, but any attempt to restrain it would be unconstitutional. In the torture memo, Bybee and Yoo invoke this power to circumvent the requirements of the anti-torture statute. But the same claim has been invoked repeatedly since 9/11 to justify every new exercise of presidential power taken in the war on terror.

On September 25, 2001, Yoo wrote a memo arguing that the commander in chief power trumped the War Powers Resolution, which Congress passed in 1973 to place limits on the president's power to use force without a declaration of war. He also argued that the commander in chief power overruled any limitation in the Congressional Authorization for the Use of Military Force, passed September 14, 2001. The Authorization gave the president the power to use force, but limited his actions to the people, groups, and nations that planned, authorized, or committed the attacks of September 11, as well as the nations that harbored them. Yoo argued that, under the commander in chief power, this limitation was unconstitutional.[30] In another memo, Yoo argued that the commander in chief power could override the Fourth Amendment protection against unreasonable searches and seizures, and could allow the president to set up military checkpoints inside an American city or use military force "to raid or attack dwellings where terrorists were thought to be despite risks that [innocent] third parties could be killed or injured by exchanges of fire."[31]

As Justice Jackson warned in *Youngstown*, a claim to inherit "power either has no beginning or it has no end."[32] More recently, we learned the president invoked the same authority to authorize the National Security Agency to intercept international telephone conversations and e-mail communications of people lawfully inside the United States, including U.S. citizens, without a warrant. This action appears to violate the Foreign Intelligence Surveillance Act of 1978, which prohibits warrantless surveillance of domestic electronic communications by citizens and lawful resident aliens. Under a still-classified presidential order signed in 2002, the NSA has monitored the messages of "hundreds, perhaps thousands, of people" inside the country.[33] On December 19, 2005, in remarks to the press, Attorney General Gonzales said the Bush Administration believes "the president has the inherent authority under the Constitution, as commander in chief, to engage in this kind of activity," a position reaffirmed December 22 in a letter to the ranking members of the House and Senate Intelligence Committees and again February 6, 2006, in Gonzales's testimony to the Senate Judiciary Committee.[34]

Though it is an outrageous document, the torture memo is not the problem with the Administration's detention policy; it is merely a symptom. Jay Bybee and John Yoo are not incompetent lawyers. Bybee is now a federal appelate judge, and Yoo is a law professor at the University of California at Berkeley. But they approached their task bent on diminishing rather than enhancing the legal protection of prisoners seized during armed conflict. Their goal was to read the anti-torture statute in a way that would ensure it did not restrain the executive branch in its overseas interrogations, no matter what techniques were employed. Its tone, content, and organization reflect a client—the Bush Administration—with a conscious desire to evade and circumvent the requirements of the law. It is a sad day when competent lawyers who are asked to play this role agree to do so. If the rule of law is to be silenced during war, lawyers should not be the ones who silence it.[35]

III

Meanwhile, the prison population at Guantánamo was rising steadily. In mid-January 2002, Camp X-Ray held fifty inmates. Three weeks later, there were 186 prisoners at the base and by the end of February there were three hundred. In early June, with the prisoners now housed at Camp Delta, the total had climbed to four hundred, and by the first day of summer, the population had reached six hundred. By this time, Brigadier General Michael

Lehnert had left the base and interrogation and detention operations were under separate commands. Major General Michael Dunlavey directed interrogations, and Brigadier General Rick Baccus was in charge of the military police. Baccus was also the base commander.[36] When Secretary Rumsfeld ordered the military to treat the prisoners "consistent with the principles of the Geneva Conventions," Baccus took him at his word. He maintained a "constant, open dialogue" with the International Committee of the Red Cross, who were welcome at the facility "any time of day or night." He authorized personnel to post signs reminding prisoners of the requirements of the Geneva Conventions. When Baccus spoke to the prison population over the camp loudspeaker, he began his remarks with, "peace be with you," and closed with, "may God be with you." He allowed prisoners a second weekly exercise period and shower, and directed his subordinates to make surprise visits throughout the camp and to report any mistreatment they observed. He also resisted attempts by interrogators to use aggressive interrogation techniques and promised the prisoners that as long as he was in charge they would be treated humanely.[37]

Naturally, given the Administration's approach to intelligence gathering, Baccus's orientation brought him into conflict with interrogators, who believed this humane treatment prevented them from creating the disorientation, anxiety, and distress necessary for productive interrogations. Dunlavey began to complain. In September 2002, Defense Secretary Rumsfeld ordered an overhaul of the operations at Guantánamo.[38] In October, Baccus's tour ended.[39] Baccus later reported constant pressure from interrogators to make the prisoners' lives "less comfortable."[40] In November, Baccus was replaced by Major General Geoffrey Miller. General Miller, who had no prior experience running a detention facility, considered it his mission "to produce actionable intelligence for the nation . . . operational and strategic intelligence to help the [United States] win the global war on terror."*[41]

On October 11, 2002, the military responded to Miller by seeking approval for a set of vastly more aggressive interrogation techniques. Lieu-

---

* Miller would later achieve notoriety as the commander of the U.S. prison at Abu Ghraib, a post he took over in April 2004. In late August 2003, he and a team from Guantánamo conducted a site visit to Abu Ghraib. They brought material describing the interrogation techniques in place at Camp Delta. Not long after Miller's visit, the abuses began at Abu Ghraib.

tenant Colonel Jerald Phifer, who was part of the interrogation group, complained in a memo to Dunlavey that "[t]he current guidelines"—which he did not identify or discuss—"limit the ability of interrogators to counter advanced resistance."[42] Phifer asked Dunlavey to approve more aggressive techniques that were divided into three categories. The proposed techniques in Category I began with direct questioning but could escalate to more coercive methods whenever an interrogator believed the prisoner was being "uncooperative." Among other strategies, interrogators could identify themselves as "from a country with a reputation for harsh treatment of detainees."[43]

In Category II, which required permission from the chief of the interrogation section, the prisoner could be subjected to solitary confinement for up to thirty days at a time. Additional solitary confinement could be approved by the commanding general at the base. Prisoners could be hooded during transportation and interrogations, which could last up to twenty hours. Interrogations could take place "in an environment other than the standard interrogation booth." Prisoners could be deprived of "light and auditory stimuli." Their "comfort items" could be removed, including religious items. Interrogators could use "forced nudity [or] forced grooming (forcibly shaving a prisoner's hair and beard)." They could take advantage of a prisoner's "individual phobias (such as fear of dogs) to induce stress." And they could order inmates to stand or sit in awkward or painful positions for extended periods.[44]

In Category III, which would require approval by the commanding general at Guantánamo as well as unspecified "legal review and information" by the commander of the U.S. Southern Command, properly trained interrogators could manufacture "scenarios designed to convince the detainee that death or serious painful consequences are imminent for him and/or his family." This, of course, is a euphemism for mock execution. Interrogators could also experiment with "[e]xposure to cold weather or water (with appropriate medical monitoring)." They could "[u]se . . . a wet towel and dripping water to induce the misperception of suffocation." And they could employ "mild, non-injurious physical contact."[45]

Phifer's request was accompanied by a legal memo from Lieutenant Colonel Diane Beaver, a military attorney. As Beaver pointed out, interrogators had been carefully trained to comply with Army Field Manual 34–52, which conforms to the Geneva Conventions and prohibits all coercive interrogations. The Administration had determined, however, that the Conventions did not apply. As a result, interrogators did not know what the "interrogation limits" were. Many of them felt "they could not do anything that could be considered 'controversial.' " Beaver determined that the "more aggressive interrogation techniques" proposed by Phifer did not violate the anti-torture statute.[46] Seizing on the statute's intent requirement, Beaver thought that any interrogation technique used in a good-faith effort to secure information was not illegal. By that reasoning, she concluded that all Category I techniques were lawful so long as there was no intent to injure. The techniques in Category II were also "legally permissible . . . because there is a legitimate governmental objective in obtaining the information . . . and it is not done for the purpose of causing harm or with the intent to cause prolonged mental suffering." Category III techniques are "not illegal for the same aforementioned reasons."[47]

It is immediately apparent that Beaver's reasoning might be made to authorize *any* interrogation technique. An interrogator could always maintain that his or her only purpose was to secure information vital to the national security, and that the efforts were certainly not undertaken "for the purpose of causing harm or with the intent to cause prolonged mental suffering." Indeed, Beaver's analysis is so sweeping that it could authorize techniques that were even more aggressive than those included in Phifer's memo—it could authorize a Category IV. And recently we learned there was in fact such a category. On November 27, 2002, an FBI agent working at the base (who was also a former New York City prosecutor) sent a memo to his superiors outlining his objections to Phifer's proposed categories. Entitled "Legal Analysis of Interrogation Techniques," his memo identified each of the proposed techniques from Categories I, II, and III, but also offered this description of the single technique contemplated by a hitherto unknown Category IV:

> Detainee will be sent off GTMO, either temporarily or permanently, to Jordan, Egypt, or another third country to allow those countries to employ interrogation techniques that will enable them to obtain the requisite information.[48]

The practice of sending prisoners to the custody of a third country known for the use of torture is called extraordinary rendition, and will be discussed in Chapter 9.

Phifer's memo (with no mention of Category IV) quickly made its way up the chain of command. Major General Dunlavey accepted Beaver's legal analysis without comment and concluded the proposed techniques, even those in Category III, "do not violate U.S. or international law." He asked General James T. Hill, commander of the U.S. Southern Command, to approve them as a way to "enhance our efforts to extract additional information."[49] Two weeks later, on October 25, 2002, Hill sent a memo to Richard B. Myers, chairman of the Joint Chiefs of Staff. Hill concluded the techniques in Category I and II were "legal and humane," and recommended their approval. He thought the Category III techniques, however, particularly the use of death threats toward the prisoner or his family, required further study.[50]

After another month, William J. Haynes, general counsel for the Department of Defense, sent a memo to Defense Secretary Rumsfeld.* Haynes recommended that Rumsfeld approve all Category I and II techniques, as well as the use of "mild, non-injurious contact" from Category III, for immediate use at General Hill's discretion. He recommended that the other Category III techniques, though "legally available," should not be given "blanket approval . . . at this time." He did not identify the circumstances that would justify their use, nor did he identify who could approve them.[51] On December 2, 2002, Rumsfeld signed off on Haynes's memo, leaving the permissible scope of Category III techniques ambiguous. In a reference to the four-hour limit on stress and duress positions, however, Rumsfeld added a handwritten note: "However, I stand for 8–10 hours a day. Why is standing limited to 4 hours? D.R."[52] It is unclear whether someone misled the Secretary to believe that stress and duress positions implied nothing more than "standing," or whether he came to this error on his own.

---

* Haynes's memo was written November 27, 2002, the same day the unnamed FBI agent wrote his objections to Category IV, suggesting the category was still in discussion at Guantánamo at the time.

IV

At the time, my colleagues and I in the litigation, like the rest of the American public, had no idea this was taking place. And that, of course, was deliberate. When al Qahtani's interrogation logs became public in June 2005, the Pentagon said these were the sort of documents "that were never meant to leave GITMO."[53] All we knew was that the Administration wanted desperately to keep Guantánamo beyond judicial scrutiny.

In March 2002, in U.S. District Court for the District of Columbia, the Administration moved to dismiss *Rasul* and *Al Odah v. United States,* the case filed by Shearman & Sterling on behalf of twelve Kuwaitis that had been consolidated with *Rasul.* Relying on *Johnson v. Eisentrager* and the argument advanced by John Yoo and Patrick Philbin in their jurisdiction memo of December 2001, the Administration's lawyers argued that Guantánamo was beyond the court's jurisdiction because Cuba retained "ultimate sovereignty" over the base. Ultimate Cuban sovereignty did not imply any practical Cuban authority, and the Administration took pains to emphasize that a Cuban court was wholly powerless at the base. That, however, was irrelevant. The Administration could not articulate what "ultimate sovereignty" meant, except one thing: it meant the cases should be dismissed. On July 30, 2002, the day before Bybee and Yoo finished their torture memo, Judge Colleen Kollar-Kotelly agreed with the Administration and dismissed *Rasul* and *Al Odah.** For now, Guantánamo would remain a prison beyond the law.[54]

Meanwhile, in a courtroom a few miles away in Alexandria, Virginia, another team of government lawyers argued that Yaser Hamdi, a U.S. citizen

---

* When two or more cases are consolidated, decisions are usually published under the name of the case filed first. In the federal district court, we filed *Rasul* in February 2002, and the lawyers at Shearman & Sterling filed *Al Odah* in May. In the district court, therefore, the court's decision was published under the name *Rasul v. Bush.* In the Court of Appeals, the Shearman team filed their case before we did, and the decision of the D.C. Circuit was published under the name *Al Odah v. United States.* In the Supreme Court, we filed our papers seeking review shortly before the team from Shearman, and the decision was eventually published under the name *Rasul v. Bush.* Though the case today is known for one of our clients, it could have just as easily been one of theirs, and the name in no way reflects the relative importance of each team's contribution to the final result.

born in Baton Rouge, Louisiana, and raised in Saudi Arabia, could be held incommunicado. Hamdi had been captured by the Northern Alliance in Afghanistan late in 2001, transferred to U.S. custody, and designated an "enemy combatant." In January 2002, he was one of the first prisoners brought to Camp X-Ray. In April, when the military confirmed his citizenship, they transferred him to the U.S. naval brig in Norfolk, Virginia. In June 2002, Hamdi's father filed a habeas petition on his son's behalf in the federal court in Alexandria, which has jurisdiction over the Norfolk brig. Hamdi's lawyer, Frank Dunham, immediately sought access to his client. The government opposed the request, submitting the declaration from Colonel Donald Woolfolk discussed in Chapter 1. Woolfolk warned that allowing Hamdi to meet with his lawyer would "crippl[e] the national security." Judge Robert Doumar was unmoved and ordered the government to let Dunham meet with his client.[55]

The government took an immediate appeal to the Fourth Circuit Court of Appeals in Richmond, widely regarded as the most conservative federal appellate court in the country. The Fourth Circuit reversed Judge Doumar and sent the case back to him with instructions to proceed with "the most cautious procedures." On remand, the Bush Administration filed a declaration from Michael Mobbs, a special advisor to the undersecretary of defense for policy, who claimed that Hamdi had entered Afghanistan during the summer of 2001 to train with, and, if necessary, fight for the Taliban. Hamdi, Mobbs said, "affiliated" with a Taliban unit and surrendered to the Northern Alliance sometime in late 2001, allegedly while armed with a Kalashnikov rifle.[56]

The information in the Mobbs declaration was third-hand hearsay, originating "with an unknown person in the Northern Alliance, who communicated it to someone within the U.S. military, who put it in a military record, which was then reviewed by Mobbs."[57] According to the Administration, however, Hamdi's lawyers were not entitled to anything else. In fact, the Administration argued that while his lawyers could see the declaration, Hamdi could not. Nor could he learn of its existence, discuss it with his lawyer, or challenge it in court. By itself, the declaration provided conclusive proof that his detention was lawful, and for that reason alone his habeas petition should be dismissed. Judge Doumar, saying he would not be a "rubber stamp" for the government, disagreed and ordered the Administration to provide him with material that would support the Mobbs declaration. In August 2002, the government again took an appeal to the Fourth Circuit. Hamdi, meanwhile, had been transferred to the naval brig in Charleston, where he remained in solitary confinement.[58]

A similar battle was under way in New York. On May 8, 2002, José Padilla stepped from a plane at Chicago's O'Hare Airport and was immediately arrested by federal authorities. A federal court in New York had issued a warrant for Padilla's arrest so he could appear as a witness before a federal grand jury investigating the attacks of September 11. Federal officials brought Padilla, a U.S. citizen born and raised in Chicago, to New York, where he too was held in solitary confinement. On May 15, 2002, Chief Judge Michael Mukasey of the Southern District of New York appointed Donna Newman, an experienced criminal defense lawyer, to represent him. Newman met with Padilla a number of times and filed several motions on his behalf, including one that challenged the material witness warrant. If that motion had been successful, Padilla would have been released from custody. Mukasey scheduled the motion to be heard June 11.[59]

Two days before the hearing, however, President Bush designated Padilla an "enemy combatant" and directed the secretary of defense to take over his custody. Rumsfeld dispatched military personnel to New York, who whisked Padilla to the same brig in Charleston that would soon house Yaser Hamdi. At the hearing two days later, instead of arguing about the material witness warrant, Newman filed a habeas petition on her client's behalf. (By the time Newman filed the petition in New York, however, Padilla had already been transferred to South Carolina, a fact that would later become important.)[60]

Chief Judge Mukasey ordered the government to explain why it was holding Padilla. On August 27, 2002, the Bush Administration filed yet another hearsay declaration from Michael Mobbs, who said that from 1998 to 2001, Padilla had lived and traveled widely in the Middle East. In Afghanistan and Pakistan in 2001 and 2002, he allegedly met with members of al-Qaeda, including Abu Zubaydah, one of Osama bin Laden's senior lieutenants. The two had discussed Padilla's plans to detonate a radiological dispersion device in the United States. Zubaydah sent Padilla to Pakistan for training in explosives. In 2002, Padilla allegedly met again with senior al-Qaeda operatives, where they again discussed his plans for terrorist operations in the U.S., including the dirty-bomb plot. At the direction of these operatives, Padilla returned to the U.S. in May, where he was arrested. As it did in Hamdi's case, the Bush Administration argued that the Mobbs declaration was conclusive proof that Padilla's detention was lawful. Padilla did not have a right to see the declaration, discuss it with counsel, or challenge its content in court.[61]

On December 4, 2002, Mukasey issued a mixed decision. He agreed that the president had a right to hold Padilla as an enemy combatant. But he said that Padilla had the right to challenge the factual basis for the president's designation in court. To facilitate this challenge, Mukasey ordered the government to allow Padilla's lawyers to meet with their client (by this time Newman had enlisted the help of Andy Patel, another experienced criminal defense lawyer). On January 9, 2003, the government asked Judge Mukasey to reconsider his order. It submitted the declaration from Admiral Jacoby first discussed in Chapter 1. Like Colonel Woolfolk, Jacoby warned against allowing Padilla to meet with counsel. Judge Mukasey, however, like Judge Doumar in Virginia, was unpersuaded. In March 2003, the Bush Administration appealed his order to the Second Circuit Court of Appeals, in New York.[62]

By the time all three cases—*Rasul* in Washington, *Hamdi* in Virginia, and *Padilla* in New York—had progressed into the appellate courts, Padilla had been held in solitary confinement since May 2002. Hamdi had been in solitary confinement since April 2002, when he was moved from Cuba to Norfolk. The prisoners in Cuba had been held incommunicado for fourteen months, most of the time in solitary confinement.

V

If you drum into a soldier's brain that certain behavior is wrong—that it is morally reprehensible, tactically counterproductive, and strategically short-sighted—you cannot expect that on the day you decide differently he will suddenly disregard all he has been taught, all he has come to believe, and behave as you would like. It is a testament to the honor and professionalism of the U.S. military that at least some of its members resisted the developments at Guantánamo Bay.

In December 2002, Dr. Michael Gelles, the chief psychologist for the

Navy Criminal Investigative Service, reported that interrogators at Camp Delta were using "abusive techniques and coercive psychological procedures." Alberto Mora, the Navy's general counsel, complained that the techniques were "unlawful and unworthy of the military services." Senior officials within the Navy were so incensed by the way prisoners were being treated that they threatened to pull their interrogators from the facility.[63] On January 15, 2003, responding to these complaints, Secretary Rumsfeld rescinded his December 2 order. He withdrew approval of all Category II techniques as well as the single authorized technique from Category III, the use of "mild, non-injurious" contact. At the same time, he established a Working Group to evaluate "the legal, policy, and operational issues relating to the interrogations of detainees held by the U.S. Armed Forces in the war on terrorism." The remarkable thing about this order is not that he created this group, or that he charged it with examining these important issues, but rather that no one in the Administration figured the issue was important enough to study until more than a year after the prisoners began to arrive at Guantánamo—and thirteen months after John Yoo and Robert Delahunty had concluded the Geneva Conventions did not apply to the prisoners. To underscore how little Rumsfeld understood the magnitude of his request, he directed the Working Group to complete its study within fifteen days. The Working Group issued its final report eighty days later, on April 4, 2003.[64]

Devoting much of their analysis to the anti-torture statute, the authors of the working group report adopt almost verbatim the most offensive features of the Bybee/Yoo torture memo. Like Bybee and Yoo, they stress that an interrogator has not committed a crime unless the pain or suffering he or she inflicts is "of such a high level of intensity that the pain is difficult for the subject to endure." Because the statute requires specific intent, an interrogator is not guilty unless he or she "acts with the express purpose of inflicting severe pain or suffering. . . ." But in any case, the president's power as commander in chief renders the whole statute irrelevant; the statute "must be construed as inapplicable to interrogations undertaken pursuant to [the] Commander in Chief authority."[65]

The Working Group included the top legal officers from each service branch of the military, all of whom objected to the use of interrogation techniques that were not authorized by Field Manual 34–52. Major General

Thomas Romig, the judge advocate general for the U.S. Army, predicted these "questionable techniques" were unlikely to produce reliable intelligence, but would almost certainly "establish a baseline for acceptable practice." The result would not only endanger U.S. military personnel, but vitiate the "POW/detainee safeguards the U.S. has worked hard to establish over the past five decades."[66] Major General Jack Rives, deputy judge advocate of the U.S. Air Force, warned that the Administration failed to appreciate "the overall impact of approving extreme interrogation techniques." He cautioned against giving "official approval and official sanction to the application of interrogation techniques that U.S. forces have consistently been trained are unlawful."[67]

Brigadier General Kevin Sandkuhler, staff judge advocate to the commandant of the Marine Corps, complained that the Working Group draft failed to "accurately portray the services' concerns that the authorization of aggressive counter-resistance techniques by servicemembers" put U.S. personnel at risk should they be captured, and diminished the "pride, discipline, and self-respect within the U.S. Armed Forces." While the draft accurately portrayed the view of the Justice Department Office of Legal Counsel, "OLC does not represent the services; thus, understandably, concern for servicemembers is not reflected in their opinion."[68] And Rear Admiral Michael Lohr, the judge advocate general for the U.S. Navy, noted that the techniques were "inconsistent with our most fundamental values." He recommended that decision-makers ask the one question that seemed to have eluded them: "is this the 'right thing' for U.S. military personnel?" Admiral Lohr also believed the report should include an acknowledgment that the prisoners were protected by the fourth Geneva Convention (the Civilian Convention), a view he said was shared by the lawyers in the Joint Chiefs of Staff and all the services. As we saw in Chapter 3, the Civilian Convention, like the POW Convention, prohibits coercive interrogations.[69]

All of these objections fell on deaf ears. The final Working Group report endorsed the use of thirty-five techniques, many of which went substantially beyond the techniques authorized by the Geneva Conventions and the Army Field Manual, including extended isolation, sleep deprivation, the continued use of prolonged interrogations ("e.g., 20 hours per day per interrogation"), hooding during an interrogation, "environmental manipulation" (prolonged exposure to extreme heat or cold), removal of clothing, the threat of transfer to a third country that would subject the prisoner "to torture or death," "false flag" (convincing a prisoner he is being interrogated by someone from another country), and "increasing anxiety by use of aversions" such as dogs.[70]

The Working Group report clearly shows the influence of the Bybee/Yoo torture memo, indicating a close collaboration between the Departments of Defense and Justice. According to one military lawyer who worked on the report, the Administration's objective in preparing the report was to place "presidential power at its absolute apex."[71] No one seemed to have thought to consult with the State Department during this process, and no one from State was in the Working Group.[72] This was an unfortunate omission. For many years, the State Department, which projects America's image and moral authority overseas, has issued scathing reports condemning countries around the world for using many of the interrogation practices endorsed by the working group. In the 2004 report on Turkey, for instance, released February 28, 2005, the State Department complained that "security officials mainly used torture methods that did not leave physical traces, including . . . exposure to cold, stripping and blindfolding, food and sleep deprivation, threats to detainees or family members . . . and mock executions." This at least appears to represent an improvement from prior years, when the State Department also criticized Turkey for using "forced prolonged standing, isolation, loud music, witnessing or hearing incidents of torture, being driven to the countryside for a mock execution, and threats to detainees or their family members."[73]

The State Department has similarly protested that "elements of the security apparatus" in China use "prolonged periods of solitary confinement [and] incommunicado detention."[74] "Common methods" of torture in Iran include "prolonged solitary confinement," "long confinement in contorted positions," the threat of execution, and sleep deprivation. Government officials in that country have created "a series of 'unofficial' secret prisons and detention centers outside the national prison system."[75] The State Department has repeatedly condemned Jordan for using "sleep deprivation [and] extended solitary confinement."[76] In Burma, security forces "routinely subjected detainees to harsh interrogation techniques designed to intimidate and disorient," and forced prisoners "to squat or assume stressful, uncomfortable, or painful positions for lengthy periods."[77] Examples like this could be readily multiplied.[78]

On April 16, 2003, Secretary Rumsfeld approved the use of twenty-four of these techniques at Guantánamo Bay, including extended isolation, sleep "adjustment" (which, they say, is not sleep deprivation), environmental manipulation, and false flag. Rumsfeld's order is undoubtedly a welcome improvement on Phifer's three categories and on the working group report. For instance, his order does not explicitly allow interrogators to threaten the prisoner or his family with death or serious injury, nor does it approve the use of wet towels across the prisoner's face to "induce the misperception of suffocation." It apparently does not allow the use of stress and duress positions or hooding during an interrogation. But prisoners still may be kept indefinitely in solitary confinement. They may be subjected to interrogations of indefinite duration. (Recall that Phifer asked for permission to conduct twenty-hour interrogations. We do not know how long interrogations may persist at present.) This is particularly worrisome since the order also allows "sleep adjustment," which refers to a reversal of sleep cycles from night to day. Though this is not intended to be sleep deprivation, it is easy to see how this technique, in combination with extended interrogations, could produce the same result.[79]

More importantly, there is a troubling qualification in the fine print: the April order allows interrogators to use *any* interrogation technique, even those not listed in the order, so long as they get prior approval from the secretary of defense. Nothing done to al Qahtani, for instance, is necessarily out of bounds. Once again, therefore, the only assurance against the abuse of these various techniques is the Administration's unenforceable promise to exercise the power wisely. As we will see, this is not a promise that will protect the prisoners.

Finally, the April order takes as its starting point the conclusion that the military has the right people in custody. It assumes, in other words, the critical fact at issue—that a competent tribunal has established by a lawful process that the prisoner belongs in custody in the first place. No amount of tinkering with the conditions of a prisoner's confinement can justify a wrongful incarceration and the April order does nothing to restore due process to Camp Delta.

•   •   •

In Chapter 2, we saw the migration of techniques developed by the CIA in the KUBARK manual to the Department of Defense. The April 2003 order completes the process. It imports a legal analysis that was originally meant for CIA interrogations outside the country and applies it to military interrogations at Guantánamo. And while the April order is limited to interrogations at Guantánamo, its guidance quickly traveled to Afghanistan and became the basis for all Defense Department interrogations in the war on terror. It remains in effect today.[80]

VI

On December 30, 2004, one week before Alberto Gonzales was scheduled to testify before the Senate Judiciary Committee on his nomination to be attorney general, the Bush Administration withdrew the Bybee/Yoo torture memo and issued a new interpretation of the anti-torture statute. The revised memo retreats from the suggestion that torture requires pain "equivalent in intensity to the pain accompanying serious physical injury, such as organ failure, impairment of bodily function, or even death," and recognizes that it had been a mistake to interpret the anti-torture statute based on a statute about medical benefits.[81] The new memo also backs away slightly from the suggestion that torture must be the interrogator's "precise objective," noting that "it would not be appropriate to rely on parsing the specific intent element of the statute to approve as lawful conduct that might otherwise amount to torture."[82]

Still, the new memo is a carefully crafted document. In a footnote, the authors make a point of saying they reviewed the prior opinions addressing "issues involving treatment of detainees"—including the torture memo—and found that none of the earlier conclusions "would be different under the standards set forth in this memorandum." Substantively, in other words, the new memo changes nothing. None of the interrogation practices developed from the advice contained in the old memo is called into question by the new memo. In addition, the new memo pointedly *does not* retreat from the position in the Bybee/Yoo memo that the commander in chief has the inherent power to overrule Congress and order the use of torture. On that score, the new memo, which was explicitly written for public release, says only that the discussion by Bybee and Yoo had been "unnecessary."[83] As we will see, the Bush Administration continues to claim the unfettered power to allow interrogators to use any technique, regardless of the will of Congress.

SIX

"THE MORE SUBTLE KIND OF TORMENT"

The Bush Administration did not concoct the techniques used against Mohammed al Qahtani from whole cloth. As the KUBARK and *Human Resource Exploitation* manuals make plain, a sustained program of secrecy, isolation, and control will eventually produce sufficient disorientation, anxiety, and dread to break the will of nearly any prisoner. And for those few who manage to resist, the calculated use of painful and debilitating techniques and, more importantly, the *threat* of such techniques, will generally tip the balance. Rarely is it necessary to resort to the more grotesque forms of physical torture and coercion that have been used to extract confessions—and false confessions—since time immemorial. But the Bush Administration should have known that even these "touchless" techniques did not originate with the United States.

I

Because of the issues that come before it, and the number of judges elevated from there to the Supreme Court, the U.S. Court of Appeals in Washington, D.C., is often described as the second highest court in the land. The judges on the court are generally among the most distinguished jurists in the country. In the 1960s and '70s, the D.C. Circuit was one of the most liberal circuit courts in the country. Over the past two decades, however, it has become increasingly conservative, a shift reflected in the court's rulings. On December 2, 2002, a three-judge panel turned its attention to Guantánamo: A. Raymond Randolph, who had been appointed by President George H. W. Bush in 1990; Merrick Garland, a Clinton appointee; and Senior Judge Stephen Williams, who had been named to the bench by Ronald Reagan. Williams had taken senior status in September 2001.

As in the district court, the court had consolidated *Al Odah* and *Rasul* into a single case. Tom Wilner from Shearman & Sterling argued for the Kuwaiti prisoners in *Al Odah* and I argued for the prisoners in *Rasul*. Deputy Solicitor General Paul Clement, now the solicitor general, made the case for the United States. Clement continued to press the Guantánamo fiction. The prisoners at Camp Delta were no different from the prisoners in *Johnson v. Eisentrager,* he said. They were all foreign nationals detained "abroad."[1] Tom and I pointed out that by the time the prisoners in *Johnson* filed in federal court they had already received the benefit of a lawful process, the very thing our clients had been denied. In any event, Guantánamo, an area subject to the exclusive jurisdiction and control of the United States for as long as we see fit, could hardly be compared to wartime Germany or China. The panel had originally reserved twenty minutes for oral argument. Ninety minutes later, the court took the case under advisement.

Twenty-four hours after the argument, President Bush spoke at the state fairgrounds in Shreveport, Louisiana. The president assured his audience, "we're making progress in this war against terror." The United States had recently captured "a guy named al Nashiri." "Let me just put it to you this way," the president said. "He no longer has the capacity to do what he did in the past. . . . He's out of action." (Abd al Rahim al Nashiri is now held by the CIA in an undisclosed location, reportedly in the North African desert.[2]) September 11 had ushered in a "new reality," he continued, one that required allegiance to a common cause: "either you're with us or you're with the terrorists." September 11 had also made the world smaller and more dangerous. Broad oceans could not protect us from "gathering threats . . . And that's why I elevated the issue of Iraq." Saddam Hussein "doesn't tell the truth. He says he won't have weapons of mass destruction; he's got them." The president then traced the thread he had divined between Iraq and 9/11:

By being tough and strong and united in the face of danger, we can bring peace to the world. . . . I believe that by doing what we need to do to secure the world from terrorist attack, to rid tyrants of weapons of mass destruction, to make sure that somebody like Saddam Hussein doesn't serve as a training base or a provider of weapons of mass destruction to terrorist networks—by doing our job, that the world will be more peaceful.[3]

In these uncertain times, it is worth recalling that the threat posed by weapons of mass destruction is not new. Nearly five decades before 9/11, the American public learned that a prisoner in military custody had confessed to participating in an elaborate conspiracy to bomb civilian targets with bacteriological weapons. His handwritten confession described in painstaking detail the origin, scope, and intended sweep of this conspiracy. He named his co-conspirators, recounted their clandestine meetings, and described their long-term plans. The goal, he said, was nothing less than "the mass annihilation of the civilian population."[4] One confession led to another, and before long, the public discovered that thirty-five other prisoners had provided similar, corroborating confessions—page upon page of chilling, meticulously detailed admissions.

But it was all a lie. Thirty-six American airmen, shot from the sky during the Korean War, falsely confessed to bombing civilian targets with bacteriological weapons. The most important of these confessions was that of Colonel Frank Schwable, the highest-ranking Marine captured during the war. Schwable was shot down July 8, 1952, shortly after he arrived in Korea. By late November, he began to cooperate with the enemy. Throughout December and the first three weeks of January 1953, he wrote, edited, and revised a remarkably detailed statement, eventually running almost six thousand words. Between February 1 and February 20, he repeatedly practiced his confession, eventually recording it in front of motion picture cameras. Finally, on February 22, 23, and 24, his statement was broadcast worldwide over Radio Peking. On March 13, Soviet Foreign Minister Andrei Vishinsky introduced Colonel Schwable's statement before the United Nations.[5]

Schwable's confession was immediately denounced in the United States. General Mark Clark, the commander of U.N. forces in Korea, called his allegations "fabricated . . . , fantastic, and utterly false."[6] A number of the military personnel named as co-conspirators in Schwable's confession denied his allegations under oath. Brigadier General Clayton Jerome, who had been Schwable's commander in Korea, denounced the allegations as "a damn lie, and I would like to go up to the U.N. and tell them so."[7] On March 27, 1953, the United States introduced the denials before the United Nations, along with a demand for an independent investigation.[8] Percy Spender, Australia's ambassador to the United States, called the charges the "most monstrous accusation that could be made by a state that calls itself civilized."[9] But behind the angry denials by the U.S. and our allies lurked a troubling question: what had the communists done to secure these confessions?

North Korea treated most American prisoners with a barbarism that simply defies comprehension, especially in the first year of the war. Hundreds of American prisoners died in forced marches. One survivor described such a march in April 1951:

> [T]hey started to double-time us from fifteen to twenty miles at night. Men who fell out were either beaten to death, shot, or pushed over cliffs. Others died of starvation during periods of rest in Korean houses. . . . I saw the interpreter tie two men and beat them with a rifle butt and bayonet; that night they fell out of column and I heard two shots fired. I looked back and saw two guards running to catch up with the rear of the column. . . . When we arrived at Camp No. 1 we had a roll call. There were 325 men left out of the original 735 men.[10]

In October 1950, sixty-eight prisoners who survived a march from Seoul to Pyongyang were gunned down outside a railroad tunnel north of Sunchon, Korea. Another American POW who survived the massacre later recalled the scene:

> The last car was unloaded and the men were told to go to the mouth of the tunnel where they would be fed. They were told to sit down in groups and then, without warning, they were machine-gunned. In the scramble a few men actually got away, but for the most part they were all murdered.[11]

Thousands of other POWs died in prison camps. Weakened by the march from the front or wounded when they were captured, they died by the scores from starvation, malnutrition, and dysentery in primitive, over-crowded camps. Men slept on the floor in rooms without latrines. In the largest camp, Camp 5, the Koreans packed twenty-five prisoners into every fourteen by nine-foot room. Those who survived in the camps were often subjected to ingenious tortures as punishment for real or imagined trans-gressions. Prisoners were beaten, hung by their hands, or forced to stand barefoot on the frozen ground for hours at a time.[12] Around Christmas 1950, the Koreans distributed seven copies of a propaganda magazine titled *People's China* to a group of prisoners. When the Koreans later came to col-lect the magazines, only two remained. One soldier recounted the punish-ment meted out to the entire group:

> [T]wo Chinese and a Korean . . . told us all to fall in outside. . . . The group consisted of approximately thirty to thirty-five men. At this time the temperature was below zero and a strong cold wind was blowing. None of the prisoners were well clothed. We were made to stand with our hands in the air. If anyone moved or lowered his arms, he was struck with a limb from a tree. We remained exposed for approx-imately four and a half hours. As a result of this exposure many of the prisoners had frozen limbs. After we returned to our room no medical aid was given. As a result approximately half of the men in this group died.[13]

Very little that we have seen from Abu Ghraib prison, Guantánamo, Bagram Air Base, or other post-9/11 U.S. facilities even approaches this sadistic cruelty. Hundreds of American prisoners "confessed" to a variety of war crimes in Korea. One should attach no significance to these confes-sions, since they establish only that a man will say anything if he believes his life depends on it. That much we have known for centuries. But Colonel Schwable's false confession, and that of the other airmen who falsely con-fessed to using weapons of mass destruction, cannot be so easily dismissed.

· · ·

Throughout their incarceration, the North Koreans kept the American air-men completely isolated.* First Lieutenant Kenneth Enoch, who was shot down January 13, 1952, spent thirteen months in solitary confinement. Major Roy Bley, who was shot down with Colonel Schwable, was in solitary confinement for ten months, during which time he was not "permitted [to] talk or even see any other prisoners of war."[14] Colonel Andrew Evans, downed March 26, 1953, later said he "never saw another person except my guards and interrogators, nor was any news of the outside world given to me." John Quinn, who flew with Lieutenant Enoch, reported much the same thing.[15] Schwable did not learn of the armistice until after he con-fessed. The North Koreans did not even begin the interrogation of Schwable and Bley until they had completed a two-week "thinking period." They were separated from each other and left completely alone in small rooms. "There is no distraction," Schwable said later. "You sit there and you just think. You reflect. You analyze. You grasp at anything your mind can concoct—any-thing—and anything you flash back as you go along is exaggerated more and more. Your judgment becomes warped."[16] "You get a feeling of utter, hopeless despair." When interrogators finally arrived, Schwable welcomed them for the human contact they provided. He remained in solitary con-finement for fourteen months.[17]†

Once the interrogations began, they did not stop. Like Mohammed al Qahtani, the airmen were kept to a relentless schedule of repetitive ques-tioning. Bley said his interrogators permitted him to sleep some nights, but on other occasions would not let him lie down. Lieutenant Paul Kniss said he was interrogated "for periods lasting up to twenty hours." Schwable and Colonel Walker Mahurin described "night raids."[18] Guards roused them out of bed in the middle of the night to begin another round of interrogations. (At Guantánamo, this is called placing a prisoner on the "frequent flier pro-

---

* The airmen included two Marines—Colonel Schwable and Major Roy Bley, who were shot down together. The rest were with the Air Force.

† After his release from Camp Delta, Shafiq Rasul described his reaction to solitary confine-ment in similar terms: "I just had to sit there waiting. I felt like I was going out of my mind. I didn't know where the others were, I didn't know why I was being held there. Nobody would talk to me. I was taken out maybe just twice for showers but that was it. I was extremely anx-ious." Composite statement, 65–66.

gram.")[19] Evans said he was kept awake for days at a time, "except for a brief few moments when I would lapse into unconsciousness and then [be] forcibly awakened."[20] Sleep deprivation was often complemented by the use of stress and duress positions. Bley was sometimes ordered to stand for six or seven hours per day. Evans was forced to stand at attention for up to twelve hours, often until he passed out. Other times, he was forced to sit "erect on a hard stool for 15 hours [per] day." During one period, Mahurin was forced to sit at attention on the edge of a stool for fifteen hours per day for thirty-three days. Another time he had to stand for thirty consecutive hours until he collapsed.[21] Schwable was required to sit at attention every day for almost ten weeks.[22]

At the same time, the North Koreans exercised an almost obsessive control over every aspect of the airmen's lives. The prisoners had to ask permission to sleep, to lie down, to bathe, and to use the latrine. Bley said he "was not allowed to leave the cave except to urinate and then only during daylight hours." Mahurin said the guards ordered him not to close the door of his cell and that "at all times two guards . . . watched my every move."[23] Schwable said he was "under the constant surveillance of a guard who was never more than perhaps ten yards away." This forced dependency produced a regression, just as the KUBARK manual would have predicted. The airmen became confused, enfeebled, their mental acuity dulled "to that of a child."[24]

Finally, the North Koreans deliberately humiliated the airmen. Schwable said the guards kept him unshaven and "growled" or "barked" at him, slopped food at him, and made him defecate in public. "They did everything to just make you feel as little and as insignificant and useless as they possibly could," he said. "Every effort was made to degrade and humiliate me and reduce me to the level of an animal wallowing around in dirt and filth, living practically the life of a beast in a cage." During an eight-month period, Bley took one bath.[25]

In the end, the psychological pressure combined to overwhelm Schwable and the other airmen and destroyed their capacity to resist. Schwable later described his ordeal as a "slow, quiet, and diabolical" poisoning of the mind.[26] Witnesses who saw him during this period said he was hallucinating, shadowboxing against imaginary foes, flailing about "like a punch drunk prize fighter," and shouting that he was surrounded by oil.[27] But Schwable and several other airmen were careful to distinguish the treatment they endured from the grotesque physical abuse heaped upon so many American GIs in Korea:

> I want to re-emphasize that I did not undergo physical torture. Perhaps I would have been more fortunate if I had, because people nowadays seem to understand that better. I didn't have that. Mine was the more subtle kind of torment. That kind is a little bit harder, I am afraid, for people to understand.[28]

Several of the other airmen said much the same thing. "It is an unpleasant memory," Lieutenant Alvert Seaver said, "[but] I was not physically tortured." Lieutenant Floyd O'Neal alluded to "physical torture of sorts," but his account of his treatment did not involve direct physical contact. Evans said that on one occasion, the North Koreans slapped and kicked him. Major William Harris said he would have preferred physical abuse instead of the "mental torture" he endured. "They don't have to lay a hand on you to make you the most miserable person in the world. I would rather take a beating any day than be subjected to their type of questioning and treatment."[29] It appears that none of these airmen were tortured as the Administration defined the term in the torture memo.

II

It is vitally important that we acknowledge the differences between the "touchless" interrogation techniques used on the American airmen in North Korea and those used on the prisoners at Guantánamo, Afghanistan, and other locations. Some of the airmen, for example, were forced to live in caves or mud hovels during significant parts of their incarceration. Schwable spent ten weeks, from early September to late November 1952, in an unheated lean-to next to a Korean house. Though he was given winter clothing and a quilt, the cold was brutal.[30] While prisoners at Guantánamo were originally kept outdoors in chain-link cages, this lasted only until the military had completed work on a permanent facility. To be sure, as we will see in the next chapter, the military has made extensive use of "environmental manipulations," subjecting prisoners to hours of extreme heat or cold, screamingly loud cacophonous sounds, or dizzying strobe lights to weaken their resistance. But the prisoners do not live outdoors (though al Qahtani was kept in the outdoor cages at Camp X-Ray during his lengthy interrogation). Likewise, the food provided to many of the airmen in Korea was horrific, and a number of the soldiers lost a significant amount of weight and became quite ill. By contrast, the United States has generally provided its prisoners with an adequate diet.

Yet for the airmen, the physical degradations were not what produced the false confessions. As they discovered, and as the KUBARK manual would later confirm, people generally have a much higher tolerance for physical discomfort than they do for psychological stress. The primitive conditions of confinement alone, though certainly illegal, probably would not have overcome their capacity to resist. But the psychological pressure— the isolation and fear, the mind-numbing, repetitive interrogations, the sense of despair, the complete lack of control over one's daily life, all of which were brought to bear on soldiers who were weak and exhausted— these were the features that drove the American airmen to confess, and it is these features that are so disturbingly similar to the techniques authorized by the Bush Administration after 9/11.[31]

In addition, there is a fundamental difference in the purpose of these interrogations. The North Koreans were extracting "confessions" they knew to be false in order to use them as a propaganda tool. Manifestly, the United States has no interest, and certainly no legitimate interest, in deliberately developing false intelligence. But while the United States has no legitimate interest in generating unreliable intelligence, the obvious concern is that interrogators will unwittingly give credence to a false confession simply because it conforms to what they believe to be true. In fact, in matters of this sort the sincere mistake is far more dangerous than the deliberate falsehood. Though the military is unlikely to act based on what it knows to be a lie, it will almost certainly go forward based on what it believes to be true, all to the nation's great regret if that information turns out to be mistaken.

Nothing would seem to confirm this more clearly, and more tragically, than the disastrous interrogation of Ibn Shaykh al Libi, another so-called high-value detainee in the war on terror. Three months after September 11, 2001, Pakistani troops captured al Libi and delivered him to the CIA, who rendered him to Egypt, but not before a CIA agent told him, "You're going to Cairo, you know. Before you get there, I'm going to find your mother and I'm going to f*** her." [32] In Egypt, al Libi confessed that he received instructions in 1998 to travel to Iraq to obtain training with poisons and gases. Al Libi also said that in December 2000, two more al-Qaeda operatives went to Iraq to train with chemical and biological weapons. [33]

Al Libi's confession would soon become a central piece of the Administration's argument in favor of the war in Iraq. On October 7, 2002, four days before Lieutenant Colonel Phifer first sought approval for the use of coercive interrogation techniques at Camp Delta, the president announced in a speech in Cincinnati that "Iraq and al Qaeda have had high-level contacts that go back a decade. . . . We've learned that Iraq has trained al Qaeda members in bomb-making and poisons and deadly gases." [34] Secretary of State Colin Powell elaborated on this claim in his now-discredited presentation to the U.N. Security Council in February 2003. Powell warned that Iraq had weapons of mass destruction and that it had formed a "sinister nexus" with "the Al Qaida network." Powell assured the council that "every statement" he made was "based on solid intelligence . . . from human sources." [35] One month after Powell's speech, partly on the basis of this "solid intelligence," the United States and its coalition partners invaded Iraq.

Coalition forces never located weapons of mass destruction. In March 2005, in a letter to the president, the Commission on the Intelligence Capabilities of the United States Regarding Weapons of Mass Destruction concluded that "the Intelligence Community was dead wrong in almost all of its pre-war judgments about Iraq's weapons of mass destruction." [36] Al Libi later recanted his confession, and looking back on his interrogation, some U.S. officials have concluded interrogators induced al Libi to say what they wanted to hear. [37]

III

The torture, murder, and abuse of U.S. prisoners of war in Korea provoked a bitter outcry in this country. The Senate appointed a committee to investigate Korean War atrocities, held extensive hearings, and issued a blistering report. [38] On November 30, 1953, Henry Cabot Lodge, U.S. ambassador to the United Nations, took to the floor of the General Assembly and recounted these atrocities in painstaking detail. At the end of his presentation,

Lodge noted with scorn and derision that North Korea, like the United States, had promised at the start of the war that it would "strictly abid[e] by the principles of the Geneva Conventions." [39] Yet their promise had come to naught. Lodge closed his remarks with a universal appeal:

> No human power can undo or retrieve the evils that have been done . . . But the United Nations should speak clearly in defense of the civilized standards of conduct which find expression in the Geneva conventions and which are here involved. We may thus at least help to reverse a deterioration in human standards of conduct which, if not checked, will lead the world straight back to the jungle. [40]

Lodge was followed by Sir Hubert Miles Gladwyn Jebb, the United Kingdom ambassador to the United Nations, who warned that the United Nations must not "lose our awareness of the direct relationship between our actions here and the sub-human cruelties which a condition of war seems to evoke among those who are not restrained by a sense of the primordial virtues enshrined in the Geneva conventions." [41]

Like the rest of the country, the CIA also took note of the Korean atrocities. But the CIA was especially interested in the confessions secured from the downed airmen. The agency was alarmed that the communists managed to extract such detailed statements from experienced American officers without resort to physical torture. The realization dramatically accelerated the research under way at universities across the United States, much of it funded by the CIA, into the psychology of coercive questioning. What makes a person confess? Are some factors more important than others, and could they be isolated, refined, and taught to U.S. agents? Between 1950 and 1962, the CIA poured millions of dollars into this and related research, which culminated in the KUBARK manual in 1963. [42]

But the experience of the downed airmen also produced a defensive program. On August 17, 1955, in response to the alarming number of POWs who confessed during the Korean War, President Eisenhower signed an executive order establishing a code of conduct for American servicemen. The code required that soldiers, even if captured by the enemy, must continue to resist by any means at their disposal. Captivity was only an extension of the battlefield, and not an end to a soldier's obligation to his country. In order to prepare soldiers for the challenges presented by captivity, the president required that each member of the armed forces at risk of capture be provided with "specific training and instruction designed to better equip him to counter and withstand all enemy efforts against him."[43]

Given its experiences in Korea, it is hardly surprising that the Air Force took the lead in this endeavor. Shortly after the Korean War, the Air Force developed a program called SERE, for Survival, Evasion, Resistance, and Escape. During the first phase, Survival, fliers are abandoned in remote areas with nothing but a flight suit and part of a parachute. In the second part, Evasion, stranded students are hunted by SERE instructors. But it was the third part of the three-week course that represented the most important innovation. With a meticulous attention to detail, the Air Force recreated the conditions in Korea that drove the airmen to confess. Prisoners were isolated, stripped of their clothing, deprived of food and sleep, subjected to prolonged stress and duress techniques, humiliated, and subjected to long hours of intense questioning.[44] Michael Durant, the downed flier whose ordeal became the basis for the book *Black Hawk Down,* said the program "was designed to demoralize, debase, and degrade us, and it was very effective."[45]

After Vietnam, SERE expanded to the Army and Navy. In 1985, the military produced a detailed set of regulations that describe the obligations of a captured soldier and the elements of SERE training.[46] The Army regulations explain why such a program is necessary: American POWs are protected by the Geneva Conventions, which specifically prohibit the use of coercive interrogation techniques. "Unfortunately," however, "captors of American personnel have not treated [American soldiers] in accordance with the spirit or letter" of the Conventions. Instead, captors have resorted to a variety of "illegal" practices in an effort to "exploit" American servicemen, including "psychological pressure," "physical mistreatment," and "medical neglect." The code of conduct, complemented by rigorous SERE training, is an attempt to provide soldiers with a "mental and spiritual defense" so that they may resist these illegal tactics.[47] Today, every branch of the U.S. Armed Forces has developed its own version of the SERE program.

For perfectly sound reasons, the SERE curriculum is classified. Training of this sort quickly loses its value if soldiers know what to expect, or if hostile forces know how American personnel have been trained. Nevertheless, SERE graduates and instructors have disclosed some of the techniques used in the training. Captured prisoners are hooded, deprived of food and sleep, and confined in a mock prison camp under harsh and primitive conditions. They are repeatedly subjected to a program of coercive interrogations. Soldiers may be forced to endure sexual and religious humiliation—devout servicemen may have to watch an interrogator rip a Bible to shreds; others may have to stand naked while female interrogators taunt and insult them.[48]

Some soldiers have been put through a modified version of water-boarding (except that the soldiers do not know the technique has been changed for their safety). One graduate of the program later became an editor for the *Washington Monthly*. He described SERE's version of water-boarding, which began when guards suddenly "swarmed" over a prisoner, cuffed his arms and legs to a board, and covered his face with a bandana:

> Then another guard started pouring water over the cloth. [The prisoner's] limbs strained at the cuffs as if he was being shocked. The groaning, gurgling sounds were . . . awful. . . . Every 20 seconds or so, the torturers would remove the cloth so the commandant could ask a question.[49]

In the early '90s, the Air Force SERE program introduced a "sexual exploitation scenario." One female trainee said she was nearly raped. A male soldier was forced to wear makeup and dress in a skirt fashioned from a plastic garbage bag. An instructor forced him to "act like a girl, curtsy, and sit on his lap." Later, he was forced to remove his "skirt" and bend over a table. Then his captors brought in another prisoner, made him disrobe, and forced him to pretend he was having sex with the first captive.[50]

According to the Pentagon, the goal of this ordeal, by now familiar from the KUBARK manual, is to "strip soldiers of their identities" by creating conditions of unbearable anxiety and stress. The rationale is simple: "Is the guy going to be under stress in captivity? You're dang straight. So we're going to put him under stress here to prepare him for that."[51]*

SERE has produced a wealth of valuable defensive strategies. Under the supervision of trained psychologists and psychiatrists, the schools have become a laboratory for the study of coercive interrogations, with a constant stream of human subjects. The advice given to American soldiers captured by terrorists, for example, is to engage in a dialogue about "non-substantive topics," like sports, family, and clothing, in order to convey the prisoner's "personal dignity." "The purpose of this dialogue is for the hostage to become a 'person' in the captor's eyes, rather than a mere symbol of his or her ideological hatred."[52] As the Army has discovered, it is much more difficult to torture a human being than a symbol.

But of course, careful study of how to *resist* "psychological pressure" and "physical mistreatment" also produces a record of how to *apply* the same techniques. In one of the more controversial aspects of the Administration's post-9/11 detention policy, experienced mental health professionals, who developed their defensive expertise at SERE programs, are now teaching interrogators at Camp Delta and elsewhere how to apply the very techniques U.S. soldiers have been taught to resist. At a press briefing in June 2004, General James Hill, then the head of the U.S. Southern Command, said that the list of coercive interrogation techniques drafted in October 2002 and approved by Secretary Rumsfeld in December resulted from a close collaboration between experts from the Army SERE school at Fort Bragg, North Carolina, and interrogation teams at Guantánamo.[53]

As a result of this collaboration, SERE principles have become an integral part of interrogations at Camp Delta and elsewhere. Nowhere is this collaboration more evident than in the role of mental health professionals at the base. In late 2002, Major General Geoffrey Miller, who replaced

---

* The CIA developed a similar program. Agents posing as prisoners "were deprived of sleep, kept doused with water in cold rooms, forced to sit or stand in uncomfortable positions for long periods, isolated from sunlight and social contacts, given food deliberately made unappetizing . . . , and subjected to mock executions. At least 10 percent of the volunteers dropped out, even though they knew it was a training exercise." See Mark Bowden, "The Dark Art of Interrogation," *Atlantic Monthly* (October 2003). Bowden says the CIA discontinued this program in the '70s.

Brigadier General Rick Baccus with a mandate to get "actionable intelligence," approved the introduction of the "Behavioral Science Consultation Teams" (BSCT, pronounced "Biscuit"). According to the Pentagon, the BSCT teams, each of which includes a psychiatrist and a psychologist, "observe interrogations, assess detainee behavior and motivations, review interrogation techniques, and offer advice to interrogators."[54] Their advice, however, derives from SERE techniques. SERE psychologists, for instance, have traveled to Guantánamo to consult with the staff on how best to overcome a prisoner's "resistance."[55] In early 2003, Colonel Morgan Banks, a senior psychologist for the Army's SERE program, provided classified guidance to the BSCT team doctors and recommended that BSCT psychologists have SERE backgrounds.[56]

Former interrogators at the base report that BSCT doctors routinely advised them how to use prisoners' psychological vulnerability in developing their techniques. On one occasion, for instance, the BSCT team helped an interrogator devise ways to take advantage of a prisoner's profound fear of the dark. Exactly what the doctors advised the interrogator to do with this knowledge is not known. On another occasion, the BSCT team helped develop a strategy that capitalized on a prisoner's intense longing for his mother. Once again, their specific recommendations are not known, nor is it known whether the prisoner involved was one of the juveniles at the base. As one interrogator summed it up, "[t]heir purpose was to help us break them."[57] In May 2004, an FBI agent wrote a memo to his superiors outlining his "objections" and "concerns" about the use of "SERE techniques to interrogate prisoners."[58]

As has often happened since 9/11, practices that began at Guantánamo have made their way to other facilities. In November 2003, CIA agents and members of a Special Forces team repeatedly beat Abed Hamed Mowhoush, a general in the Iraqi army. Eventually, a U.S. Army interrogator and a military guard stuffed Mowhoush inside a sleeping bag, wrapped him in an electrical cord, laid him on the floor, and piled onto his chest. Mowhoush died of asphyxiation inside the sleeping bag. According to his autopsy, the fifty-six-year-old had "contusions and abrasions with pattern impressions" over much of his body. He also had six fractured ribs. Hours after his death, the Army falsely reported he had died of natural causes.[59] One of the interrogators involved in that incident was a former SERE trainer who claims to have received command authorization for the use of what he has called "the sleeping bag technique." (The Pentagon denied this.)[60] As this interrogator explained, "[a] cord was used to limit movement within the bag and help bring on claustrophobic conditions." In SERE, he said, this technique had proven "very effective." Those who squirmed or screamed in the sleeping bag were "allowed out as soon as they start to provide information."[61]

By 2004, the use of SERE techniques against prisoners in U.S. custody had become so widespread that the military began to insist that SERE graduates sign a statement promising not to apply the techniques against enemy prisoners. "We did this when we learned people were flipping it," Colonel Banks explained.[62] There is no indication that the prohibition against the use of SERE techniques extends to interrogations conducted by the CIA.

IV

Were the American airmen in Korea tortured? Probably not as the Administration defined the term in the torture memo. They were not, for instance, beaten with "iron barks, truncheons, and clubs," or subjected to "electric shocks to genitalia," some of the techniques considered torture by Bybee and Yoo. Obviously, this suggests something important about the definition. Any definition that allows such treatment to escape legal and moral condemnation in the strongest possible terms is a disgrace. But it suggests something even more important about the significance we have attached to the term "torture" (or, perhaps more precisely, "torturer"). We have laden it with moral, legal, and historical implications. Because so much rides on the result, debates about torture frequently devolve into legalistic quibbling, a testament either to the creativity of imaginative lawyers or the curse of inartful drafters. We seem to take comfort if we can plausibly argue that the conduct was something less than torture, which explains the Administration's repeated insistence that torture is done by others, and not by American soldiers or CIA agents. But the devil is in the details, and we must be careful when apparent absolutes are qualified by the lawyer's whispered footnote: "We do not torture *as our lawyers have defined the term.*"

To avoid this quibbling, I prefer to rely on the understanding formerly employed by the United States military. The Army Field Manual on interrogations, FM 34–52, defines torture as "the infliction of intense pain to

body or mind to extract a confession or information, or for sadistic pleasure." This language is obviously not self-defining, and I have no doubt
that some lawyer could argue, however implausibly, that nothing we
have seen at Camp Delta amounts to torture under this definition. But
wisely, the military does not content itself with the definition. Instead, it
provides concrete examples of prohibited behavior. Physical torture includes "[f]orcing an individual to stand, sit, or kneel in abnormal positions
for prolonged periods of time"—notwithstanding Secretary Rumsfeld's
protestation that he stands eight to ten hours a day. Mental torture includes
"[m]ock executions" and "[a]bnormal sleep deprivation." Unlawful coercion includes "[t]hreatening or implying physical or mental torture to the
subject, his family, or others to whom he owes loyalty."[63] The Administration authorized the military to use all these techniques, and all of them have
been used (albeit some more than others) at Guantánamo and in
Afghanistan. In addition, FM 34-52 offers practical guidance for those who
would be tempted to test the limits of this definition. As we saw in Chapter
2, when considering a new or controversial approach, the military directs its
interrogators to ask whether they believe the proposed technique should
also be used against a U.S. POW. If not, then the interrogator must restrain
himself.[64]

What about Mohammed al Qahtani, whose interrogation was described
in the last chapter? After *Time* released the records of his interrogation, the
Pentagon said his treatment fell considerably short of torture. In fact, it said
his interrogation plan was consistent with the Pentagon's "unequivocal
standard of humane treatment for all detainees."[65] Statements like this, of
course, tell us less about what happened to al Qahtani than they do about
the Administration's definitions of "torture" and "humane treatment." Perhaps the more important question is whether we would object if an American soldier were subjected to the same treatment, which used to be (but is
no longer) the question asked by the U.S. military.

Frank Schwable and the other airmen were repatriated at the end of the Korean War. The Air Force conducted quiet investigations and determined
that the prisoners, as a group, would not be punished for collaborating with
the enemy. In February 1954, Schwable was brought before a Marine Corps
Board of Inquiry to determine whether he would be disciplined for his col-

laboration. After hearing days of testimony, the board decided against it. "The communists," the board wrote, "have developed, and perfected, a diabolic method of torture which combines degradation, deprivation and mental harassment, and which is aimed at the destruction of the individual's will to resist." Though Schwable "resisted this torture to the limit of his ability," the treatment he experienced was "of such severity and compelling nature as constituted reasonable justification" for his actions.[66] Upholding this conclusion, General Lemuel C. Shepherd, commandant of the Marine Corps, observed that "[t]he methods of collecting military intelligence are universal."

> They rely not on the spectacular revelations of a single prisoner *but on the painstaking creation of a related mosaic of fact created out of fragments of seemingly unimportant information* gleaned from the patient questioning of thousands of captives, few of whom possess even rudimentary military knowledge. The raw material for the process is found in the prisoner who can be gotten to extend his answers beyond the zone of safety established by the [Geneva C]onvention.[67]

It is ironic that the mosaic theory can trace its historic lineage back in time to a set of elaborate, but false, confessions given by American servicemen, who claimed to have taken part in a vast conspiracy to use weapons of mass destruction against civilian targets. But it is painful to learn that the techniques adopted by the Administration in the anxious weeks and months after 9/11 are an echo of the same techniques used against these all but forgotten soldiers, who falsely confessed because their captors would not give them shelter in the "zone of safety" provided by the Geneva Conventions.

V

On March 11, 2003, the federal court of appeals in the District of Columbia handed the Administration a decisive victory. In *Al Odah v. United States,* named for the first of the Kuwaiti prisoners represented by Shearman & Sterling, the court held that the prisoners at the base had no rights that could be vindicated by a federal court. According to the appellate panel, even if the prisoners were blameless, they still had no rights because they were foreign nationals beyond the sovereign territory of the United States.[68]

Note that this result does not depend on a state of war. The fact that the prisoners were aliens beyond the sovereignty of the United States meant they had no rights, constitutional or otherwise, without regard to the temporary demands of military necessity. This is a permanent disability imposed on the prisoners as long as they were at the prison, depriving them forever of the right to seek judicial review no matter how they were treated. In fact, the Administration candidly acknowledged in another case that its position would be the same "even if the claims were that it was engaging in acts of torture or that it was summarily executing the detainees."[69]

We had argued before the D.C. Circuit December 2, 2002. Though we did not know it at the time, on that same day, while a knot of uniformed military lawyers sat nervously behind the government's table in the courtroom, Secretary of Defense Donald Rumsfeld stood at his custom-built desk a few miles away and signed off on the coercive interrogation techniques that had made their way up the military's chain of command. Over the course of the next ninety days, while the D.C. Circuit grappled with the Guantánamo fiction, interrogators at Camp Delta applied what the Chief Psychologist for the Navy's Criminal Investigative Service described as "abusive techniques and coercive psychological procedures." By March 2003, when the court issued its decision in *Al Odah*, Rumsfeld had appointed the working group, whose report in April would endorse the sweeping claim to executive branch authority first proposed in the torture memo drafted by Jay Bybee and John Yoo in August 2002. As we saw in the last chapter, this report was an attempt by the Administration to place "presidential power at its absolute apex."[70] *Al Odah* marked their greatest success. One can only wonder whether the court would have decided differently had it known then what we know now.

Part Three

☆

"OUR EXECUTIVE DOESN'T"

SEVEN

"WAR IS NOT A
BLANK CHECK"

I

Every year, the Supreme Court agrees to review only a tiny fraction of the cases clamoring for its attention. For that reason, many lawyers believe, not without reason, that the most important document in a case is the one that asks the Court to accept review, called the petition for writ of certiorari. The petition in *Rasul,* drafted in the summer of 2003, went through more than a dozen drafts, and in the final product, my colleagues and I tried to capture not simply the legal reasons for review, but the moral consequences if the Court were to remain silent. My greatest fear was that the Bush Administration would simply forget about the prisoners, in the vain hope the world would too. In time, the country would turn its attention elsewhere. Eventually, the prisoners would settle into the mind-numbing routine that characterizes prison life everywhere. Nameless and faceless, lost to a world that would gradually grow indifferent, the men and boys at Camp Delta would be left, in the words of Albert Camus, to "drift through life rather than live, the prey of aimless days and sterile memories."[1]

The document would have been very different had we known what was taking place at Camp Delta and other post-9/11 facilities. Since at least the fall of 2002, military interrogators in Cuba had used "aggressive interrogation practices" that went far beyond both what the FBI had successfully used in its criminal investigations, and what the military had been authorized to use in the past.[2] FBI agents complained about these practices in memos to their superiors, which came to light when some of those memos—usually heavily redacted—were disclosed to the ACLU in response to requests the organization had filed under the Freedom of Information Act.[3] The letter quoted in the Introduction that described the interrogation techniques used by Sergeant Lacey, who apparently grabbed a prisoner's genitals and bent his thumbs back violently during an interrogation, was among the documents disclosed during this litigation.

But Sergeant Lacey's behavior was no isolated act of thuggery and reflected a common practice of abuse by interrogators. On a number of occasions, an FBI agent entered an interrogation room only to discover "a detainee chained hand and foot in a fetal position to the floor, with no chair, food, or water." Most times, these prisoners "had urinated or defacated (sic) on themselves and had been left there for 18, 24 hours or more," which the agent found "not only aggressive, but personally very upsetting." * Other times, "the air conditioning had been turned down so far and the temperature was so cold in the room, that the barefooted detainee was shaking with cold." The agent "was told that interrogation from the day prior had ordered this treatment, and the detainee was not to be moved." On another occasion, the air-conditioning had been turned off, "making the temperature in the unventilated room probably well over 100 degrees. The detainee was almost unconscious on the floor, with a pile of hair next to him. He had apparently been literally pulling his own hair out throughout the night."[4]

Another agent happened upon an "interview" where there "wasn't much talking going . . . because the lights had been turned off and a strobe light was flickering on and off, and loud rock music was being played."[5] Sometimes, military interrogators combined these techniques. In one room, "not only was the temperature unbearably hot, but extremely loud rap music was being played in the room, and had been since the day before, with the detainee chained hand and foot in the fetal position on the tile floor."[6] According to the FBI, these practices, which the Pentagon euphemistically calls "environmental manipulation," were "quite common."[7]

---

* As a rule, the government redacted the name of the FBI agent who had written the memo before disclosing the document to the ACLU. The FBI agents were at the base to conduct their own interrogations. According to the FBI, their agents did not use, and refused to participate in, the tactics employed by the Department of Defense.

As seen in Chapter 5, Lieutenant Colonel Jerald Phifer, in his memo of October 11, 2002, ranked environmental manipulation as a Category II technique. It remains among the techniques approved by Secretary Rumsfeld in his April 2003 order.

Some interrogation techniques involved a systematic assault on the prisoners' religion or culture. An FBI agent saw a shackled prisoner chained to the floor of an interrogation room, with loud music playing and a strobe light flashing. The prisoner had been draped with an Israeli flag. On another occasion, an interrogator became impatient with an inmate who was chanting the Koran. He directed a guard to wrap the prisoner's head and mouth in duct tape. Prisoners were subjected to "the close physical presence of a woman" in order to increase their stress. Female interrogators straddled prisoners and gyrated over them. A female guard rubbed lotion on a prisoner's hands and arms during Ramadan. My client Mamdouh Habib was one of the prisoners smeared with fake menstrual blood.[8]

Other methods reported by the FBI were more ominous. Members of the FBI Behavioral Assessment Unit described "sleep depravation (sic) . . . and utilization of loud music/bright lights/growling dogs."*[9] Other agents were also aware "of detainees being threatened (either in person or aurally) by dogs" and some prisoners were apparently "subjected to considerable pain" and "manhandling." At least one prisoner "was told that his family had been taken into custody and would be moved to Morocco for interrogation if he did not begin to talk."[10] In late 2003, the FBI discovered that at least one team of military interrogators had been representing themselves as FBI agents. On December 5, an agent sent an e-mail to his superiors with the subject line, "Impersonating FBI at GTMO." When disclosed to the ACLU, the e-mail had been heavily redacted, but the redactions were themselves telling:

Of concern, DOD interrogators impersonating Supervisory Special Agents of the FBI told a detainee that [one-half line redacted]. These same interrogation teams then [two-thirds line redacted]. The detainee

---

* In the memo from the Behavioral Assessment Unit, the description of at least one other technique had been redacted when the document was released to the ACLU.

was also told by this interrogation team [one and one-half lines redacted]. . . .

If this detainee is ever released or his story made public in any way, DOD interrogators will not be held accountable because *these torture techniques* were done [by] the "FBI" interrogators. The FBI will [be] left holding the bag before the public.[11]

The memo concludes that these unknown tactics "have produced no intelligence of a threat neutralization nature" and have "destroyed any chance of prosecuting this detainee."[12]

The futility of these techniques is a recurring theme of the FBI memos. In a May 10, 2004, e-mail to T. J. Harrington, the deputy assistant director of the FBI Counterterrorism Division, an agent at Camp Delta recalled weekly meetings with the Department of Justice. Agents discussed the military's techniques "and how they were not effective or producing intel that was reliable." Agents repeatedly protested to Generals Dunlavey and Miller, but to no avail. "Both agreed the Bureau has their way of doing business and DOD has their marching orders from the Sec Def." In one instance, the FBI apparently provided DOD with information suggesting a prisoner might have useful intelligence, the details of which are redacted. DOD then gave the FBI "a so called deadline to use our traditional methods. Once our timeline [approximately two words redacted] was up [one word redacted] took the reigns (sic)." In a meeting with the Pentagon Detainee Policy Committee, the FBI "voiced concerns that the intel produced [by the DOD] was nothing more than what FBI got using simple investigative techniques." The conversation became "somewhat heated" but "[name redacted] agreed with me" and "[name redacted] finally admitted the information was the same info the Bureau obtained. It still did not prevent them from continuing the [one word redacted] methods."[13]

The techniques described by the FBI have been independently corroborated by a number of other sources. Former guards and intelligence agents at the base, for example, described a "regular procedure" at Camp Delta. "Uncooperative" prisoners were stripped to their underwear. Interrogators then forced them to "sit in a chair while shackled hand and foot to a bolt in the floor [while] strobe lights and screamingly loud rock and rap music played through two close loudspeakers, while the air-conditioning was turned up to maximum levels." As one observer recalled, "it fried them." [14] And as the FBI observed, the prisoners were not routinely permitted a chair. In another common practice, prisoners were forced to participate in the "frequent flier program." An inmate was awakened and interrogated in the middle of the night in another facility, then returned to a different cell. As soon as guards determined he had fallen into a deep sleep, he was awakened again, brought back to interrogation, and then returned to yet another cell. This continued throughout the night.*[15] In June 2004, the International Committee of the Red Cross (ICRC) reported that interrogators at Guantánamo had developed a system intended to make prisoners entirely dependent on their interrogators, precisely as contemplated by the KUBARK manual. According to the ICRC, interrogators subjected prisoners to "humiliating acts, solitary confinement, temperature extremes, [the] use of forced positions," loud and persistent noise, and "some beatings." The methods had become "more refined and repressive" over time, and were "tantamount to torture." †[16]

Many of the same practices were also taking place at U.S. facilities in Afghanistan. As in Guantánamo, interrogators in Afghanistan operated without specific guidance throughout 2002. While the Administration had decided that interrogations would not be constrained by the Geneva Conventions, it was not clear what restraints, if any, would fill the void. At the same time, the pressure to produce "actionable intelligence," combined with the conviction that some of the prisoners in U.S. custody were hardened terrorists masquerading as innocent civilians, made it inevitable that interrogators would begin to use more aggressive techniques. In order to

---

* In response to these reports, a spokesman with the Defense Department said the military provided a "safe, humane and professional detention operation at Guantánamo" in which interrogators "gain valuable information from detainees because they have built a relationship of trust, not fear." See Neil A. Lewis, "Many Guantánamo Detainees Treated Harshly, Witnesses Say," *New York Times,* Oct. 17, 2004, quoting Defense Department spokesman Lieutenant Commander Alvin Plexico.

† When asked about the accusations leveled by the ICRC, a Pentagon spokesman said, "The United States operates a safe, humane and professional detention operation at Guantánamo that is providing valuable information in the war on terrorism." See Neil A. Lewis, "Red Cross Finds Detainee Abuse in Guantánamo," *New York Times,* Nov. 30, 2004.

maximize and prolong the trauma associated with the initial capture, a policy quickly developed that prisoners would be "hooded, shackled and isolated for at the least the first 24 hours, sometimes 72 hours of captivity." [17] Thereafter, according to the military, interrogators in Afghanistan were trying to extract information by "removing clothing, isolating people for long periods of time, using stress positions, exploiting fear of dogs, and implementing sleep and light deprivation." [18] Environmental manipulation of the sort described by the FBI at Guantánamo was also common. According to a spokesman for the U.S. military in Afghanistan at the time, it was "legitimate to use lights, noise and vision restriction, and to alter, without warning, the time between meals, to blur a detainee's sense of time" and that sleep deprivation "was probably within the lexicon." [19]

In at least one respect, interrogations in Afghanistan went well beyond anything at Camp Delta: no prisoner has been killed in Cuba. As of February 2006, ninety-eight prisoners have died in U.S. custody in Iraq and Afghanistan, and thirty-four of these deaths are being investigated by the military as suspected or confirmed homicides. [20] At least six prisoners have been killed at U.S. prisons in Afghanistan. [21] In November 2002, at a CIA-run prison north of Kabul, Afghanistan, code-named the Salt Pit, a young case agent on his first assignment ordered Afghani guards to strip a prisoner naked, chain him to a concrete floor, and leave him outside overnight. By morning, the prisoner had frozen to death. Recently, the Justice Department indicated it would not bring charges against the case agent because it would have been impossible to prove the prisoner had not been abused by guards during the night. The prisoner, who was in his early twenties, has never been identified. He was buried in an unmarked grave. At the time of his death, interrogators had not yet determined whether he had done anything wrong, or whether he had any connection to terrorism. One government official speculated, "He was probably associated with people who were associated with al Qaeda." The CIA case officer, meanwhile, was later promoted. [22]

In June 2003, at a site near Asadabad, Afghanistan, a prisoner was kept without water for several days of an extended hot spell. On the fourth day, an interpreter saw the prisoner lying on the ground, handcuffed, with spittle around his mouth. He alerted a guard, who brushed it off as malingering. "But when he checked the guy," the interpreter said, "he found he was dead."

The military reported the prisoner died of a heart attack. He was eighteen. The interpreter no longer works for the U.S. military.[23]

According to Army documents, two prisoners killed at Bagram Air Base in December 2002 had been chained to the ceiling, kicked, and beaten over a period of several days. One U.S. soldier admitted striking the prisoner thirty-seven times, "destroying his leg muscle tissue with repeated unlawful knee strikes." Three other interrogators participated in the assault on these prisoners with "kicks to the groin and leg, shoving or slamming him into walls/table, forcing the detainee to maintain painful, contorted body positions during interview and forcing water into his mouth until he could not breathe." One of these two prisoners had been captured by Afghan militiamen, who stopped him driving a vehicle at a checkpoint near Khost, Afghanistan. They turned him and his three passengers over to the United States. The passengers were sent to Guantánamo, where they were held for more than a year before being released without charges. But the driver remained in Afghanistan, where he was beaten so severely that, even if he had survived, doctors determined he would have lost both his legs.[24] Yet by the time the interrogators were finished, most of them "were convinced that the detainee was innocent."[25]

Initially, American military officials said the two prisoners died of natural causes. Lieutenant General Daniel McNeill, the American commander of allied troops in Afghanistan at the time, emphatically denied the prisoners had been chained to the ceiling or that they had been mistreated. Only after an investigation by the New York Times did the military acknowledge that the prisoners had been killed by U.S. soldiers, who had, among other things, suspended them from the ceiling of their isolation cells.[26] A guard at Bagram at the time reported later that the climate of abuse developed in response to the initial decision that the prisoners were beneath the protection of the Geneva Conventions. "We were pretty much told that they were nobodies, that they were just enemy combatants," he said. "We called them hajis, and that psychology was really important."[27] A total of twenty-eight U.S. soldiers have been implicated in these two deaths; some of them were with the military intelligence unit that later transferred to Iraq and was involved in the scandal at Abu Ghraib.[28]

• • • •

Yet, at least at Camp Delta, the coercive interrogations and oppressive conditions were not the source of the prisoners' greatest anguish. Within months of their arrival—after the military finally told the prisoners they would not be shot—the prisoners began to suffer the chronic despair that comes from indefinite detention. Administration officials were quick to point out that detention during an armed conflict is inherently indefinite, since military planners cannot predict in advance when a conflict will end. But this misses the mark. The point is not that conventional conflicts have a predetermined length, but that prisoners in a conventional conflict can identify what constitutes the ending. They, like everyone else, can describe the events that mark the end of war and the beginning of peace, whether it be a surrender, the capture of certain territory, etc. This allows a prisoner to set his thoughts on these events, knowing that when they arrive, he goes home. This focus nurtures and sustains the most precious commodity in any prisoner's life—hope. But the war on terror makes hope impossible. Even today, the Administration cannot say when the war will end. In fact, it cannot even say how it will know that the end has come.[29]

And it is this gnawing uncertainty that drives men mad. In late February 2002, prisoners at the base began a hunger strike. By mid-March, three prisoners who had refused food and water for roughly two weeks were admitted to the camp hospital and given fluids intravenously. Prison officials attributed the protest to "the fact that they don't know what is happening to them." At the same time, military officials reported rising frustration and anger among the prisoners caused by anxiety over their uncertain fate.[30] In the summer of 2002, four prisoners tried to commit suicide by hanging themselves from bedsheets tied to the bars of their cells. At least thirty other prisoners made what officials described as less serious attempts. By September 2002, near the end of Brigadier General Baccus's tenure, fifty-seven prisoners were being treated for mental illnesses, and many more were taking antidepressants or antipsychotic medication.[31] The next month, an FBI agent reported, "[t]he mental condition of the detainees is to the point where [they] are all participating in a hunger strike."[32] This was *before* the most coercive interrogation practices began.

The number of attempted suicides rose steadily for the next year. In January 2003, a young Saudi prisoner named Mashaal hung himself in his cell. By the time guards cut him down he had lapsed into a coma. He suffered irreversible brain damage. After three and a half months he regained consciousness but is now permanently disabled and will never walk again.[33] James Yee, the former Muslim chaplain at the base, estimates Mashaal was about twenty-three when he tried to take his own life.[34] By June 2003, the number of prisoners under mental health supervision had risen to about ninety, with roughly half regularly receiving psychiatric drugs.[35] The number of serious suicide attempts had climbed to thirty-two by August, and the Administration stopped reporting the less serious attempts. The following month, the number rose to thirty-four. Prison officials attributed these attempts "to the effects of the indefinite detentions on prisoner morale."[36] By that time, over 20 percent of the inmates at the base—more than 120 prisoners—were taking Prozac or other antidepressants. An entire cellblock was reserved for the most severely traumatized inmates. According to Yee, the inmates on this block responded to him "in a childlike voice, talking complete nonsense." Many sang "childish songs, repeating the song over and over." They were allowed paper and crayons and spent their days lying on the floor or bed of their cells, drawing pictures. The nurses let them hang the pictures on their walls.* [37]

In late 2003, the International Red Cross reported a "worrying deterioration in the psychological health of a large number of the internees" and warned the Bush Administration that indefinite detention would continue to take its toll.[38] In June 2004, the ICRC found an increasing incidence of

---

* Chaplain Yee was arrested in September 2003 and accused of mishandling classified documents. Anonymous military officials accused him of being part of a vast and dangerous conspiracy that had infiltrated Camp Delta. He spent seventy-six days in solitary confinement—in the same facility as Yaser Hamdi and José Padilla—before he was eventually exonerated. He has since left the service. Yee, *For God and Country,* 138–61, 211–13. Meanwhile, the military has not brought a new Muslim chaplain to the base. Yee's duties were taken over by Colonel Stephen Feehan, who describes himself as "from the conservative strand of the Southern Baptist Church." In an interview in October 2003, the month after Yee's arrest, Feehan told British journalist David Rose he believed the Bible was "literally true," and that "the world was created in seven days." See Rose, "Operation Take Away My Freedom," *Vanity Fair,* Jan. 2004. When asked about nonbelievers, Feehan said "without believing in and accepting Christ, without faith, you cannot be redeemed. It's impossible." *Id.* I should hasten to add that I do not know Colonel Feehan, and have no reason to believe he is anything other than a man of the deepest personal integrity. That is not the point. The point is that the military has not seen fit to make a Muslim chaplain available either to the prisoners or to the Muslim soldiers serving their time at Camp Delta.

mental illness, "much of it caused by prolonged solitary confinement."[39] A source familiar with conditions at the base during this period confided to representatives from Physicians for Human Rights, a Nobel Prize–winning organization, that the combination of sensory deprivation during solitary confinement and sensory overstimulation during interrogations (loud music, strobe lights, etc.) was causing "spatial and temporal disorientation," leading to "self-harm and suicide attempts."[40] The military later announced plans to build a permanent psychiatric wing at Guantánamo.[41]

In September 2003, we filed our petition asking the Supreme Court to review the case. At about this time, after we had called the Court's attention to the suicide attempts at the base, the military started to report an inexplicable decline in such incidents. We were at a loss to explain it, since we were not aware of a change in conditions that would account for any sudden improvement in the prisoners' mental state. As it turns out, officials at the prison began to call the suicide attempts "manipulative self-injurious behavior," or SIB, a previously unknown psychiatric category. According to the chief surgeon at the base, a prisoner's attempt at suicide would be classified as SIB if the prison staff decided "the individual's state of mind is such that they did not sincerely want to end their own life."[42] How the prison made this assessment has not been disclosed. Recalculating old numbers, the military now says there were forty incidents of SIB in the last six months of 2003, including twenty-one of the twenty-three attempted suicides between August 18 and 26, 2003.[43] The military also reported 350 "self-harm" incidents during the year, almost three times as many as in 2002. This included 120 "hanging gestures."[44]

During this period, the prison at Guantánamo had become an international pariah. In the days after the September 11 attacks, much of the world stood shoulder to shoulder with the United States. There were candlelight vigils outside the U.S. embassy in Tehran, despite police orders to disperse.[45] The liberal French daily Le Monde declared, "Nous Sommes Tous Américains" [We Are All Americans], and the left-leaning German chancellor called the attacks "a declaration of war against the civilized world."[46] This was not just rhetoric. On September 13 NATO voted that the murders in New York, Washington, and Pennsylvania were an attack against all nineteen of its members.[47] It was inevitable that this sense of solidarity would fade with time. But it was not inevitable that it would disintegrate so completely, and so quickly. By the fall of 2003, the rift between the United States and the rest of the world, including our closest allies, was wider than it had been prior to the attacks. There is no doubt that Guantánamo (and the claim of unlimited presidential power that it symbolizes) acted as a powerful wedge, driving the United States away from the Muslim world on whose behalf we claimed to wage this war, and from the Western democracies whose standard we claimed to bear.[48]

Europe was uneasy about the prison almost from the start. The first protests came after President Bush's November 13, 2001, executive order, which authorized trial by military commissions instead of civilian courts. Spain promptly refused to extradite eight terrorism suspects to the United States.[49] The controversy intensified when the first prisoners began to arrive at the base. As we have seen, Defense Secretary Rumsfeld told reporters January 11, 2002, that the prisoners were "unlawful combatants" who "do not have any rights under the Geneva Convention." On January 17, the Administration released the now-infamous photographs of shackled prisoners kneeling on the gravel wearing orange jumpsuits, thick gloves, blackened goggles, surgical masks, and heavy earmuffs, an environment of complete sensory deprivation. Combined with newspaper reports that British, French, Belgian, and Australian citizens were among the prisoners, the pictures sparked an outcry in Europe. The controversy was most intense in England, where the *Daily Mail*, a conservative paper, ran the photographs under the headline "Tortured"[50] and editorialized that, "Even the SS Were Treated Better Than This."[51] British Foreign Minister Jack Straw asked for an explanation of the photographs, and warned the United States to treat prisoners "humanely."[52]

Guantánamo increasingly placed the United States in the position of international outlier. On January 16, 2002, the United Nations high commissioner for human rights called on the Administration to provide the prisoners with a competent tribunal to determine their status. The Administration refused. On March 12, 2002, the Inter-American Commission on Human Rights, part of the Organization of American States (of which the United States is a member), indicated that the Guantánamo prisoners must not be held "entirely at the unfettered discretion of the United States government" and urged the United States to create competent tribunals to determine the legal status of the prisoners under its control. The Administration refused to acknowledge the court's jurisdiction.[53] On November 6, 2002, the English Court of Appeal noted its "deep concern that, in apparent contravention of fundamental principles of law, [the prisoners] may be subject to indefinite detention in territory over which the United States has exclusive control with no opportunity to challenge the legitimacy of [their] detention before any court or tribunal."[54]

During 2002 and 2003, disturbing reports leaked out of Guantánamo that contributed to international concerns: suicide attempts; reports that the prisoners included children under the age of sixteen and frail old men with no teeth; allegations of torture in the prisoners' letters to their families. The United States insisted the prisoners were being treated humanely, but refused to give independent monitors, like the U.N. special rapporteur on torture, access to the base. As the months of incommunicado detention dragged into years, and as it became clear that most prisoners would never be charged with any wrongdoing, the import of the Bush Administration's legal position became apparent—this was a prison deliberately placed beyond the law. The international community became increasingly skeptical about the Administration's insistence that it could be trusted to do the right thing.

At the same time, a number of international groups condemned the detentions at Camp Delta, including the U.N. Working Group on Arbitrary Detention, the U.N. special rapporteur on the independence of judges and lawyers, and the European Parliament.[55] On November 25, 2003, Lord Johan Steyn, a judge on Great Britain's highest court, denounced the prison at a conference in London. Lord Steyn acknowledged that there was very little public information about how the United States was treating prisoners at the base, but stated, "what we do know is not reassuring." "The purpose of holding the prisoners at Guantánamo Bay," he said, "was and is to put them beyond the rule of law, beyond the protection of any courts, and at the mercy of the victors. . . . As a lawyer brought up to admire the ideals of American democracy and justice, I would have to say that I regard this as a monstrous failure of justice."[56] By the time of Steyn's speech, much of the world agreed.

On the other hand, the international condemnation was not unanimous and several countries took great comfort from the prison at Guantánamo. In Liberia, then-President Charles Taylor announced shortly after 9/11 that opposition to his rule was in fact part of the global terrorist threat. Taylor designated Hassan Bility, a respected journalist and critic of Taylor's policies, an "unlawful combatant." Bility was arrested in June 2002, held without trial or access to counsel, and tortured during interrogations. The United States protested, but Taylor insisted Bility was being treated "in the same manner in which the U.S. treats terrorists." When an American journalist pressed the point, the Liberian information minister replied, "It was you guys who coined the phrase. We are using the phrase you coined."[57] In Zimbabwe, President Robert Mugabe lashed out at foreign journalists who reported on political attacks against white Zimbabweans, calling them "terrorist sympathizers." "We agree with President Bush," he said. "Anyone who in any way finances, harbors, or defends terrorists is himself a terrorist."[58] One week after September 11, the Eritrean government arrested a group of dissident politicians and later suggested they were agents of Osama bin Laden. Eritrea is one of the countries criticized by the State Department for its coercive interrogation practices.

In March 2002, shortly after Camp X-Ray opened, the State Department criticized Namibia for human rights violations committed by its security forces. Namibia's Permanent Information Secretary Mocks Shivute waved off the criticism, citing the indefinite detentions at Guantánamo Bay as proof "the U.S. government was the worst human rights violator in the world."[59] Egypt, the Ivory Coast, Cameroon, and Burkina Faso, a small, landlocked country in West Africa, all invoked the indefinite detentions at Guantánamo when they locked up human rights campaigners as threats to national security.[60] In May 2003, Indonesian President Megawati Sukarnoputri announced plans to create an island prison with a maximum capacity of one thousand to hold separatist rebels without trial or charge, a plan immediately likened to the prison at Guantánamo Bay. Also in 2003, Malaysia's law minister, when called to explain the detention of alleged militants without trial, said the practice in his country was "just like the process in Guantánamo. What happened to the cases that are still there and there was no due process? Similarly we have got the same treatment." The United States responded to this rebuke by dropping its criticisms. Explaining its deafening silence, one senior State Department official said, "with what we're doing in Guantanamo, we're on thin ice to push." Another explained that Camp

Delta had established a new baseline for human rights: the U.S. government could only act on cases of abuse that were "worse than Guantanamo."[61]

II

On November 10, 2003, the Supreme Court agreed to review the case, once again consolidating *Rasul* and *Al Odah*. On January 9, 2004, the Court agreed to review the Fourth Circuit decision in *Hamdi* and on February 20, added *Padilla* to its docket. Formally, the cases asked whether, and to what extent, the judiciary could police the bounds of the commander in chief power to detain people seized in ostensible connection with the war on terror. But on the level of most immediate concern to the prisoners, the Court would determine whether the Administration could detain people beyond the law.

The briefing in *Rasul, Hamdi,* and *Padilla* occupied the winter and early spring of 2003–2004. But the most telling events took place outside the Court. Throughout the litigation in *Hamdi,* the Defense Department had insisted the fate of the union required that Hamdi, like the prisoners at Camp Delta, be held in solitary confinement and virtually incommunicado, unaware that litigation had been filed on his behalf or that lawyers had been working for him since April 2002. Yet on December 2, 2003, the day before the Administration filed its papers opposing Hamdi's petition for certiorari, the Defense Department suddenly decided that the urgent demands of national security no longer required these conditions, and announced that he would be permitted to meet with counsel. The Defense Department allowed the meeting to take place the day before Hamdi's lawyers filed their brief in the Supreme Court.[62]

Padilla enjoyed a similar spring. Recall that after his arrest in Chicago, Padilla had been held as a possible witness before the grand jury investigating the 9/11 attacks in the Southern District of New York. Chief Judge Michael Mukasey appointed Donna Newman, who challenged Padilla's detention. In June 2002, two days before Newman's challenge was scheduled to be heard, the president designated Padilla an "enemy combatant" and whisked him to South Carolina, where, despite his previous contact with counsel, national security suddenly required that he be held incommunicado, under the same conditions (and at the same facility) as Hamdi, though the two had no contact with each other. On February 11, 2004, the same day the Bush Administration filed a brief asking the Supreme Court to review the case, the Defense Department decided that the demands of military necessity were such that Padilla would be allowed to meet with his attorneys.[63]

In *Rasul,* three weeks after the Supreme Court agreed to hear the case, a Bush Administration official announced that 140 prisoners would be released within the next two months, more than double the number that had been released up to that point. In January 2004, the teams in *Rasul* and *Al Odah* filed our briefs in the Supreme Court, arguing the prisoners could not be held beyond the law. On February 13, 2004, in a speech in Miami, Defense Secretary Rumsfeld announced that the Administration was contemplating the creation of "administrative review boards," which would review the cases of every prisoner at the base.[64] On the same day, a Defense representative held a press conference at the Pentagon, repeating the plans for an "administrative review" of each case, and insisting the prisoners were not held "in some legal black hole." On March 2, 2004, the department prepared a memorandum outlining the procedures to be followed by this board.[65]

The next day, the Bush Administration filed its brief in the Supreme Court, describing at some length the legal process contemplated for the prisoners. Sadly, the Administration failed to point out to the Supreme Court that, according to the Pentagon, the process would be established "solely as a matter of discretion and does not confer any right or obligation enforceable by law."[66] And on March 9, the department released Shafiq Rasul and Asif Iqbal, the two British citizens in the litigation. They were flown home to England, along with three other British nationals, and released. The five have never been charged with any wrongdoing and are all free men today. In just another odd twist to the litigation, *Rasul* became a case about the lawfulness of executive detention named for a person who was no longer in custody.[67]

When we began the litigation in *Rasul,* barely five months after the 9/11 attacks, it is fair to say we had relatively few allies. I was based in Minneapolis at the time, and my colleagues at the Center for Constitutional Rights were in New York. We asked a number of Washington, D.C., lawyers to act as our local counsel. All of them turned us down, some more quickly than others.* In fact, it is probably fair to say we had more than a few enemies. After we filed in *Rasul,* one of our partners in the litigation, Clive Stafford Smith, received a death threat at his home in New Orleans. I did not attach much significance to this hostility. I had discovered from my years in capital defense that lawyers who represent unpopular clients often encounter a certain amount of misunderstanding, which more than anything reflects the public's natural tendency to associate the lawyer with his client. In this case, the tendency was amplified both by the enormity of 9/11 and by the Administration's overwrought hyperbole that our clients were "trained killers." With the nation still reeling from the attacks, it was unlikely that our clients would be viewed sympathetically.

But I also knew this would change. Ours is not a culture that sits well with shrill but untested accusations of wrongdoing; we would expect instead that at some point, and preferably sooner rather than later, a jailer would produce some proof that his prisoner has done something wrong. As it became increasingly clear the Bush Administration had no intention of coming forward with such proof, and in fact hoped to prevent the courts even from inquiring into whether this proof existed, an increasing number of people and organizations became concerned. The decision by the Supreme Court to review the case gave these groups the opportunity to voice those concerns in amicus curiae briefs to the Court.

Amicus curiae, or "friend of the court" briefs, have become an important feature of Supreme Court litigation. By illuminating aspects of the case that may not be fully explored by the parties, or by communicating how the issue will affect groups that are not before the Court, amicus briefs help the Court understand a case in all its complexity. Ideally, these briefs deliver more than one message. The first is communicated by the persuasive force of the brief itself—by the quality and originality of its argument. But another message is the one delivered by the people or organization on whose

---

* Eventually, Barry Boss, at the time with a small firm specializing in criminal defense, agreed to be our local counsel. As a criminal defense lawyer, Barry immediately understood that deciding whether a prisoner is entitled to legal process is not a choice properly entrusted to the jailer. I owe Barry a great debt for his courage at a time when others were timid.

behalf the brief is submitted. They may have special expertise or familiarity with the issue, which makes their opinion particularly useful to the Court. Or they may be the unexpected ally. When responsible officials take a position that seems contrary to type—the former prosecutors who take the side of a suspect in a criminal case or the prison wardens who support greater protections for inmates, for example—it can send a powerful signal to the Court.

In *Rasul*, we benefited from a number of such briefs. One of the first was presented on behalf of several retired federal judges. Even before the Supreme Court agreed to review the case, these jurists—Republicans as well as Democrats—had filed a brief supporting our petition for certiorari. In retrospect, their action is easily understood: the Administration's position amounts to an assault on the competence of the judiciary to scrutinize the executive's claim of military necessity, and it is not surprising that at least some judges would take umbrage. At the time, however, their position was extremely important because it demonstrated that support for our case transcended political affiliation, and that our view was shared not just by the lawyers in the case, but by responsible jurists with no stake in the outcome.[68]

We also won the support of some unexpected allies. Brigadier General David Brahms was a U.S. Marine for twenty-five years and the senior Marine Corps legal advisor from 1985 through 1988. During the 1970s, Brahms served as the principal legal officer for POW affairs. Rear Admiral John Hutson was in the Navy for nearly thirty years and served as judge advocate general, the Navy's senior legal officer, from 1997 to 2000. Today he is the dean of Franklin Pierce Law Center in New Hampshire. Rear Admiral Donald Guter was the Navy's judge advocate general from June 2000 through June 2002. Guter was in the Pentagon on 9/11 when the third jet exploded into the building. He was also one of the officials who recommended that the Administration hold prisoners at Guantánamo. Today he is the dean of Duquesne Law School in Pittsburgh. Supporting our position, their brief recounted the military's historic commitment to the laws of war, and responded to the Bush Administration's contention that due process for the prisoners at Camp Delta imperiled national security.[69]

One of the most emotionally powerful amicus briefs was written by a Washington law firm on behalf of former American prisoners of war. At the time of the brief, Leslie Jackson was the executive director of the American Ex-Prisoners of War, a nonprofit, congressionally chartered organization representing roughly fifty thousand former POWs and their families. On April 24, 1944, Jackson was captured by the German army when his B-17 bomber crashed. He was held for thirteen months in Stalag 17. Edward Jackfert and Neal Harrington were part of the American force in the Philippines that surrendered to the Japanese in 1942. Both survived the infamous Bataan Death March. Jackfert is the former national commander of the American Defenders of Bataan & Corregidor, an organization supporting former POWs held by the Japanese during World War II.[70]

As we saw in Chapter 4, Germany generally complied with the Conventions in its treatment of U.S. prisoners (though not in its treatment of Soviet prisoners). As a POW, Jackson enjoyed the bare necessities: shelter, minimally adequate food, and the opportunity to socialize with other American POWs. He was never tortured or otherwise mistreated by German guards. Jackson believes, not without reason, that Germany's determination to abide by the Conventions saved his life, a view widely shared by scholars of the period. The death rate of U.S. POWs held by the Germans was just over 1 percent.* His brothers in Japan, however, were not so fortunate. Japan had not ratified the Geneva Conventions and made no pretense of following them. Harrington "was forced into slave labor in a Japanese coal mine, and saw his compatriots starved, beaten, and killed."[71] Jackfert was also forced into slave labor, and in a matter of months shed thirty-five pounds from his slender 125-pound frame. "No one can adequately impart the suffering most Allied prisoners endured [in Japan]. . . . They were beaten, kicked, robbed . . . and were buried alive. . . . [T]he overwhelming majority endured 'hell on earth.' . . ." Four in ten American servicemen did not survive captivity in Japan.[72] These ex-POWs reminded the Court what can scarcely be doubted: not only does the Administration's position cast doubt on this country's well-deserved reputation "as the standard-bearer for democracy and human rights," it also "puts at risk the safety of the men and women of the U.S. armed forces."[73]

---

* Russia, by contrast, had not ratified the Conventions, and Germany treated soldiers of the Red Army with unabashed cruelty. Nearly 60 percent of Soviet prisoners died in German custody.

In another brief, one hundred seventy-five members of the British Parliament supported our position, which apparently marked the first time members of the Parliament of Westminster had submitted a brief to the Supreme Court. "The exercise of executive power without judicial review," they wrote, "jeopardizes the keystone of our existence as nations—namely, the rule of law."[74] Nearly two dozen retired American diplomats, who served in Republican and Democratic administrations alike, offered the Court the benefit of their experience with "that vast external realm." "Power counts," they said. "But values count too. And, for this nation, there is no benefit in the exercise of our undoubted power unless it is deployed in the service of fundamental values: democracy, the rule of law, human rights, and due process."[75]

Undoubtedly, however, the amicus brief that resonated with the most historical significance was written by Geoffrey Stone, my former colleague at the University of Chicago Law School. In twenty-eight pages, Stone summarized a tragic pattern of American history: in war, the executive branch typically reacts to perceived threats by curtailing civil liberties much more than necessary. Every major conflict has contributed to this sad tale—from the nearly forgotten Alien and Sedition Acts of 1798 to the loyalty oaths and McCarthyism of the Cold War. In time, the nation comes to recognize and regret its excesses, but for those whose lives have been upended, belated regrets offer cold comfort. "The challenge," Stone said, "is to identify excess when it occurs."[76] *Rasul* was such a case.

Stone wrote on behalf of Fred Korematsu, whose personal experience has come to symbolize this recurring phenomenon. A U.S. citizen, Korematsu was among the nearly 120,000 people of Japanese descent forcibly relocated during World War II from their homes in California, Oregon, Washington, and Arizona to one of ten camps dotted throughout the nation's interior. Korematsu challenged the constitutionality of President Roosevelt's executive order, which authorized internment based on ancestry alone, with no proof of disloyalty and no opportunity to be heard. He was convicted and sent to prison. In *Korematsu v. United States,* the Supreme Court upheld his conviction.[77]

The decision in *Korematsu* is a judicial embarrassment. The Supreme Court has never cited the result with approval. Francis Biddle, who was Roosevelt's attorney general at the time, wrote in 1962 that he had always opposed the relocations, and that internment demonstrated "the power of suggestion which a mystic cliché like 'military necessity' can exercise on human beings."[78] In 1976, President Gerald Ford issued a proclamation recognizing that internment had been one of our "national mistakes." In 1984, the federal court in California that presided over Korematsu's trial vacated his conviction, based in substantial part on evidence, unearthed decades after his trial, that the War Department had knowingly misrepresented the military justification for the program.[79] In vacating the conviction, the court said his case "stands as a caution that in times of distress the shield of military necessity and national security must not be used to protect governmental actions from close scrutiny and accountability."[80] And during his presidency, Ronald Reagan signed into law the federal Civil Liberties Act of 1988, which acknowledged internment as a "grave injustice" "carried out without adequate security reasons." *[81]

III

No lawyer wants to pass up an opportunity to argue before the Supreme Court, and Tom Wilner of Shearman & Sterling and I are no different. We had led our respective teams from the beginning—developing the legal issues, presenting the arguments in the lower courts, and pressing the litigation at a time when few others were willing to come forward. We both had earned the right to stand before the Court. We knew, however, that the Court was unlikely to hear arguments from more than one lawyer for the prisoners. At a meeting in New York shortly after the Supreme Court agreed to review the case, I quipped to Tom that we should arm wrestle for the honor. Tom quickly agreed, having been a champion wrestler in high school. I pointed out that he had since taken up smoking, but he was undeterred. Cooler heads eventually prevailed, and we decided to bring a new member into our group.

---

* In December 2004, I attended a conference marking the sixtieth anniversary of the Supreme Court decision in *Korematsu*. Though visibly infirm and confined to a wheelchair, Fred Korematsu spoke to a rapt audience with a simple eloquence, reminding us by his presence that turbulent times will always test our resolve. Fred passed away March 30, 2005, at the age of eighty-six.

We recruited retired federal judge John Gibbons to argue the case. President Nixon had appointed Judge Gibbons to the Third Circuit Court of Appeals in Philadelphia in 1970. He eventually became chief judge before retiring in 1990 and returning to private practice in New Jersey. He had earned a reputation as a rigorously fair advocate whose personal and political views defied categorization. On the bench, he had been seen as conservative, and certainly not sympathetic to criminal defendants. A lifelong Republican, Judge Gibbons had testified in support of Clarence Thomas's nomination to the U.S. Supreme Court. Yet since his retirement, he had devoted most of his time to public interest litigation. He had defended a number of death row inmates, including one in Virginia whose appeal he handled successfully in the U.S. Supreme Court. His participation in *Rasul* demonstrated that the principle at stake in the litigation—that no person can be held without some lawful process—transcended political affiliation. (As an added wrinkle, Judge Gibbons had volunteered as a young man to serve in the U.S. Navy and was stationed briefly at Guantánamo, a tidbit he never ceased to remind us of as we helped him prepare for the argument.)

The Court heard arguments April 20, 2004. The courtroom was filled to overflowing. Tom and I sat nervously with Judge Gibbons at counsel table, a few feet in front of the Court. Chief Justice William Rehnquist called the case: "We'll hear argument now on 03-334, *Shafiq Rasul v. George W. Bush* and a companion case. Mr. Gibbons." Judge Gibbons rose from his seat, moved to the podium, and addressed the Court:

> What is at stake in this case is the authority of the federal courts to uphold the rule of law. Respondents assert that their actions are absolutely immune from judicial examination whenever they elect to detain foreign nationals outside our borders. Under this theory, neither the length of the detention, the conditions of their confinement, nor the fact that they have been wrongfully detained makes the slightest difference. Respondents would create a lawless enclave insulating the executive branch from any judicial scrutiny now or in the future.[82]

Theodore Olson, the solicitor general, represented the Bush Administration. "The United States is at war," he began. "Over ten thousand troops are in Afghanistan." Almost immediately he was cut off. His argument, Justice John Paul Stevens pointed out, did not depend on a state of war. It turned on the fact that the prisoners were aliens beyond the "ultimate sovereignty." Olson agreed, but thought the existence of the war made the question "even more forceful" since it made the case more analogous to *Johnson v. Eisentrager*. Justice Sandra Day O'Connor pointed out that the prisoners in *Eisentrager* were citizens of a country at war with the United States, and that they had been tried and convicted, "which makes it worlds different from our case." Olson had to agree, but held to his position.[83]

Justice Stephen Breyer, who has a knack in oral argument of getting to the bottom of things, then struck at the core of the case: "if we go with you," he said, "it has a virtue of clarity." If you're not a citizen and you're held outside the United States, "you don't get your foot in the door." But that, he said, is also the problem: "It seems rather contrary to an idea of a Constitution with three branches that the executive would be free to do whatever they want without a check. . . . [T]here would be a large category of unchecked and uncheckable actions dealing with the detention of individuals . . . in a place where America has the power to do everything."[84]

Eight days later, on April 28, 2004, before another packed gallery, the Court heard oral argument in *Hamdi* and *Padilla*. Jennifer Martinez, a professor at Stanford Law School, argued for Padilla. Frank Dunham, a federal public defender in Virginia, handled the argument for Hamdi. Two-thirds of the way through the government's argument in *Padilla*, Deputy Solicitor General Paul Clement, who argued for the United States in both cases, was asked what would prevent the executive from ordering that a prisoner be tortured. Clement answered that the United States would court-martial a soldier that committed an "atrocity" against a "harmless, detained enemy combatant." Justice Ruth Bader Ginsburg pressed Clement further. "Suppose," she said, "the executive says mild torture will help get this information. . . . [I]t's an executive command. Some systems do that to get information." Clement answered quickly: "Well, our executive doesn't."[85]

Some eight hours later, the CBS news program *60 Minutes II* broadcast the first photos from Abu Ghraib prison in Baghdad.* These photos proved

---

* There is no reason to believe Clement knew about the abuse at Abu Ghraib prison when he answered Justice Ginsburg's question.

to be the most powerful amicus brief of all. Throughout the spring and summer of 2004, precisely when the Court was preparing its opinions in the three terrorism cases, the world was subjected to a seemingly endless series of nauseating disclosures. The haunting vision of helpless prisoners humiliated and tortured by American servicemen and women hung over the Court like an apparition, proving once and for all that the power over a prisoner's life cannot be left to the caprice of his jailer.

On June 28, 2004, the next-to-last day of the Supreme Court term and two months to the day after we first saw the Abu Ghraib photos, the Court issued its decisions in all three cases. In *Rasul,* the Court, by a six-to-three margin, decided that the prisoners could challenge the lawfulness of their detention in federal court. The Court quickly dispatched the "Guantánamo fiction" that had succeeded in the lower courts, concluding that Cuba's "ultimate sovereignty" did not deprive the federal courts of the power to act. For more than two years, we had argued the courts should look to the reality of events at Guantánamo, rather than some mythical notion of Cuban sovereignty. The Supreme Court agreed. "What matters," Justice Anthony Kennedy explained in a concurrence, "is the unchallenged and indefinite control that the United States has long exercised over Guantanamo Bay. From a practical perspective, the indefinite lease of Guantanamo Bay has produced a place that belongs to the United States." [86] The Court also made short work of *Johnson v. Eisentrager,* the case involving the German prisoners convicted of war crimes:

> Petitioners in these cases differ from the *Eisentrager* detainees in important respects: They are not nationals of countries at war with the United States, and they deny that they have engaged in or plotted acts of aggression against the United States; they have never been afforded access to any tribunal, much less charged with and convicted of wrongdoing; and for more than two years they have been imprisoned in territory over which the United States exercises exclusive jurisdiction and control. [87]

The Administration fared no better in *Hamdi,* where eight members of the Court rejected the Administration's position. Writing for a plurality of four, Justice O'Connor upheld the president's power to detain prisoners in the war on terror, but categorically rejected the suggestion that prisoners could be held without legal process. "A state of war is not a blank check for the President," she noted tersely, and the commander in chief power is not a license to "turn our system of checks and balances on its head."[88] Yaser Hamdi's undisputed right to liberty cannot be taken from him unless the Bush Administration has established by a fair process that he was, in fact, an enemy combatant. At a minimum, Justice O'Connor said, this required substantially more than an affidavit from Michael Mobbs, an official in the Defense Department with no firsthand knowledge of the facts. Hamdi must be given prompt notice of the allegations against him and a meaningful opportunity to be heard in federal court by an impartial judge. And if the Administration failed to prove its allegations, Yaser Hamdi must be released.[89]

Justice David Souter, speaking for himself and Justice Ginsburg, would have gone even further. The president, Justice Souter observed, seems to have forgotten that he "is not Commander in Chief of the country, only of the military."[90] The president may not claim for himself the unilateral power to define the offense, prove that it occurred, and determine the consequences:

> In a government of separated powers, deciding finally on what is a reasonable degree of guaranteed liberty whether in peace or war (or some condition in between) is not well entrusted to the Executive Branch of Government, whose particular responsibility is to maintain security. For reasons of inescapable human nature, the branch of the Government asked to counter a serious threat is not the branch on which to rest the Nation's entire reliance in striking the balance between the will to win and the cost in liberty on the way to victory; the responsibility for security will naturally amplify the claim that security legitimately raises.[91]

Justice Souter believed the president did not even have the authority to detain a U.S. citizen without bringing criminal charges. But since that view did not command a majority of the Court, he and Justice Ginsburg agreed with the plurality that Hamdi must be given at least the opportunity to offer evidence that he is not an enemy combatant.[92]

But the most passionate rebuke to the Bush Administration's position in *Hamdi* came from perhaps its most conservative member. Joined by Justice John Paul Stevens, Justice Antonin Scalia dissented. "[I]ndefinite imprisonment at the will of the Executive," Scalia wrote, strikes at "[t]he very core of liberty," and freedom from such imprisonment is a treasured legacy of "our Anglo-Saxon system of separated powers."[93] The principle has survived unchanged for centuries, and the articulation by William Blackstone, the famous English jurist that Scalia quoted, can scarcely be improved upon:

> To bereave a man of life, or by violence to confiscate his estate, without accusation or trial, would be so gross and notorious an act of despotism, as must at once convey the alarm of tyranny throughout the whole kingdom. But confinement of the person, by secretly hurrying him to gaol, where his sufferings are unknown or forgotten; is a less public, a less striking, and therefore a more dangerous engine of arbitrary government.[94]

"If civil rights are to be curtailed during wartime," Justice Scalia warned in closing, "it must be done openly and democratically, as the Constitution requires, rather than by silent erosion through an opinion of this Court." Democracy dies in the dark.*

Praise for *Hamdi* and *Rasul* was immediate, and very nearly unanimous, as editorial pages from every corner of the country cheered the rulings. "This week courage and good sense graced the U.S. Supreme Court," the *Pittsburgh Post-Gazette* wrote, "and the justices said enough is enough." The *Milwaukee Journal Sentinel* said, "American citizens who are distrustful of unchecked government power—and we should all be members of that club—have reason to cheer [the] two decisions." The *Boston Globe* said the rulings "struck decisively at Bush Administration assertions of sweeping power over combat detainees . . . [and] kept the Bill of Rights from being a collateral victim of the war on terror." The *Buffalo News* hailed, "The king is dead. So said the U.S. Supreme Court this week in knocking down the Bush Administration's monarchist pretensions."[95]

"At last," the Fort Lauderdale *Sun-Sentinel* commented, "President Bush

---

* Unlike Yaser Hamdi and the petitioners in *Rasul,* José Padilla suffered a setback. In a 5–4 decision, the Court in *Padilla* held that the case should have been filed in South Carolina, where Padilla was incarcerated at the time his lawyers filed their habeas petition, instead of New York. The Court sent Padilla back to start again. As we will see, there would be significant subsequent developments in *Padilla.*

is being taught some valuable lessons about the limits of his power by the U.S. Supreme Court." The *San Antonio Express-News* welcomed the decisions: "Not only was the U.S. Supreme Court right to reject President Bush's policy of holding 'enemy combatants' in prison indefinitely without trial or access to lawyers, a majority of the court also was refreshingly decisive on the issue." The *St. Louis Post-Dispatch* wrote, "The U.S. Supreme Court soundly rejected on Monday President George W. Bush's extraordinary claim that he could classify people as enemy combatants and order them held indefinitely without access to a lawyer or a day in court." The *Houston Chronicle* praised the Supreme Court "for exerting the rule of law in this country," and the *Los Angeles Times,* in an editorial titled, "It's Called Democracy," wrote, "It is hard to see what is left of American freedom if the government has the authority to make anyone on its soil—citizen or noncitizen—disappear and then rule that no one can do anything about it." [96]

For more than two years, the Administration had said Yaser Hamdi was so dangerous that he had to be held in solitary confinement without access to family or counsel. Yet days after the Supreme Court ordered the Administration to defend Hamdi's detention in open court, the government's lawyers began negotiating the terms of his release with his lawyer, Frank Dunham. As the negotiations continued throughout the summer of 2004, Judge Doumar of the federal district court in Richmond, Virginia, grew frustrated that Hamdi remained in solitary confinement with no legal process, despite the Supreme Court's decision. Finally, on October 5, 2004, Doumar ordered the government to defend Hamdi's detention in open court on October 12. He also ordered the government to bring Hamdi to the hearing. On October 11, Hamdi was released and returned to his home in Saudi Arabia. No evidence was ever presented in open court to justify his nearly three-year imprisonment. He remains a free man today. [97]

EIGHT

A PATTERN OF DECEIT

In *Rasul*, the Supreme Court rejected the Administration's core legal argument that the prisoners could be held indefinitely based on nothing more than the president's word. It was no longer sufficient for the Administration to claim, as it had since the base opened in January 2002, that the prisoners were all "the worst of the worst," as though that overheated description alone demonstrated the lawfulness of their confinement. After *Rasul*, the Administration could no longer content itself with untested hyperbole.

Or so we thought. While *Rasul* may have changed what the law allowed, it did nothing to change what the Administration wanted. The Administration built Camp Delta to be the ideal interrogation chamber and developed an elaborate legal strategy to insulate the prison's operation from judicial scrutiny. *Rasul* may have stripped away the legal defense, but it did nothing to make the architects of the policy reexamine their judgment. From the Administration's perspective, therefore, the challenge after *Rasul* was to make sure the winds of change blowing into Cuba from the north did as little damage as possible.[1]

I

The day after the decision in *Rasul*, Judge Kollar-Kotelly, the district judge on the case, held a conference call with the lawyers to discuss the next steps in the litigation. We sought immediate access to our clients, who by this time had been held virtually incommunicado for more than two years. (Shafiq Rasul and Asif Iqbal had been released in March 2004. Mamdouh

Habib and David Hicks were still at the base, as were the twelve Kuwaiti prisoners represented by Shearman & Sterling.) The government's attorney seemed surprised by the Supreme Court ruling and did not have a response to our request. He asked for time to research the issue and file a brief, which the judge was not inclined to give. He asked for a week; she scheduled another call in three days. During the second call, the government's attorney said the Administration would allow us to travel to the base and meet with our clients, provided we first got a security clearance from the Justice Department and the FBI.* But he chose his words carefully. The Administration did not concede we had a right to meet with our clients, or that the prisoners had a right to counsel. In fact, he did not concede the prisoners had *any* rights, only that the government would permit a meeting in this instance. This was consistent with the position the Administration had taken since the litigation began: the prisoners had no rights, only the process grudgingly extended to them as a matter of Executive grace.[2]

Meanwhile, a host of new cases was getting under way. While we were waiting for the Supreme Court in *Rasul,* my co-counsel Clive Stafford Smith had quietly been gathering authorizations to proceed on behalf of several dozen other prisoners at the base, and the Center for Constitutional Rights had recruited a score of prominent law firms to handle these new cases free of charge. (All our work in *Rasul* has been uncompensated.) As the summer progressed, these lawyers filed habeas petitions in Washington for approximately fifty-five additional prisoners at the base. The government agreed that the new lawyers would also be allowed to go to the base once they were cleared by Justice and the FBI. Litigation that began in February 2002 on behalf of three prisoners now included nearly seventy, but there were still more than five hundred prisoners at the base.

At the same time, the Administration unveiled its response to *Rasul,* making two arguments. First, the government argued that because the prisoners were foreign nationals held outside the sovereign territory of the United States, they had no rights that could be enforced in court. If this sounds familiar, it is: before *Rasul,* the Administration used the same facts to argue the prisoners had no right to seek relief in federal court. Having

---

* I had applied for a security clearance in 2003, but the government took no action on it until the Supreme Court decided *Rasul.*

lost that argument, the Administration now repackaged it to say that while the prisoners could *seek* relief, none could be provided.

This argument, however, ignores the determination by the Supreme Court in *Rasul* to focus on the reality of U.S. control at Guantánamo, rather than the myth of Cuban sovereignty. It also fails to account for the majority's statement that

> Petitioners' allegations—that although they have engaged neither in combat nor in acts of terrorism against the United States, they have been held in Executive detention for more than two years in territory subject to the long-term, exclusive jurisdiction and control of the United States, without access to counsel and without being charged with any wrongdoing—*unquestionably describe custody in violation of the Constitution or laws or treaties of the United States.*[3]

In its pleadings filed after *Rasul,* the Administration dismissed this language as "oblique."[4]

The government's position suggests that *Rasul* was nothing more than a fire drill, a meaningless exercise. Though the Supreme Court held that the prisoners could rely on the habeas statute, and remanded the case for a determination on the merits of the allegations, the Administration thought the federal courts had no other authority than to dismiss the petitions. Before *Rasul,* the Administration argued the courthouse doors were closed to the prisoners; now, it argued the doors were open, but the building was empty.

Anticipating that the courts were likely to reject the suggestion that *Rasul* was an empty ritual, the Bush Administration proposed an alternative that, at least at first blush, had more substance. On July 7, 2004, nine days after the Supreme Court's decision in *Rasul,* the Administration announced that it had created "Combatant Status Review Tribunals," or CSRTs, to determine whether the prisoners at Camp Delta were enemy combatants. Each tribunal would consist of three commissioned officers who would base their decision on information presented by the military and the prisoner. If he chose, the prisoner could testify before the panel. The panel's decision would then be reviewed by a senior officer. According to the Administration, whatever rights these prisoners had—and the government insisted they have none—were adequately provided for by the CSRTs.[5]

The Administration developed this argument from a passage in *Hamdi*, where the Court noted that the military had drafted detailed regulations to implement the requirement in Article 5 of the Third Geneva Convention that doubts about a prisoner's status be resolved by a "competent tribunal." Article 5 hearings, like the CSRT, involve a panel of three officers who hear information from the military and the prisoner. These hearings, the Court said, had proven successful in resolving doubts about the status of prisoners captured in conflicts governed by the Geneva Conventions. From this, the Administration argued that something akin to an Article 5 hearing—the CSRT—would be sufficient to resolve doubts about the status of prisoners at Camp Delta.

But as the Administration so often reminds us, this is not a conventional conflict. In a conventional conflict—and by that I mean a conflict in which the United States complies with the Geneva Conventions—the Army regulations implementing Article 5 serve as a sorting mechanism. These regulations, as discussed in Chapter 3, call for prompt, streamlined proceedings shortly after capture, while the prisoner is still in the theater of operations. The hearing determines which of several groups the prisoner belongs to. Is he innocent? Take him back to the point of capture and let him go. Is he a lawful combatant? Hold him as a POW and give him the benefit of the Third Geneva Convention. Is he an unlawful combatant who is not entitled to treatment as a POW? Give him the benefit of the Fourth Geneva Convention (the Civilian Convention) and "further proceedings to determine what acts [he] may have committed and what penalty should be imposed." And while these decisions are being made, treat him as a POW.[6]

The streamlined proceedings of an Article 5 hearing were developed in response to the unique circumstances presented in the field. Field commanders do not have the time or resources to impose carefully calibrated standards onto battlefield determinations. Yet they need to separate the wheat from the chaff. Article 5 hearings provide an acceptable balance, given the circumstances. Admittedly, these hearings are extremely summary, which creates a significant risk of error. But the consequences of a mistake are mitigated by the fact that prisoners will be confined under conditions that comply with the Geneva Conventions. More onerous conditions, like those that could be imposed if the prisoner were convicted of war crimes, can only come about if the prisoner receives "further proceedings."[7] And finally, the duration of a prisoner's confinement in a conventional conflict—at least if the past is any predictor—will be measured in years, and not decades.

But all these considerations unravel in the present context. The prisoners at Camp Delta are held thousands of miles from the theater of operations and some were captured thousands of miles from the battlefield in Afghanistan. The government has interrogated the men and boys at Guantánamo for years and has had ample opportunity to marshal the evidence against them, if any exists. Circumstances no longer make it impossible to conduct a thoughtful and deliberate review of the allegations. As importantly, the likelihood that an innocent person was captured by mistake is extremely high, and the consequences of an adverse decision are without parallel in U.S. military history: confinement under uniquely severe conditions, unprotected by the Geneva Conventions, and subject to virtually incommunicado detention for what may be the rest of the prisoner's natural life. In short, the same conditions that permit us to be casual in an Article 5 hearing now require that we be careful; what we tolerate at an Article 5 hearing tells us nothing about what we can tolerate in a CSRT.

Yet the CSRT, while it bears a glancing resemblance to an Article 5 hearing, actually provides fewer procedural protections. The ostensible purpose of the CSRT is to determine whether the prisoner is an enemy combatant. In the Supreme Court in *Hamdi* and *Rasul,* the Administration defined an "enemy combatant" as "an individual who . . . was part of or supporting forces hostile to the United States or coalition partners in Afghanistan *and* who engaged in an armed conflict against the United States there."[8] The Court in *Hamdi* endorsed this definition repeatedly, and underscored that it applied without regard to alienage.[9] Restricting the category to people who were "part of or supporting forces hostile" to the U.S. or its allies in Afghanistan, *and* "who engaged in armed conflict against the United States *there*" helps to minimize the risk that the military will incarcerate a person who took no belligerent action.

But in the CSRT proceedings, the Administration took it upon itself to expand the definition. Now, an "enemy combatant" is an individual who was part of or supporting Taliban or al Qaeda forces. . . . This includes any person who has committed a belligerent act or has directly supported hostilities in aid of enemy forces.[10]

This definition is no longer limited to prisoners who have "committed a belligerent act." It is not limited to the conflict in Afghanistan. In fact, it is not subject to any geographic limitation and conceivably reaches anywhere in the world. Finally, because the definition does not tell us what it means to be "supporting" al Qaeda or the Taliban, we are left to wonder whether it includes inadvertent, or involuntary support.

The answers to these questions soon became apparent, as press accounts of CSRT proceedings appeared through the end of 2004 and early 2005. One Afghani prisoner testified at his CSRT that he was "captured by the Taliban while buying tea and sugar in his village," and forced to work as a cook. As we saw in Chapter 4, the Taliban routinely resorted to forced conscriptions to fill out its ranks. The prisoner asked to call four witnesses who could verify his report. The military conceded that the man, like many others at the base, had been "conscripted" to join the Taliban, and that he had served as a cook, but they nonetheless refused his request for witnesses. According to the panel's presiding officer, "Whether or not the detainee was forced to join the Taliban, or in what role they served the Taliban, is not relevant."[11]

Another Afghani prisoner testified he was kidnapped from his wife and six children and forced to join the Taliban. He never fought for the Taliban and was held under armed guard for the month he was with them. He too asked that the tribunal summon witnesses who would support his testimony, but his request was summarily denied: "how or why the individual joined the Taliban is not a consideration," the presiding officer explained.[12] Although an officer involved in this case described it as "gut-wrenching" to find against this prisoner, he felt he had no choice. The question before the tribunal was simply whether the person was "part of or supporting Taliban or al Qaeda forces," as that term had been defined by the Administration. Constrained by their own inquiry, the result of the tribunal's deliberation was foreordained. Many prisoners testified, without contradiction by the military, that they had been forced to work for the Taliban under threat of death. As one official involved in the process explained, however, the definition of enemy combatant "does not address consent or intent."[13]

In short, the inflexible and expansive definition of enemy combatant made it inevitable the CSRT would rule against a number of prisoners who should have been released. Yet this problem was exacerbated by the procedural rules governing the CSRTs. To begin with, the tribunals based their decision on secret evidence kept from the prisoner. This sometimes produced absurd spectacles, fit for Lewis Carroll, like the exchange between Mustafa Ait Idir, a Bosnian-Algerian, and the officers at his CSRT. Idir was asked to respond to a charge that he had "associated with a known Al Qaida operative" while living in Bosnia. "Give me his name," Idir said.

Tribunal President: I do not know.
Idir: How can I respond to this?
Tribunal President: Did you know of anyone that was a member of Al Qaeda?
Idir: No, no. . . . This is something the interrogators told me a long while ago. I asked the interrogators to tell me who this person was. Then I could tell you if I might have known this person but not if this person was a terrorist. Maybe I knew this person as a friend. Maybe it was a person that worked with me. Maybe it was a person that was on my team. But I do not know if this person is Bosnian, Indian, or whatever. If you tell me the name, then I can respond and defend myself against this accusation.
Tribunal President: We are asking you the questions and we need you to respond to what is on the unclassified summary.

Idir was read another charge accusing him of involvement in a plan to attack the U.S. embassy in Sarajevo. He again denied the allegations and asked to see the evidence against him. Once more the panel refused; once more Idir asked how he could defend against charges he could not see:

I am prepared now to tell you, if you have anything or any evidence, even if it is just very little . . . , then I am ready to be punished. I can just tell you that I did not plan anything. . . . I was hoping you had evidence that you can give me. If I was in your place—and I apologize in advance for these words—but if a supervisor came to me and showed me accusations like these, I would take these accusations and I would hit him in the face with them. Sorry about that.

At this, everyone in the room began to laugh. The presiding officer assured Idir it was okay for him to continue:

> Because these are accusations that I can't even answer. I am not able to answer them. You tell me I am from Al Qaida, but I am not an Al Qaida. I don't have any proof to give you except to ask you to catch Bin Laden and ask him if I am a part of Al Qaida. . . . I don't have proof regarding this. What should be done is you should give me evidence regarding these accusations because I am not able to give you any evidence. I can just tell you no, and that is it.

In fact, however, Idir did have some evidence to support his protestations: the allegations against him had been investigated by the Bosnian Government, which cleared him of the charges. The tribunal did not consider the evidence of his exoneration.[14]

At the same time, the tribunal must presume that the evidence presented by the military, including the secret evidence, is genuine and accurate. This distinguishes the CSRT from an Article 5 hearing, where the prisoner is presumed to be a POW until proven otherwise, and there is no presumption in favor of the military's evidence. In addition, the CSRT panel may rely on "any information it deems relevant and helpful," including any degree of hearsay. Furthermore, and for the first time in U.S. military history, the tribunal may rely on information secured by torture, coercive interrogations, or cruel and degrading treatment. The interrogations of Mohammed al Qahtani, for instance, may be used by the CSRT. Article 5 hearings, by contrast, rely on evidence secured in compliance with the Geneva Conventions, which prohibit torture and unlawful coercion and thereby minimize the risk of error caused by unreliable confessions.

In one of the earliest CSRT proceedings, a Tunisian prisoner claimed his confession—that he had voluntarily gone to Afghanistan to take part in military training—was false, and that he only said it because he was being tortured after his capture in Afghanistan. The tribunal found him to be an enemy combatant, with no apparent inquiry (at least, no public inquiry) into whether his allegations were correct.[15]

Farouq Ali Ahmed, a Yemeni detainee who was eighteen years old when he was captured, was found to be an enemy combatant in part because of evidence supplied by the interrogations of Mohammed al Qahtani. As the *National Law Journal* reported, "[a]t some point after facing a snarling dog, donning women's underwear, and gibbering under a sheet, Kahtani had apparently pointed to a mug shot of Farouq" and identified him as a mujahedeen fighter.[16] Ahmed's lawyers, Marc Falkoff and David Remes of the law firm Covington and Burling, have said that al Qahtani was also a source of allegations against two of their other clients.[17]

CSRTs have sometimes relied on evidence that is even more dubious than al Qahtani's coerced confessions. The government has accused at least ten prisoners partially on the basis that they own a Casio watch similar or identical to a model whose parts have been used in explosives. But the same watch is "sold in sidewalk stands around the world."[18] A Yemeni prisoner "confessed" during one interrogation that "I saw bin Laden five times: Three times on Al Jazeera and twice on Yemeni news." His CSRT file now states that "[d]etainee admitted to knowing Osama bin Laden."[19] Another prisoner "slammed his hands on the table during an especially long interrogation and yelled, 'Fine, you got me; I'm a terrorist.' " His interrogators recognized it as sarcasm but the military used the remark against the prisoner at his CSRT, which dutifully recorded that the prisoner "admitted he is a terrorist."[20]

The tribunal is also apparently free to ignore exculpatory evidence, even when that evidence is overwhelming. Murat Kurnaz is a German Muslim of Turkish descent. He was traveling through Pakistan with Islamic missionaries when he was pulled off a bus by local police in October 2001. The Pakistanis questioned Kurnaz and turned him over to U.S. officials, who eventually transferred him to Cuba. He told the tribunal he was innocent and virtually all the information presented to the CSRT supported his position. In one memo, the Command Intelligence Task Force, the investigative arm of the U.S. Southern Command, reported it was "not aware of evidence that Kurnaz was or is a member of Al Quaeda[sic] ." The task force, it said, "has no definite link/evidence of detainee having an association with Al Qaida or making any specific threat against the U.S." German intelligence offered an even more unequivocal assessment: "this detainee has no connection to an al-Qaida cell in Germany."[21]

The only evidence to the contrary was a single, unsigned document authored by an unnamed military official who wrote, without supporting evidence, that Kurnaz was a member of al-Qaeda, and that a friend of his—a person named Selcuk Bilgin—had been a suicide bomber in Turkey. Whatever merit there is to the suggestion that a person should be classified an enemy combatant based on a friend's behavior, the suggestion is particularly worrisome in this case because Bilgin is alive and well and living in Germany. He is not under suspicion by the German authorities, who remain mystified by the suggestion that he was a suicide bomber. Yet the CSRT, since it was required to accept the military's evidence as accurate, credited the single page against Kurnaz and disregarded the evidence that he was innocent. When confronted with the facts of this case, the military said only that the exculpatory evidence had been declassified by mistake and should not have been made available to the public.[22]

Nor are the tribunals administered by impartial decision-makers. Like an Article 5 hearing, each tribunal consists of three commissioned officers. But in an Article 5 hearing, the prisoner is presumed a POW. In these tribunals, by contrast, the president, the secretary of defense, and the secretary of the Navy (who convenes the tribunals and selects the member officers) have all repeatedly announced that each detainee is an enemy combatant. In fact, the order establishing the tribunals declares that "each detainee . . . has been determined to be an enemy combatant through multiple levels of review by officers of the Department of Defense."[23] Unlike in a conventional hearing, where the tribunal listens to the evidence and then announces its result, in a CSRT, the superiors announce the result, and then convene a hearing. At the same time, this explicit prejudgment is presumed correct, and it is the prisoner's burden to prove otherwise. When combined with the panel's reliance on secret evidence, this has repeatedly led to maddening exchanges. When told that he could not see the classified information that established his status as an enemy combatant, one prisoner replied, "I know that the accused is innocent until proven guilty. First prove that I am a criminal, and then after that I will prove I am innocent."[24]

Furthermore, it is not at all clear how a prisoner at Camp Delta could possibly rebut the presumption against him. He is allowed to testify, but presumably the military—after interrogating him for literally hundreds of hours and concluding he is in fact an enemy combatant—has already heard and discounted whatever protestation of innocence the prisoner could provide, as happened with Shafiq Rasul and Asif Iqbal, my British clients. "I've been here for three years," one Afghani prisoner told his panel, "and the past three years, whatever I say, nobody believes me. They listen but they don't believe me."[25] Prisoners also have the right to call "reasonably available" witnesses and produce "reasonably available" documents, but how they may exercise this right is not immediately apparent.[26] Availability is determined by the tribunal, which as we have seen, takes a dim view of these requests.

In any event, the rules do not explain how a prisoner who cannot communicate with the outside world could locate and secure witnesses or produce documents from halfway around the globe, nor is it evident how that witness could be brought to Guantánamo Bay, since foreign nationals are allowed on the base only under extremely unusual circumstances. Perhaps for that reason, former Navy Secretary Gordon England predicted when the hearings began that few such requests would be honored.[27] Witnesses from the armed forces—including the person who may have tortured the detainee—will *not* be considered reasonably available (even if the witness's identity were somehow known to the prisoner), if their commanding officer, in his exclusive discretion, determines their presence at a hearing would "affect combat or support operations."[28] Ait Idir, the Bosnian-Algerian who quizzed his panel how he could be expected to answer allegations he could not see, told the CSRT that he lived in Croatia. The panel told him it would be helpful if he could document that fact: "I do not know how or what the procedure is, but you should really take the opportunity to get that information." "How," Idir replied, "when I am at GTMO?"[29]

Finally, the prisoners—all of whom are foreign nationals unfamiliar with the American system of justice—must navigate the various obstacles at a CSRT without counsel. Even the habeas lawyers who represent the prisoners in federal court are not allowed to consult with their clients about, or to attend, the CSRT proceedings. Instead, the prisoners are assigned a "personal representative," who is not a lawyer and who cannot provide legal advice. These representatives do not enjoy a confidential attorney-client relationship with the prisoners, and have been instructed that they must disclose to the tribunal anything the prisoner tells them. And while the personal representative can review the secret evidence, he cannot share it with the prisoner.[30]

To their credit, some personal representatives have done their best to help the prisoners despite these constraints. One nineteen-year-old Syrian prisoner, a young man named Mohammed al-Tumani, told his CSRT he had simply never been to the terrorist training camp he was accused of attending. Tumani's personal representative looked at the secret evidence in the case, and found that the only evidence against him came from a single prisoner who had given evidence against more than sixty fellow prisoners. This man, whose name has not been publicly reported, accused Tumani of attending the camp several months before the teenager entered Afghanistan. The personal representative examined the accuser's classified file, learned that he had accused more than five dozen prisoners, and then studied the files of every prisoner implicated by the man. None of them had been in Afghanistan at the time the accuser placed them at the camp.[31] In the end, however, the personal representative's efforts were to no avail. The tribunal found that Tumani was an enemy combatant.[32]

Nor can these accounts be dismissed as merely anecdotal. In February 2006, a team of scholars at Seton Hall University Law School completed the first systematic analysis of the government's evidence.[33] They examined the files in 517 cases, including almost every case in which the CSRT concluded the prisoner was an enemy combatant. Their findings were remarkable. Recall that Secretary Rumsfeld once described the prisoners as "among the most dangerous, best trained, vicious killers on the face of the earth."[34] In fact, however, only 8 percent of the prisoners at the base are even alleged to be al-Qaeda fighters. Fifty-five percent of the prisoners, or roughly 280 people, are not alleged to have engaged in any hostile act against the United States or coalition forces, and for the remaining 45 percent, the "hostile act" included conduct like fleeing from U.S. bombing or being captured in Pakistan.[35] In one case discussed by the authors, the entire record against the prisoner was that he was a cook's assistant who fled "from Narim to Kabul during the Northern Alliance attack and surrendered to the Northern Alliance."[36] Only 5 percent of the prisoners were captured by the United States military; the rest were seized under unknown circumstances by the Northern Alliance, Pakistani Intelligence, or Afghan warlords who, in many cases, sold their captives for bounty.[37] To be sure, a small number of prisoners appear to be the sort of person for whom the base was intended. These cases, however, are "atypical." According to the Pentagon's own data, "[t]here are only a very few individuals who are actively engaged in any activities for al-Qaeda or the Taliban."[38]

In short, the conclusion is simply inescapable that these tribunals were created for no other purpose than to validate a predetermined result. For years, the Administration has told the world that the prisoners at the base were "enemy combatants," and now a "hearing" will come to precisely that conclusion. Not surprisingly, Secretary England confidently predicted that only a few prisoners at the base would prevail at their hearing.[39] He was right. All but thirty-eight were found to be enemy combatants. And even in these cases, the military refuses to acknowledge that it made a mistake. Instead, it has given these thirty-eight prisoners yet another label, calling them NLECs, or "No Longer Enemy Combatants," to signify that every one of them was properly captured and correctly designated as an enemy combatant up until the moment the CSRT determined they were not.[40]

It is important to understand the combined effect of the government's two-pronged response to *Rasul*. Its first contention—that the prisoners have no rights that can be enforced in court—obviously preserves Camp Delta in its pristine, pre-*Rasul* state. Its second, alternative argument—that the CSRT provides an adequate substitute for habeas—does the same thing, only in a more subtle fashion. The CSRT relies on a black box of information provided by the military and withheld from the prisoner, who must confront this unseen information without counsel. The military controls what information passes into the box, and orders the tribunal to presume that information to be correct. While a prisoner may add his contrary account, it is not likely to be different from the information the military has already heard and discounted. Moreover, there is no meaningful opportunity for the prisoner to gather and present contrary evidence. The net effect of the CSRT procedures, therefore, is to ensure that the particulars of any given detention remain shielded from outside scrutiny, and that the prisoner remains in a black hole.

But more importantly, the CSRT, with its superficial similarity to Article 5 hearings, creates the impression that the Administration has fixed the problem identified in *Rasul*. The CSRT appears to blunt the most pointed criticism of Camp Delta: that the prisoners are being held beyond the law with no meaningful opportunity to demonstrate that the military has made a mistake. Appearances, however, can be misleading: any proceeding that forces an alien prisoner unfamiliar with our justice system and held incommunicado to disprove allegations he cannot see, and whose reliability he cannot test, before a military panel whose superiors have repeatedly pre-judged the result, all without counsel, does not deserve to be called a hearing. In court, I once described them as the perfect storm of procedural inadequacy. Yet it is undoubtedly easier for the Administration to defend a process that shares some distant kinship with an Article 5 hearing than it is to defend detentions with no process at all.

Finally, the CSRTs offer another example of the Administration's selective use of the laws of war. As we have seen, we tolerate summary Article 5 proceedings for a number of reasons: more elaborate procedures are not practicable in the field, the consequences of a mistake are mitigated by the application of the Geneva Conventions, and adverse decisions are followed by additional proceedings. In that way, though the executive has the power to hold people based on a summary process, that power is constrained by the obligation to comply with the Geneva Conventions and provide additional process to prisoners who are not given POW status. In the CSRT, however, the situation is exactly the reverse: circumstances no longer present the same need for summary proceedings, the consequences of an adverse decision are uniquely severe, and no additional proceedings protect against the risk of error. Yet the Administration provides even less process than that contemplated by Article 5. Once again, the Administration asserts the power associated with the laws of war, but accepts none of the restraints.

II

By creating the appearance of an open and impartial process, the CSRT fits within a broader pattern of events at Camp Delta and other post-9/11 detention centers. The Administration often touts Camp Delta as an open and transparent facility and invites journalists and members of Congress to visit the base. But when these people take them up on the offer, the visits are scripted, tightly controlled affairs. James Yee, the former Muslim chaplain, referred to these visits as the "dog and pony show."[41] Media and congressional delegations are given controlled access only to Camp Four, the medium (and lowest) security wing of the base. No visitor is given a tour of Camp Five, the high-security wing where prisoners spend more than twenty-three hours a day in solitary confinement. No member of the media or congressional delegation is allowed to speak with any prisoner, and should an inmate attempt to holler out to a journalist during a tour, the two are quickly separated.[42] The few reporters who have tried to speak with a prisoner have been summarily expelled from the facility.[43] No congressman has ever seen a "stress and duress" position, and no reporter has ever spoken with a prisoner about the "atmosphere of dependency and trust" between him and his interrogators. And this of course is deliberate; as we saw in Chapter 5, al Qahtani's interrogation log "was never meant to leave Gitmo."[44]

At the same time, visitors are treated to fake interrogations, at least according to one person familiar with the practice.[45] According to Erik Saar, a linguist and former interpreter at Camp Delta, the military routinely staged bogus interrogations to dupe congressional delegations. When members of Congress or other important officials visited the base to watch interrogations, the military would manufacture mock interrogations with compliant prisoners. In these sessions, the prisoner would simply repeat the answers he had given before and the congressional delegation would watch what appeared to be nothing more than a casual conversation. Saar makes clear, however, that these staged events were hardly representative of actual interrogations, and says that if the members of Congress wanted to witness what actually took place during a session, they needed to come back "unannounced . . . at 2:00 in the morning."[46]

In the summer of 2005, Pennsylvania Republican Senator Arlen Specter, chairman of the Senate Judiciary Committee, traveled to Guantánamo hoping to conduct hearings into both the conditions of confinement and the allegations by former prosecutors that the system for military commissions had been rigged against the defendants. In negotiations prior to leaving for the base, Specter acceded to the military's demand that any witness called at the hearing not be under oath, although why the military would insist on this is unclear. At the base, however, Specter was told that a hearing would not be allowed, apparently because Specter wanted to create a transcript of the witnesses' statements so they could be reviewed by other senators. Instead of a hearing, Specter was given a tour of the facility and allowed to meet with some of the interrogators.[47]

Some of these attempts at deception have been inexplicably clumsy, arising in cases where they were certain to be uncovered. At Camp Delta, if an inmate does not leave his cell when ordered, the military sends in the "initial reaction force," or IRF squad.* So many inmates have described the aggressive tactics used by this squad that "IRF" has become a verb in the prisoners' vocabulary. The public got a rare window into the operation of the IRF squad after a botched drill involving a U.S. soldier.

On January 24, 2003, Army Specialist Sean Baker volunteered to participate in a training exercise for the IRF squad, which routinely conducts trainings with U.S. soldiers posing as prisoners. In training, however, the volunteer is always dressed in his Army uniform and the squad knows it is only a drill. But on this occasion, Baker, who volunteered for the Army after 9/11 and had been at Guantánamo for only a few months, was asked by his commanding officer to wear the orange jumpsuit of a Camp Delta inmate. Four members of the IRF team later swore they believed they were extracting an actual inmate who had not responded to pepper spray. To heighten the sense of reality, an Army linguist yelled loudly, in English and Arabic and within earshot of the IRF squad donning riot gear down the hall, for the "prisoner" (Baker) to leave his cell. Baker, however, did as he had been instructed: he refused the order to come out and cowered under the bunk of his cell, waiting for the extraction team. He was given a code word— "red"—if he wanted to stop the drill at any time. The IRF team stormed into his cell:[48]

> My face was down. And of course, they're pushing it down against the steel floor, you know, my right temple, pushing it down against the floor. And someone's holding me by the throat, using a pressure point on me and holding my throat. And I used the word, "red." At that point I, you know, I became afraid. And when I said the word "Red," he forced

---

* This squad is sometimes also referred to as the "Immediate Reaction Force," and the "Extreme Reaction Force."

my head down against the steel floor and was sort of just grinding it into the floor. The individual then, when I picked up my head and said, "Red," slammed my head down against the floor. I was so afraid, I groaned out, "I'm a U.S. soldier." And when I said that, he slammed my head again, one more time against the floor. And I groaned out one more time, I said, "I'm a U.S. soldier." [49]

The beating stopped only when a member of the team noticed Baker's Army-issued uniform and boots.

Baker began having seizures within hours of the beating. He was transferred to Walter Reed Medical Center in Washington, where he was diagnosed with a complex partial seizure disorder as a result of a traumatic brain injury. In April 2004, he was honorably discharged from the service. Yet despite all Baker endured, the military initially denied that his discharge had anything to do with the injuries he suffered during the exercise. Only months later, after the press had publicized the matter, did the military reverse itself and acknowledge the contributing role of the beating Baker received. As a final codicil to this episode, all IRF team extractions at Camp Delta are videotaped, but the tape of Specialist Baker's extraction and beating was somehow lost. [50]

Nor is this pattern of deception confined to Camp Delta. As we saw in Chapter 6, Colin Powell in his February 5, 2003, presentation to the U.N. Security Council, and President Bush in an October 2002 speech about Iraq training al-Qaeda members, were both relying on information learned from the coercive questioning of Ibn Shaykh al Libi, who told his interrogators that he and other al-Qaeda operatives had traveled to Iraq, where they received training in the use of chemical and biological weapons. [51] Recently, however, we learned that as early as February 2002—eight months before the president's speech and a year before Powell's presentation to the U.N.—the Defense Intelligence Agency had concluded that al Libi's account was not credible and that al Libi was probably "intentionally misleading the debriefers." [52] The DIA report, which would have been circulated throughout the Administration at the time it was written, did not become known to the public until November 2005, when declassified portions were made available by Senator

Carl Levin of Michigan, the ranking Democrat on the Armed Services Committee.* [53]

Only the Administration's most partisan advocates could defend these deceptions. The argument, to the extent one can be made, is that the truth invites unwanted inquiry by unqualified observers who will not understand the justification for especially aggressive interrogation practices. Perhaps from ignorance, perhaps from misplaced sensitivities, observers would misconstrue these techniques as abusive when in fact they are essential to the successful prosecution of the war on terror. To prevent this, the military and the CIA must shield us from reality, even if it means lying, because only the executive branch can see these techniques for what they are.

This justification, however, is obviously inadequate, for a number of reasons. First, observers may have found particular techniques abusive *because they were.* One recoils at the thought of an interrogator suspending a prisoner from the ceiling and beating him to death—not out of any particular squeamishness, but because it is reprehensible, criminal behavior. Moreover, the very elaborateness of some of these deceptions suggests a consciousness of guilt. Like the decision to create a bogus set of financial records to conceal an elaborate accounting fraud, one does not stage phony interrogations except to conceal wrongdoing.

Second, the argument rests on a now familiar claim to the unilateral

---

* I focus on al Libi because of the connection between his false confession and the Administration's detention policy. I do not mean to suggest, however, this was the only, or even the most important misrepresentation in the run-up to the war in Iraq. For instance, the president warned ominously in his 2003 state of the union address that Iraq had "mobile biological weapons labs" that could produce "germ warfare agents," a charge he repeated in a number of prewar speeches. Similarly, in his presentation to the U.N. Security Council, Secretary of State Powell relied on an "eyewitness" report that Iraq's mobile labs could manufacture enough chemical weapons in a single month "to kill thousands upon thousands of people." In fact, however, their intelligence came principally from an Iraqi defector, codenamed Curveball, whose handlers in Germany had repeatedly warned the Administration that he was unreliable and mentally unstable, and that his claims could not be confirmed. The Administration did not admit its error until 2004, more than a year after the invasion. See Bob Drogin & John Goetz, "How U.S. Fell Under the Spell of 'Curveball,'" *Los Angeles Times* (Nov. 20, 2005); Commission on the Intelligence Capabilities of the United States Regarding Weapons of Mass Destruction at 48, 80–111 (March 31, 2005), available at http://www.wmd.gov/report/wmd_report.pdf.

power of the commander in chief. Apparently, no one outside the executive branch is qualified to judge the wisdom or utility of its detention policy. The Administration claims for itself not simply the power to devise the policy, but to control its implementation—even to the point of deceiving other organs of government, the press, and the American electorate. But a constitutional democracy cannot function if one branch of government is permitted to emasculate the others.

Finally, and most significantly, the deceptions do not simply shield the reality of the Administration's detention policy from public view. Instead, they are an attempt to create a *new* reality. It would be one thing if the Administration were to exclude all visitors from Camp Delta, including congressional delegations. Then we would be left to wonder what is taking place. But it is something altogether different to stage mock events that create a false or distorted picture of what takes place behind the wire. These deceptions, like the Combatant Status Review Tribunals, can have no other goal than to induce members of Congress, the judiciary, and the public into believing, mistakenly, that all is well at Guantánamo, and that the Administration deserves our trust. But of course, bringing these deceptions to light demonstrates precisely the opposite.

III

Sometimes the attempt to obscure the details of the detention policy relies not on deception, but on outright resistance to oversight. Human Rights Watch, whose reporting about prison conditions in other countries has been relied upon by the State Department, has requested access to the Guantánamo base every year since 2002, without success.[54] Also since 2002, the U.N. special rapporteur on torture has asked to visit Guantánamo but until very recently had not received a reply from the United States.[55] In October 2005, the Bush Administration finally announced it would allow this delegation to visit the base, and said it had nothing to hide. Yet Secretary Rumsfeld attached a qualification to the Administration's announcement: the U.N. monitors would not be allowed to speak with any prisoners about their treatment. In fact, they would not be allowed to speak with any prisoners for any reason. The special rapporteur said he could not accept this restriction on his inspection and canceled his planned trip.[56] There is a rich irony in these events: the State Department has repeatedly criticized other countries for refusing to grant the special rapporteur access to their prisons.

Other U.S. detention facilities are even more impenetrable than Camp Delta. As noted, the Administration's legal response to *Rasul* was to argue that the prisoners had no rights, and that whatever rights they had were adequately provided by the CSRT. At the same time, however, the Administration developed a contingency plan: the Pentagon created a new Guantánamo at Bagram Air Base in Afghanistan. At a cabinet-level meeting September 14, 2004, the National Security Counsel essentially cut off the transfer of prisoners to Guantánamo. The last delivery of ten prisoners took place eight days later. Since then, the prison population at Bagram, described as "a cavernous former machine shop" built by the Soviets forty miles north of Kabul, has exploded, from one hundred in early 2004, before the Supreme Court decision in *Rasul,* to as many as six hundred in 2005 and approximately five hundred in early 2006.[57]

Conditions at Bagram are primitive, even worse than in Cuba. "Men are held by the dozen in large wire cages . . . , sleeping on the floor on foam mats and, until about a year ago, often using plastic buckets for latrines." Until recently, prisoners at Bagram rarely saw daylight, "except for brief visits to a small exercise yard." One former prisoner, a sixty-year-old tribal elder released in June 2005 after nearly two years, said it was "like a cage. Like the cages in Karachi [Pakistan] where they put animals." The Geneva Conventions have no more force at Bagram than they do at Camp Delta. Prisoners at Bagram do not even receive the benefit of a CSRT. The Pentagon has created "Enemy Combatant Review Boards," which review the allegations against the prisoners on an annual basis. The prisoners, however, are not told what the allegations are and have no role in the review process.[58]

And unlike Camp Delta, Bagram is all but closed from public scrutiny. There are no media visits to the base and the prison itself may not even be photographed. The Administration repeatedly rebuffed the U.N. Human Rights Commissioner's independent expert for Afghanistan when he tried to visit Bagram and in 2005 forced him from his job. (The monitor also tried unsuccessfully to visit the U.S. air base at Kandahar, Afghanistan, which has since been closed.) As a result, Bagram remains a pre-*Rasul* prison. Who is being held, for what reason, and based on what evidence? We do not know. Some of the prisoners have been there more than two years.

According to the military, the current average length of detention is fourteen and a half months.[59]

But at least these prisons are operated by the Defense Department, which acknowledges their existence. Since 2002, the CIA has operated a small network of secret, overseas detention centers that, by official accounts, do not even exist. Described in highly classified documents as "black sites," these centers trace their origin to a presidential order signed December 17, 2001, which gave the CIA broad power to kill, capture, or detain suspected members of al-Qaeda all over the world. An early plan to engage in a series of covert assassinations was briefly considered and rejected as impractical, and the CIA decided instead to hold prisoners in these secret sites, which have operated at various times in eight countries. The first of these sites, in Thailand, closed when its existence became known.[60] Another facility operated briefly at Guantánamo Bay, but that site closed sometime in 2004 to make sure none of the prisoners held by the CIA came within the jurisdiction of the federal courts under *Rasul.* A third facility, known as the Salt Pit, operated for a time near Kabul, Afghanistan, but was later closed and moved to a more secure location north of the Kabul airport. Another CIA prison, code-named Bright Light, is used for prisoners who will probably never be released. According to one CIA official, "The word is that once you get sent to Bright Light, you never come back."[61] The *Washington Post* reported the CIA was operating additional sites in several Eastern European democracies. At the Administration's request, the *Post* agreed not to identify these countries. Human Rights Watch, however, reported that CIA facilities were located in Poland and Romania—a charge denied by those countries.[62] After the *Post* article appeared, the Administration apparently closed the European facilities and moved the prisoners yet again—reportedly to a spot in the North African desert.[63]

Little is known about the "black sites," and even less about the condition of the prisoners within them. The CIA does not even acknowledge that the covert program exists, although its operation has been repeatedly confirmed by a number of senior administration officials, as well as current and former intelligence officers. The facilities themselves are among the Administration's most closely guarded secrets. We do not know who is being held, although published accounts indicate the CIA has held approximately three thousand people since 9/11, and that it is currently holding approximately thirty prisoners, including senior al-Qaeda operatives Khalid Sheikh Mohammed (one of the suspected masterminds behind the September 11 attacks and the self-proclaimed head of al-Qaeda's military committee), Ramzi Binalshibh (a suspected coordinator of the September 11 attacks), Abu Zubaydah (the former operations director for al-Qaeda), and Omar al-Faruq (al-Qaeda's top operative in Southeast Asia).[64]

In these clandestine facilities, prisoners are apparently kept in total isolation, sometimes in dark, underground cells.[65] No one except CIA interrogators may see or speak with the prisoners. In addition to the techniques used by the military, the CIA may use a number of "enhanced interrogation techniques." Among other tactics approved for use by the CIA, a prisoner may be forced to stand with his feet shackled to the floor and his hands cuffed together for more than forty hours. He may be doused with cold water and left to stand naked in a cell that is kept near fifty degrees. Or he may be water-boarded: strapped to an inclined board, with his feet raised and his head slightly below his feet. His face is wrapped with cellophane and water is poured over his head and mouth, which produces a sensation that he is drowning.[66] Prisoners have also "been forced into coffin-like boxes, forced into cells where they are alternately denied all light and put in brightly lit rooms and denied sleep for long periods."[67]

Agents have apparently used some or all of these and other aggressive techniques against a dozen senior members of al-Qaeda. Ibn Shaykh al Libi was subjected to a number of these tactics during two weeks of questioning by the CIA before he was rendered to Egypt in January 2002.[68] As we saw in Chapter 6, under the force of these tactics, al Libi falsely confessed that he traveled to Iraq and received training in chemical weapons and explosives, the claim that would later become a central part of the Administration's case for the war in Iraq. Abu Zubaydah was shot in the chest, groin, and thigh when he was captured in Pakistan on March 28, 2002, and agents initially withheld pain medications until he agreed to cooperate with interrogators.[69]

Khalid Sheikh Mohammed was captured at a house in Rawalpindi, Pakistan, in March 2003. Over a two-week period, interrogators reportedly subjected him to "several types of harsh interrogation techniques approximately a hundred times," including the repeated use of water-boarding.[70] In April 2003, American intelligence agencies concluded his interrogation program had led him to spin an elaborate web of lies.[71] For three months, al-Faruq was "subjected to sleep and light deprivation, prolonged isolation, and room temperatures that varied from 100 degrees to 10 degrees." One official characterized his treatment as "not quite torture, but about as close as you can get." Other officials familiar with CIA interrogation techniques believe al-Faruq was left naked most of the time with his hands and feet bound. (In an embarrassing codicil, al-Faruq and three other senior al-Qaeda operatives escaped from their prison at Bagram in July 2005, and remain at large as of this writing.[72])

Treatment of this sort is clearly prohibited by the Convention Against Torture, which the United States ratified in 1994. In addition to prohibiting torture, this treaty requires that we "undertake to prevent . . . other acts of cruel, inhuman or degrading treatment or punishment." Because these words are not part of our legal lexicon, the Reagan Administration urged the Senate to ratify the treaty subject to a reservation: the words, "cruel, inhuman, or degrading treatment or punishment" would be interpreted to mean the same thing as the similar words in the Eighth Amendment, which prohibits "cruel and unusual punishment." This was a sensible reservation, since the courts had interpreted the Eighth Amendment for many years and had developed an understanding about its content. Linking the Torture Convention to the Eighth Amendment meant that both would be given the same substantive scope.

Unfortunately, the Administration's lawyers have transformed this substantive understanding into a geographic loophole. The Eighth Amendment, they say, does not protect foreign nationals outside the sovereign United States. Because the Torture Convention is linked to the Eighth Amendment, the prohibition against "cruel, inhuman, or degrading treatment" also does not apply outside the United States. But this is just bad lawyering. As Abraham Sofaer, the legal advisor to the State Department when the Reagan Administration signed the Convention, explained in a letter to Vermont Senator Patrick Leahy, the obvious purpose of the Senate reservation was to give "cruel, inhuman and degrading treatment" the same substantive meaning as "cruel and unusual punishment." It was never meant to define or restrict the Convention's geographic reach. Yet the Administration took the position that interrogators could subject prisoners to cruel, inhuman, and degrading acts that would be illegal under the Convention and the Eighth Amendment, so long as they are not committed in the U.S.[73]

The Administration has vigorously, and so far successfully, resisted any attempt to shed light on these secret CIA prisons. The memo authorizing "enhanced interrogation techniques" remains classified, and the Administration refuses to show it to the Senate Intelligence Committee, even though its members could not make the memo public. Senator Carl Levin of Michigan, a member of the committee, recently told the *New Yorker* that "[t]he refusal to give us these documents is totally inexcusable. . . . The Administration is getting away with just saying no. There's no claim of executive privilege. There's no claim of national security—we've offered to keep it classified. It's just bullshit. They just don't want us to know what they're doing, or have done." *[74]

The International Red Cross, which enjoys limited access to Defense Department facilities, has not been allowed to monitor the black sites, although it was apparently given some access to the CIA site that formerly operated at Guantánamo.[75] The 9/11 Commission, which was charged by Congress with conducting a complete investigation into the facts surrounding the attacks, sought to question a number of senior members of al-Qaeda, including Khalid Sheikh Mohammed and Abu Zubaydah. The CIA flatly refused to make them available to the commission. Even the ranking members of the House and Senate intelligence committees, who receive regular briefings on all covert activity, have not been told more about the

---

* Because so many of the documents remain classified, it is difficult to know precisely when the CIA received approval to use these techniques. ABC News reports it was mid-March, 2002. See Brian Ross and Richard Esposito, "CIA's Harsh Interrogation Techniques Described," ABC News, Nov. 19, 2005. Other reports suggest the Justice Department did not sign off on these techniques until the summer of 2002, possibly August. The difference is probably attributable to the layers of review within the Administration. Agents in the field apparently began using these techniques not long after the CIA began holding prisoners. In March 2002, these techniques were apparently approved by CIA headquarters. As the year progressed and the use became more widespread, the CIA may have sought further review from Justice, which offered its opinion in August.

program than its broad outlines. West Virginia Senator Jay Rockefeller, the ranking Democrat on the Committee, has repeatedly sought to hold hearings on the CIA's role in detentions since 9/11, but his efforts have been rebuffed.[76] As a result, the black site prisons have emerged as the ultimate refinement of the Administration's post-9/11 detention policy, the quintessential black hole.

NINE

"FINDING SOMEONE ELSE TO DO YOUR DIRTY WORK"

N early three years to the day after Mamdouh Habib was arrested, the Administration finally disclosed what he had supposedly done to justify his capture and continued imprisonment. In early October 2004, lawyers from the Justice Department, which represents the Administration in these cases, filed the unclassified portion of Mamdouh's Combatant Status Review Tribunal in federal court in Washington. The allegations were extremely serious. According to the Administration, Mamdouh had been within al-Qaeda's inner circle. He supposedly had advance knowledge of the 9/11 attacks, had trained the hijackers in the martial arts, and in an earlier stage of the planning had meant to be with them on their suicide mission. The Administration said he had attended al-Qaeda training camps in Afghanistan and had conducted video surveillance of potential terrorist targets. On one occasion, he and other members of al-Qaeda had allegedly unloaded a truck full of chemical weapons at a secret location in Afghanistan.[1]

But the record of his CSRT revealed something else as well. The evidence against Mamdouh consisted entirely of "confessions" he gave after the United States transferred him to Egypt, where he spent six months in prison prior to his incarceration at Camp Delta. Terek Dergoul, a British prisoner released from Camp Delta in 2003, was one of several people who saw Mamdouh when he was at Guantánamo:

> [H]e was telling me stuff about Egypt, he'd been taken to Egypt. . . . He told me he'd been electrocuted, put in water. . . , he'd been stripped,

been punched, kicked and punched . . . He said something about a dog being put on him as he was naked.

I

Legal visits at the Guantánamo base take place in Camp Echo, a separate facility across from the main prison. Echo is a collection of small concrete boxes, each of which serves as both a temporary prison cell and an attorney's visiting quarters. The inside of the box is divided by a concrete and wire wall. On one side of the wall, the prisoner spends his entire day and night, coming out only long enough to sit at a small rectangular table, shackled and with his back to the door, where he meets with his lawyer. Prisoners in these boxes cannot see another living soul and can hear only the continuous drone of electric fans and fluorescent lights. Most prisoners are brought to Echo several days before their lawyer arrives at the base, and remain there until a day or two afterward.

Before my first visit with Mamdouh in November 2004, I had met with his wife, Maha. We talked about the risk that Mamdouh wouldn't trust me. Even the Army Field Manual permits interrogators to lie to prisoners, and Mamdouh, like all the prisoners at the base, had been lied to repeatedly as part of the interrogation process. Though I had worked on Mamdouh's case for years, he didn't know me, and had no reason to believe my visit wasn't some ruse manufactured by the military. Maha had provided me with a letter of introduction that encouraged Mamdouh to trust me, but, not knowing his mental state, we worried he would think the letter had been forged or secured from her under duress. I encouraged Maha to share with me some of the small, personal details from their history that I could tell Mamdouh to convince him I was genuine. There was a risk, of course, that Mamdouh would think that these too had been extracted from Maha against her will, but I asked Maha to search her memory for events that were insignificant to others yet memorable to the two of them, events that would have escaped the attention of even the most patient interrogator. We settled on the location of their first date, the first gift he gave her, and the people who looked after their youngest son when their oldest boy was ill. There is no reason to repeat those private reminiscences here, but suffice it to say, they worked. When I shared that information with Mamdouh, he began to cry.

• • •

In 2001, Mamdouh and Maha owned a small coffee shop in Sydney, Australia. Born in 1955 in the Egyptian port city of Alexandria, Mamdouh left Egypt when he turned eighteen. Like many teenagers, he roamed a bit around Europe, living for a time in Italy, where he learned to speak Italian and developed a fondness for Italian wine and food. Eventually Mamdouh, a small, slightly built man with receding hair and a wry smile, emigrated to Australia, where he made his home and became a citizen. In Sydney, he met and married Maha, and the two of them began a family. In time, Mamdouh became more religious. As his convictions grew, he tired of secular Australia, and began considering a move to Pakistan, where he thought he could find a more rigorous Islamic community. In the summer of 2001, he said goodbye to his family and traveled to Pakistan, where he hoped to find a job for himself and a school for his four children.[2]

In early October 2001, in the anxious aftermath of September 11, Pakistan was not a safe place for foreigners, especially devout Muslims. As in the United States, security forces in Pakistan were arresting hundreds of people on suspicion that they might have had something to do with the 9/11 attacks. Mamdouh telephoned his wife to tell her he was coming home. He boarded a bus in Quetta and headed for Karachi with a ticket in his pocket for his return flight to Sydney. But the police were looking for militants fleeing the approaching conflict in neighboring Afghanistan, and people leaving the country were particularly suspicious. Mamdouh's bus was stopped and searched near the small town of Khuzdar and he was arrested.[3]

He was eventually taken to a facility near Islamabad, where he was tortured and interrogated by Pakistani agents. When I visited him at the base, he described one of the techniques used by his Pakistani interrogators. Mamdouh said that he was suspended from hooks on the wall with his feet resting on the side of a large cylindrical drum. Down the middle of this drum ran a metal rod, with wires attached to both ends. The wires ran to what appeared to be an electric battery. When Mamdouh did not give the answers that his Pakistani questioners wanted, a guard threw a switch and a jolt of electricity ran through the rod, electrifying the drum on which Mamdouh stood. The action of Mamdouh "dancing" on the drum forced it to rotate, which caused his feet to slip, leaving him suspended by only the hooks on the wall. Instinctively, he struggled to regain his balance by placing his feet squarely on the drum, which of course sent another excruciating jolt of electricity into his feet. Eventually, he was forced to raise his legs, leaving him to hang by his outstretched arms until he could stand it no longer and, exhausted, he dropped his legs back onto the electrified drum. This lasted until he finally fainted.[4]

After approximately a week in Islamabad, Pakistani guards handcuffed him, took him from his cell, placed a blindfold over his eyes, and drove him to a nearby airfield. At the field, someone approached him and began to cut away his clothes. Unsure of what was happening to him, Mamdouh, who was still blindfolded and restrained, tried to resist. Several people knocked him to the ground, yelling at him and to each other as they grappled. Mamdouh speaks English and could tell that his attackers were American. During the struggle, his blindfold was knocked askew, which allowed him to see his assailants. They all wore black, short-sleeve T-shirts with grey or khaki pants. A number of them had distinctive tattoos. One had a colorful tattoo of a woman on the inside of his forearm. Another—a large, muscular man—had a cross tattooed on his upper arm. And a third had a tattoo of an American flag on or near his wrist. The flagpole was in the design of a finger, with the flag unfurled to the right of this "finger."[5]

After the men subdued Mamdouh, they brought him to his feet. Someone continued to cut his clothes from his body while someone else took a video. Then they dressed him in a blue tracksuit and transferred him to a plane. From their voices, Mamdouh could tell that the Americans who had attacked him sat at the front of the plane. They took him to Cairo, but not at the request of the Egyptian government. Makhdoom Hayat, who was Pakistan's interior minister at the time, later reported that this was an entirely American operation. "The U.S. wanted him for their own investigations," he said, and he was taken by U.S. agents acting on U.S. orders.[6] On the plane, Mamdouh had duct tape placed over his mouth, a hood placed over his head, and heavy, opaque goggles strapped over his eyes—the same type of goggles he would wear when he first arrived at Camp Delta.[7]

Mamdouh spent six months in an Egyptian cell, most likely at the state security headquarters in Lazoughli Square, in the heart of Cairo. Throughout his imprisonment, he lived in a windowless cell, roughly six by eight feet and illuminated by a bare yellow bulb that hung from the ceiling. He slept on a concrete floor with nothing but a single blanket. Cockroaches and other insects crawled across the floors and walls. Except for his interrogations, he remained in his cell twenty-four hours a day, though occasionally guards would allow him to use the bathroom down the corridor. For weeks on end, he did not see natural light. Three times a day he received a single glass of milk and a scrap of bread.[8]

Interrogators came for him at unpredictable times. Since he could not see outdoors, he could only estimate the time from the heat inside the prison. Sometimes it seemed they came for him in the middle of the night, other times in the heat of the day. Sometimes they would come for him not long after the last session had ended; sometimes they came for him less frequently. The sessions lasted for hours and beatings were routine. Mamdouh, who was almost always handcuffed, was kicked, punched, beaten with a stick, and rammed with what, based on Mamdouh's descriptions, must have been an electric cattle prod. If he lapsed into unconsciousness, they would revive him and continue the beatings. If they discontinued the "interrogations" and he fell asleep on the floor, they would douse him with water or kick him in the ribs and start again. These sessions typically ended only when he admitted whatever they were questioning him about at the time. Mamdouh "confessed" to it all.[9]

Beatings were only part of the abuse. The Egyptian authorities were also adept at psychological torture. Mamdouh told me he was brought to three different rooms. In one, the guards would slowly fill the room with water. Helpless and handcuffed, Mamdouh could only watch as the water rose steadily up his body until, if he stood on the tips of his toes, he could keep the water just below his chin. He was left in this room for hours. In another room, guards filled the water to his knees. But the room had an extremely low ceiling and Mamdouh, still in handcuffs, could only stoop. If he tried to sit in the water or rest on his knees, a guard would force him to his feet. In a third room, the water only came up to his ankles. But in this room, he could see through a window to another room containing a large lever or switch. His interrogators told him the switch was wired to an electric current, and that unless he confessed, they would throw the switch and electrocute him.[10]

The threat of violence was common throughout his Egyptian imprisonment. On several occasions, Mamdouh was threatened with assault by German shepherd dogs. But this was not simply the assault we have seen at Guantánamo and Abu Ghraib prison. In Egypt, they told Mamdouh they could induce the dogs to sexually assault him. He does not know whether his captors had actually trained a dog to act in this fashion, as he never allowed the interrogations to reach that sadistic point. In fact, he believes the interrogations could have been even worse than he was made to endure, judging from the screams he heard from other prisoners throughout his detention. But in Mamdouh's case, he signed a number of papers, some of which were blank, and credits these "confessions" with saving his life by bringing particularly horrific sessions to a close.[11]

The torture Mamdouh endured in Egypt did not end until days before he left the country. Without explanation, but apparently in order to allow time for his bruises to heal, the interrogations and beatings abruptly stopped. He began to receive a far better diet. He started getting meat, sweets, cigarettes, and coffee. He was taken from his cell and moved to a regular room with a bed. He was allowed to sleep as much as he wanted. He was examined by a doctor. His guards told him he was going home. Instead, he was retrieved by the Americans and brought to Bagram Air Base in Afghanistan. Three weeks later, he was transferred to Guantánamo Bay. There, he was seen by several prisoners, including Shafiq Rasul, who would later report that Mamdouh was in "catastrophic shape, mental and physical. . . . [H]e used to bleed from his nose, mouth, and ears when he was asleep." Jamal al Hirith, an English prisoner released in 2003, had similar recollections of the slight, balding, middle-aged Australian. He "seemed to be in pain. He was haggard-looking. I never saw him walk. He always had to be held up."[12]

The U.S. agents who took Mamdouh to Egypt undoubtedly knew what was in store for him. For years, the State Department has criticized Egypt as a practitioner of official, state-sponsored torture. In its 2003 country report on human rights, covering most of the period when Mamdouh was in prison, the State Department found there were "numerous, credible reports that security forces tortured and mistreated detainees" and that "torture and abuse of detainees by police, security personnel, and prison guards remains frequent." Victims reported "being stripped and blindfolded; suspended from a ceiling or doorframe with feet just touching the floor; beaten with fists, whips, metal rods, or other objects; subjected to electric shocks; and doused with cold water. Victims also frequently reported being subjected to threats and forced to sign blank papers for use against them in future proceedings." Some victims reported they were sexually assaulted or threatened with sexual assault. Nor is this report anomalous. Every year for the past decade, the State Department has made the same complaint: Egypt tortures prisoners.[13]

II

Mamdouh was sent to Egypt as part of a controversial practice known as extraordinary rendition. The rendition program has become an integral part of the Administration's detention policy. Since 9/11, prisoners have been rendered to countries renowned for torture, including, among others, Syria, Jordan, Morocco, Egypt, and Uzbekistan.

Like so much of the Administration's detention policy, the origin and scope of the rendition program is shrouded in secrecy. Renditions began in the 1980s during the Reagan Administration. U.S. law enforcement agents, frustrated with what they perceived as the glacial pace of diplomatic efforts to extradite suspected terrorists and members of drug conspiracies, began to snatch suspects overseas and bring them to the United States for trial. The U.S. Supreme Court approved this version of rendition in 1992 and it has been used approximately twenty times.[14]

During this first phase of the program, renditions played an important part in bringing terrorists to justice. In February 1995, for instance, Ramzi Yousef was rendered from Pakistan to New York by U.S. law enforcement agents, where he was tried, convicted, and sentenced to life imprisonment for his role in the first World Trade Center bombing. Three years later, after simultaneous explosions ripped through the U.S. Embassies in Nairobi, Kenya, and Dar es Salaam, Tanzania, FBI agents rendered most of the bombing suspects to New York, where they too were prosecuted and sentenced to life imprisonment.[15]

Because these prisoners were tried in the United States, renditions during this period were also subject to important restraints. Prisoners rendered from a third country and tried in the United States enjoyed all the protections that the U.S. legal system extends to any criminal defendant, including the right to counsel, the presumption of innocence, the right to a public trial by jury, and the right to confront one's accusers. This acted as a bulwark against the risk of a wrongful rendition. In fact, in the very case in which the Supreme Court approved the practice, involving a Mexican doctor abducted from his home in Guadalajara and tried in this country for his alleged role in the murder of a DEA agent, the defendant was acquitted at trial and released.[16] Because prisoners in this early version of the program faced trial in the United States, renditions that took place during this period are often called renditions to justice.

The program changed dramatically under President Bill Clinton, who authorized the CIA to render prisoners to Egypt and Middle Eastern countries that practiced torture, rather than to bring them to the United States to face trial. According to former CIA agent Michael Scheuer, the original purpose of the program was not to have al-Qaeda suspects tortured, though the CIA knew what Egypt did to prisoners. The purpose was to get them "off the street" when a criminal conviction was not feasible. Scheuer stated that in every case the suspect had been convicted *in absentia* by a foreign government—most often Egypt—and that no prisoner was rendered without a prior interagency review by the Justice Department, the National Security Council, the CIA, and the White House.[17]

After 9/11, the Bush Administration quickly developed other ways to get terrorist suspects "off the streets," with Defense Department prisons at Bagram and Guantánamo and CIA "black sites" in unknown locations. The rendition program, however, not only continued, but expanded, and began operating under fewer legal constraints. On September 17, 2001, President Bush signed an order that gave the CIA the unilateral authority to render prisoners without the prior knowledge, participation, or approval of the White House or other executive branch agencies. This order, which remains classified, also gave the CIA the power to render prisoners solely for the purpose of detention and interrogation. In fact, prisoners could be rendered to a third country that had not even sought the person's extradition. In Habib's case, for instance, Pakistan's interior minister reported that Egypt had not asked that he be delivered to that country. In other cases, the request by the foreign country may be a sham; as one government official involved in the process has put it, "sometimes a friendly country can be invited to 'want' someone we grab." [18]

In this way, foreign intelligence services have become a proxy for U.S. interrogators. The Administration attempts to direct the interrogation by providing the receiving country with a list of questions it would like answered. On some occasions, CIA agents are allowed to monitor the interrogations through one-way mirrors. More often, however, the prisoner is left to endure whatever interrogation techniques the foreign agency may devise. Egyptian intelligence officers, for example, do not allow American interrogators to participate in their questioning. [19]

Even when CIA agents are present, they do not have the legal authority to tell foreign agents how to do their job. As CIA Director Porter Goss told the Senate Intelligence Committee, "once [prisoners are] out of our control, there's only so much we can do." [20] And in this regard, it seems the CIA does not want to do very much. As one Arab diplomat put it, "[i]t would be stupid to keep track of them because then you would know what's going on. . . . It's really more like, 'Don't ask, don't tell.' " [21] A U.S. official involved in the practice took a similar view: "If we're not there in the room, who is to say?" [22]

Because the United States has rendered prisoners to countries with a richly deserved reputation for torture, the question put to the president at a press conference in March 2005 naturally arises: "what is it that Uzbekistan can do in interrogating an individual that the United States can't?" The president declined to answer this question. [23] While the number of people rendered after 9/11 is a closely guarded secret, reported estimates put the total at one hundred to two hundred prisoners. In most cases, prisoners are transferred in executive jets, usually a Gulfstream, owned or chartered by CIA front companies. The prisoners transferred are generally considered low-level members of al-Qaeda. [24]

III

As the number of renditions has increased since September 11, the kind and quality of evidence needed to effect a prisoner's disappearance has declined. No cases illustrate this better than those of Maher Arar and Khaled Masri.

On September 26, 2002, Arar, a Syrian-born Canadian citizen, was changing planes at John F. Kennedy International Airport during a trip from Tunisia to Montreal when he was stopped by U.S. immigration officials. He was arrested and kept in solitary confinement for thirteen days and interrogated at length about al-Qaeda. The questions focused on Arar's relationship with two other Canadians: Ahmad el-Maati and Abdullah Al-malki. Arar was confused by the questions because he barely knew the two men. Though Arar didn't know it at the time, both had been arrested and tortured by Syrian authorities. During their interrogations, the two had identified Arar as a compatriot.[25]

At three in the morning on October 8, 2002, guards woke Arar in his cell and read him a decision by Immigration and Naturalization Service Eastern Region Director J. Scott Blackman stating that he was a member of al-Qaeda and would be deported to Syria, apparently because of the statements made by Almalki and el-Maati. Arar was never given an opportunity to challenge this decision in court. Arar was driven to Newark and placed on a private jet. He was flown to Amman, Jordan, and then driven in a van to Syria. For the first twelve days of his imprisonment, his interrogators beat him with their fists and a two-inch-thick electrical cable. He was threatened with more severe forms of torture, and could hear other prisoners' screams. The beatings stopped after the Canadian Embassy made contact with Arar on October 20, but he spent most of the next year in a dark, underground cell that was three feet wide, seven feet high, and six feet long—the size of a grave.[26]

Arar was released from prison and returned to Canada in October 2003. He has never been charged with any wrongdoing. The Syrian ambassador to the United States has stated that his government considers Arar completely innocent. No evidence against him has ever been produced beyond his acquaintance with el-Maati and Almalki, both of whom were also freed from prison and never charged.[27] Arar has since filed a lawsuit against the United States. On January 18, 2005, the Bush Administration moved to dismiss his case on several grounds, among them the claim that going forward would require that the Administration reveal state secrets, and that doing so could "cause exceptionally grave or serious damage" to national security. Trying Arar's case, the Administration claims, risks "the disclosure of information that may have been received from foreign governments pursuant to an understanding of confidentiality."[28]

• • •

On New Year's Eve 2003, Khaled Masri traveled by bus from his home in Ulm, Germany, to Macedonia, after he and his wife got into an argument. There, he was taken off the bus by the border police in Macedonia because he and the associate of a 9/11 hijacker have similar names. The police took him to a motel room with darkened windows and questioned him about al-Qaeda. Masri produced his passport and insisted he was innocent. The police thought the passport could have been a convincing fake and ignored his claim of innocence. They contacted the CIA station in Skopje. Because the station chief was on vacation, the matter fell into the hands of the deputy chief, a junior officer. Because the CIA's European Division chief was also on vacation, the deputy contacted the Counterterrorist Center in Virginia and the head of its al-Qaeda unit, a woman described by the *Washington Post* as "a former Soviet analyst with spiked hair that matched her in-your-face personality." According to one former CIA official, the head of the unit "believed [Masri] was someone else. . . . She didn't really know. She just had a hunch." Without adequately investigating this "hunch," she ordered Masri rendered to Afghanistan. Flight logs of a plane registered to a CIA front company show a flight out of Macedonia on the day Masri says he was taken to Afghanistan.[29]

In March 2004, the CIA determined Masri had been telling the truth and that his passport was genuine. For two more months, the agency and the State Department dithered over what to do with him. The CIA wanted to conduct a "reverse rendition," sending him back to Macedonia, dropping him off in the middle of nowhere, and leaving him, without telling the German government. The State Department favored more complete disclosure, a view backed by former National Security Advisor Condoleezza Rice and eventually endorsed by George Tenet, then-director of the CIA. The CIA and State Department apparently quibbled over whether the disclosure should include an apology. After the debacle of the first rendition, Macedonia refused to let the CIA fly Masri back into the country. In May 2004, more than four months after his initial arrest, the CIA took him to Albania, where he was taken to a narrow country road at dusk and told to start walking without looking back. Soon he was met by three armed men who drove him to an airport, where he was eventually returned to Germany. Meanwhile, his wife and five children, who had no idea where Masri had been, had moved to Lebanon. He has since been reunited with his family, and they have returned to Germany. The same month, the U.S. ambassador to Germany, Daniel Coats, advised the German interior minister, Otto Schily, that the CIA had made a mistake. Coats, however, asked Germany not to reveal anything about the matter.[30]

Although it is no longer allowed, when lawyers first began to arrive at the Guantánamo base in September 2004, the military used to let us check our e-mail at a small library near the commercial center of the base. While I was at the base, I had been sent a news report that the Egyptian government was negotiating for the return of five prisoners who it claimed were Egyptian nationals. One of those five was Mamdouh. I had no way of knowing whether this was an actual request by the Egyptian government, or whether Egypt had been induced to "want" Mamdouh, as had apparently happened in the past. What mattered, however, was that Mamdouh now faced the prospect of being sent back to Egypt, where he had been so brutally tortured before.

I returned from the base November 21 and immediately drafted a request to block Mamdouh's possible rendition, arguing that sending him back to the same country that tortured him would violate the Convention Against Torture, especially in light of the treatment he endured the first time. Because this request included the information I learned from Mamdouh at the base, I had to prepare it at a secure facility set up for us by the court, and treat it as a classified document, which was filed under seal November 24, 2004. The government was then supposed to review the papers and decide whether they could be disclosed to the public. Ordinarily, this review takes about two weeks. Even allowing for the Thanksgiving holiday, however, the review in this case took much longer.

Throughout December, I heard nothing from the Justice Department. So long as the documents were under seal, I could not share them or discuss their content with anyone who did not have a security clearance and a need to know. On the morning of January 4, 2005, I decided the government had taken long enough and contacted a court security officer. I told her that if I had not heard from the government by the close of business, I would ask the district court to unseal the pleadings. At 4:00 P.M., I got a phone call from the court security officer: the documents had been cleared for public filing.

I filed them the following day, January 5, 2005. Then I called Dana Priest, a reporter with the *Washington Post*. Priest has done some of the best reporting in the country on different aspects of the Administration's detention policy, particularly rendition,[31] and I guessed—correctly, it turned out—that she would be interested in what had happened to Mamdouh. I e-mailed her the documents that afternoon.

The next morning, the *Post* ran a front-page story about Mamdouh's rendition.[32] As it happened, the story appeared the same day Attorney General-designate Alberto Gonzales testified at his Senate confirmation hearings. Illinois Democratic Senator Richard Durbin had read the article in the *Post* and questioned Gonzales sharply about Mamdouh's treatment:

> **Q.** And so this morning we read in the paper about rendition, an argument made that we took a prisoner whom we could not, should not torture legally and turned him over to a country that would torture him. That would be illegal . . . would it not?
>
> **A.** Under my understanding of the laws, yes sir, that we have an obligation not to render someone to a country that we believe is going to torture them; that is correct.[33]

Five days later, in the predawn hours of January 11, 2005, my co-counsel Michael Ratner woke me up with a phone call. The Australian media was reporting that Mamdouh would be released from Guantánamo. An hour later, I received a call from the Australian Embassy in Washington. Mamdouh was indeed going home.

IV

Gonzales was certainly right about the law. Article 3 of the Convention Against Torture—the same treaty John Yoo and Jay Bybee discussed in their torture memo of August 1, 2002—could hardly be more explicit: "No State party shall expel, return or extradite a person to another state where there are substantial grounds for believing that he would be in danger of being subjected to torture." The United States interprets this article to prohibit rendition when it is more likely than not the prisoner would be tortured.

Under the treaty, no country can send a prisoner to another country unless it first takes into account *"all relevant considerations* including, where applicable, the existence in the State concerned of a consistent pattern of gross, flagrant or mass violations of human rights."[34] One hundred and thirty-five countries, including the United States and Egypt, have pledged to abide by the Torture Convention.[35]

The Administration claims it has satisfied its obligations under the Torture Convention by securing assurances from the receiving country that the prisoner will not be tortured. These so-called "diplomatic assurances," unenforceable and unverifiable, are apparently quite informal. Typically, the CIA station chief of the country that will receive the prisoner asks for a verbal assurance from the foreign intelligence service that the prisoner will not be tortured, and notifies CIA headquarters in Langley when he gets it. CIA Director Porter Goss told Congress that the agency has an "accountability program" to monitor rendered prisoners, but as we have often seen in the war on terror, the executive is accountable only to itself. There are no publicly available executive orders or regulations that describe how such an assurance should be evaluated or by whom the evaluation is made.[36]

Government officials have repeatedly ridiculed these assurances. By and large, those who remain involved in the practice have expressed their doubts anonymously. One such official with the CIA, for example, bluntly dismissed diplomatic assurances as "a farce." After visiting a number of prisons where suspects had been rendered by the CIA since 9/11, another U.S. official described it as "beyond" farcical: "They say they are not abusing them, and that satisfies the legal requirement, but we all know they do." "It's widely understood," he added, "that interrogation practices that would be illegal in the U.S. are being used." One official who has supervised the capture and transfer of alleged terrorists seemed exasperated by the restraints imposed on him by the law. "If you don't violate someone's human rights some of the time," he said, "you probably aren't doing your job." Another official involved in the process put it rather more bluntly. "We don't kick the [expletive] out of them. We send them to other countries so *they* can kick the [expletive] out of them."[37]

But a number of officials who have left law enforcement have spoken more freely. In 2002, Vincent Cannistraro, former head of the CIA's counterterrorism division, said that "Egyptian jails are full of guys missing toenails and fingernails. It's crude, but highly effective, although we could never con-done it publicly. The Egyptians and Jordanians are not that squeamish." In 2004, when asked about the Arar case, Cannistraro said, "[y]ou would have to be deaf, dumb and blind to believe that the Syrians were not going to use torture, even if they were making claims to the contrary." [38] Michael Scheuer, the former head of the bin Laden unit at the CIA, has defended the use of ex-traordinary rendition. "[T]he idea that we're gonna suddenly throw our hands up like Claude Rains in 'Casablanca' and say, 'I'm shocked that justice in Egypt isn't like justice in Milwaukee,' there's a certain disingenuousness to that." Eschewing this disingenuousness, Scheuer sees extraordinary rendi-tion for what it is: "It's finding someone else to do your dirty work." [39]

V

In mid-January 2005, I got another call from the Australian Embassy. Nego-tiations were under way with the United States to let Australia fly Mamdouh home from Guantánamo to Sydney. They could not tell me when the nego-tiations would be finished, but when the time came, would I be willing to accompany Mamdouh on the flight? So it was that I found myself at the Miami International Airport two weeks later. Embassy officials had in-structed me to meet them in the lobby of an airport hotel shortly before midnight, January 26, 2005. The Australian government had chartered a private jet that would fly me and several Australian officials to the base, where we would retrieve Mamdouh. From there, we would fly to Sydney.

The guards took Mamdouh from his cell on the morning of January 26 and moved him to a small room, where he waited for several hours. No one told him anything and he knew better than to ask. Eventually, a guard brought him a change of clothes—blue jeans, tennis shoes, and a white T-shirt. It was the first time in nearly three years he had worn anything other than the ill-fitting orange jumpsuit made famous in pictures of Camp Delta prisoners. As evening approached, the guards moved him again, this time to the rear of a small, enclosed truck. They shackled his hands together and chained his feet to the truck's floor. Still, no one told him anything. Fi-nally, a guard opened the rear door of the truck. He was holding some pa-pers. He glanced down at them, then back at Mamdouh. "You Habib?" he asked, though he surely knew.

"Yes," Mamdouh told him, "I am Habib."

"You're leaving. Goin' to Egypt."

Mamdouh's heart stopped. Egypt. But he would not give the guard the satisfaction of seeing him react. "I am Australian. My home is Australia."

"Sorry." The guard waved the papers, as though they contained the answer. "Says here you're going to Egypt. Transport should be here directly." And with that, he closed the door and left Mamdouh alone. Some time later several guards climbed into the rear of the truck, which began to move. Mamdouh, of course, had no idea where they were, or where they were going. After all, this could just be an elaborate ruse, another "psychological technique." Perhaps it would end at any minute. Someone would tell him it was a mistake, they had meant to take another prisoner. In an hour, he could be back in his cell, dressed in the familiar orange jumpsuit. Or he could be on a plane to Egypt.

After a few minutes, the truck stopped. All the guards but one jumped out. As the last guard climbed past him, he whispered to Mamdouh, "Don't worry, Habib. It's OK. You're going to Australia." Mamdouh nodded, but knew better than to react or respond. If the guard were lying, he was no better than the guard who told him he was going to Egypt. And if he were telling the truth, Mamdouh knew he would get in trouble if the other guards discovered his kindness. He still did not know what was going to happen.

By this time, our plane had arrived at the base. It was after 1:00 A.M. Though I had been to the base several times and had a security clearance, the United States would not let me off the plane to greet Mamdouh or accompany him to the plane. Fortunately, the Australian officials had anticipated that Mamdouh might be disoriented or confused when he got to the plane. They asked if I would wait at the open cabin door so Mamdouh could see me as he approached the plane.

I stood in the doorway as Mamdouh climbed down from the rear of the truck with his hands cuffed. His eyes were not adjusted to the darkness and for a time he seemed uncertain of his surroundings. One of the guards turned him toward the plane and helped him walk toward the metal steps. Another guard videotaped the whole scene, the light from her camera shining like a spotlight in the darkness. As Mamdouh got closer to the plane, he saw me and smiled faintly. Later he told me that was the first time he allowed himself to believe he was actually going home. He waited while the guards removed his cuffs for the last time. He started to climb the half dozen steps to the plane, and as he came within earshot I called to him, shouting to be heard over the low rumble of the engines: "Mamdouh, we're going to Sydney. Wanna come?"

For nearly three years, U.S. officials had promised the Australian government they would charge Mamdouh and prosecute him before a military commission. Just weeks before he was released, the Administration had accused him of having a prominent role in the 9/11 hijackings. Yet in the early morning hours of January 27, 2005, he flew home to his wife and family.[40] When asked to explain the sudden change of heart, American officials refused to comment on the record. But they told the Australians they had decided to release him "because the C.I.A. did not want the evidence about Mr. Habib being taken to Egypt, and his allegations of torture, raised in court."[41]

VI

Several things about the rendition program should be noted. First, the CIA has substantially more power under the present iteration than it did in the past. When renditions were used to bring prisoners back to this country, the risk of error was mitigated by the legal protections extended to suspects in a criminal trial. When the CIA began to render prisoners to third countries, each transfer was subject to interagency review. After 9/11, however, the CIA began to operate the rendition program entirely on its own prerogative, with no external check, often with disastrous results, as the Masri rendition makes plain. Second, the CIA has exercised its newly expanded power over substantially more people. In the first fifteen years of the program, the CIA rendered about seventy prisoners; in the last four years, the CIA has rendered about two hundred. While exact figures are hard to come by because the CIA refuses to disclose this information, no one doubts that the numbers have increased dramatically. Finally, and perhaps most importantly, rendition now serves a radically different purpose. Originally, rendition brought prisoners *into* the legal process. Today, however, it keeps them *outside* the legal process. It allows the CIA and compliant third countries to hold prisoners indefinitely, solely for the purpose of interrogation and detention. And all the while, prisoners are held in countries with a well-earned reputation for torture.

The *Washington Post* reported that the CIA inspector general would be investigating a "growing number" of "erroneous" renditions such as those of Khaled Masri and Mamdouh Habib. One official put the number of cases to be examined at about three dozen, although others claim it is fewer. The list apparently includes several people who were identified by alleged members of al-Qaeda while they were being subjected to the CIA's "enhanced interrogation" practices, and includes one person who turned out to be an innocent college professor who had given the accused al-Qaeda member a bad grade.[42]

Despite everything that happened to him, there is a sense in which Mamdouh Habib was lucky. He could remember crucial details that allowed me to describe the people involved in his rendition in some detail. Armed with this information, it would have been a relatively simple matter for the federal court to order the government to identify these people—after all, how many U.S. employees who were operating in Pakistan and participating in extraordinary renditions in October 2001 have the U.S. flag tattooed on their wrist? Once these people had been identified, the judge could direct them to explain themselves, under oath, in open court. Compounding his good fortune, the details surrounding Mamdouh's rendition were published on the front page of the *Washington Post* the same day Alberto Gonzales testified before the Senate, which provided an occasion for Senator Durbin to quiz Gonzales about the practice of extraordinary rendition in general, and about Mamdouh's case in particular. This turned a national spotlight on the issue, and on a single prisoner at the base, which made it even more likely that a court would start asking questions. Mamdouh Habib is home with his wife and family because the Bush Administration did not want to answer these questions.

But what of the people for whom the stars do not align so fortunately? What, for instance, of Binyam Mohamed? Born in Ethiopia, Mohamed moved to London at age fifteen, when his father sought asylum. He grew up in Notting Hill and traveled to Afghanistan in June 2001 to see for himself whether it was "a good Islamic country or not." He returned to Pakistan after 9/11 and was arrested at the airport in Karachi as he tried to board a plane for Zurich, on his way home to London. He was held in Pakistani custody until late July 2002, when the U.S. rendered him to Morocco. (Flight logs of a Gulfstream jet used by the CIA confirm a flight in and out of Morocco July 22.) In Morocco, interrogators repeatedly used a scalpel to cut inch-long incisions in his penis. "I was in agony," Mohamed said. "There was blood all over."[43] Mohamed has been at Guantánamo since September 2004.

Mamdouh Habib's flight to Sydney went without incident. He was not restrained and the four Australian security officers who flew with us seemed bored. They, like Mamdouh, slept much of the way. Officials from Australia's Foreign Affairs and Attorney-General's departments joined us on the flight. One of the pilots told me he typically flew corporate executives, but that sometimes the plane was chartered by government officials. The Gulfstream was emblazoned with an American flag.

Part Four

☆

THE FUTURE OF
CAMP DELTA

TEN

WHAT IF HE'S A SHEPHERD?

———————

I

Getting to Guantánamo is no small struggle. Two commercial airlines charter twin-engine prop planes that make the three-hour flight from Fort Lauderdale four days a week. They fly the long way around to the southeast corner of the island, being careful not to cross into Cuban airspace. Lined with two rows of tattered seats, and with barely room to stand, the planes have a maximum capacity of nineteen passengers. Typically, the planes carry military personnel and their families back and forth from the base, though on my first trip to the island most of the passengers were members of a rugby team from Oklahoma, flying in for a few exhibition matches against the base's squad. No one flies into Guantánamo without permission from the U.S. military. And even those allowed aren't afforded many luxuries—it's a good idea to use the bathroom before boarding because there are no facilities on the plane.

Habeas attorneys began traveling to the base in September 2004. The first was Gita Gutierrez, a young lawyer then with Judge John Gibbons's firm in New Jersey, who represented British residents Moazzam Begg and Feroz Abbasi. Both have since been released and Gita is now a staff attorney with the Center for Constitutional Rights in New York. When lawyers started to arrive, the Pentagon began to complain. Counsel disrupted the sense of isolation and despair—the interrogators would say "dependency and trust"—that the interrogators had created.[1] Lawyers represented "a visible link to the outside"—a link that, in a KUBARK-inspired world, the interrogators were working feverishly to sever.[2] It was feared that the presence of counsel made the prisoners feel "less cut-off" and nurtured a desperate hope in the detainees that their interrogators *did not* "control [their] ultimate destiny."[3]

Given this, I was not at all surprised when reports began to trickle back from the base that interrogators were trying to drive a wedge between prisoners and their lawyers. Interrogators began to tell prisoners that their lawyers' advice was wrong, or that their attorneys could not be trusted. Lawyers, they said, only delay the process; the prisoners who go home are the ones without lawyers. On other occasions, interrogators misrepresented themselves as lawyers, just as they earlier had misrepresented themselves as FBI agents. One prisoner, who was a juvenile when he came to the base, told his attorney that a female interrogator said she was his lawyer and bragged about her experience litigating in the U.S. Supreme Court. Other prisoners have said they were later questioned about their conversations with counsel.[4]

But some of the most disturbing allegations in this vein came from several Kuwaiti prisoners represented by Shearman & Sterling. In February 2005, Tom Wilner met with Fayez al Kandari, one of the twelve Kuwaitis represented by his firm. Al Kandari said he had been warned by his interrogator—a woman who identified herself as Megan—that if he were returned to Kuwait he would be tortured. Al Kandari said his lawyer had assured him otherwise. The interrogator scoffed and said, "don't trust your lawyers. Did you know your lawyers are Jews?" She told al Kandari that Shearman & Sterling represented the government of Israel. The next month, Tom met with Fouad Mahmoud al Rabiah, another client, who asked Tom his religion. When Tom answered that he was Jewish, al Rabiah said his interrogator—this time a man—had told him, "Your lawyers are Jews. How could you trust Jews? Throughout history, Jews have betrayed Muslims. Don't you think your lawyers . . . will betray you?" On another occasion, al Rabiah's interrogator asked him, "What will other Arabs and Muslims think of you Kuwaitis when they know the only help you can get is from Jews?"[5] The Pentagon denies these allegations and insists its interrogators have not interfered with attorneys.

Interference of this sort is not confined to counsel. Brent Mickum is an attorney with the Washington, D.C., law firm of Keller & Heckman. He represents Jamil El-Banna and Bisher al Rawi, two businessmen who had been granted refugee status and were living in London. They were arrested in August 2002 on a business trip to the African country of Gambia. When Brent visited the prison, Jamil, a father of five, complained that his wife and children had not written. He was confused and felt they had abandoned him. Brent made inquiries and discovered the military had been withholding Jamil's mail. Soon, after Brent's intercession, sixteen letters from Jamil's family were delivered at once to his small, windowless cell. Someone had taken the time to censor the letters, painstakingly redacting the language where Jamil's children told him they loved and missed him.[6] A former military interrogator not involved in this case told Brent that both the refusal to deliver the mail and the redactions were a calculated part of the interrogation plan developed for Jamil. The Pentagon said it was a misunderstanding. Oddly, the same misunderstanding happened with David Hicks's mail. Portions of the letters Hicks received from his father were similarly excised.

As lawyers began heading to the base, all the judges but one in the federal court in Washington, D.C., agreed to consolidate their cases before a single judge, Senior District Court Judge Joyce Hens Green, who was coaxed out of retirement by her colleagues on the D.C. bench to preside over the government's renewed motion to dismiss the cases. (Judge Richard Leon initially transferred his cases to Judge Green but later pulled them back.) As we saw in Chapter 8, the government responded to *Rasul* with two arguments: the prisoners still had no right to any legal process, but even if they did, the CSRT gave them all the process they deserved. Judge Green heard arguments on December 1, 2004.

Brian Boyle, from the office of the Attorney General, represented the government. Judge Green questioned Boyle about the government's definition of "enemy combatant." In *Hamdi* and *Rasul*, the Administration had limited the category to people who were "part of or supporting forces hostile to the United States or coalition partners in Afghanistan *and* who engaged in an armed conflict against the United States there." In the CSRT, however, the Administration broadened the definition to include any person "who was part of or supporting Taliban or al Qaeda forces." What it meant to "support" the Taliban or al-Qaeda was not made clear, and Judge Green posed a series of hypothetical questions to identify the limits of the Administration's position.

What about, she asked, "a little old lady in Switzerland who writes checks to what she thinks is a charity that helps orphans but really is a front to finance al-Qaeda activities. Would she be considered an enemy combatant?" She could be, Boyle answered, noting that the military would not be "disabled" from detaining her even if she did not intend that the money go to terrorism. A "resident of London who collects money from worshippers at mosques to support a hospital in Syria, but entrusts the money for that purpose to someone who is an al-Qaeda member?" She, too, could be legally categorized as an enemy combatant under the Administration's definition. Or "a resident of Dublin . . . who teaches English to the son of a person who the CIA knows to be a member of al-Qaeda?" Yes, Boyle said, because unbeknownst to the teacher, the al-Qaeda agent might be learning English as part of his plot to launch an attack.[7]

Judge Green pressed further. Suppose a hypothetical "Mr. Smith" has a cousin, she said. "Let's assume that his cousin has spoken favorably about a leader of al-Qaeda, and [Mr. Smith] has reason to believe that his cousin is in fact a member of al-Qaeda. If Mr. Smith does not pick up the telephone and report to the police that he believes his cousin is a member of al-Qaeda and his cousin's whereabouts, could Mr. Smith be considered" an enemy combatant? While Boyle found it "inconceivable" that the military would detain such a person, he said they did not lack the power to do so. Green continued. "A *Wall Street Journal* reporter, working in Afghanistan, who knows the exact location of Osama bin Laden but does not reveal it to the United States government in order to protect her source?" Boyle labeled this a "tougher case" but said he could not rule it out.[8] It became apparent that, in the Administration's view, the power to designate a person an enemy combatant is, as a practical matter, unlimited, bound only by the president's unenforceable promise to exercise it wisely.

A handful of lawyers spoke for the prisoners. Brent Mickum, the lawyer for El-Banna and al Rawi, argued last. Though his remarks were the briefest by far, he said what all of us should have. Courtroom arguments typically turn on the stuff of lawyering. Distinctions are made and language is parsed. Arguments are carefully crafted but quickly forgotten. Lawyers can easily lose themselves in these arcane ruminations and forget the people on whose behalf they claim to labor. The risk is particularly acute when the clients cannot be in the courtroom, unable to remind lawyers by their presence that an ancient but ambiguous concept like "due process" can mean the difference between prison and freedom. But law is not an abstraction, and the challenge for any lawyer is to ensure that it does not become lifeless.

Brent understood this, and tried to communicate it to Judge Green. Because El-Banna and al Rawi had been arrested during a business trip to Gambia, the legal question in their case was whether the definition of an enemy combatant reaches people arrested thousands of miles from any battlefield, with no connection to hostilities. Brent, quite properly, made it clear that the legal question does not arise in a vacuum:

> Your Honor, it's easy to forget that we're talking about human beings here, who've been in prison for three years in horrendous conditions. They've been beaten, they've been abused, they've been degraded, short-shackled, subjected to temperature extremes of hot and cold, sometimes with screaming loudspeakers, and facing strobe lights for as long as 14 hours. . . . The government [said] the prisoners were the worst of the worst. We now know . . . that the worst of the worst were cooks, farmers, businessmen, civilians, husbands and fathers. Petitioner El-Banna is the father of five children, the youngest of whom is eight years old.[9]

I was one of the lawyers who argued before Judge Green. After the argument, Boyle crossed the courtroom and congratulated me. It was a gracious gesture and we chatted privately for a few minutes. Perhaps it was my imagination, but he seemed visibly uncomfortable with the legal positions his job had forced him to take. He has since left the government and entered private practice.

On January 31, 2005, Judge Green announced her decision. To begin with, she rejected the Administration's contention that *Rasul* established only a procedural right—the right to file a petition only to see it dismissed the next day. Speaking with the sense of sardonic restraint that characterizes much judicial writing, Judge Green found it "difficult to imagine" the Supreme Court would bother to point out that the prisoners' allegations "unquestionably describe custody in violation of the Constitution, laws or treaties of the United States" unless they also believed a court could do something about it. "Indeed," she wrote, had the Court meant for the cases to be dismissed "it is reasonable to assume that the majority would have included in its opinion at least a brief statement to that effect." [10] Because the Supreme Court did not intend its decision to be meaningless rhetoric, the government's reading of *Rasul* was nonsensical. The prisoners, Judge Green held, had a right under the Due Process Clause of the Fifth Amendment ("No person shall be . . . deprived of life, liberty, or property without due process of law") to challenge their detention.

Judge Green also held that the CSRT had not provided the process demanded by the Constitution. Any tribunal that relied on secret information suffered from "an inherent lack of fairness." It is simply unfair to demand that a prisoner fight what he could not see. To be sure, the government may want to withhold classified information from some prisoners. But if it does, it must at least share the information with an attorney who can advocate on the prisoner's behalf. Yet the CSRT forced prisoners to challenge secret information without a lawyer. At the same time, Judge Green said, the CSRT allowed the government to rely on information secured by torture with no inquiry into its reliability. Judge Green pointed specifically to the allegations of torture made by my client, Mamdouh Habib—allegations the government has never denied. Any process that allowed the government to imprison a man for the rest of his life based on a confession literally wrung from him against his will, cannot be sanctified as lawful. And finally, Judge Green said the government's definition of "enemy combatant" was much too broad, as demonstrated so convincingly by the hypothetical questions she posed to Boyle during the oral argument, and confirmed in practice by the detention of Brent's clients, who were picked up in Africa. [11]

"Of course," Judge Green acknowledged, "it would be far easier for the government to prosecute the war on terror" without having to comply with the law. "That, however, is not the relevant legal test." It is emphatically not the judiciary's duty to make life "easier" for the commander in chief. Instead, in a divided government, it is the judiciary's duty to ask whether his actions are lawful. "Although this nation unquestionably must take strong action . . . that necessity cannot negate the existence of the most basic fundamental rights for which the people of this country have fought and died for well over two hundred years." [12]

·   ·   ·

Judge Green handed down her decision nearly three years after we began the litigation in *Rasul* and seven months after the Supreme Court decision. Her ruling held out the hope that, finally, the Administration would be put to its proof, and the promise of *Rasul* would at last be fulfilled. But those hopes were dashed when Judge Leon, the one judge who did not transfer his cases to Judge Green, announced in a separate decision that the Administration was correct after all: the prisoners had no constitutional rights that could be vindicated in court. Notwithstanding the decision in *Rasul,* the cases before him should be dismissed. To resolve the conflict between Leon and Green, the cases had to go back to the Court of Appeals a second time. It meant, at least, another year of litigation.

II

As the cases progressed, a familiar dance was taking place in the public theater. Senior Administration officials continued to insist the prisoners were all dangerous terrorists, while former and current officials at the base continued to tell them otherwise. In April 2004, a former CIA asset who spent a year at Guantánamo reported that "only like 10 percent of the people [there] are really dangerous, that should be there and the rest are people that don't have anything to do with it . . . don't even understand what they're doing here."[13] In June, Lieutenant Colonel Anthony Christino, a twenty-year veteran Pentagon intelligence officer, retired after spending more than a year reviewing the information gathered from Guantánamo. During its first ten months of operation, Christino said, interrogations at Camp Delta produced "information of only minimal to moderate intelligence value."[14] While the *number* of interrogations increased dramatically after Major General Geoffrey Miller arrived in November 2002 (Shafiq Rasul and Asif Iqbal, for instance, estimate they were interrogated only five times during all of 2002, but more than two hundred times from January 2003 until their release in early 2004), Christino "saw nothing that indicated a dramatic improvement in the quality of intelligence" coming from the base.[15] According to Christino, the Administration's claims about the men at the base and the quality of the intelligence they have provided are "wildly exaggerated."[16]

In August 2004, a former interrogator put the matter bluntly: "[t]here are a large number of people at Guantanamo who shouldn't be there," he said, because they have "no meaningful connection to al Qaida or the Taliban." [17] Two months later, Brigadier General Martin Lucenti, the deputy commander at the base, told the *Financial Times,* "most of these guys weren't fighting, they were running." Lucenti later said he was misquoted, though the *Financial Times* stood by its reporting. In any event, Lucenti has not retracted the statement he made days later to the German magazine *Der Spiegel,* where he described most of the prisoners as "little fish." [18] Brigadier General Jay Hood, Camp Delta's commander, now concedes that initial expectations about intelligence from the base "may have been too high" and says that many of the prisoners should never have been brought to the facility: "Sometimes, we just didn't get the right folks." [19] In 2003, he said, officials at Guantánamo had recommended that more than one hundred of the prisoners be immediately released. In January 2005, they were still in prison. By that time, officials at the base estimated that 40 percent of the prison's population—then numbering 549—posed no threat and had no significant intelligence value, and that the majority of the prisoners in Cuba were no longer being interrogated. [20]

In April 2005, the Pentagon quietly released Abdul Rahim Muslim Dost and Badr Zaman Badr, two Afghan brothers who had been at Guantánamo since May 2002. Throughout the 1990s, the two brothers had written scores of satirical lampoons criticizing Afghan mullahs who enriched themselves while their country sank into poverty. One of the mullahs was not amused, and when the U.S. invasion began, his allies took the opportunity to denounce the brothers as supporters of al-Qaeda and the Taliban. Their accusers seized on another satire Dost had written in 1998 that poked fun at President Clinton. After the Clinton Administration offered a five-million-dollar reward for the capture of Osama bin Laden, Dost wrote an article offering five million Afghanis—roughly $110—for the capture of Bill Clinton. He would be easy to identify, Dost said, should any Afghani happen upon him: "clean-shaven . . . light-colored eyes . . . [recently seen] with Monica Lewinsky." This article, their accusers said, was actually a threat against the president. (In an ironic twist, some of their accusers have themselves been accused, this time by Pakistani intelligence agents, who say they falsely named their enemies as terrorists. One is now a prisoner at Guantánamo.) [21]

At Camp Delta, the two university-educated brothers were questioned hundreds of times. Badr, who has a master's degree in English literature and a fondness for Jonathan Swift's *Gulliver's Travels* and Geoffrey Chaucer's *Canterbury Tales,* estimates he was interrogated 150 times by twenty-five different lead interrogators. Over and over again, interrogators from the CIA, the FBI, and the Defense Department asked them about the Clinton satire. Dost, a poet, wrote twenty-five thousand lines of verse during his incarceration. Along with thousands of poems, he translated the Koran into Pashto, his native language, and completed a reference book with an alphabetical list of rhymes. Before the International Red Cross provided him with paper and a pen, he scratched his verses into a Styrofoam cup with his fingernail. When Dost was released, the military kept all but a small fraction of his poetry.[22]

Dost was the 234th prisoner freed from Guantánamo. Officially, the Pentagon maintains that every single one of the released prisoners had been correctly designated as an "enemy combatant." In fact, the military maintains that every prisoner was a threat to the United States up until the moment he was set free. Yet in May 2005, Erik Saar, the former Army linguist who participated in interrogations at the base, estimated that "[a]t best, I would say there were a few dozen" out of the five hundred at Guantánamo who had any connection with terrorism.[23] Of the remainder, he said, "[s]ome of them were conscripts who actually were forced to fight for the Taliban, so actually had taken up arms against us, but had little or no choice in the matter." Others "were individuals who were picked up by the Northern Alliance, and we have no idea why they were there, and we didn't know exactly what their connections were to terrorism."[24] In July 2005, the current head of interrogations at Guantánamo said that 75 percent of the prisoners are no longer being questioned.[25] Unfortunately, however, the same mind-set that brought them to Cuba has made it almost impossible to release them. "Nobody wants to be the one who signs the release papers," Commander Hood said. "There's no muscle in the system."[26]

And so the prisoners are left to languish. A series of hunger strikes hit the camp in 2005. Omar Deghayes, a British resident and a prisoner at the base since 2002, told his lawyer, Clive Stafford Smith, that a strike began June 21, 2005, when prisoners refused one meal a day for a week. On June 28, they began to refuse two meals. Starting July 2, they refused all food. Because the military controls the flow of information at the base and refuses to allow outside monitors, it is impossible to know how many prisoners participated in the June/July strike. The Pentagon reports that fifty-two prisoners refused at least nine consecutive meals, which is the military's definition of a hunger strike. But lawyers who have been to the base estimate that approximately two hundred prisoners—40 percent of the prison population—refused to eat through most of July 2005.

To end the strike, the military negotiated for several days in late July with a group of prisoners who had been chosen to speak on behalf of the other inmates. The strike ended July 28, after the military promised the inmate representatives that conditions at the base would improve within ten days. But the strike began again in mid-August after the military failed to make good on the promised improvements.[27] The strike continued into 2006. Once again, it is impossible to know how many prisoners refused to eat. The Pentagon reported a high of 131—more than a quarter of the prison population—and that thirty-two were being force-fed by a tube passed through the nose and into the stomach. The military also says it never promised to change the conditions at the base, and that the prisoners' determination to starve themselves is evidence of their affiliation with al-Qaeda.[28]

In April 2004, the prison opened Camp Five, a permanent facility removed from the rest of Camp Delta. According to the Defense Department, Camp Five is reserved for "high-value intelligence assets," though it appears that prisoners deemed "uncooperative" are also held there. Camp Five is modeled after a "super-max" prison in Indiana. Prisoners "are held in concrete isolation cells with 24-hour lighting and large, loud fans designed to prevent detainees talking with each other." When Camp Five first opened, prisoners were confined to their cells up to twenty-four hours a day, "only being allowed out to exercise once a week or every two weeks." Often, they were allowed from their cells "in the middle of the night, so that detainees go for months without seeing the sun."[29] A camera in each cell monitors every inmate, all the time.[30] Camp Five has a maximum capacity of one hundred. At least three prisoners who were juveniles at the time of their capture, including one who was fourteen, have been housed in Camp Five at various times during their imprisonment.[31]

The conditions at Camp Five have exacted an especially heavy toll. On

October 15, 2005, Joshua Colangelo-Bryan, an attorney with the law firm of Dorsey & Whitney, was visiting with Jumah al Dossari, a Bahraini citizen and one of six prisoners represented by Dorsey. Josh was part of the group of lawyers that joined the litigation in the summer of 2004, after the Supreme Court decision in *Rasul*. At the time of the visit, al Dossari had been in Camp Five since May 2004. For five months before that, he was housed in a special isolation block at the base. Al Dossari wants to learn English, and Josh had sent him a number of English/Arabic children's books, including *Jack and the Beanstalk, Cinderella,* and *Beauty and the Beast.* The titles were returned with the notation, "these items were not cleared for delivery to the detainee."

During the legal visit, al Dossari had to use the bathroom, which required that he be taken by the military police to another cell. Several minutes later, when al Dossari did not return, Josh "knocked on the cell door, calling out his client's name. When he did not hear a response, Colangelo-Bryan stepped inside and saw a three-foot pool of blood on the floor. Numb, the lawyer looked up to see Dossari hanging unconscious from a noose tied to the ceiling, his eyes rolled back, his tongue and lips bulging, blood pouring from a gash in his right arm."[32]

> I immediately yelled for M.P.s, who arrived quickly. I called Jumah's name several times, but he did not respond, and as best I could tell, appeared to be unconscious. The M.P.s arrived, cut him down from the noose that was holding him and put him on the floor. Still didn't seem that he was conscious . . . Within a moment or so, I was . . . ordered to leave the room . . . , and as I did I saw Jumah seeming to gasp, which at least struck me as a good sign.[33]

One thing has emerged clearly enough since the litigation in *Rasul* first began. Public scrutiny, and especially the threat of judicial review, is the mechanism that puts "muscle in the system." Josh had to leave the base after Jumah's suicide attempt, but promptly tried to schedule a return visit. Through the last two weeks of October, however, he was unable to get a response from the base. On November 1, 2005, the *Washington Post* ran a front-page story about the attempted suicide. On the same day, Josh filed papers with the court protesting the conditions of Jumah's confinement and asking that he be moved out of isolation. Later that day, the Pentagon approved Josh's return visit, which took place November 11 and 12. On November 14, Jumah tried to kill himself again, this time by attempting to reopen the gash he had made a month earlier.

The court scheduled oral argument on Josh's request for December 16, 2005. On December 15, Josh received a letter from the government informing him that Jumah had been moved out of Camp Five. He was put in Camp One, a less oppressive environment. The Pentagon offered no explanation for why he could be moved in December 2005, but not sooner. The Pentagon also reports that it now "dims" the lights in Camp Five between 10:00 P.M. and 5:00 A.M., and that a prisoner can "request" that lights be dimmed on other occasions. Camp officials also say they have begun giving prisoners additional recreation time, and that, "with a raised voice," prisoners can communicate the length of the cellblock, which, they say, is not discouraged.[34] Meanwhile, the prison opened a new psychiatric unit containing sixteen inpatient cells and completed at a cost of $2.65 million.[35]

I have been to death row in Texas, South Carolina, Missouri, Mississippi, Arkansas, and Indiana (the last being the site of the federal death row). I have been to more maximum-security prisons than I can recall. I have delivered the saddest news to men and women behind bars—parents have passed, children have been diagnosed, appeals have been denied. I have broken the news that a client's last chance for a reprieve has been turned down and his execution has been scheduled for a date in the near future. I have visited with clients late at night, in holding cells near execution chambers. Some paced nervously, others sat with a quiet dignity and peace. I have, only once, watched as a client of many years—a sixty-two-year-old great-grandmother—was put to death. But I have never been to a more disturbing place than the military prison at Guantánamo Bay. It is a place of indescribable sadness, where the abstract enormity of "forever" becomes concrete: *this* windowless cell; *that* metal cot; *those* steel shackles.

III

In June 2005, four months after Judge Green and Judge Leon issued their conflicting decisions, the Pentagon released the results of its internal investigation into the FBI's allegations of abusive interrogations at Guantánamo. The Pentagon did not commission the investigation until after the allegations became public.[36]

Almost without exception, the Pentagon, under the direction of Lieutenant General Randall Schmidt, confirmed the FBI's allegations.* "Environmental manipulation"—the Pentagon euphemism for leaving prisoners in extremely hot or cold rooms, sometimes with strobe lights or blaringly loud music, and sometimes short shackled—was widespread. On some occasions, prisoners were left alone in the interrogation booths "for an indefinite period."[37] Other times, they were placed in a room called "the freezer." The report confirmed that prisoners were routinely put on the "frequent flier program," moved from cell to cell throughout the night "to disrupt the sleep patterns and lower the ability to resist interrogation." And on "several occasions" in 2003, "various DoD interrogators" impersonated FBI agents and State Department employees.[38] (In the Schmidt Report, no prisoner is ever identified by name, nor is any FBI agent or Defense Department official.)

The Schmidt Report also confirmed the sexual humiliation reported by the FBI. On one occasion, a female interrogator "approached a detainee from behind, rubbed against his back, leaned over [him and] touch[ed] him on his knee and shoulder and whispered in his ear that his situation was futile." She also "ran her fingers through his hair." On another occasion, an interrogator removed her blouse during an interrogation, "approached the detainee from behind, touched him on his knee and shoulder, leaned over him, and placed her face near the side of his." The goal was "to create stress and break his concentration." On "at least one occasion," an interrogation chief directed a female interrogator to rub perfume on a prisoner's arm. (Though the Schmidt Report omits this fact, this took place during Ramadan, when the contact would have been particularly offensive.) Another

---

* An FBI agent had reported seeing a prisoner shackled to the floor of an interrogation room draped in an Israeli flag, with loud music blaring and strobe lights flashing. General Schmidt apparently did not investigate this particular allegation, though he confirmed that a number of techniques could have been construed by the prisoner as "religious humiliation" (Schmidt Report, at 21). He found no evidence that military personnel interfered with FBI interrogators, or that prisoners were denied food and water (*id.*, at 12–13).

time, a female interrogator wiped fake menstrual blood on a prisoner. "The detainee [then] threw himself on the floor and started banging his head."[39]

In some cases, the Schmidt Report was able to shed new light on old allegations. While an FBI agent had reported that a prisoner's head had been wrapped in duct tape, General Schmidt confirmed that this had been ordered by an interrogation chief, who directed an MP to wrap the prisoner "twice around the head and mouth and three times under the chin and around the top of [his] head." The chief then summoned two FBI agents and, laughing, told them "they needed to see something." Much later, after the incident became public, the chief told Schmidt's investigators the prisoner had been "screaming resistance messages" and that he feared "a riot." At the time, however, he told FBI agents the prisoner had been "chanting" passages from the Koran. The chief received a "verbal admonishment" for his actions but no formal discipline.[40]

The Schmidt Report described one unnamed prisoner's interrogation in some detail. Throughout the summer and fall of 2003, like many other prisoners, he was subjected to what had become the standard interrogation practice: on "repeated occasions" from July to October, he was placed in "the freezer." On "at least" two occasions in July he was placed in a sweltering interrogation booth with no ventilation and the air-conditioning off. (Recall that the Pentagon says the average summer temperature at Guantánamo is 90° to 100°F, "with a heat index of over 100°F."[41]) A number of times, female interrogators "used their status as females to distract" the prisoner, though Schmidt does not describe what they did. In August 2003, the prisoner was involved in "an altercation" with the MPs and was treated for "rib contusions," "an edema of the lower lip," and a "laceration" on his head.[42]

During this time, interrogators devised a particularly elaborate deception for this prisoner. On July 17, 2003, he was brought to a small booth and confronted by a masked interrogator. The interrogator told the prisoner he had had a dream. In his dream, four prisoners were chained together at the feet. They were digging a grave, six feet long, six feet deep, and four feet wide. After they finished, they put down their shovels and stooped to raise a plain, pine casket. The casket had been marked in orange paint with the prisoner's identification number. They slowly lowered the prisoner's casket into the ground. In case the import of this "dream" was not apparent to the prisoner, the masked interrogator then took the time to interpret its meaning: the prisoner was never going to leave Guantánamo unless he started to talk; he would grow old and die in prison, and be buried on "Christian . . . sovereign American soil."[43]

Three days later, the prisoner was brought back to the booth, where the same masked interrogator told him his family had been taken into custody. Then he was left to wonder about his family's fate for two weeks until finally, in early August 2003, he was brought back to the interrogation booth. This time, he was confronted by a senior interrogator dressed in the uniform of a captain in the U.S. Navy, who told the prisoner he worked in the White House. He said he had come from Washington, D.C., to speak with the prisoner, and to deliver an official letter. The letter confirmed that the prisoner's mother had been arrested, and that unless he "cooperated," his mother would be interrogated by "U.S. authorities in conjunction with authorities from [the prisoner's] country of origin."[44] The letter itself has never been disclosed and we do not know whether the military used White House letterhead when it communicated this threat. We also do not know the interrogation techniques that were threatened against the prisoner's mother, but the captain made it clear that she and his family were "in danger," and that if she were uncooperative, the interrogators—once they were finished with her—would bring her to Guantánamo.[45]

Finally, the captain said the interrogators had asked him to deliver a "message." They were getting fed up, he said, and were "considering washing their hands of him. Once they do so, he will disappear and never be heard from again." The captain then encouraged the prisoner "to use his imagination to think of the worst possible scenario he could end up in." Obviously trained in "touchless torture," the captain assured him that "beatings and physical pain are not the worst thing in the world" and that there are much "worse things than physical pain." "[A]fter being beaten for awhile, humans tend to disconnect the mind from the body and make it through." In time, "he will talk, because everyone does."

> But until then, he will very soon disappear down a very dark hole. His very existence will become erased. His electronic files will be deleted from the computer, his paper files will be packed up and filed away, and

his existence will be forgotten by all. No one will know what happened
to him and, eventually, no one will care.[46]

When questioned about this interrogation, the chief interrogator said that a
senior military lawyer had approved both the threat and the fake letter.
When asked, the lawyer at first said he did not recall. When questioned a
second time, he invoked the military equivalent of the Fifth Amendment
and refused to answer questions.[47]

The Schmidt Report also described the interrogation of Mohammed al
Qahtani, discussed in Chapter 5. General Schmidt concluded that "the cumulative effect" of al Qahtani's interrogation—which included 160 days of
isolation and "48 of 54 consecutive days of 18 to 20-hour interrogations,"
during which time he was "led around by a leash tied to his chains," had a
thong placed on his head, was forced to wear a bra, forced to stand naked in
front of a female interrogator for five minutes, made to endure strip
searches as an interrogation technique, and repeatedly doused with water—
had been "abusive and degrading." Schmidt recommended that the commanding general at Guantánamo at the time, Major General Geoffrey
Miller, be reprimanded for failing to supervise the interrogation.[48] Army
General Bantz Craddock, Commander of the U.S. Southern Command,
overruled the recommendation, concluding that al Qahtani's interrogation
did not violate U.S. policy.[49]

IV

On September 8, 2005, we once again appeared in the federal Court of Ap-
peals in Washington, D.C. The cases from Judge Green and Judge Leon had
been consolidated and were argued before a three-judge panel that included
Judge A. Raymond Randolph, who wrote the court's earlier decision in
2003; Judge David Sentelle, appointed by President Reagan in 1987; and
Judge Judith Rogers, who had been appointed by President Clinton in 1994.
Tom Wilner argued for the prisoners whose cases were consolidated before
Judge Green, and Stephen Oleskey, from the Boston office of the law firm
WilmerHale, handled the appeal from Judge Leon. Tom once again pressed
the point we had been making for nearly three years: our clients were not

enemy combatants "no matter how broadly that term may be defined." They were innocent men who had been caught up in the fog of war, like so many of the prisoners, and they were entitled to their day in court. Almost immediately, the court asked Tom whether the prisoners had rights under the Constitution—the issue that had divided Judges Leon and Green. Tom answered that even if the prisoners had no constitutional rights, they could still challenge the legality of their detentions, coming up with an ingenious hypothetical to make his point.

Suppose, he said, the United States passed a constitutional amendment that allowed the military to detain any person of Japanese descent. A person arrested under this regime could not complain that his constitutional rights had been violated, because, by hypothesis, the constitution now permitted his arrest. But what if the military simply arrested the wrong guy? "I'm not of Japanese descent," Tom said, assuming the role of the wronged prisoner in his own hypothetical. "My name isn't Hara, it's O'Hara, and I'm Irish, and you've just made a mistake here." That person would have a right under the habeas statute to challenge the *factual* accuracy of the military's judgment in federal court, without regard to the existence of a constitutional right. In a nutshell, that's what habeas is—a challenge to the validity of the executive's judgment. And so it is with our clients, Tom argued. The military claims the right to detain any person who is an "enemy combatant," as they have defined the term. Regardless of whether the prisoners have rights under the Constitution, the habeas statute gives them the right to challenge the factual accuracy of the military's judgment in federal court. That challenge had not yet taken place, and it was past time for the delay to end.[50]

It was a brilliant hypothetical that immediately crystallized our position for the court: if, as we allege, they simply caught the wrong guy, the writ of habeas corpus is the answer. The Administration was represented by Deputy Attorney General Gregory Katsas, who began his prepared remarks with an extended argument on why the Constitution does not apply at Guantánamo. But the court now understood this was irrelevant if the prisoners also had rights under the habeas statute. Suppose the Fifth Amendment doesn't apply, they asked Katsas. Does that mean there's nothing left? "[S]uppose they simply picked up a shepherd and said you look like you might be al Qaeda and dragged him over to Guantanamo. . . . If somebody was held by the military [and] it was clear they had no connection with 9/11, no connection with al Qaeda, no connection with the Taliban, why," the court asked, "aren't they entitled to . . . habeas corpus?"[51]

By the time these arguments took place, Tom Wilner and I had been representing prisoners at Guantánamo Bay for three and a half years. None of our clients had yet received an opportunity to contest their detention in open court. A lucky few had been released, but the rest remained in legal limbo. The litigation was beginning to remind me of the Greek myth of Sisyphus, who was destined to push a rock up a mountain only to see it roll back down again. We had pressed our contentions throughout 2002 and 2003, until the decision in *Rasul* in June 2004, hoping that the decision would finally bring a lawful process to Camp Delta. But the hope proved short-lived because it failed to anticipate the Administration's continuing hostility to judicial oversight. Along with the other legal teams, we rolled the rock up the hill a second time before Judge Green, convincing her in January 2005 that the prisoners' rights were not adequately protected by the CSRT. But Judge Leon disagreed, forcing us to roll the rock up the hill once more, this time going back to the Court of Appeals. But I hoped, and believed, the third time would be the charm: though appearances could be deceiving, the D.C. Circuit in September 2005 certainly seemed to agree that the habeas statute guaranteed the right to demand that the government prove the prisoners were something other than shepherds. Sisyphus, after all, was only a myth.

ELEVEN

ASKING WHY

I

Why did this happen? For the first time, the United States had made a deliberate decision that its armed forces—and interrogators—would not be constrained by the Geneva Conventions. Recall that General Tommy Franks, commander of the U.S. forces in Afghanistan, did not think "military necessity" demanded this unprecedented step. On October 17, 2001, shortly after the hostilities in Afghanistan began, Franks ordered all U.S. troops to comply with the Conventions and existing military rules regarding the treatment of prisoners. In fact, among senior military officers, there seems to have been little support for the so-called new paradigm. There is nothing in the history of coercive interrogations that should have led the Administration to conclude that Franks and his staff were being overly cautious. Why then, within weeks of when the first prisoners were captured in Afghanistan, and before the first prisoners even arrived at Guantánamo, did the Bush Administration decide the old rules could not be squared with the new conflict?

The answer has something to do with the nature of war, and something to do with the nature of this Administration.

In 1942, Justice Robert Jackson described the war power as "the Achilles Heel of our constitutional system."[1] In his choice of imagery, Jackson may have been responding to the well-publicized remarks of the California attorney general, a Republican, who in January 1942 warned ominously that the large number of Japanese-Americans living on the West Coast "may be the Achilles Heel of the entire civilian defense effort. Unless something is done it may bring about a repetition of Pearl Harbor."[2] Not long after this remark, the California attorney general was among the first to suggest that the very absence of sabotage by Japanese-Americans proved that sabotage was imminent: "It seems to me that it is quite significant that in this great state of ours we have had no fifth column activities and no sabotage reported. It looks very much to me as though it is a studied effort not to have any until the zero hour arrives."[3] Over the next several months, he maintained a steady, and influential, drumbeat in favor of internment.

Later, however, in his memoirs, he confided that he "deeply regretted the removal order and [his] own testimony advocating it," admitting that "[i]t was wrong to react so impulsively without positive evidence of disloyalty, even though we felt we had a good motive in the security of our state. It demonstrates the cruelty of war when fear, get-tough military psychology, propaganda, and racial antagonism combine with one's responsibility for public security to produce such acts."[4] In an interview shortly before his death, he was moved to tears as he recalled the faces of children separated from their parents during the relocations.[5]

That attorney general, whose bellicose and racist rhetoric helped propel one of the great civil liberties disasters of U.S. history, was Earl Warren, whose eventual tenure as chief justice would become synonymous with a liberal, activist Supreme Court dedicated to the protection of minorities, even in the face of fierce public opposition.[6] As chief justice, Warren cautioned against the danger of an unchecked war power, reminding us that "[e]ven the war power does not remove constitutional limitations safeguarding essential liberties."[7]

Warren's experience cautions us not to view wartime behavior solely through a partisan lens. During these periods, honorable, well-intended public servants who, under normal circumstances, are steadfast in their commitment to the Constitution and the rule of law, nonetheless find themselves capable of reprehensible conduct. Even observers who seem mindful of the forces distorting their judgment are likely to falter. It is worth recalling, for instance, that Justice Jackson's "Achilles Heel" metaphor occurs in a draft opinion in *Hirabayashi v. United States*. Gordon Hirabayashi had been convicted of violating a curfew imposed during World War II that applied only to people of Japanese descent. Despite the warning implicit in his metaphor, Jackson never published his draft opinion. Instead, he joined the majority, which affirmed the conviction. The Court's decision in *Hirabayashi* set the stage for the disastrous decision two years later in *Korematsu v. United States,* which upheld the Japanese internments.[8] As Justice Louis Brandeis lamented in the extended shadow of World War I, "You might as well recognize that during a war . . . all bets are off."[9]

We look back at these periods with deep and abiding regret, berating ourselves in public displays of contrition. But we do not contribute to our understanding if we cast these episodes in moralistic or partisan terms, as though the actors, faced with a clear choice between good and evil, calmly chose the latter for malicious or political reasons. Instead, it seems to me more accurate to describe these episodes as moments when the people charged with the responsibility for our national security simply lost their moral compass. And this in turn suggests a more useful metaphor, one that likens political actors to pilots. Flying can be extremely dangerous. During certain maneuvers, pilots may become so disoriented that they cannot trust their senses. Every instinct in their body will tell them that their life depends on taking a certain action. And yet, their instincts during these periods are wrong, and—tragically—what they believe to be their only safe option becomes precisely what kills them. By some estimates, this phenomenon, called spatial disorientation, accounts for 10 percent of all general aviation accidents. Perhaps 90 percent of the accidents attributable to it are fatal. (It is the most likely explanation for the crash that killed John F. Kennedy, Jr.) In these moments, pilots must learn to disregard their instincts and to trust their instruments instead.[10]

I find spatial disorientation a useful metaphor. It captures the essence of the hysteria that periodically grips the nation, without casting it in pejoratives. Political actors trapped in a tightening spiral of wartime hysteria simply cannot trust their instincts. They make their choices not because they fail to appreciate what they are doing, but because they believe they are doing precisely what must be done to preserve the nation—that the ends they seek justify the means they endorse, since (at least in their view), the life of the nation is at stake.[11] They cling to their choices with a confidence that may be perceived as arrogance—even when they are terribly mistaken and long after the ostensible justification for their choices has passed. With notable exceptions, these actors choose their folly much in the same way that pilots who suffer from spatial disorientation choose to crash—with grim, deadly determination, fully convinced of the rightness of their actions.[12]

This metaphor goes a long way toward explaining the Administration's detention policy. The policy came about not because the principal actors failed to understand their actions. On the contrary, they knew exactly what they were doing: they deliberately created a network of prisons beyond the law in order to evade existing legal constraints, and to allow the military and the CIA to conduct interrogations that had always been thought to be illegal. It was not an accident, nor was it the unintended consequence of some other policy preference: it *was* the policy preference. It is pointless to impugn the motives of the participants in this debate, at least on the current state of the record.[13] They did what they thought best. Timothy Flanigan, the former deputy White House counsel and a leading architect of the detention policy, said, "Everybody who was involved in this process had . . . a white hat on."[14]

But we must be careful with this metaphor. It would be wrong to attribute the Administration's detention policy to nothing more than the cold, impersonal forces of history, as though actors were irrelevant and events foreordained. Such an emphasis on the predictive power of the past unfairly diminishes the significance of the present. Today, the occupant of the Oval Office and his most senior advisors share an abiding belief in the value of a powerful, unified executive. It is a legitimate political philosophy, neutral and nonpartisan in and of itself, perhaps no better and arguably no worse than any other approach to national government. But on September 11, 2001, this philosophy was summoned into service, rising above other competing approaches and quickly achieving dominance in presidential deliberations. In this way, the disorienting power of war was brought to bear on personalities strongly predisposed to embrace its central, and most seductive message: if a country at peace requires a strong chief executive, then a country at war cannot survive without a dominant commander in chief. September 11 crystallized and made urgent what this Administration already believed.

Viewing events through the prism of this political philosophy, and pressed on by the moral disorientation of war, the Administration almost immediately set about disabling the very instruments that mark our commitment to the rule of law: that the military must always be subject to civilian rule; that the proper limits of military discretion are ultimately, and always, judicial questions; that armed conflict—and particularly the treatment of prisoners—is not a descent into lawless anarchy but instead is governed by carefully negotiated and reciprocal obligations; and that restraints on individual liberty must be subject to review by some impartial tribunal. Precisely when history cautions us that we are least likely to be thinking clearly, the Administration believed it could see, with the false clarity that sometimes comes from strong conviction, exactly what must be done.

But in disabling the essential instruments of a constitutional democracy, the Administration invested the military with a power its leaders did not seek. General Tommy Franks ordered his troops to comply with the Geneva Conventions. Secretary of State Colin Powell, the former chairman of the Joint Chiefs, pleaded with the president not to abandon the Conventions. The most senior lawyers in the Pentagon and the State Department told the leaders of the Administration they were making a mistake. It was civilian politicians and Justice Department lawyers, unschooled in the realities of armed conflict but believers in the mystic power of a strong commander in chief, who insisted that the military should be unmoored from the Conventions.[15]

In fact, the White House did more than reject the judgment of career military and diplomatic professionals. It deliberately excluded them from the debate. Secretary of State Powell and National Security Advisor Condoleezza Rice did not find out about the president's November 13, 2001, order establishing military commissions and authorizing indefinite detentions until it was released to the public.[16] The State Department's top legal adviser, William Howard Taft IV, was "shunned" by the White House and Justice Department lawyers developing the detention policy. According to one former White House official, Taft, who had been a deputy secretary of defense during the Reagan Administration, was seen as "ideologically squishy." Retired Rear Admiral Donald Guter, who was then the Navy's most senior lawyer and who had been in the Pentagon on 9/11, would later complain that he and other Pentagon experts on military justice were largely kept in the dark as the policy was developed.[17]

Rather than solicit input from the people with the broadest range of relevant experience, the Administration leaned heavily on a small circle of young civilian lawyers in the White House and Justice Department. By and large, these lawyers had impeccable academic credentials. Several had clerked for Supreme Court justices Clarence Thomas or Antonin Scalia. Still more had clerked for Lawrence Silberman, a prominent conservative jurist formerly on the federal Court of Appeals for the District of Columbia. Many were members of the Federalist Society, a conservative legal group.[18] While no one doubts the intellectual firepower of these lawyers, there is a well-known tendency for like-minded people to overlook or ignore the pitfalls and risks that may be evident to those who do not share their ideological orientation. In fact, they may push one another to take increasingly radical views. As Cass Sunstein has observed, "like-minded people go to extremes."[19]

Yet the same perspective that created Camp Delta prevents it from changing. As I write, the four-year anniversary of Camp Delta's first planeload of twenty prisoners has recently come and gone. The prison has now been open longer than our involvement in World War II. Today, no one can credibly maintain that the prisoners in Cuba are "the worst of the worst." A steady stream of interrogators, translators, and analysts attests to exactly the opposite. More than two hundred fifty prisoners have been released with no intimation that they did anything wrong. The chief interrogator at the base says 75 percent of the prisoners are no longer being questioned. Even the camp commander says many of the five hundred who remain could be released tomorrow at no risk to the United States. Nor can anyone seriously suggest that Guantánamo has provided the storehouse of intelligence for which it was built. One senior American official who has closely reviewed the intelligence gathered from the base summed it up succinctly: "When you have the overall mosaic of all the intelligence picked up all over the world, Guantánamo provided a very small piece of that mosaic. It's been helpful and valuable in certain areas. Was it the mother lode of intelligence? No."[20]

At the same time, balanced against whatever limited benefit Guantánamo provides is the enormous cost it inflicts. Camp Delta has become a symbol of American hubris and hegemony, indelibly linked with Abu Ghraib and a rallying cry for terror. "You who shirk jihad," asked one Saudi sheikh on a radical Islamist Web site, "How can you enjoy life and comfort while your noble sisters are being raped and their honor defiled in the Abu Ghraib prison? . . . You who shirk jihad, what excuse can you give Allah while your brethren in the prisons of Abu Ghraib and Guantánamo . . . are stripped naked?"[21] In October 2003, Defense Secretary Rumsfeld complained that "we lack metrics to know if we are winning or losing the global war on terror. Are we capturing, killing or deterring and dissuading more terrorists every day than the madrassas and the radical clerics are recruiting, training and deploying against us?"[22] By almost any "metric," the answer to this question is no.

Since 1986, the State Department has published *Patterns of Global Terrorism,* an annual survey of terrorist activity worldwide, which includes a compilation of terrorist attacks for the preceding year. In 2005, the State Department abruptly canceled publication of this report. According to Larry Johnson, a former CIA analyst and State Department terrorism expert, the 2005 report showed 625 "significant" terrorist attacks in 2004. This represents the largest number of attacks since 1985 and more than three times the number in either 2002 or 2003. And this does not include attacks on U.S. troops in Iraq. Johnson did not disclose how he obtained his information, but his account was confirmed by U.S. intelligence officials familiar with the issue, who spoke on the condition of anonymity. The State Department maintains that it discontinued publishing the data because it overstated the number of terrorist attacks. It has declined, however, to provide what it believes is the more accurate number.[23]

Meanwhile, terrorist violence in Iraq is on the rise and shows no sign of abating. Insurgent attacks climbed steadily in 2005 and by October numbered more than five hundred per week.[24] But the magnitude of the violence in Iraq threatens to overshadow the deteriorating conditions in Afghanistan, where the war on terror began. The year 2005 proved the deadliest for U.S. forces in that country since the ground war started in October 2001. In the first eleven months of 2005, there were at least sixteen suicide bomb attacks, nearly three times the number in 2004. In the past, the Afghan belief that suicide is inconsistent with the teachings of Islam had kept such attacks to a minimum. Yet defense analysts now believe that insurgent tactics used in Iraq are migrating to Afghanistan.[25]

Some may protest that we cannot back down in the face of terror, and that no war is won by appeasement. That much may be true, but it is certainly beside the point. Guantánamo is not simply a rallying cry for our enemies; it is a defining symbol for our friends. As Daniel Benjamin and Steven Simon recently observed, "Guantánamo has become a word that arouses rage for millions of Muslims."[26] The great majority of these people are not, by upbringing or temperament, either opposed to the United States or hostile to our goals. Yet for them and millions of others around the world, Guantánamo symbolizes a litany of complaints that, in years past, would never have been linked to the United States: that people may be held for the rest of their lives based on evidence secured by torture; that people may be incarcerated under uniquely severe conditions based on secret evidence, without charges or an opportunity to be heard by an impartial tribunal; that prisoners may be subjected to the disabilities of war but given none of the protections of international conventions; that the treatment of Mohammed al Qahtani was, in the U.S. view, "humane."

I do not mean to suggest that Guantánamo, or even the Administration's detention policy as a whole, is the only explanation for the venomous anger presently directed toward the United States. The war in Iraq, for instance, contributes powerfully to this sentiment. An exhaustive account of the current policies and historical events that collectively explain this hatred is beyond the scope of the book. My point is more elemental. Guantánamo has become a symbol, a word that transcends its own literal importance as a prison. While many factors account for the diffuse hostility that buffets us from all corners of the globe, the Administration's detention policy, and particularly the prison at Guantánamo, is one of the very few that concentrates this rage, giving it a pure and dangerous intensity.

Today, these facts challenge even our most faithful allies. Two years ago, and then again more recently, British Prime Minister Tony Blair, an ardent supporter of the Administration, described Guantánamo as "an anomaly that at some point has to be brought to an end."[27] But for those whose support is wavering, who find themselves on the knife edge between moderation and extremism, Guantánamo provides powerful "evidence of how America and the West make the war on terrorism synonymous with the war against Islam."[28] As Guantánamo endures, their support withers and their anger grows. And it is for them that we must be most concerned. It is for them that the future of Camp Delta is the most urgent. We adhere to the rule of law not to coddle those who would do us harm, but to reassure those who would wish us well.

II

But the Administration's detention policy has done more than alienate allies and enrage enemies. Since September 11, the military has opened nearly six hundred investigations into allegations of prisoner abuse, which includes thirty-four suspected homicides. The Defense Department takes pride in these numbers, citing them to show a determination to root out misconduct within the ranks. What should be said of the soldiers charged with implementing the Administration's vision—of the men and women charged with prying loose the intelligence that the Administration claimed would keep America safe (which, after all, is the *raison d'être* of these prisons)? Some of them indisputably committed violent criminal acts. Others—many others—deliberately treated prisoners like animals, engaging in a systematic pattern of debasement and cruelty. What accounts for this behavior?

The Administration maintains that the abuses are simply the misdeeds of a few rogue soldiers—the proverbial bad apples—whose actions are unconnected to the policy itself. The detention policy no more caused their behavior than the availability of alcohol causes a person to drink and drive. Blaming the policy for their behavior overlooks their intervening act of will. More importantly, this blame creates the risk that we will scrap an otherwise sound policy when all we really need is to root out and punish a small number of miscreants.[29] Or so the argument goes.

In 1960, a group of students from Yale University volunteered to participate in an experiment. They were told the study would measure the relationship between punishment and learning. Volunteers were divided into "teachers" and "learners." The teachers asked the learners a series of questions and administered an electric shock in steadily increasing voltage for each wrong answer. Unbeknownst to the volunteers, however, this landmark study, designed and carried out by Stanley Milgram, was meant to test the hypothesis that normal people will not inflict pain on undeserving strangers. The learners were actually Milgram's confederates and were not really shocked, although the teachers did not realize this. Milgram was careful to ensure that the teachers and learners were strangers to each other, so the teachers had no reason to bear any ill will toward their unfortunate charges. Yet fully 60 percent of the teachers freely delivered the highest voltage—what they believed to be 450 volts—even though a label next to the dial warned of the risk caused by such a shock.[30]

Milgram eventually conducted eighteen variations on this study. He recruited more than a thousand volunteers from all walks of life. Men and women of all ages participated in his experiments. He altered the appearance and location of the test site. He varied the distance between the teacher and the learner. In one variation, he directed the learner to beg and plead with the teacher to stop. Yet so long as an authority figure was present during the study—creating the impression that the punishment had been approved by someone in charge—the teachers proved themselves willing to inflict pain on blameless strangers. To be sure, the teachers were somewhat less willing to administer shocks when the learners were immediately at hand, but when the teachers asked questions and a *third* person (also a confederate of Milgram's) administered the shock—that is, if the test was conducted in a way that placed a buffer between the act and its consequences—more than 90 percent of the teachers, all of whom were adults living in New Haven, Connecticut, were prepared to deliver the maximum voltage.[31]

Eleven years after Milgram's initial study, Craig Haney, Curtis Banks, and Philip Zimbardo conducted the famous Stanford prison study. Stanford college students who volunteered to participate and who were screened for their "normalcy" were randomly assigned to act as either prisoners or guards in a mock prison set up in the basement of the psychology building on Stanford's campus. Both groups were given uniforms: guards wore khakis and carried nightsticks and whistles; prisoners wore ill-fitting smocks imprinted with an ID number on the front and back, without underwear. They wore rubber sandals and a nylon stocking cap.[32] The prisoners were to remain in the mock prison for two weeks, the duration of the experiment. The guards came to the prison for an eight-hour shift but were otherwise free to carry out their normal lives. They were also given a brief orientation at the start of the experiment and told their mission was to "maintain the reasonable degree of order within the prison for its effective functioning."[33] They were not told how to accomplish this goal, although they were instructed against using physical punishment or aggression.

The results were extraordinary. Almost immediately, the two groups became negative toward each other. "Despite the fact that guards and prisoners were essentially free to engage in any form of interaction (positive or negative, supportive or affrontive, etc.), the characteristic nature of their encounters tended to be negative, hostile, affrontive, and dehumanizing." In fact, guards became increasingly hostile as the two-week study progressed. Zimbardo described a "rise in aggressive responding over time" that was "experienced as increasingly pleasurable." The "guards repeatedly stripped their prisoners naked, chained them, denied them food or bedding privileges, put them into solitary confinement, and made them clean toilet bowls with their bare hands." Toward the end of the Stanford study, guards "began using the prisoners as their playthings, devising ever more humiliating and degrading games for them to play." Eventually, the guards forced the prisoners "to simulate sodomy on each other." When Zimbardo became aware of this behavior, he shut the planned two-week study down after only six days.[34]

From this and other similar research, an understanding has emerged, an awareness that the capacity for cruelty lurks within us all, needing only the right combination of events to release it. It is a combustible mix that begins with a studied effort to dehumanize the victim[35]:

> Detainee was compared to the family of banana rats and reinforced that they had more love, freedom, and concern than he had. . . . Began teaching the detainee lessons such as stay, come and bark to elevate his social status up to that of a dog.

> We called them hajis, and that psychology was important.

Soon, preexisting moral standards are replaced with a new and avowedly superior moral perspective[36]:

The war on terror "ushers in a new paradigm" in which coercive interrogation techniques are "legally permissible . . . because there is a legitimate governmental objective in obtaining the information."

Problematic actions are minimized and their consequences downplayed:

I stand for 8–10 hours a day. Why is standing limited to 4 hours?

Accountability is obscured; perpetrators tell themselves that superiors, who
are schooled in these matters and presumably have access to more and better information, approve of what is being done:

Interrogators "are developing information of enormous value to the
nation, enormously valuable intelligence. . . . We have an enormously
thorough process that has very high resolution and clarity." [37]

Shortly after his retirement, William Howard Taft IV, who had vigorously but unsuccessfully opposed the Administration's detention policy
from his position as legal advisor for the State Department, was the key-
note speaker at a March 2005 conference organized by the Washington College of Law at American University in Washington, D.C., on the Geneva
Conventions and the laws of war after 9/11. Taft described his "considerable
disappointment" that lawyers at the Justice Department had concluded the
Conventions do not apply in the war on terror, a conclusion that overruled
the Pentagon:

This unsought conclusion unhinged those responsible for the treatment of the detainees in Guantanamo from the legal guidelines for interrogation of detainees reflected in the Conventions and embodied in
the Army Field Manual for decades. Set adrift in uncharted waters and
under pressure from their leaders to develop information on the plans
and practices of al Qaeda, it was predictable that those managing the interrogation would eventually go too far. [38]

What has happened is exactly what had been predicted by so many from
within the Administration's own ranks. But those people, who perhaps did

not share the same vision of the commander in chief, no longer had a significant voice in the Administration. Did the architects of the Administration's detention policy intend for things to go so badly? Perhaps not. Did they mean for prisoners to be abused? I grant that, in the main, they did not.* But was it predictable, a foreseeable consequence of the regime they created? Absolutely. And for that they are to blame.

---

* I say "in the main" because of at least one case. Vice President Dick Cheney, speaking about the prisoners at Guantánamo shortly after the base opened, said, "Nobody should feel defensive or unhappy about the quality of treatment they've received. It's probably better than they deserve." See Katharine Q. Seelye, "A Nation Challenged: Captives; Criticized, U.S. Brings Visitors to Prison Camp," *New York Times*, Jan. 26, 2002.

TWELVE

"JUST SHUT IT DOWN AND
THEN PLOW IT UNDER"

I

Throughout the summer and fall of 2005, the clamor for change at Camp Delta grew gradually louder, the volume increasing with each embarrassing disclosure. On May 9, *Newsweek* reported that a guard at the base had put a copy of the Koran in a toilet. The allegation sparked a wave of violent protests in Afghanistan and other Muslim countries that left sixteen people dead and dozens injured. The Pakistani legislature denounced the desecration and in London, five hundred people marched in protest. The Administration vowed to undertake a complete investigation. Secretary of State Rice promised that "[d]isrespect for the Holy Koran is not now, nor has it ever been, nor will it ever be tolerated by the United States." On May 16, *Newsweek* retracted the story, saying that its source—an unnamed, senior government official—was no longer certain of his account. The Administration castigated *Newsweek* for its shoddy reporting, and blamed it for the violence that erupted.[1]

But the Administration's angry denunciations overlooked the fact that similar allegations had been reported for years. James Yee, the onetime Muslim chaplain at the base who was accused and cleared of allegations that he mishandled classified documents, said that guards at the base routinely abused the Koran.[2] On May 19, 2005, in the midst of the *Newsweek* scandal, the International Committee of the Red Cross confirmed that it had given the Pentagon "multiple" reports documenting prisoners' allegations that U.S. personnel had mishandled the Koran at Camp Delta. At the same time, the American Civil Liberties Union released documents from its Freedom of Information Act litigation showing that the FBI had fielded numerous complaints from prisoners about abuse of the Koran. And scores of released prisoners reported, independently of each other, that guards often desecrated the Koran in a number of ways, including ripping it to shreds or throwing it in the toilet. One prisoner released from a facility in Iraq reported that a guard allowed a dog to carry the Koran in its mouth.[3]

The Administration was quick to point out that the prisoners' allegations could not be confirmed, though this is hardly surprising given the circumstances of their confinement. Still, on June 3, 2005, the Administration acknowledged that its internal investigation confirmed that guards and interrogators at the base had, on a number of occasions, "kicked, stepped on, and splashed urine on the Quran, in some cases intentionally and in others accidentally." The incident involving urine was one of the accidents.[4] But *Newsweek*'s retraction, coupled with the Administration's angry denials that a Koran had ever been flushed down the toilet, threatened to obscure the more significant lesson of the whole affair: when the *Newsweek* article appeared, almost no one—and particularly no one in the Muslim world—dismissed the allegation as inconceivable. In the immediate aftermath of September 11, when the Administration still had the opportunity to demonstrate that its response would be constrained by the rule of law, and before it jettisoned the Geneva Conventions, this allegation would have been dismissed out of hand by all except the most ardent anti-Americans. Instead, the allegation was given immediate credence all over the world, even among our allies. And how could the Administration fairly expect otherwise? Wiping fake menstrual blood on a prisoner is only a short step away from flushing the Koran down a toilet. The whole affair provided a telling measure of how deeply our global credibility had suffered.

On May 20, just after the riots over the *Newsweek* article, the *New York Times* reported the grisly details of the interrogation, beating, and murder of two Afghani prisoners held by the United States at Bagram Air Base in Afghanistan, described in Chapter 7.[5] Afghan President Hamid Karzai was shocked by the account in the *Times*. He denounced the abuse of prisoners and demanded that citizens of his country be transferred to Afghan custody. He repeated the demand in a meeting with President Bush May 23. The president demurred.[6] The next day, in a speech to the Foreign Press Association, Irene Khan, the secretary general of Amnesty International (the first woman, and the first Muslim, to hold that post), described Guantánamo as "the gulag of our times."[7] Khan's attempt to link Guantánamo to one of the worst features of Soviet-era repression provoked a bitter outcry in the United States. The president called the accusation "absurd."[8] Khan's choice of words was certainly unfortunate; no fair reading of the evidence can support the implication that Guantánamo is equivalent in kind or degree to the Soviet system of gulags. But it was also unnecessary. The issue is not whether our actions in Guantánamo are as bad as the actions of other countries, and we should not take much comfort in the knowledge that the Soviet regime was worse. Instead, it should be sufficient to note that we can be—and have been—considerably better. Still, Khan's remarks obviously struck a chord. The intensity of the response—for and against, at home and abroad—signaled the depth of the feeling surrounding this issue, and just how divisive it had become.

On May 29, 2005, *New York Times* columnist Thomas Friedman weighed in on Guantánamo Bay for the first time. An influential author and an early supporter of the war in Iraq, Friedman wrote that Guantánamo was having a "toxic effect" on our position in the international community, "inflaming sentiments against the U.S. all over the world and providing recruitment energy on the Internet for those who would do us ill." Writing from London, and observing firsthand the anger inspired by Guantánamo even among our closest allies, Friedman said the prison "has become worse than an embarrassment." Supporters of the United States, who argue that "American values must be emulated and America is a bastion of freedom . . . get Guantánamo thrown in [their] faces." As a result, he said, Guantánamo "is becoming the anti–Statue of Liberty," a powerful and indelible symbol of American hypocrisy and abuse. Friedman proposed a typically succinct solution: "If we have a case against any of the [prisoners], then it is high time we put them on trial, convict as many as possible (which will not be easy because of bungled interrogations), and then simply let the rest go home. . . ." After that, "[j]ust shut it down and then plow it under."[9]

Friedman's commentary was extremely important. His early pro-war stance and centrist credibility accelerated a trend toward mainstream domestic criticism of the base that has continued to this day. On June 7, 2005, former President Jimmy Carter called for the Administration to close Camp

Delta and abandon the most controversial aspects of its detention policy, including the practice of rendition to torture and holding people at secret CIA prisons. Speaking at a human rights conference in Atlanta, Carter warned that these policies had caused us to suffer "terrible embarrassment and a blow to our reputation," all of which was unnecessary: "combating terrorism, defending human rights, and ensuring our collective security go hand in hand." [10] The next day, President Bush announced for the first time that his Administration was open to exploring alternatives to incarcerating prisoners at the base.

Three days later, Florida Republican Senator Mel Martinez became the first high-profile Republican to enter the fray. Martinez, a former member of the president's Cabinet, said Camp Delta had "become an icon for bad news," and that he supported closing the prison. But the "bad news" was about to get worse. The next day—Sunday, June 12, 2005—*Time* magazine published its account of al Qahtani's interrogation, recounted in Chapter 5. The treatment of al Qahtani, combined with the Administration's unapologetic insistence that his interrogation had been entirely professional, sparked broad, bipartisan protest. Nebraska Republican Senator Chuck Hagel said the interrogation was "not only wrong, [but] dangerous and very dumb and very shortsighted. This is not how you win the people of the world over to our side, especially the Muslim world." Hagel, a decorated Vietnam veteran, said al Qahtani's treatment should offend "any straight-thinking American, any straight-thinking citizen of the world." Senator Dianne Feinstein, a California Democrat, said it made the United States look "ludicrous." "I don't know what tree we're barking up," she said, but it was "a terrible mistake." [11] Pennsylvania Republican Congressman Curt Weldon, a member of the House Armed Services Committee, thought it was finally time for Congress to determine "whether or not this facility has, in fact, lost its viability." [12]

On June 15, 2005, Congress held its first hearings on Guantánamo Bay. The widely anticipated session before the Senate Judiciary Committee drew an overflow crowd, and a number of observers, including some of my colleagues, were forced to watch the hearing on video in a nearby room. The committee chairman, Pennsylvania Republican Senator Arlen Specter, had invited me and seven other witnesses to testify. I directed my remarks to the deficiencies in the CSRT, using Mamdouh Habib's case to make the point.

After recounting the torture he endured in Egypt, and noting that the CSRT relied on those statements to conclude he was an "enemy combatant," I said what would have seemed self-evident in any other time: "Any process that relies on information secured in this way is just not worthy of American justice. It is as simple as that. . . . [I]f you look at them fairly, the CSRTs are a sham. . . . [T]hey mock this nation's commitment to due process and it is past time for this mockery to end." [13]

Immediately after the hearings, editorial pages throughout the country called on Congress to make major changes at the base. Guantánamo had "become a symbol of U.S. arrogance and lawlessness," *USA Today* said. The editors called for "radical transparency" and urged the Administration to "disclose who these detainees are, why they're being held and why they can't be returned to face charges in their home nations." The *New York Times* called on the Administration to shut down the prison, and urged Congress to enact rules governing the detention of any prisoner seized in ostensible connection with the war on terror, including their rights under both the Geneva Conventions and domestic law. "Those steps would help fix a system in which prisoners have been declared enemy combatants on the basis of confessions extracted under torture by countries working in behalf of American intelligence." The *Washington Post* urged Congress to clarify the rules governing interrogations. Some of the interrogation tactics sanctioned by the Administration, the *Post* said, were "beyond the pale and ought to be banned by law—and evidence obtained by such means kept out of adjudications of enemy combatant status." [14]

On June 18, 2005, former President Bill Clinton added his voice to the debate. Speaking from London, Clinton said the base in its current form, with widespread reports of prisoner abuse and hundreds of people subject to indefinite detention without charges, was at odds with the "fundamental nature" of American society. He called for the base to be "closed down or cleaned up." Two days later, the State Department announced it was studying how the prisoners' legal status would change if the base were closed. [15]

The breadth and depth of this criticism spurred the Administration to act. To meet the accusation that the detentions were abusive, some of the Administration's most ardent backers began to boast about the exceptional quality of life enjoyed by the prisoners, who receive whole-wheat bagels, fresh fruit, baklava, yams, veggie patties, and nearly ten pounds of halal-certified meat every month. California Republican Congressman Duncan Hunter, the chairman of the House Armed Services Committee, went on national television to read from the menu served to prisoners one particular evening, taking note of the fact that they had apparently been served orange glazed chicken.[16] Hunter's remarks prompted *Miami Herald* columnist Carl Hiaasen to point out what the congressman certainly understood, and would demand for any American citizen in custody overseas: "Democracies aren't supposed to lock up people for years on a hunch, no matter how well you feed them. The Gitmo Diet is heavy on carbs but lean on basic human rights."[17] Proving Hiassen's point, at the same time the Pentagon was bragging about the prisoners' diet, it failed to note that approximately two hundred prisoners at the base were on a hunger strike and that the military was force-feeding a number of prisoners to keep them alive. At the same time, the Administration renewed its invitation to journalists and members of Congress to tour the base, insisting the base was open and transparent.[18] But the years spent shielding every aspect of its detention policy from congressional, judicial, and public scrutiny had finally caught up with the Administration; the *New York Times* quipped that the Administration had apparently confused transparency with invisibility.[19]

II

On July 25, 2005, Arizona Republican Senator John McCain, a former POW in Vietnam, offered two amendments to a Defense Department authorization bill.[20] The first provided that "[n]o person in the custody or under the control of the Department of Defense or under detention in a Department of Defense facility shall be subject to any treatment or technique of interrogation not authorized by and listed in the United States Army Field Manual on Intelligence Interrogation."[21] The second prohibited the infliction of cruel, inhuman, or degrading treatment upon any person "in the custody or under the physical control of the United States Government, regardless of nationality or physical location."[22] Taken together, these two amendments were intended to rein in some of the worst excesses caused by the Administration's detention policy. (According to one published report, McCain was also considering a ban on the practice of extraordinary rendition and a requirement that all prisoners be registered with the ICRC.[23] His eventual legislative proposal, however, was silent on these two matters.)

The first amendment was meant to bring the U.S. military back into compliance with Army Field Manual 34–52. In his extended remarks in support of the amendment, Senator McCain carefully outlined the arguments in favor of the Field Manual. While it has "proven effective in extracting lifesaving information from the most hardened prisoners," it also prohibits torture and coercive interrogations—methods that yield unreliable intelligence by inducing "prisoners to say what their interrogators want to hear, even if it is not true."[24] As a result, the manual allows us to protect national security in a way that "is consistent with our laws and, more importantly, our values." It is of no moment, McCain said, that al-Qaeda or rogue states may abuse or torture their prisoners; "what differentiates us, the United States of America, from other countries is the fact that we do not." Finally, McCain stressed that adherence to the manual would set a single, uniform standard for all Defense Department interrogations, which would cut down on the "significant level of confusion" regarding permissible interrogation techniques in the war on terror.[25]

The second amendment closed the geographic loophole opened by the Bush Administration in its interpretation of the Convention Against Torture. The Administration said the prohibition against cruel, inhuman, and degrading treatment of foreign nationals did not apply if the prisoners were overseas because the definition of such treatment was linked to the Eighth Amendment ban on cruel and unusual punishment. According to the Administration, since the Eighth Amendment did not apply outside the country, neither did the ban on cruel, inhuman, and degrading treatment. Senator McCain's second amendment eliminated this argument by requiring that all people in the custody or control of any agency of the U.S. government, regardless of nationality or physical location, be free from such treatment.[26]

McCain supported his amendments with a letter from fourteen retired high-ranking military officers. It was an impressive document. The retired military officers who signed an amicus brief in *Rasul*—Rear Admirals John Hutson and Don Guter, who had both served as the Navy's judge advocate general, and Brigadier General David Brahms, the former senior legal advisor in the Marines—signed the letter, as did Brigadier General James Cullen, the former chief judge of the U.S. Army Court of Appeals. They were joined by Brigadier General David Irvine, a former Army intelligence officer who taught prisoner interrogation and military law for eighteen years; General Joseph Hoar, who had served as commander in chief of the U.S. Central Command; Lieutenant General Claudia Kennedy, the first and only woman to achieve the rank of three-star general in the U.S. Army and former deputy chief of staff for Army Intelligence; and former Ambassador Douglas "Pete" Peterson, who served as ambassador to the Republic of South Vietnam and was incarcerated more than six years as a POW in Vietnam.* [27]

These officers attributed the abuse of enemy prisoners, "at least in part," to the "ambiguous instructions" that authorized treatment "that went beyond what was allowed by the Army Field Manual," as well as the determination "that U.S. personnel are not bound by longstanding prohibitions of cruel treatment when interrogating non-U.S. citizens on foreign soil." "As a result, we suddenly had one set of rules for interrogating prisoners of war, and another for 'enemy combatants'; one set for Guantánamo, and another for Iraq; one set for the military, and another for the CIA. Our service members were denied clear guidance, and left to take the blame when things went wrong." The solution lay in Senator McCain's amendments, which restored the Field Manual as the basis for all Defense Department interrogations, and made the prohibition against cruel, inhuman, and degrading treatment the irreducible minimum for all others. FM 34-52, "the gold standard" for interrogating enemy prisoners, allowed the military to conduct "effective, lawful, and humane" interrogations. Had the manual been followed "across the board" in the war on terror, the United States "would have been spared the pain of the prisoner abuse scandal. It should be followed consistently from now on. And when agencies other than DoD detain and interrogate

---

* Other signers of the letter to McCain included Commander Frederick Baldock (Ret. USN), who spent seven years as a POW in Vietnam; Commander Phillip Butler (Ret. USN), who spent nearly eight years as a POW in Vietnam; Brigadier General Richard O'Meara (Ret. USA), a former member of the Army's Judge Advocate General Corps; Brigadier General Evelyn Foote (Ret. USA), former commanding general of Fort Belvoir; and Major General Melvyn Montano (Ret. USAF Nat. Guard), a Vietnam veteran and former adjutant general in charge of the New Mexico National Guard.

prisoners, there should be no legal loopholes permitting cruel or degrading treatment." [28]

With these two amendments, Senator McCain tried to make it clear that no government interrogation was beyond congressional control. Any ambiguity about whether the Torture Convention placed limits on CIA authority, or whether the Army Field Manual placed limits on military authority, would be removed. But if events since September 11, 2001, have proven anything, it is that perfectly clear intentions by a coordinate branch of government can be frustrated by a determined executive branch. The White House tried to block Senator McCain's amendments even before he introduced them. On July 21, 2005, the White House sent a bluntly worded warning to Capitol Hill that it would veto any bill that included the McCain Amendments. On the same day, the Administration sent Vice President Cheney to lobby Senator McCain, urging him to abandon his position. [29] On July 26, when these clumsy attempts failed, Tennessee Republican Senator and Majority Leader Bill Frist, acting on instructions from the White House, tried to cut off further debate on the amendments and bring the bill to a vote. When that attempt failed, he scuttled further consideration of the bill until after Congress's summer recess. [30]

As we have seen, the litigation in *Rasul, Padilla,* and *Hamdi* has always followed a readily discernible pattern: favorable developments in the litigation are met by assurances from the Administration that it is ready to take steps that will ameliorate the prisoners' plight. The pattern has continued. On August 5, 2005, with Congress out of town but apparently poised to restrain the military in its interrogations, and a growing portion of the American public expressing dissatisfaction with the detentions at Camp Delta, the Administration suddenly announced that it had entered into an "understanding" with the government of Afghanistan to transfer 110 Afghani prisoners at the base, as well as 350 Afghanis at Bagram Air Base near Kabul, to the custody and control of the Afghan government. At the same time, the Administration said negotiations were under way to reach similar understandings with Saudi Arabia and Yemen, whose nationals account for the great majority of prisoners in Cuba. The Administration said that over the next several months, it planned to reduce the population of Camp Delta by approximately 70 percent. The few remaining prisoners would be held in two facilities: Camp Five, the maximum security unit opened in spring 2004, with a capacity of one hundred; and a newly constructed Camp Six, a prison for 220 inmates modeled after a county jail in Michigan. According to the Administration, Camp Six would have "more concern for the quality of life" and "more compliance with the Geneva Conventions." Prisoners there would "for the most part" eat and sleep in a communal setting.[31] The rest of Camp Delta would be demolished. Though built only three years ago, it is decaying beyond repair "because of its exposure to the elements and because it was built on unstable coral."[32]

Life has changed for José Padilla as well. In June 2004, the Supreme Court said Padilla's lawyers should have filed his habeas petition in South Carolina instead of New York, which meant they had to start all over again. On February 28, 2005, the federal district court in South Carolina ruled that Padilla's detention as an "enemy combatant" was illegal and that he had to be charged with a crime or be set free. On September 9, 2005, the Fourth Circuit Court of Appeals disagreed, giving the Administration the power to hold Padilla without charges so long as it could prove the allegations against him. The appeals court sent the case back to the district court, which ordered the parties to submit briefs on the process to be used to determine whether Padilla was, in fact, an enemy combatant. Padilla asked the Supreme Court to review his case a second time.[33]

But two business days before the Administration had to respond in the Supreme Court, and days before it was supposed to file its briefs in the district court, the Administration indicted Padilla in Miami, giving him what he had sought all along—a chance to defend himself in a regular court.[34] The Administration then asked the Supreme Court to reject Padilla's request for review, arguing that his indictment made his case irrelevant.

Since his arrest in 2002, the Administration has consistently leveled extremely serious charges against Padilla, claiming, among other things, that he had met in Pakistan with senior al-Qaeda operative Khalid Sheikh Mohammed, who directed him to travel to the United States to blow up apartment buildings and detonate a radiological bomb, and that he received specialized training, cash, travel documents, and communication devices prior to his flight to Chicago. It was on the strength of these allegations that the Fourth Circuit upheld his detention as an enemy combatant. The indictment in Miami includes none of these inflammatory charges. The Administration has offered no explanation either for the timing, or for its change of heart. But its sudden and unexplained about-face prompted a stinging rebuke from the Fourth Circuit, which accused the Administration of creating "at least an appearance that the government may be attempting to avoid consideration by the Supreme Court."[35] At this writing, Padilla's request for review in the Supreme Court remains pending, as does his indictment in Florida.

Early in October 2005, Senator McCain reintroduced his proposed amendments. The White House renewed its veto threat. Meanwhile, the list of retired admirals and generals supporting the McCain Amendments doubled from fourteen to twenty-eight, and editorial pages from every corner of the country came out in support of Senator McCain. On October 5, 2005, former Secretary of State Colin Powell lent his support to the senator's position.[36] Later that evening, the McCain Amendments finally came before the full Senate. They passed by a vote of 90–9.[37] The next day, the president renewed his threat to use the first veto of his Administration to scuttle the entire defense bill rather than accept the McCain provisions. The White House complained that the language endorsed by this overwhelming majority of the Senate, including forty-six Republicans, would "restrict the President's authority." As the *New York Times* observed dryly, "Yes, exactly."[38] "Let's be clear," the *Washington Post* said:

> Mr. Bush is proposing to use the first veto of his presidency on a defense bill needed to fund military operations in Iraq and Afghanistan so that he can preserve the prerogative to subject detainees to cruel, inhuman and degrading treatment. In effect, he threatens to declare to the world his administration's moral bankruptcy.[39]

The House version of the legislation did not contain anything comparable to Senator McCain's amendments, and as the two chambers prepared for conference, the White House began a new attack on McCain's proposal. Through late October and into November, the White House began an effort to exempt the CIA from its coverage. Yet the CIA was precisely the intended target of the prohibition on cruel, inhuman, and degrading treatment, and this attempt was also rebuffed.[40] McCain vowed to hold the line and President Bush renewed his threat to veto any bill that contained the McCain Amendments.

So the matter stood on November 10, 2005, when Republican South Carolina Senator Lindsey Graham introduced a new amendment to the Defense Authorization Act. Graham's proposed amendment stripped the federal courts of all jurisdiction over habeas claims brought by prisoners at Guantánamo, replacing it with a limited review in the District of Columbia Court of Appeals to determine merely whether the CSRT had correctly followed its own procedures.[41] With precious little debate and no congressional hearings, the Graham Amendment passed by a vote of 49–42. But over the next several days, the Graham Amendment generated intense controversy and on November 14, Graham introduced a new amendment, co-sponsored by Senator Carl Levin, D-Mich., and Senator Jon Kyl, R-Ariz. The new amendment, according to Graham, corrected "some of the weaknesses" in his original proposal. Although the original amendment would have stripped the courts of jurisdiction over pending cases, effectively wiping out the litigation filed in *Rasul* and its aftermath, the new amendment included language that made it effective only upon enactment, meaning it would apply only to cases filed after the amendment became law.[42]

On November 15, 2005, the Senate approved the proposed Graham-Levin-Kyl Amendment by a vote of 84–14. The Defense Authorization Act then went to conference with House negotiators. When the bill emerged from conference December 18, 2005, it included, in successive sections, both of the McCain Amendments and the Graham-Levin-Kyl Amendment, collectively entitled the Detainee Treatment Act of 2005, or the DTA. (An identical version of the DTA was also included in the Department of Defense Appropriations Act of 2006, which also emerged from conference December 18.[43]) The various provisions of the DTA were clearly meant to be read as a set: the first part, which codified the McCain Amendments, attempted to restrain interrogators in the treatment of prisoners, while the second part, which codified the Graham-Levin-Kyl Amendment, attempted to limit federal court review of new cases brought by prisoners at the base.

The ostensible logic of the DTA is apparent enough. When the Supreme Court decided *Rasul* in June 2004, the Pentagon was holding prisoners under uniquely severe conditions with no legal process. But since that time, the Pentagon had created the CSRT, which supposedly guarded against the risk of a wrongful detention, and Congress had adopted the McCain Amendments, which protected against abusive interrogations. Under this view, the justification for *Rasul* had been eclipsed by events; the imbalance between power asserted and power restrained had been corrected without judicial involvement, and *Rasul* was a needless anomaly.

But the assumptions embedded in this logic are equally apparent. Fundamentally, the DTA assumes the McCain Amendments will act as an effective restraint against abusive interrogations, and that the CSRTs will correctly identify those who do not belong in custody. As to the latter, little need be added to the discussion in Chapter 8; the CSRT is a mockery of military justice. The DTA continues this mockery, allowing the military to detain people based on evidence secured by torture or unlawful coercion. But the former assumption—that the McCain Amendments can restrain a resolute executive branch bent on conducting aggressive, and abusive, interrogations—deserves closer scrutiny.

The first of McCain's two amendments, codified in the DTA, requires that military interrogators conform themselves to the requirements of the Army Field Manual. That is all well and good. But the Field Manual is not written in stone and even as Senator McCain extolled the virtues of the Field Manual on the floor of the Senate, even as the retired military officials praised it as "the gold standard" for conducting interrogations, the Army was rewriting it to allow more aggressive interrogation techniques. Unlike its predecessors, the revised Field Manual on interrogations is classified. But according to military officials familiar with the revisions, the new version "goes right up to the edge" in the techniques interrogators may use. "This is a stick in McCain's eye," one official said. "He's not going to be comfortable with this." [44] The new manual apparently prohibits nudity, mock executions, stress positions for extended periods, the use of police dogs during interrogations, and sleep deprivation. It is not known, however, whether the other aggressive interrogation techniques used at Camp Delta, including twenty-hour interrogations, "sleep adjustment," "environmental manipulation," solitary confinement, and sexual humiliation are allowed under the new version. [45] In short, while the first McCain Amendment may have been intended to put interrogators on a tight leash, the new Field Manual, depending on its content, may have relaxed the leash considerably.

The second McCain Amendment, which is also part of the DTA, requires that prisoners in the overseas custody of other U.S. agencies not be subjected to cruel, inhuman, or degrading treatment. According to a still-classified report prepared by CIA Inspector General John L. Helgerson, at least some of the "enhanced interrogation techniques" used by the CIA would be illegal under this provision.[46] Because Helgerson's report has not been made public, it is impossible to know which methods would be prohibited. It is difficult to imagine, however, that water-boarding would remain on the list of approved tactics. On the other hand, it would be dangerous to assume this amendment will work a wholesale change in CIA interrogation practices. After all, the Administration said the interrogation of Mohammed al Qahtani, which included 160 days of isolation, "48 of 54 consecutive days of 18 to 20-hour interrogations," and repeated humiliation was *not* cruel or inhuman. In fact, the Pentagon described it as professional and humane. And while the Schmidt Report (the military's internal investigation of interrogation practices at Guantánamo) found the "cumulative effect" of al Qahtani's interrogation to be "degrading," the Pentagon disagreed.[47] If the CIA can legally replicate al Qahtani's interrogation, it is hard to see what good will come from the second McCain Amendment.

But the most pernicious challenge to the McCain Amendments lies not with interpretive squabbles about the meaning of "cruel, inhuman, and degrading," or about the details of the new Army Field Manual. The greater risk comes from a direct challenge to congressional authority. On December 30, 2005, the president signed the Defense Authorization Bill into law, including the DTA. In his signing statement, however, President Bush cautioned that his Administration would construe the DTA "in a manner consistent with the constitutional authority of the President . . . as Commander in Chief and consistent with the constitutional limitations on the judicial power."[48] In other words, the Bush Administration would comply with the DTA only so long as the act did not interfere with the president's unilateral power as commander in chief. As we have seen, the president claims that his inherent authority as commander in chief authorizes him to instruct interrogators to use any technique, including torture, and that congressional attempts to restrain the president are unconstitutional. According to one senior Administration official, the president's signing statement signaled the Administration's intention to use "harsher methods" as it sees fit, notwithstanding the language of the statute.[49] Thus, the president's assault on the bedrock principles of divided government continues.

In short, any assessment of whether the McCain Amendments will actually restrain interrogators must take into account this sequence of events: in the summer of 2005, the Bush Administration pressured McCain not to introduce his amendments. When McCain persevered, the Administration tried parliamentary maneuvers to prevent his amendments from coming to a vote. When that proved unsuccessful, President Bush vowed to veto any legislation that contained the amendments. When the legislation passed by a veto-proof margin, the Administration tried to exempt the CIA from its coverage. Finally, when that attempt failed, the president signed the legislation, but reserved the right as commander in chief to ignore it.

These events demonstrate the elemental flaw in the logic of the DTA. Under our constitutional structure, Congress makes the laws and the president executes them. The authors of the DTA presumably acted on the settled expectation that the president would comply with statutory limits imposed by Congress. But this expectation has been upset in the war on terror. As we have seen, the president claims the right to ignore limits imposed by Congress, whether it be the limits contained in the Foreign Intelligence Surveillance Act, the War Powers Resolution, the Authorization for the Use of Military Force passed September 14, 2001, the federal anti-torture statute, or the Detainee Treatment Act. (And those are only the provisions we know about; when asked at a Senate hearing whether there were others, Attorney General Gonzales declined to answer.[50]) The net effect of this claim is to marginalize Congress's power to restrain the commander in chief—or, as Senator Graham himself put it, to "neuter the Congress."[51] The imbalance that led to the decision in *Rasul* has not been corrected at all, and the courts remain an essential check on the abuse of presidential power.

And so the rock has rolled back down the hill. The sweeping transformation promised by the Administration in August 2005, when it appeared Congress might take meaningful action to restrain interrogators, has yet to take place. The status of the Administration's supposedly imminent plan to transfer 70 percent of the prisoners to their home countries, with most of the remainder moved to a facility that provided "more compliance with the

Geneva Conventions," is uncertain. Approximately five hundred prisoners remain at the base.

In late 2005, senior officials from every branch of the Armed Forces met at the Pentagon to discuss a proposal to treat prisoners in accordance with Common Article Three of the Geneva Conventions. As we saw in Chapter 3, this Article prohibits cruel, inhuman, and degrading treatment, as well as outrages to human dignity. According to the *New Yorker,* which first reported on this meeting in February 2006, every military officer in the room endorsed the proposal.[52] But Stephen Cambone, the undersecretary of defense for intelligence, and William Haynes, the general counsel at the Defense Department and one of the original architects of the Administration's detention policy, spoke against it. The proposal, they said, would limit the military's "flexibility," and possibly expose Administration officials to prosecution. Their objections carried the day and the proposal died.[53]

Challenges to the Detainee Treatment Act are pending in the federal courts. Contrary to the effective date of the DTA, the Administration has moved to dismiss even those cases that predate the act. While these challenges unfold, the Administration says the DTA allows the military to exclude all lawyers from the base. In fact, it has refused to authorize new lawyers to travel to the base, even in cases that began months before the DTA became law. It is clear that, if the Administration's argument is successful, the Pentagon will restore Camp Delta to its pre-*Rasul* state.

On February 16, 2006, five independent U.N. experts, including the U.N. Special Rapporteur on Torture, released the results of their eighteen-month investigation of the prison at Guantánamo. Because the Administration refused to let the U.N. investigators speak to any prisoners, the report is based on interviews with a number of the 260-plus prisoners who have been released or transferred from the base, as well as lawyers for the prisoners and U.S. officials. The report concluded that the simultaneous use of the interrogation techniques authorized and employed at Guantánamo—prolonged solitary confinement; exposure to extreme temperatures, noise, and light; the use of dogs; and forced shaving and other techniques that exploit religious beliefs or cause intimidation and humiliation—constituted degrading treatment. Indeed, if they caused severe pain, as many former prisoners reported, they "amounted to torture."[54]

The report called upon the United States to try the prisoners or release them, and to close the prison at Guantánamo Bay "without further delay." The next day, U.N. Secretary General Kofi Annan echoed the call to close the base "as soon as possible." [55] Speaking the same day, Archbishop Desmond Tutu agreed, saying that the rule of law at Guantánamo had been "subverted horrendously," and denouncing the prison as "a stain on the character of the United States." [56] The Administration brushed these criticisms aside. White House Press Secretary Scott McClellan dismissed the U.N. report as "a discredit" to the organization. The prisoners, he said, were treated "humanely." In any case, "these are dangerous terrorists [who were] picked up on the battlefield." They have been trained, he said, "to disseminate false information." [57]

Meanwhile, the hunger strikes continue. On February 9, 2006, the *New York Times* reported that an Iowa company had shipped twenty-five "restraint chairs" to Guantánamo. These narrow, straight-backed chairs allow prison officials to bind prisoners by the head, arms, legs, and feet. On January 11, 2006, exactly four years after the first prisoners arrived at the base, the Pentagon began force-feeding "recalcitrant" prisoners by strapping them into these chairs and inserting a feeding tube into their stomach through their nose. The Pentagon also began using a wider feeding tube than it had used in the past, causing great pain and waves of nausea when inserted and removed. Prisoners are kept in the chair for hours at a time, sometimes to the point that they soil themselves. Government officials said they were concerned about the international reaction should a prisoner die at the base. [58]

On March 2, lawyers for Mohammed Bawazir, a Yemeni prisoner who had been subjected to this treatment, asked federal district judge Gladys Kessler to intervene. They argued—and the medical records from the base confirmed—that their client had cooperated in being fed through the smaller nasal tube and that his weight had stabilized. Using the larger tube and leaving Bawazir strapped to the chair until he urinated and defecated on himself deliberately inflicted gratuitous pain and humiliation, they argued, in violation of the McCain Amendment's prohibition against cruel, inhuman, and degrading treatment. Kessler said the allegations "describe disgusting treatment that if proven, is . . . cruel, profoundly disturbing and violative of" U.S. law. The Justice Department countered that the new feeding process had been designed for the prisoner's "comfort and protection," but that even if the allegations were true, the DTA meant the prisoner had no right to bring his complaint to court.[59]

And so it goes. Camp Delta continues in 2006 much as it began in 2002, except the world is less safe, the future more uncertain, and the global solidarity of September 12, 2001, when the United States stood as one with the civilized world, has faded to a distant memory.

ACKNOWLEDGMENTS

Writing a book is an act of great conceit, made even worse if the reader is left at the end with the unfortunate impression that the finished product was delivered from the author's mind without so much as a midwife to help it along. I have accumulated a great many debts writing this book, and it is a pleasure to repay them here, however inadequately. A number of people read all or part of this manuscript, and I have benefited from their insightful comments: Eric Freedman, Clive Stafford Smith, Steven Schulhofer, Eugene Fidell, Katherine Hawkins, Spencer Short, Karen Greenberg, Jonathan Hafetz, Aziz Huq, Elizabeth Wilson, Celia Rumann, Michael O'Connor, Baher Azmy, Jeff Urdangen, Brody Greenwald, Brent Mickum, Josh Colangelo-Bryan, and Gita Gutierrez. Several students (some of whom have since gone on to much better things) provided excellent research and editorial assistance: Spencer Short, Katherine Hawkins, Lauren Skalina, Joshua Segal, Karen Selking, Sarah Rashid, and Janaan Hashim. Katherine, Spencer, and Josh were really partners in the writing, and not simply my assistants. I should also give a particular nod to Margaret Schilt, faculty librarian at the D'Angelo Law Library at the University of Chicago Law School. She has an astounding gift for tracking down even the most obscure material.

If I were asked to identify the one person with the clearest understanding of the various issues raised by the detentions at Guantánamo, I would not hesitate long: Clive Stafford Smith. He has been a friend for many years, since our days defending death penalty cases in the South. Though one is well advised not to come between Clive and a news camera, the fact is that he deserves the credit he has received around the world for giving a voice to those who would otherwise have none. My understanding of Camp Delta has been much improved by many long conversations with Clive.

I could not have written this book without the generous support of the MacArthur Justice Center, my employer since January 2004. Locke Bowman and David Bradford have been far more patient with me than I probably deserve, and I am grateful to them, and to Rick and Solange MacArthur, without whom the MacArthur Center would not exist.

On a number of occasions over the past few years, I have marveled at the beauty of a free and aggressive press. It is customary nowadays, on the political left and right, to trash the press, and much of that criticism is well earned. But on the issue addressed by this book, several reporters have been excellent. Their work brought to light many of the worst abuses, and helped force many of the most important reforms, in the Administration's detention policy. In one case, which I discuss in the book, I am convinced that a client of mine was released because of a well-timed article written by one of these reporters. Because they care about this sort of thing, I would point out that this list is alphabetical: Ray Bonner, *New York Times;* Tim Golden, *New York Times;* Douglas Jehl, *New York Times;* Carol Leonnig, *Washington Post;* Jane Mayer, *New Yorker;* Dana Priest, *Washington Post;* and Adam Zagorin, *Time.*

I learned the wisdom of the old saw about forests and trees from Peter Matson, my literary agent at Sterling Lord Literistic, and from Bob Bender, my editor at Simon & Schuster. They had a much clearer vision of this book than I could have hoped to achieve without them.

Finally, my most profound thanks go to my wife, Sandra Babcock, without whom I certainly would not have completed this work. If it has merit, much of the credit goes to her. She is the perfect partner, and incidentally the finest lawyer I know.

Joe Margulies
Chicago, Illinois
2006

NOTES

Introduction

1. President George W. Bush, Address to a Joint Session of Congress and the American People, Sept. 20, 2001, transcript available at http://www.whitehouse.gov/news/re leases/2001/09/20010920-8.html.

2. President George W. Bush, "Statement by the President in His Address to the Nation," September 11, 2001, available at http://www.whitehouse.gov/news/releases/2001/09/ 20010911-16.html.

3. The Administration consistently refers to the people captured in the war on terror as "detainees." It avoids the term, "prisoners" to prevent any intimation that they are prisoners of war within the meaning of the Geneva Conventions. I refer to them as prisoners for two reasons. First, as discussed in Chapter 3, the Geneva Conventions require that people seized during an armed conflict be treated as prisoners of war until a competent tribunal resolves any doubt about their status. Because the prisoners have not yet had that hearing, the Administration has no right to denominate them anything else. Second, and more simply, people held in prisons are prisoners.

4. Tim Golden and Eric Schmitt, "The Struggle For Iraq: Prison Policies; General Took Guantanamo Rules to Iraq For Handling Prisoners," *New York Times,* May 13, 2004, A1. The Administration's original plan to use the base for war crimes prosecutions has fallen by the wayside. As of April 2006, only ten prisoners have been charged with alleged violations of the laws of war. Though the military commissions—as the prosecutions are called—have attracted a great deal of attention, they have become a minor part of the Administration's detention policy and are not the subject of this book.

5. T. J. Harrington, Deputy Assistant Director, Counterterrorism, "Letter to Major General Donald J. Ryder, DOA Criminal Investigation Command, re Suspected Mistreatment of Detainees," July 14, 2004, available at http://www.aclu.org/torturefoia/ released/FBI_4622_4624.pdf. This memo was among the thousands of documents obtained by the American Civil Liberties Union in litigation against the Department of Defense and other government agencies under the Freedom of Information Act. See *ACLU, et al. v. Department of Defense, et al.,* No. 04-cv-4151 (AKH) (S.D.N.Y. 2004). The original complaint is available at http://www.aclu.org/torturefoia/complaint.pdf.

The memo released to the ACLU had Sergeant Lacey's name redacted. An un-redacted version naming Sergeant Lacey was obtained by the Associated Press and has become part of the public record. See, e.g., Paisley Dodds, "FBI Letter Complains of Aggressive Interrogation Techniques at Guantanamo Starting in 2002," *Associated Press*, Dec. 7, 2004; "FBI reports Guantanamo 'abuse'," *CNN*, Dec. 8, 2004, available at http://www .cnn.com/2004/US/12/08/guantanamo.abuse/. A copy of the un-redacted memo is on file with the author.

6. Melissa Jamison, "Detention of Juvenile Enemy Combatants at Guantanamo Bay: The Special Concerns of Children," 9 *University of California at Davis Journal of Juvenile Justice Law and Policy* 127, 136–36 (2005); James Astill, "Cuba? It Was Great, Say Boys Freed From US Prison Camp," *Guardian*, March 6, 2004, 18; Pamela Constable, "An Afghan Boy's Life in U.S. Custody," *Washington Post*, Feb. 12, 2004, A1; Sonia Verma, "The Lost Childhood of Asadullah," *Toronto Star*, Feb. 11, 2004, A3; Ted Conover, "In the Land of Guantanamo," *New York Times Magazine*, June 29, 2003.

7. Harrington, "Letter to Ryder."

8. *Rasul v. Bush*, 542 U.S. 466 (2004).

9. Defense Secretary Donald Rumsfeld, remarks at a Department of Defense news briefing, Jan. 11, 2002, available at http://www.dod.gov/transcripts/2002/t01112002 _t0111sd.html; Charles Aldinger, "Geneva Convention Doesn't Cover Detainees," Reuters, Jan. 11, 2002.

10. *Olmstead v. U.S.*, 277 U.S. 438, 468 (1928) (Brandeis, J., dissenting).

11. Alan M. Dershowitz, "Is There a Torturous Road to Justice," *Los Angeles Times*, Nov. 8, 2001, B19; *CNN Access: Dershowitz: Torture Could Be Justified* (CNN television broadcast), March 3, 2003, transcript available at http://www.cnn.com/2003/LAW/03/03/ cnna.Dershowitz; "The Vice President Appears on 'Meet the Press' with Tim Russert," Sept. 16, 2001, transcript available at http://www.whitehouse.gov/vicepresident/news- speeches/speeches/up20010916.html.

12. *Hirabayashi v. United States*, 320 U.S. 81, 109 (1942) (Murphy, J., concurring).

13. Eric Schmitt and Thom Shanker, "Washington Recasts Terror War as 'Struggle,' " *International Herald Tribune*, July 27, 2005.

14. *Youngstown Sheet & Tube Co. v. Sawyer*, 343 U.S. 579, 645–46 (1952) (Jackson, J., concurring).

15. *Ex Parte Milligan*, 71 U.S. 2, 125 (1866).

16. *United States v. Robel*, 389 U.S. 258, 264 (1967) (quoting *Home Bldg. & Loan Assn. v. Blaisdell*, 290 U.S. 398, 426 [1934]).

17. James Madison, *The Federalist*, No. 47, at 2:92–93 (1788).

18. Bush, "Address to a Joint Session of Congress," *supra*.

PART ONE: UNDERSTANDING CAMP DELTA

Chapter One: "An Atmosphere of Dependency and Trust"

1. Carol D. Leonnig and Dana Priest, "Detainees Accuse Female Interrogators," *Washington Post*, Feb. 10, 2005, A1. See also "Torture, Cover-Up At Gitmo," *60 Minutes*, CBS television broadcast, May 1, 2005.

2. Leonnig, "Detainees Accuse Female Interrogators."

3. Human Rights First, "Command's Responsibility: Deaths in U.S. Custody in Iraq and Afghanistan," Feb. 22, 2006, available at http://www.humanrightsfirst.info/pdf/ 06221-etn-hrf-dic-rep-web.pdf; "News Briefing with Secretary Rumsfeld and Gen. Pace," Jan. 12, 2006, available at http://www.defenselink.mil/transcripts/2006/ tr20060112-12303.html. The number of homicides reported by the military almost certainly understates the actual number in Iraq and Afghanistan. See Steven H. Miles, "Medical Investigations of Homicides of Prisoners of War in Iraq and Afghanistan," *MedScape General Medicine E-Journal,* July 5, 2005, available at http://www.medscape .com/viewarticle/507284.

4. National Commission on Terrorist Attacks Upon the United States, *Final Report,* Executive Summary (2004), 10–11 ("9/11 Commission Report"). The report can be viewed in its entirety at http://govinfo.library.unt.edu/911/report/index.htm.

5. 9/11 Commission Report, Executive Summary, 12.

6. For some of the many accounts of the various intelligence failures contributing to 9/11, see, e.g., 9/11 Commission Report; Curt Weldon, *Countdown to Terror* (Washington, D.C.: Regency, 2005); Anonymous, *Imperial Hubris: Why the West Is Losing the War on Terror* (Washington, D.C.: Brassey's, 2004) (written by Michael F. Scheuer, who led the CIA unit that tracked bin Laden from 1996 to 1999); Anonymous, "How Not to Catch a Terrorist," *Atlantic Monthly,* December 2004, 50–54 (also written by Scheuer, itemizing specific failures of the intelligence community in the run-up to 9/11); Ned Zeman, "The Path to 9/11," *Vanity Fair,* November 2004, 326–403 (discussing evidence that 9/11 could have been prevented but for the petty infighting and territoriality of competing members of the intelligence community); Douglas Jehl, "Republicans Join in Call for Release of Report on CIA," *New York Times,* Sept. 17, 2005, A8 (discussing classified report by CIA Inspector General John L. Helgerson regarding lapses by CIA before September 11); Philip Shenon, "Officer Says Military Blocked Sharing of Files on Terrorists," *New York Times,* Aug. 17, 2005, A12; Eric Lichtblau, "State Department Says It Warned About Bin Laden in 1996," *New York Times,* Aug. 17, 2005, A12.

7. Authorization for Use of Military Force Joint Resolution, Public Law 107-40, 115 Stat. 224 (2001).

8. President George W. Bush, Address to a Joint Session of Congress and the American People, Sept. 20, 2001, available at http://www.whitehouse.gov/news/releases/2001/ 09/20010920-8.html.

9. Department of the Army, Field Manual 34–52, *Intelligence Interrogation,* Sept. 28, 1992, 2–17, available at http://www.fas.org/irp/doddir/army/fm34-52.pdf. I liken this to counterinsurgency operations because the great majority of the prisoners at Guantánamo were not captured by the U.S. military in conventional battlefield operations. As we will see, more than 90 percent of the prisoners at the base were captured by Pakistani Intelligence officers, the Northern Alliance, or tribal warlords who sold them to the United States for bounty.

10. *Id.*

11. "Al Qaeda Training Manual," 30, available at http://www.fas.org/irp/world/para/manu alpart1.html. This manual was introduced into evidence in the embassy bombing trials in New York. It is important to note that a number of paramilitary organizations, in-

cluding at one time the Provisional IRA, adopted a "cell" structure, and the use of this structure by al-Qaeda does not imply a greater justification for the resort to military force. See Zachary E. McCabe, "Northern Ireland: The Paramilitaries, Terrorism, and September 11th," 30 *Denver Journal of International Law and Policy* 547, 566 n. 147 (2002), citing Graham Ellison and Jim Smyth, *The Crowned Harp* (London: Pluto Press, 2000), available at http://cain.ulst.ac.uk/issues/police/docs/ellison/ellison00bx .htm.

12. The KUBARK manual, the CIA text on coercive interrogations discussed in the next chapter, describes the difference between a criminal and a counterintelligence interrogation in these terms: "Unlike a police interrogation, the CI [counterintelligence interrogation] is not aimed at causing the interrogatee to incriminate himself as a means of bringing him to trial. Admissions of complicity are not, to a CI service, ends in themselves but merely preludes to the acquisition of more information." See CIA, *KUBARK Counterintelligence Interrogation* (July 1963), 5, available at http://www.gwu.edu/~nsarchiv/NSAEBB/NSAEBB122/#kubark (KUBARK manual).

13. For similar reasons, this book also does not devote significant space to detentions taking place in Iraq. Unlike in the war on terror, the Administration professes to be following the Geneva Conventions in Iraq. The detentions, therefore, are taking place within an established legal framework. While the abuses at Abu Ghraib prison and other facilities in Iraq were undoubtedly a violation of the Geneva Conventions, the difference between the treatment of prisoners in Iraq and Guantánamo is the difference between actions taken *in spite of* policy, and actions taken *because of* policy.

14. The success rate of these detentions bears noting. In June 2003, the inspector general of the Justice Department issued a report on the post-Sept. 11 immigration detentions of foreign nationals in this country. The Administration detained 762 people in connection with ongoing investigations into the terrorist attacks, 738 of whom were arrested between Sept. 11, 2001 and August 6, 2002. None of these people was charged with an offense related to Sept. 11, and the overwhelming majority were cleared of any connection to terrorism. U.S. Department of Justice, Office of the Inspector General, *The September 11 Detainees: A Review of the Treatment of Aliens Held on Immigration Charges in Connection with the Investigation of the September 11 Attacks* (April 2003, released June 2, 2003) (hereinafter *September 11 Detainees*); David Cole, *Enemy Aliens* (New York: New Press, 2003), 30.

15. See Declaration of Michael E. Rolince, 5, submitted in *Matter of Al-Maqtari,* reproduced as Appendix B to Human Rights Watch, *Presumption of Guilt: Human Rights Abuses of Post-September 11 Detainees,* (August 2002), available at http://hrw.org/reports/2002/us911/aamfbi.pdf; U.S. Department of Justice, Office of the Inspector General, i, 79, 89 (affidavit relied on in eighty-nine immigration cases); Amy Goldstein, "A Deliberate Strategy of Disruption: Massive, Secretive Detention Effort Aimed Mainly at Preventing More Terror," *Washington Post,* Nov. 4, 2001, A1 (Rolince affidavit used "repeatedly by prosecutors in detention hearings across the country").

16. Declaration of Michael E. Rolince, 5–6.

17. *Center for National Securities Studies, et al. v. U.S. Dept. of Justice,* 215 F. Supp. 2d 94, 96 (D.D.C. 2002).

18. *Id.* at 94–95, 98 ("Plaintiffs are the Center for National Security Studies, American Civil Liberties Union, Electronic Privacy Information Center, American-Arab Anti-

Discrimination Committee, American Immigration Law Foundation, American Immigration Lawyers Association, Amnesty International USA, Arab-American Institute, Asian-American Legal Defense and Education Fund, Center for Constitutional Rights, Center for Democracy and Technology, Council on American Islamic Relations, First Amendment Foundation, Human Rights Watch, Multiracial Activist, Nation Magazine, National Association of Criminal Defense Lawyers, National Black Police Association, Inc., Partnership for Civil Justice, Inc., People for the American Way Foundation, Reporters Committee for Freedom of the Press, and the World Organization Against Torture USA").

19. *Center for National Security Studies, et al. v. Department of Justice,* Civil Action No. 01-2500 (D.D.C. 2002) (Declaration of James Reynolds), available at http://www.cnss.org/dojreynoldsdeclaration.htm.

20. See *September 11 Detainees.*

21. *Center for National Security Studies, et al. v. Department of Justice,* Civil Action No. 01-2500 (D.D.C. 2002) (Declaration of James Reynolds), available at http://www.cnss.org/dojreynoldsdeclaration.htm.

22. R. Jeffrey Smith, "U.S. Must Charge Padilla With Crime or Release Him," *Washington Post,* March 1, 2005, A2.

23. See Declaration of Donald J. Woolfolk, available at http://files.findlaw.com/news.findlaw.com/hdocs/docs/hamdi/hamdi61302wlflkdec.pdf, and Declaration of Vice Admiral Lowell E. Jacoby (USN), Director of the Defense Intelligence Agency, available at http://www.justicescholars.org/pegc/archive/Padilla_vs_Rumsfeld/Jacoby_declaration_20030109.pdf.

24. Woolfolk Declaration, at 1.

25. *Id.*

26. Jacoby Declaration, at 2.

27. *Id.,* at 4.

28. *Id.*

29. Woolfolk Declaration, at 2 ("As new information is learned from other sources it serves as a new avenue of interrogation with detained enemy combatants."); Jacoby Declaration, at 5–6 ("There is a constant need to ask detainees new lines of questions as additional detainees are taken into custody and new information is obtained from them and from other intelligence-gathering methods").

30. Woolfolk Declaration, at 2.

31. *Id.;* see also Jacoby Declaration, at 3 ("Any interruption to the intelligence gathering process, especially from an external source, risks mission failure").

32. Jacoby Declaration, at 5.

33. *Id.,* at 8.

34. Evidence of this default position appears in a number of post-9/11 detention programs. For instance, the FBI adopted a "hold until cleared" policy regarding the immigration detentions in this country. See *Oversight Hearing: Lessons Learned—The Inspector General's Report on the 9/11 Detainees: Hearings Before the Senate Judiciary Committee,* 108th Cong., 1st sess., at 257 (2003). Inspector General Glenn A. Fine testified, "Although never communicated in writing, this 'hold until cleared' policy was clearly understood and applied throughout the Department. As a result, the September 11

detainees were not allowed to be released on bond according to normal INS procedures and were not allowed to depart or be removed from the United States before FBI clearance, even if an Immigration Judge ordered their removal or the detainee voluntarily agreed to leave." See also *September 11 Detainees,* 37–41. The same mind-set would later surface in Iraq. See Jess Bravin, "Army Report Omitted Prison Details," *Wall Street Journal,* June 4, 2004, A6. The *Journal* quotes a report prepared by Lieutenant Colonel Robert Chamberlain, intelligence chief for the Army's Joint Readiness Training Center, who found that prisons in Iraq were severely overcrowded but that approximately 80 percent of the prisoners were innocent. According to Colonel Chamberlain, "It's like the Roach Motel, 'They can check in but they never check out!' " Colonel Chamberlain's assessment was omitted from the portion of the report originally made public by the Department of Defense.

35. Woolfolk's Declaration offers yet another institutional reason why the military would, as a default, always opt for continued detention: "[I]nformation from, or concerning, detainee Hamdi could be brought to the attention of terrorists who later themselves become detainees in Guantanamo Bay. Armed with any such knowledge, such "new" detainees may be able to poison the interrogation environment currently being maintained in Guantanamo Bay. . . ." (Woolfolk Declaration, at 3). But of course any time a prisoner is released he may "poison the interrogation environment" by telling the whole world how he was treated at the base. If he were tortured or otherwise mistreated, I would argue this disclosure is a good thing.

36. *September 11 Detainees,* 46, 51.

Chapter Two: "Debility, Dependence, and Dread"

1. Department of Defense, "Army Regulation 15-6: Investigation of the Abu Ghraib Detention Facility and 205th Military Intelligence Brigade" ("Fay Report"), available at http://www.defenselink.mil/news/Aug2004/d20040825fay.pdf. See also Independent Task Force on Post-Conflict Iraq, Council on Foreign Relations, *Iraq: One Year After* (March 2004), available at http://www.cfr.org/content/publications/attachments/ Iraq_year after.pdf. The history of the military's approach to interrogations is discussed in more detail in Chapter 4 herein.

2. Department of the Army, Army Field Manual 34–52, *Intelligence Interrogation* (Sept. 28, 1992), at 1–8 (emphasis added), available at http://www.fas.org/irp/doddir/army/ fm34–52.pdf.

3. *Id.,* at 1–8.

4. *Id.,* at 3–14.

5. *Id.*

6. *Id.,* at 3–15, 3–16, 3–18.

7. *Id.,* at 3–10, 3–11.

8. *Id.,* at 3–11.

9. *Id.*

10. *Id.,* at 3–1.

11. *Id.*

12. *Id.,* at 3–14, 3–16, 3–18.

13. *Id.*, at 1–9.

14. CIA, *KUBARK Counterintelligence Interrogation* (July 1963), available at http://www.gwu.edu/~nsarchiv/NSAEBB/NSAEBB122/#kubark (Kubark manual); Mark Bowden, "The Dark Art of Interrogation," *Atlantic Monthly*, October 2003, 57–58. For a discussion of the link between the KUBARK manual and the interrogation techniques used after 9/11, see Alfred W. McCoy, "Cruel Science: CIA Torture & U.S. Foreign Policy," 19 *New England Journal of Public Policy* 210, 220–54 (Winter 2005); Walter Pincus, "Iraq Tactics Have Long History with U.S. Interrogators," *Washington Post*, June 13, 2004, A08; Mark Matthews, "U.S. Practices at Abu Ghraib barred in 80s, Interrogators now taught psychological methods," *Baltimore Sun*, May 11, 2004; Vikram Dodd, "Torture by the book," *The Guardian*, May 6, 2004. "KUBARK" is a cryptonym for the CIA itself.

15. Bowden, "Dark Art," 58.

16. KUBARK manual, 4.

17. For the same reason, while some of the Army's revised interrogation manual will be public, the descriptions of the various psychological ploys in use will be classified and unavailable to the public. See Eric Schmitt, "Army, in Manual, Limiting Tactics in Interrogations," *New York Times*, April 28, 2005, A1; see also chapter 12.

18. KUBARK manual, 52–53.

19. *Id.*, at 85–86.

20. *Id.*, at 48–49.

21. David Rose, *Guantánamo: The War on Human Rights* (New York: New Press, 2004), 15.

22. *Id.*, at 21.

23. Shafiq Rasul, Asif Iqbal, and Rhuhel Ahmed, "Composite Statement: Detention in Afghanistan and Guantanamo Bay," July 26, 2004 ("Composite Statement"), available at http://www.ccrny.org/v2/reports/report.asp?ObjID=4bUT8M23lk&Content=424.

24. KUBARK manual, 65–66.

25. *Id.*, at 83.

26. "Composite Statement," 65.

27. KUBARK manual, 90.

28. "Composite Statement," 80.

29. *Id.*, at 66.

30. KUBARK manual, 90–92.

31. "Composite Statement," 46.

32. *Human Resource Exploitation Training Manual* (1983), F-20, L-7, and L-8, at http://www.gwu.edu/~nsarchiv/NSAEBB/NSAEBB122/#hre.

33. Ginger Thompson and Gary Cohn, "Torturers' Confessions," *Baltimore Sun*, June 13, 1995, A1.

34. Central Intelligence Agency, *Human Resource Exploitation Training Manual* (1983), F-20, available at http://www.gwu.edu/~nsarchiv/NSAEBB/NSAEBB122/#hre.

35. "Composite Statement," 69–70.

36. David Rose, *Guantánamo*, 121.

37. Douglas Jehl, "White House Has Tightly Restricted Oversight of C.I.A. Detentions, Officials Say," *New York Times*, April 6, 2005, A21.

38. See, e.g., McCoy, "Cruel Science."

39. As further indication of the increasing merger between the CIA and the Pentagon, a na-

tional reorganization of intelligence gathering approved in 2005 by President Bush calls for the creation of a national human intelligence manager. This post is to be filled by a senior CIA official who will coordinate all overseas intelligence-gathering activities, whether carried on by the CIA, the FBI, or the Pentagon. See Walter Pincus, "CIA, Pentagon Seek to Avoid Overlap," *Washington Post,* July 4, 2005, A2.

Chapter Three: "The System That Has Been Developed"

1. George H. Aldrich, *Human Rights and Armed Conflict: Conflicting Views,* 67 A.S.I.L. Proc. 141, 143 (1973). Aldrich was criticizing the decision by North Vietnam to deny the protection of the Geneva Convention to American and South Vietnamese soldiers on the ground that they were war criminals.
2. Memorandum for Alberto R. Gonzales, counsel to the president, from Jay Bybee, "Re: Status of Taliban Forces Under Art. 4 of the Third Geneva Convention of 1949," February 7, 2002. Gonzales was arguing the president could unilaterally conclude that Taliban prisoners did not deserve the protection of the Convention because they were all war criminals.
3. Katherine Q. Seelye, "A Nation Challenged: The Detention Camp; U.S. to Hold Taliban Detainees in 'the Least Worst Place,' " *New York Times,* Dec. 28, 2001, A1.
4. Tim Golden, "Threats and Responses: Tough Justice; After Terror, a Secret Rewriting of Military Law," *New York Times,* Oct. 24, 2004, A1.
5. Deputy Assistant Attorney General Patrick F. Philbin and Deputy Assistant Attorney General John C. Yoo, "Memorandum for William J. Haynes, II, General Counsel, Department of Defense, Re: Possible Habeas Jurisdiction over Aliens Held in Guantanamo Bay, Cuba," Dec. 28, 2001 ("Jurisdiction Memo"), reprinted in *The Torture Papers: The Road to Abu Ghraib,* ed. Karen J. Greenberg and Joshua L. Dratel (New York: Cambridge University Press, 2005), 29.
6. *Harris v. Nelson,* 394 U.S. 286, 290–91 (1969).
7. *Id.*
8. *Bowen v. Johnston,* 306 U.S. 19, 26 (1939). For a discussion of the history of habeas corpus, see Eric M. Freedman, *Habeas Corpus: Rethinking The Great Writ of Liberty* (New York: New York University Press, 2003).
9. 18 U.S.C. § 2241(c)(1); (c)(3).
10. Philbin and Yoo, Jurisdiction Memo, 29, 36.
11. Philbin and Yoo, Jurisdiction Memo, 33 and n. 4. The December 28, 2001, jurisdiction memo refers to an earlier memo about jurisdiction at Midway and Wake islands, but that memo has not yet become public. The Administration apparently also vetted plans to hold prisoners at Guam, which they rejected because "prisoners there might have to be granted the same rights as defendants in the United States," and U.S. ships at sea, which they rejected because of space constraints. See Seelye, "U.S. to Hold Taliban Detainees in 'the Least Worst Place.' "
12. *Johnson v. Eisentrager,* 339 U.S. 763 (1950), Index to Pleadings filed in Supreme Court, Ex. F—"Regulations Governing the Trial of War Criminals in the China Theater," at 34; *Ex Parte Quirin,* 317 U.S. 1, 28 (1942) ("Congress has explicitly provided, so far as it may constitutionally do so, that military tribunals shall have jurisdiction to try offenders or

offenses against the law of war in appropriate cases."); *In Re Yamashita,* 327 U.S. 1, 7–12 (1948).

13. *Johnson,* 339 U.S. at 790.

14. *Id.,* at 788.

15. Gerald Neumann, "Closing the Guantanamo Loophole," 50 *Loyola Law Review* 1, 65 (2004) ("at the beginning of the twentieth century, the Insular Cases forged a compromise between the forces of constitutionalism and the forces of empire by guaranteeing that the most fundamental constitutional rights would be honored whenever the United States rules as sovereign. Courts have since enforced this historic compromise in other areas where the United States has enjoyed complete jurisdiction and control. They have recognized that the exercise of sovereign power, not nominal sovereignty, makes the United States responsible for recognizing fundamental rights.").

16. Leland H. Jenks, *Our Cuban Colony* (New York: Vanguard Press, 1928), 77–79. President William McKinley signed the Platt Amendment on March 2, 1901, and it was presented to the Cuban government the following day.

> *Their relations to the United States had been settled forever. They had only to vote the articles into their constitution. Until they did so, Cuba was clearly to be regarded as unpacified. The American Army of occupation would remain. The Cubans were entirely free to agree or disagree. They were entirely free to secure such independence as was possible under the Platt Amendment or to continue under the military administration. After several vain attempts to find a more palatable alternative, they added the provisions, word for word, as an "appendix" to their constitution, June 12, 1901. Two years later, in accordance with its own terms, the Platt Amendment was embodied in a permanent treaty between the two countries, and received the formal accolade of two-thirds of the Senate. (77–78)*

17. *Id.,* at 80–84.

18. Agreement for the Lease to the United States of Lands in Cuba for Coaling and Naval Stations, Feb. 23, 1903, Art. 3, T.S. No. 418 (Agreement).

19. Neuman, "Closing the Guantánamo Loophole," 50 *Loyola Law Review,* at 36. In 1934, the United States and Cuba entered into another treaty providing that, absent a subsequent agreement, the lease would remain in effect "[s]o long as the United States of America shall not abandon the . . . naval station of Guantanamo." See Treaty Defining Relations with Cuba, May 29, 1934, U.S.-Cuba, Art. 3, 48 Stat. 1683, T.S. No. 866 (hereinafter 1934 Treaty); see also *Rasul v. Bush,* 542 U.S. 466, 471 (2004).

20. *Rasul v. Bush,* No. 03-334, *Al Odah v. United States,* No. 03-343, Brief *Amicus Curiae* of Retired Military Officers in Support of Petitioners, Jan. 14, 2004.

21. *Opinions of the Attorneys General* 157 (1905).

22. *Opinions of the Office of Legal Counsel of the Department of Justice* 236, 242 (1982) (opinion of Assistant Attorney General Theodore Olson).

23. See, e.g., *Kirchdorfer, Inc. v. United States,* 6 F.3d 1573, 1583 (Fed. Cir. 1993) (finding violation of Takings Clause by Navy at Guantánamo); *Burtt v. Schick,* 23 M.J. 140 (U.S.C.M.A. 1986) (granting writ of habeas corpus and holding that impending court-martial proceeding on Guantánamo would constitute double jeopardy, in violation of 10 U.S.C. § 844[a]).

24. See, e.g., *United States v. Lee,* 906 F.2d 117 (4th Cir. 1990).

25. *Bird v. United States,* 923 F. Supp. 338, 341 n.6 (D. Conn. 1996); Anita Snow, "Cuba Attacks Guantanamo Use for Prisoners," *Washington Post,* Dec. 27, 2003, A14.

26. Neuman, "Closing the Guantánamo Loophole," 50 *Loyola Law Review,* 39.

27. *Id.,* at 34 (citing Wayne S. Smith, "The Base From the U.S. Perspective, in Subject to Solution: Problems in Cuban-U.S. Relations," 97, 98 Navy Office of Information, Statistical Information, U.S. Naval Base, Guantanamo Bay, Cuba (1985) (Wayne S. Smith and Esteban Morales Dominguez, eds., 1988).

28. Neuman, "Closing the Guantánamo Loophole," 34–35.

29. See, e.g., *Ex Parte Merryman,* 9 Am. Law Reg. 524, C. C. Md. 1861 (president does not have unilateral authority to suspend the writ of habeas corpus; only Congress may suspend the writ); *Ex Parte Milligan,* 71 U.S. (11 Wall.) 2 (1866) (president may not order military trials for disengaged civilians captured outside the battlefield when civil courts are open and functioning).

30. U.S. Const. Art II, § 2; *Youngstown Sheet & Tube v. Sawyer,* 343 U.S. 579, 644 (1952) (Jackson, J., concurring).

31. *Sterling v. Constantin,* 287 U.S. 378, 401 (1932); *Duncan v. Kahanamoku,* 327 U.S. 304, 336 (1946) (Stone, C.J., concurring).

32. See, e.g., *Little v. Barreme,* 6 U.S. (2 Cranch) 170 (1804) (president exceeded constitutional authority by directing naval action contrary to statute); *Brown v. United States,* 12 U.S. (8 Crancy) 110 (1814) (striking down wartime seizure on the ground that Congress alone could authorize action); *Mitchell v. Harmony,* 54 U.S. (13 How.) 115 (1852) (forces in the field improperly seized goods from civilian without compensation); *Jecker v. Montgomery,* 54 U.S. (13 How.) 498 (1852) (nullifying condemnation proceeding begun by military commander because only Congress could establish such a proceeding); *Ex Parte Milligan, supra; Dooley v. United States,* 182 U.S. 222 (1901) (Congress, but not the president, could impose duties on goods shipped from New York to San Juan after the Spanish-American War); *Youngstown Sheet & Tube v. Sawyer, supra* (despite claim to national emergency, president could not seize steel mills in contravention of statute).

33. "[T]he classical function of habeas corpus was to assure the liberty of subjects against detention by the executive or the military without any court process at all. . . ." See Paul Bator, "Finality in Criminal Laws and Federal Habeas Corpus for State Prisoners," 76 *Harvard Law Review* 441, 475 (1963).

34. The literature on the application of the laws of war in the present context has quickly become voluminous. See, e.g., William H. Taft IV, "The Law of Armed Conflict After 9/11: Some Salient Features," 28 *Yale Journal of International Law* 319 (2003) ("The law of armed conflict is, above all, a vast framework of general principles, specific laws, and detailed rules that *matter.* This framework stands for the idea that the law can and should protect all persons caught up in war—making the difference between life and death, between humanity and inhumanity—whether they are civilians, prisoners of war (POWs), the wounded, the sick, the *hors d'combat,* or soldiers on the battlefield."); Derek Jinks, "September 11 and the Laws of War," 28 *Yale Journal of International Law* (2003); Rosa Ehrenrich Brooks, "War Everywhere: Rights, National Security Law, and the Law of Armed Conflict in the Age of Terror," 153 *University*

of Pennsylvania Law Review 675 (2004); Derek Jinks, "The Declining Significance of POW Status," 45 *Harvard International Law Journal* 367 (2004); Ingrid Brunk Wuerth, "Authorizations for the Use of Force, International Law and the Charming Betsy Canon," 46 *Boston College Law Review* 293 (2005); Derek Jinks and David Sloss, "Is the President Bound by the Geneva Conventions," 90 *Cornell Law Review* 97 (2004).

35. See Theodor Meron, "Geneva Conventions as Customary International Law," 81 *American Journal of International Law* 348, 350; Jean-Marie Henckaerts, "ICRC Study on Customary International Humanitarian Law," March 2005, available at http://www .icrc.org/Web/eng/siteeng0.nsf/htmlall/review-857-p175/$File/irrc_857_Henckaerts .pdf; Army Field Manual § 506(b); Jordan J. Paust, M. Cherif Bassiouni, Michael Scharf, et al., *International Criminal Law*, 2nd ed. (Durham, N.C.: Carolina Academic Press, 2000), *Prosecutor v. Tadic*, Trial Chamber [10 Aug. 1995], 51–52, 689, 692–93, 695; International Criminal Tribunal for the Former Yugoslavia [ICTY], noting especially the same recognition by the International Court of Justice in *Nicaragua v. United States*, 1986 I.C.J. 4, at paras. 218, 255), 814, 823, 829–31 (ICTY, *Prosecutor v. Tadic*, Appeals Chamber [2 Oct. 1995], recognizing that Common Article 3 violations, if serious, are war crimes).

36. See generally *The Laws of War: Constraints on Warfare in the Western World*, ed. Michael Howard et al. (New Haven, Conn.: Yale University Press, 1994); Howard Levie, *Prisoners of War in International Armed Conflict* (Newport, R.I.: Naval War College Press, 1978), 2–11.

37. A full listing of the signatories to the 1949 Geneva Conventions can be found at http://www.icrc.org/Web/eng/siteeng0.nsf/htmlall/party_gc/$File/Conventions%20 de%20Geneve%20et%20Protocoles%20additionnels %20ENG.pdf.

38. GPW, Art. 118 ("Prisoners of war shall be released and repatriated without delay after the cessation of active hostilities.").

39. Civilian Convention, Art. 5. A combatant cannot be punished for alleged violations of the laws of war without a fair trial, the elements of which are also regulated by the Conventions.

40. GPW, Art. 4.

41. GPW, Art. 13.

42. GPW, Art. 17.

43. Civilian Convention, Art. 4 (emphasis added). The Civilian Convention is subject to one relevant exception: it does not protect nationals of a co-belligerent.

44. Civilian Convention, Arts. 27–34; International Committee of the Red Cross, *Commentary: IV Geneva Convention Relative to the Protection of Civilian Persons in Time of War*, ed. Jean S. Pictet (Geneva: ICRC, 1958), 4–5 ("In general . . . the regulations applicable to civilians reproduce almost word for word the regulations relating to prisoners of war."); see also Derek Jinks, "The Declining Significance of POW Status," 45 *Harvard International Law Journal* 367 (2004).

45. ICRC, *Commentary*, 51 (emphasis in original). See also *id.* at 50 ("if, for some reason, prisoner of war status—to take one example—were denied to them [persons who find themselves in the hands of a party to the conflict], they would become protected persons under the [Civilian] Convention.") Founded nearly a century and a half ago, the

ICRC is a neutral, impartial, and independent humanitarian organization with an explicit mandate, codified in the Geneva Conventions and agreed to by member States, to protect and assist the victims of armed conflict. See International Committee of the Red Cross, "US Detention Related to the Events of 11 September 2001 and its Aftermath-the Role of the ICRC," July 26, 2004, available at http://www.icrc.org/Web/Eng/siteeng0 .nsf/iwpList74/D8B5101EE13FCDD6C1256EDD004C580F; International Committee of the Red Cross, *Discover the ICRC* (Geneva 2005), 6.

46. Department of the Army, FM 27-10 (Law of Land Warfare), at par. 73 (if a person is determined not to be a POW, he is still a "protected person" under the Civilian Convention); see also *id.* at par. 60 ("The enemy population is divided in war into two general classes: a. Persons entitled to treatment as prisoners of war upon capture, as defined in Article 4 [of the POW Convention]," and "b. The civilian population [as defined in the Civilian Convention]"; *id.* at par. 246–48.

47. GPW, Art. 3.

48. See, e.g., remarks of Michael J. Matheson, Deputy Legal Advisor, U.S. Department of State, "The United States Position on the Relation of Customary International Law to the 1977 Protocols Additional to the 1949 Geneva Conventions," 2 *American University Journal of International Law and Policy* 419, 430–31 (1987) ("common article 3 of the 1949 conventions . . . is . . . a part of generally accepted customary international law"); see also Theodor Meron, *Human Rights and Humanitarian Law as Customary Law* (Oxford: Clarendon Press, 1989).

49. The relevant provision of the Convention can be found at Geneva Convention III, art. 5, 6 U.S.T. at 3324, 75 U.N.T.S. at 142; the military regulation is codified at *Enemy Prisoners of War, Detained Personnel, Civilian Internees, and Other Detainees*, U.S. Army Regulation 190-8 (applicable to the Departments of the Army and Navy, the Air Force, and the Marine Corps [Oct. 1, 1997]). For a discussion of the history and current use of these provisions, see Frederic L. Borch, *Judge Advocates in Combat* (Office of the Judge Advocate General, 2001); Levie, *Prisoners of War.*

50. Deputy Assistant Attorney General John Yoo and Special Counsel Robert J. Delahunty, "Memorandum for William J. Haynes, II, General Counsel, Department of Defense, Re: Application of Treaties and Laws to Al Qaeda and Taliban Detainees," Jan. 9, 2002, reprinted in Greenberg and Dratel, eds., *Torture Papers,* 71.

51. *Id.,* at 76.

52. Civilian Convention, Art. 4.

53. Department of the Army, FM 27-10, at par. 73

54. GPW, Art. 3

55. See Bureau of Consular Affairs, U.S. Department of State, Consular Notification and Access, Instructions for Federal, State, and other Local Law Enforcement and Other Officials Regarding Foreign Nationals in the United States and the Rights of Consular Officials to Assist Them (no date of publication available, "[t]he Department of State expects to update it every 2–5 years"), 44, available at http://travel.state.gov/law/ consular/consular_744.html ("the United States . . . looks to customary international law as a basis for insisting upon adherence to the right of consular notification, even in the case of countries not party to the VCCR or any applicable bilateral agreement. Consular notification is in our view a universally accepted, basic obligation that should be

extended even to foreign nationals who do not benefit from the VCCR or from any other applicable bilateral agreement."); Daily Press Briefing, Phillip T. Reeker, Deputy Spokesman, Washington, D.C., August 14, 2001, at 9–12, available at http://www .state.gov/r/pa/prs/dpb/2001/4546.htm; CNN, "Afghan Prison Ordeal Ends Happily for U.S. Aid Workers," available at http://www.cnn.com/CNN/Programs/people/ shows/curry.mercer/profile.html.

PART TWO: UNLIKE ANY OTHER WE HAVE EVER SEEN

Chapter Four: "You Are Now the Property of the U.S. Marine Corps"

1. Christopher Cooper, "Detention Plan: In Guantanamo, Prisoners Languish In a Sea of Red Tape," *Wall Street Journal*, Jan. 26, 2005, A01.
2. James Yee, *For God and Country: Faith and Patriotism Under Fire* (New York: Public Affairs, 2005), 50.
3. Carol Rosenberg, "Taliban Prisoners Arrive at Guantanamo to Sparse Conditions," *Miami Herald*, Jan. 12, 2002.
4. *Id.*
5. "Composite Statement," 16, 21.
6. *Id.*, at 24; Cooper, "Detention Plan," (humane but not comfortable).
7. Katherine Q. Seelye, "A Nation Challenged: Captives; An Uneasy Routine at Cuba Prison Camp," *New York Times*, March 16, 2002, A1.
8. Rose, *Guantánamo*, 52–53. Rose quotes a memo written by an anonymous official at the base: "Should we continue not to tell them what is going on and keep them scared? ICRC [the International Committee of the Red Cross] says they are very scared. What are the benefits in keeping them scared vs. telling them what is happening? . . . The detainees think they are being taken to be shot."
9. Statement of Defense Secretary Donald Rumsfeld (Jan. 27, 2002) ("trained killers"), available at http://www.dod.gov/transcripts/2002/t01282002_t0127enr.html; Statement of Gen. Richard Myers (Jan. 11, 2002) ("hydraulic lines"), available at http://www .pbs.org/newshour/bb/asia/jan-june02/afghan_update_1-11.html; Tim Golden and Don Van Natta, Jr., "U.S. Said to Overstate Value of Guantánamo Detainees," *New York Times*, June 21, 2004, A1 ("worst of a very bad lot").
10. Statement of Defense Secretary Donald Rumsfeld (Jan. 11, 2002), available at http://www.dod.gov/transcripts/2002/t01112002_t0111sd.html; "Geneva Convention Doesn't Cover Detainees," Reuters, Jan. 11, 2002.
11. U.S. Department of Defense, DefenseLINK, "Secretary Rumsfeld Media Availability en route to Camp X-Ray," Jan. 27, 2002, available at http://www.defenselink.mil/tran scripts/2002/t01282002_t0127sd2. html.
12. Tim Golden, "Administration Officials Split Over Stalled Military Tribunals," *New York Times*, Oct. 25, 2004, A1.
13. Golden and Van Natta, Jr., "U.S. Said to Overstate Value"; Seelye, "Uneasy Routine," A8.
14. Greg Miller, "Many Held at Guantanamo Not Likely Terrorists," *Los Angeles Times*, Dec. 22, 2002, A1.
15. Golden, "Administration Officials Split."

16. Miller, "Not Likely Terrorists."

17. *Id.*

18. Golden, "Administration Officials Split."

19. Department of Defense Press Kit, Fact Sheets, *supra:* Media Information, Guantanamo Bay, Cuba, May 2004; Fact Sheet: Joint Task Force GTMO, May 2004; Fact Sheet: Camp Delta, May 2004, available at http://www.defenselink.mil/news/Aug2004/d2004 0818PK.pdf.

20. Ted Conover, "In the Land of Guantanamo," *New York Times Magazine,* June 29, 2003.

21. Charles Savage, "For Detainees At Guantanamo, Daily Benefits—and Uncertainty," *Miami Herald,* Aug. 24, 2003; see also David Rose, "Operation Take Away My Freedom: Inside Guantanamo Bay," *Vanity Fair,* January 2004, 88; Nancy Gibbs and Joanna McGeary, "Inside 'The Wire,' " *Time,* Dec. 8, 2003; Conover, "In the Land of Guantanamo."

22. Savage, "Daily Benefits—and Uncertainty"; Rose, "Operation Take Away My Freedom"; Gibbs and McGeary, "Inside 'The Wire.' "

23. Rose, "Operation Take Away My Freedom"; Gibbs and McGeary, "Inside 'The Wire.' "

24. Department of Defense Press Kits, Fact Sheets, *supra.*

25. Jamison, "Detention of Juvenile Enemy Combatants at Guantanamo Bay"; Astill, "Cuba? It Was Great," 18; Constable, "An Afghan Boy's Life in U.S. Custody," A1; Verma, "Lost Childhood of Asadullah," A3; Conover, "In The Land of Guantanamo." It is unclear when these boys arrived at the prison. Some reports say February 2002, not long after the base first opened, meaning they spent two years in custody; other reports say February 2003. See Ian James, "Group: Teens Still Held at Guantanamo," Associated Press, Jan. 30, 2004.

26. Jamison, "Detention," 136.

27. Clive Stafford Smith, "The Kids of Guantánamo Bay," *Cageprisoners.com,* June 15, 2005, available at http://www.cageprisoners.com/articles.php?id=7880.

28. Bob Drogin, "No Leaders of Al Qaeda Found at Guantánamo," *Los Angeles Times,* Aug. 18, 2002, A1.

29. Golden, "Administration Officials Split."

30. David Rohde, "Threats and Responses: The Detainees; Afghans Freed from Guantánamo Speak of Heat and Isolation," *New York Times,* Oct. 29, 2002, A18.

31. Seymour M. Hersh, *Chain of Command: The Road From 9/11 to Abu Ghraib* (New York: HarperCollins, 2004), 8.

32. Kathleen T. Rhem, "Four Detainees Released, New Group Brought to Cuba," American Forces Press Service, Oct. 28, 2002, available at http://www.dod.mil/news/Oct2002/ n10282002_200210282.html.

33. Ahmed Rashid, *The Taliban* (New Haven, Conn.: Yale University Press, 2000), 55.

34. Daniel Bergner, "Where the Enemy Is Everywhere and Nowhere," *New York Times Magazine,* July 20, 2003.

35. *Id.,* quoting Special Forces Commander Chris Allen.

36. *Id.,* quoting Captain Mike Gonzalez.

37. Secretary of Defense Donald H. Rumsfeld and Chairman of the Joint Chiefs of Staff General Richard Myers, remarks at Department of Defense news briefing, Feb. 12, 2002, available at http://www.defenselink.mil/transcripts/2002/t02122002_t212sdv2. html.

38. Denbeaux, Mark and Denbeaux, Joshua W., "Report on Guantanamo Detainees: A Profile of 517 Detainees through Analysis of Department of Defense Data," February 2006, available at http://law.shu.edu/news/guantanamo_report_final_2_08_06.pdf; Secretary of Defense Donald H. Rumsfeld and Chairman of the Joint Chiefs of Staff General Richard Myers, remarks at Department of Defense news briefing, Feb. 12, 2002, available at http://www.defenselink.mil/transcripts/2002/t02122002_t212sdv2.html.

39. "Secretary of Defense Donald Rumsfeld, remarks at Department of Defense news briefing," Nov. 19, 2001, available at http://www.defenselink.mil/transcripts/2001/t11192001_t1119sd.html.

40. The leaflets may be viewed at http://www.psywarrior.com/afghanleaf40.html.

41. See, e.g., Jan McGirk, "Pakistani Writes of His U.S. Ordeal," *Boston Globe,* Nov. 17, 2002, A30 ("Pakistani intelligence sources said Northern Alliance commanders could receive $5,000 for each Taliban prisoner and $20,000 for a[n] [al] Qaeda fighter. As a result, bounty hunters rounded up any men who came near the battlegrounds and forced them to confess."); Chris Mackey and Greg Miller, *The Interrogators: Inside the Secret War Against Al Qaeda* (New York: Back Bay Books, 2005), 114 ("Afghan warlords [were] pocketing a nice wad of American cash for every prisoner they turned over."); Neil A. Lewis, "U.S. in Talks to Return Scores Held at Cuba Site," *New York Times,* Dec. 1, 2003, A7 ("American officials [say] that some of the detainees being considered for release [from Guantánamo] had been captured by Afghan warlords and sold for the bounty offered by Washington for Al Qaeda and Taliban fighters."); Gibbs and Novak, "Inside 'The Wire' " ("U.S. officials concluded that some detainees were there because they had been kidnapped by Afghan warlords and sold for the bounty the U.S. was offering for al-Qaeda and Taliban fighters.").

42. Rashid, *The Taliban,* 53, 100, 103.

43. Miller, "Not Likely Terrorists."

44. Rashid, *The Taliban,* 35 ("Many surrenders [to the Taliban] had been facilitated by pure cash, bribing commanders to switch sides—a tactic that the Taliban were to turn into a fine art form in later years.").

45. Golden, "Administration Officials Split."

46. Jane Mayer, "The Experiment," *New Yorker,* July 11 and 18, 2005. See also Tim Golden, "After Terror, A Secret Rewriting of Military Law," *New York Times,* Oct. 24, 2004 (quoting State Department official Pierre-Richard Prosper: "the operating assumption was that we would capture a significant number of al Qaeda operatives.").

47. Gibbs and McGeary, "Inside 'The Wire.' "

48. Tim Golden, "Slow Pace of Pentagon's Courts Sets Off Friction at White House," *New York Times,* Oct. 25, 2004, A01.

49. U.S. Department of Defense, "Release/Transfer of Detainees Completed," news release, May 16, 2003, available at http://www.dod.mil/news/May2003/b05162003_bt33803.html; Department of Defense, "Transfer of Detainees Completed," news release, July 18, 2003, available at http://www.defenselink.mil/releases/2003/nr20030718-0207.html.

50. Prisoners held by the military in another country may challenge their detention in Washington, D.C. See, e.g., *McElroy v. United States ex rel. Guagliardo,* 361 U.S. 281, 282–83 (1960) (habeas filed in the District of Columbia by prisoner detained in Mo-

rocco at time of filing); *Toth v. Quarles,* 350 U.S. 11, 13 n. 3 (1955) (habeas filed in D.C. against secretary of the Air Force by sister of prisoner detained in Korea).

51. Secretary of State Colin L. Powell, "Memorandum re Draft Decision Memorandum for President on the Applicability of the Geneva Conventions to the Conflict in Afghanistan," Jan. 26, 2002, in Greenberg and Dratel, eds., *Torture Papers,* 123.

52. William H. Taft IV, "Memorandum re Comments on Your Paper on the Geneva Convention," Feb. 2, 2002, *Torture Papers,* 129.

53. *Id.,* at 131.

54. Howard S. Levie, "Prisoners of War in International Armed Conflict," 60 *International Law Studies* (1977).

55. Treaty Between His Majesty the King of Prussia and the United States of America, Art. 24 (1785), available at http://usa.usembassy.de/etexts/gal-860606.htm. The 1848 treaty between the United States and Mexico contained almost identical language. See Treaty of Peace, Friendship, Limits, and Settlement Between the United States of America and the United Mexican States Concluded at Guadalupe Hidalgo, Art. 22, Feb. 2, 1848, available at http://www.yale.edu/lawweb/avalon/diplomacy/mexico/ guadhida.htm#art22.

56. Michael Howard, "Constraints on Warfare," in *The Laws of War: Constraints on Warfare in the Western World,* eds. Michael Howard, George J. Andreopoulos, and Mark R. Shulman (New Haven, Conn.: Yale University Press, 1994), 6.

57. *Instructions for the Government of Armies of the United States in the Field,* General Order No. 100, Arts. 15, 16, 49, 56, 75, 80 (1863).

58. S. Doc. 331, 57 Cong., 1st Sess. (1903), at 1767–68 (testimony of Lieutenant Grover Flint).

59. *Court-Martial of Major Edwin F. Glenn,* Samar, Philippines, April 1902, reprinted in *The Law of War: A Documentary History,* ed. by Leon Friedman (New York: Random House, 1972), 814–19.

60. "War Captives in U.S. to Be Gone by Spring; Total of Prisoners Here Is Put at 417,034," *New York Times,* Sept. 13, 1945; Arnold Krammer, *Nazi Prisoners of War in America* (New York: Stein & Day, 1979).

61. Krammer, *Nazi Prisoners,* 27.

62. See, e.g., Gary K. Reynolds, Congressional Research Service, "U.S. Prisoners of War and Civilian American Citizens Captured and Interned by Japan in World War II: The Issue of Compensation by Japan," July 27, 2001, available at http://www.house.gov/bor dallo/gwcrc/RL30606.pdf, at 2.

63. Committee on Military Affairs, *Investigation of the National War Effort,* H.R. 728, 79th Cong., 1st Sess., June 12, 1945, 18–19, quoted in Krammer, *Nazi Prisoners,* 257.

64. President Franklin D. Roosevelt, Statement to the American People, reprinted in *New York Times,* April 21, 1943. Several months later, the Americans captured a Japanese soldier in New Guinea. He had been present at one of the executions and had recorded the scene in his diary in grisly detail. See "U.S. Flier Beheaded by Japanese, Says Diary Revealed by MacArthur," *New York Times,* Oct. 5, 1943.

65. United States Department of State Reply to the Japanese Government, April 12, 1943, reprinted in *New York Times,* April 21, 1943.

66. Reynolds, "U.S. Prisoners of War," 3 (citing Charles A. Stenger, *American Prisoners of War in WWI, WWII, Korea, Vietnam, Persian Gulf, Somalia, Bosnia, and Kosovo,* [2000]).

67. Army Field Manual 30-15, *Military Intelligence Examination of Enemy Personnel, Repa-*

triates, Documents, and Materiel (Washington, D.C.: War Department, 1943), at 5. Army Field Manual 19-5, *Military Police* (Washington, D.C.: War Department, 1944), contained a similar admonition: "Coercion will not be used on prisoners or other personnel to obtain information relative to the state of their Army or country. Prisoners or others who refuse to answer such questions may not be threatened, insulted, or unnecessarily exposed to unpleasant treatment of any kind." *Id.,* at 163.

68. See Geneva Conventions for the Protection of War Victims: Hearing Before the Senate Committee on Foreign Relations, 84th Cong., 1st Sess., at 3–4 (1955) ("Senate Hearing") (statement of Robert Murphy, Deputy Under Secretary of State) (United States played "a major role both in the preparatory steps and in the conference proceedings.").

69. General MacArthur, commander of United Nations forces in Korea, announced that he had been instructed "to abide by the humanitarian principles of the 1949 Geneva Conventions, particularly the common Article three. In addition, I have directed the forces under my command to abide by the detailed provisions of the prisoner-of-war convention, since I have the means at my disposal to assure compliance with this convention by all concerned and have fully accredited the ICRC delegates accordingly," quoted in Joseph P. Bialke, "United Nations Peace Operations: Applicable Norms and the Application of the Law of Armed Conflict," 50 *Air Force Law Review* 1, 50 n. 235 (2001).

70. Senate Hearing, at 61, 68.

71. 101 Cong. Rec. 9960 (July 6, 1955).

72. *Id.,* at 9962.

73. George S. Prugh, *Law at War: Vietnam 1964–1973* (Washington, D.C.: Department of the Army, 1975), 63.

74. Prugh, *Law at War,* 61–63; Frederic L. Borch, *Judge Advocates in Combat* (Washington, D.C.: Office of the Judge Advocate General, 2001), 11–12.

75. Borch, *Judge Advocates in Combat,* 11–12, 20–21 (An Article 5 tribunal "was needed only for a detained person whose legal status was in doubt. This was often the case in Vietnam, however, as rarely did the Viet Cong wear a recognizable uniform, and only occasionally did the guerrillas carry their arms openly. Additionally, some combat captives were compelled to act for the Viet Cong out of fear of harm to themselves or their families. Despite these complications, however, the tribunal could still find that such a person merited POW status. Or it could determine that an individual was a 'civil defendant' subject to Vietnamese courts or an innocent civilian who should be released."); Prugh, *Law at War,* 62–63 ("The battlefield was nowhere and everywhere, with no identifiable front lines, and no safe areas. Fighting occurred over the length and breadth of South Vietnam, on the seas, into Laos and Cambodia, and in the air over North Vietnam. It involved combatants and civilians from a dozen different nations.").

76. Prugh, *Law at War,* 75–76. Major General Prugh reprints the card distributed to all U.S. troops at 143, Appendix H.

77. Department of the Army, Field Manual 34-52, *Intelligence Interrogation,* May 8, 1987, at 2-17 (reporting that in Vietnam, only one in six detainees were enemy prisoners of war).

78. Military Assistance Command, Vietnam, Directive Number 20-5, Inspections and Investigations—Prisoners of War—Determination of Eligibility, March 15, 1968, reprinted in 62 *American Journal of International Law* 768–74.

79. *Id.* The current version of the military regulation is codified at *Enemy Prisoners of War, Detained Personnel, Civilian Internees, and Other Detainees,* U.S. Army Regulation 190-8 (applicable to the Departments of the Army and Navy, the Air Force, and the Marine Corps [Oct. 1, 1997]). For a discussion of the history and current use of these provisions, see Borch, *Judge Advocates in Combat;* Levie, *Prisoners of War.*

80. Military Assistance Command, Vietnam, Directive Number 381-11, "Exploitation of Human Sources and Captured Documents," Aug. 5, 1968, reprinted in Prugh, *Law At War,* 127–31.

81. Department of the Army Army Field Manual 30-15, *Intelligence Interrogation* (Washington, D.C.: U.S. Government Printing Office, 1967), 35–36. This field manual was amended twice in the next six years; the succeeding editions contained the same caution. See James F. Gebhardt, *The Road to Abu Ghraib: U.S. Army Detainee Doctrine and Experience* (Fort Leavenworth, Kan.: Combat Studies Institute Press, 2005), 49.

82. Senator John McCain, Speech to the American Red Cross Promise of Humanity Conference, May 6, 1999, available at http://mccain.senate.gov/index.cfm?fuseaction= Newscenter.ViewSpeech&Content_id=1459.

83. Quoted in Prugh, *Law at War,* 66–67. Major General Prugh does not identify the ICRC delegate.

84. Borch, *Judge Advocates in Combat,* 66 (in Grenada, "DOD and State Department Authorities . . . determined that the 1949 GPW Convention and that all persons captured should be treated as prisoners of war. . . . [A]ll individuals taken into military custody were regarded as prisoners of war and treated as such until a more informed determination of their status could be accomplished."); *id.* at 97, 103–04 ("the rules of engagement [in Panama] required that all those detained or captured be treated as prisoners of war. Under these rules, captured Panamanians would receive treatment as prisoners of war until their actual status could be determined." Military conducted Article 5 hearings to determine "actual status."); Center for Law & Military Operations, U.S. Army, *Law and Military Operations in Haiti, 1994–95: Lessons Learned for Judge Advocates,* Dec. 10, 1995, at 68–70, 54 ("as a matter of policy rather than legal obligation, United States forces elected to treat potentially hostile prisoners detained during the operation [in Haiti] as if they were prisoners of war"), available at http://www/global security.org/military/library/report/1995/OL_Haiti_Lessons_19951211.pdf. One arguable exception is the military operation in Somalia. The U.N. forces had not been invited into the country, nor had they invaded. The Somalis were not considered enemies of the U.N. or hostile to U.N. troops. As Professor Borch points out, "arguably, there were no 'belligerents.'" Under these unusual circumstances, the Conventions were deemed not to apply. Nonetheless, the military continued to apply Common Article 3 and all provisions of Customary International Law in Somalia. See Borch, *Judge Advocates in Combat,* 206–7.

85. See Department of Defense, Conduct of the Persian Gulf War: Final Report to Congress Pursuant to Title V of the Persian Gulf Conflict Supplemental Authorization and Personnel Benefits Act of 1991 (Public Law 102-25) App. L. at 577 (April 1992); War Briefing, Army Col. John Della Jacono, Enemy Prisoner of War Briefing from Umm Qar, Iraq, May 8, 2003, available at 2003 WL 1864306.

86. Gebhardt, *Road to Abu Ghraib,* 124.

87. Finley Peter Dunne, *Mr. Dooley on Making a Will* (New York: Charles Scribner & Sons, 1920), reprinted in John Gross, ed., *The Oxford Book of Aphorisms* (New York: Oxford University Press, 1983), 322.

88. See, e.g., John Conroy, *Unspeakable Acts, Ordinary People: The Dynamics of Torture* (New York: Alfred A. Knopf, 2000), 113–21.

89. See, e.g., Alfred W. McCoy, "Cruel Science: CIA Torture & U.S. Foreign Policy," 19 *New England Journal of Public Policy* 210 (Winter 2005); Alfred W. McCoy, "Cruel Science: The Long Shadow of CIA Torture Research," *Boston Globe,* May 15, 2004.

90. John Barry, Michael Hirsh, and Michael Isikoff, "The Roots of Torture," *Newsweek,* May 24, 2004.

91. Naomi Klein, "The U.S. Has Used Torture for Decades," *Guardian,* Dec. 10, 2005, available at http://www.guardian.co.uk/usa/story/0,12271,1664174,00.html (attributing "original sinlessness" to commentator Garry Wills).

92. Neil A. Lewis, "Red Cross Finds Detainee Abuse in Guantanamo," *New York Times,* Nov. 30, 2004, A1.

93. Testimony of Ambassador William E. Colby, Deputy to the Commander of U.S. Military Assistance Command, before the Committee on Foreign Relations, U.S. Senate, 91st Congress, 2nd Session on Civil Operations and Rural Development Support Program, Feb. 17, 1970, at 60–61, available at http://homepage.ntlworld.com/jksonc/docs/phoenix-scfr-19700217.html.

94. "Report of the Independent Panel to Review Department of Defense Detention Operations, August 2004" (Schlesinger Report), reprinted in *Torture Papers,* 947; William Howard Taft IV, remarks at American University, Washington College of Law, March 24, 2005, available at http://www.humanrightsfirst.org/us_law/PDF/taft-amer-uni-32405.pdf.

95. Rose, *Guantánamo,* 28.

96. Secretary of Defense Donald Rumsfeld, "Memorandum for Chairman of the Joint Chiefs of Staff, re Status of Taliban and Al Qaeda," Jan. 19, 2002, reprinted in *Torture Papers,* 80.

97. President George W. Bush, "Memorandum for The Vice President, *et al.,* re Humane Treatment of Al Qaeda and Taliban Detainees," Feb. 7, 2002, reprinted in *Torture Papers,* 134.

Chapter Five: Debating Torture

1. Department of Defense, "Army Regulation 15-6: Investigation Into FBI Allegations of Detainee Abuse at Guantanamo Bay, Cuba Detention Facility," June 9, 2005, 17–18 ("Schmidt Report"), available at http://www.globalsecurity.org/security/library/report/2005/d20050714report.pdf.

2. Adam Zagorin and Michael Duffy, "Inside the Interrogation of Detainee 063," *Time,* July 20, 2005, 26. Time's press release on the subject can be accessed at http://www.time.com/time/press_releases/article/0,8599,1071230.html. According to the military, interrogators doused al Qahtani with water seventeen times between Dec. 13, 2002, and Jan. 14, 2003. See Schmidt Report, 19. *Time* originally published only a

portion of the interrogation log in its possession, but published the remainder March 2, 2006, which is available at http://www.time.com/time/2006/log/log.pdf.

3. Zagorin and Duffy, "Inside the Interrogation." One of these occasions took place before Rumsfeld authorized the use of dogs during interrogations. The military offered the excuse that the dog was used "to discourage the detainee from attempting to escape." How al Qahtani, who was shackled, exhausted, and surrounded by military police and interrogators at a secure facility in Cuba, could have escaped is not further elaborated on; Schmidt Report, 14–15.

4. Zagorin and Duffy, "Inside the Interrogation"; Schmidt Report, 15–20.

5. Neil A. Lewis, "Fresh Details Emerge on Harsh Methods at Guantánamo," *New York Times,* Jan. 1, 2005, A11.

6. Zagorin and Duffy, "Inside the Interrogation."

7. Lewis, "Fresh Details."

8. Department of Defense, "Guantanamo Provides Valuable Intelligence Information," news release, June 12, 2005, available at http://www.dod.mil/releases/2005/nr2005 0612-3661.html.

9. Tim Golden, "U.S. Said to Overstate Value of Guantánamo Detainees," *New York Times,* June 24, 2004, A1.

10. Zagorin and Duffy, "Inside the Interrogation."

11. U.S. Department of Defense, news release, June 12, 2005, available at http://www.de fenselink.mil/releases/2005/nr20050612-3661.html.

12. Michael John Garcia, Congressional Research Service, "The U.N. Convention Against Torture: Overview of U.S. Implementation Policy Toward the Removal of Aliens," March 11, 2004, available at http://www.fas.org/sgp/crs/misc/RL32621.pdf, at 4.

13. See Eric Lichtblau, "Justice Nominee is Questioned on Department Torture Policy," *New York Times,* July 27, 2005, A18 ("the review was initiated in the summer of 2002 when the Central Intelligence Agency sought input on how torture statutes should be read to apply to the interrogation of top Qaeda leaders and whether certain techniques 'beyond the normal Q. and A. approach' were allowed.").

14. Dana Priest, "Wrongful Imprisonment: Anatomy of a CIA Mistake," *Washington Post,* Dec. 4, 2005, A1.

15. Assistant Attorney General Jay S. Bybee, "Memorandum for Alberto R. Gonzales, Counsel to the President, re Standards of Conduct for Interrogation Under 18 U.S.C. §§2340-2340A," Aug. 1, 2002, reprinted in Karen J. Greenberg and Joshua L. Dratel, eds., *The Torture Papers: The Road to Abu Ghraib* (New York: Cambridge University Press, 2005), 172.

16. *Id.*

17. *Id.,* at 193.

18. *Id.*

19. *Id.,* at 174.

20. *Id.,* at 175.

21. *Id.,* at 202–4. In an interview with David Frost after his resignation, Richard Nixon once observed, "When the president does it, that means that it is not illegal." See David Frost, *I Gave Them a Sword* (New York: Morrow, 1978); Nixon interview with David Frost, May 19, 1977. In the torture memo, this became, "If the commander in chief directs someone else to do it, that means it is not illegal."

22. Harold Koh, "World Without Torture," 43 *Columbia Journal of Transnational Law* 641, 647 (2005); David Luban, "Liberalism and the Unpleasant Question of Torture," in Karen J. Greenberg, ed., *The Torture Debate in America* (New York: Cambridge University Press, 2005), 57; Jeremy Waldron, "Torture and Positive Law: Jurisprudence and the White House," available at http://www.columbia.edu/cu/law/fed-soc/otherfiles/waldron.pdf; Ruth Wedgwood and James R. Woolsey, "Law and Torture," *Wall Street Journal,* June 28, 2004, A10 ("The president's need for wise counsel is not well served by arguments that bend and twist to avoid any legal restrictions."). See also Kathleen Clark and Julie Mertens, "Torturing the Law: The Justice Department's Legal Contortions on Interrogation," *Washington Post,* June 20, 2004, B3 ("Judge Bybee's actions stand in stark contrast to the best traditions of the bar."). The criticism is not unanimous, however. See Eric Posner and Adrian Vermeule, "A 'Torture' Memo and Its Tortuous Critics," *Wall Street Journal,* July 6, 2004, A22 (defending the torture memo as "standard lawyerly fare, routine stuff").

23. Luban, "Liberalism," in *The Torture Debate,* 57–58.

24. *Id.,* 49.

25. Jane Mayer, "Outsourcing Torture," *New Yorker,* Feb. 14, 2005, available at http://www.newyorker.com/fact/content/?050214fa_fact6.

26. Executive Order 10340, Directing the Secretary of Commerce to take possession of and operate the plants and facilities of certain steel companies (April 8, 1952), reproduced in *Youngstown Sheet & Tube Co., et al. v. Sawyer,* 343 U.S. 579, 589–592 (1952).

27. See *Youngstown,* Nos. 744, 745, Brief for Armco Steel Corp. and Sheffield Steel Corp., at 12–17, quoting Assistant Attorney General Baldridge (reprinted in Philip Kurland, Gerhard Casper, eds., 48 *Landmark Briefs and Arguments of the Supreme Court of the United States* 538–43 [1975]); *Youngstown,* Brief for Plaintiff Companies, Petitioners in No. 744 and Respondent in No. 745, quoting Assistant Attorney General Baldridge: "there are [only] two limitations on the Executive power. One is the ballot box and the other is impeachment" (reprinted in *Landmark Briefs and Arguments,* 446–47).

28. *Youngstown v. Sawyer,* 343 U.S. 579 (1952).

29. *Id.,* at 635, 637 (Jackson, J., concurring).

30. Deputy Assistant Attorney General John C. Yoo, "Memorandum for Deputy Council to the President Timothy Flanigan, re The President's Constitutional Authority to Conduct Military Operations Against Terrorists and Nations Supporting Them," Sept. 25, 2001, reprinted in *Torture Papers,* 3, 20–23.

31. This memo has not yet been released to the public. A copy was leaked to the *New York Times,* however, which has quoted it in several articles. See Tim Golden, "After Terror, A Secret Rewriting of Military Law," *New York Times,* Oct. 24, 2004, A1.

32. *Youngstown v. Sawyer,* 343 U.S. at 653 (Jackson, J., concurring).

33. James Risen and Eric Lichtblau, "Bush Lets U.S. Spy on Callers Without Courts," *New York Times,* Dec. 16, 2005, A1. It appears the NSA may have begun their domestic spying within weeks of September 11, 2001, even before President Bush gave them specific authority to do so. See Eric Lichtblau and Scott Shane, "Files Say Agency Initiated Growth of Spying Effort," *New York Times,* Jan. 4, 2006, A1.

34. Attorney General Alberto Gonzales and General Michael Hayden, Principal Deputy Director for National Intelligence, remarks at White House press briefing, Dec. 19, 2005,

available at http://www.whitehouse.gov/news/releases/2005/12/20051219-1.html; Assistant Attorney General William E. Moschella, letter to the Honorable Pat Roberts, the Honorable John D. Rockefeller, IV, the Honorable Peter Hoekstra, and the Honorable Jane Harman, Dec. 22, 2005, available at http://www.nationalreview.com/pdf/12% 2022%2005%20NSA%20letter.pdf; "U.S. Senate Judiciary Committee Holds a Hearing on Wartime Executive Power and the NSA's Surveillance Authority," *Washington Post,* Feb. 6, 2006, transcript available at http://www.washingtonpost.com/wp-dyn/content/article/2006/02/06/AR2006020600931.html. In 2002, the Bush Administration argued that "the Constitution vests in the President inherent authority to conduct warrantless intelligence surveillance (electronic or otherwise) of foreign powers or their agents, and Congress cannot by statute extinguish that constitutional authority." Foreign Intelligence Surveillance Court of Review, Supplemental Brief for the United States, No. 02-001 (Sept. 25, 2002), available at http://www.fas.org/irp/agency/doj/fisa/092502sup.html. The Bush Administration also relies on the Congressional Authorization for the Use of Military Force to justify the surveillance. See Letter from Moschella. The AUMF authorizes the Administration to use "all necessary and appropriate force against those nations, organizations or persons [the President] determines planned, authorized, committed or aided" the attacks of September 11. According to former Senator Tom Daschle, however, moments before the Senate voted on this language, the White House sought to insert the words, "in the United States and" after "appropriate force." This would have allowed the Administration to use "all necessary and appropriate force *in the United States* and against those nations . . ." Had the Administration believed the AUMF authorized domestic surveillance it would not have tried to add this language. The Senate refused to accept this change and it does not appear in the final text. See Tom Daschle, "Power We Didn't Grant," *Washington Post,* Dec. 23, 2005, A21.

35. Anthony Lewis, the legal commentator, may have said it best. He thought the memo reads "like the advice of a mob lawyer to a mafia don on how to skirt the law and stay out of prison. Avoiding prosecution is literally a theme." See Anthony Lewis, "Making Torture Legal," *New York Review of Books,* July 15, 2004. I should point out that support for the torture memo, and for its claim to unilateral executive power, was not at all unanimous within the Administration. See Daniel Klaidman, Stuart Taylor, Jr., and Evan Thomas, "Palace Revolt," *Newsweek,* Feb. 6, 2006 (recounting dissension within the ranks of Administration lawyers. The dissenters identified in the article have since left government service.).

36. Rudi Williams, "GITMO General Rates Force Protection High With Detainee Care," *American Forces Press Service,* June 21, 2002; "The Torture Question," *Frontline,* PBS television broadcast, transcript available at http://www.pbs.org/wgbh/pages/frontline/torture/etc/script.html.

37. Scott Shane and Tom Bowman, "Behind Iraq Abuses, a Desperate Need to Gather Information," *Baltimore Sun,* May 16, 2004, 1A; Edward Alden and Joshua Chaffin, "Chain of Command: Can Torture in Iraq be Linked to the White House?," *Financial Times,* June 17, 2004, 21 (Baccus "faced constant pressure from military intelligence officials to bend army doctrine for the treatment of prisoners"); Bill Gertz and Rowan Scarborough, "Inside the Ring," *Washington Times,* Oct. 4, 2002, A8; "The Torture Question," *Frontline.*

38. Tim Golden, "Administration Officials Split Over Stalled Military Tribunals," *New York Times,* Oct. 25, 2004, A1.

39. Gertz and Scarborough, "Inside the Ring"; Shane and Bowman, "Iraq Abuses"; Alden and Chaffin, "White House"; Hersh, *Chain of Command,* 9; "The Torture Question," *Frontline.*

40. Alden and Chaffin, "White House."

41. Testimony of Major General Geoffrey Miller, Senate Armed Forces Committee, *Hearing on Iraq Prisoner Abuse,* May 19, 2004, transcript available at http://www.washington post.com/ac2/wp-dyn/A39851-2004May19?language=printer.

42. A number of sources indicate that interrogators were already using these more aggressive techniques at Guantánamo throughout 2002, even before they were formally approved. See, e.g., Tim Golden and Eric Schmitt, "General Took Guantanamo Rules to Iraq for Handling of Prisoners," *New York Times,* May 13, 2004, A1 ("According to several officers who served at Guantánamo, the methods, begun in early 2002, included depriving detainees of sleep; leaving them in cold, air-conditioned rooms; placing them in 'stress positions'; and forcing them to stand or crouch for long periods, sometimes with their arms extended, until exhausted."). In 2004, when the White House released these memos (some of which had already been leaked to the press), Daniel Dell'Orto, principal deputy counsel for the Department of Defense, explained that the interrogators began to feel they needed to use more aggressive techniques at Guantánamo during the summer of 2002, particularly for the interrogation of Mohammed al Qahtani. See Daniel Dell'Orto, remarks at White House briefing, June 23, 2004, available at http://us info.state.gov/xarchives/display.html?p=washfile-english&y=2004&m=June&x=2004 0623203050cpataruk0.1224024&t=livefeeds/wf-latest.html.

43. Lieutenant Colonel Jerald Phifer, "Memorandum for Commander, Joint Task Force 170, re Request for Approval of Counter-Resistance Strategies," Oct. 11, 2002, reprinted in *Torture Papers,* 227–28.

44. *Id.*

45. *Id.*

46. Judge Advocate Diane Beaver, "Memorandum for Commander, Joint Task Force 170, re Legal Review of Aggressive Interrogation Techniques," Oct. 11, 2002, in *Torture Papers,* 229–35.

47. *Id.,* at 234–35.

48. Michael Isikoff, "Secret Memo—Send to Be Tortured," *Newsweek,* Aug. 8, 2005, available at http://msnbc.msn.com/id/8769416/site/newsweek/?rf=technorati. Isikoff claims the techniques listed in the memo, including Category IV, had all been approved for use by the Pentagon. A copy of the FBI memo is on file with the author.

49. Major General Michael B. Dunlavey, Commander, Joint Task Force 170, "Memorandum for Commander, United States Southern Command, re Counter-Resistance Strategies," Oct. 11, 2002, reprinted in *Torture and Truth,* 178.

50. General James T. Hill, Commander, United States Southern Command, "Memorandum for Chairman, Joint Chiefs of Staff, re Counter-Resistance Strategies," Oct. 25, 2002, reprinted in *Torture Papers,* 223.

51. William J. Haynes, General Counsel, "Memorandum for Secretary of Defense Donald

Rumsfeld, re Counter-Resistance Strategies," Nov. 27, 2002, reprinted in *Torture Papers*, 237.

52. *Id.*

53. Zagorin and Duffy, "Inside the Interrogation."

54. *Rasul v. Bush*, 215 F. Supp. 2d 55 (D.D.C. 2002).

55. *Hamdi v. Rumsfeld*, Brief for Respondents, March 29, 2004, 2004 WL 724020.

56. *Id.*, at 4.

57. *Hamdi v. Rumsfeld*, 542 U.S. 507 (2004), Brief for Petitioners, 4.

58. *Id.*, at 5.

59. *Padilla v. Rumsfeld*, Brief for Respondent-Appellant, 2003 WL 23622382.

60. *Id.*, at 6.

61. *Id.*

62. *Id.*, at 10.

63. Charlie Savage, "Abuse Led Navy to Consider Pulling Cuba Interrogators," *Boston Globe*, March 16, 2005, A1. For a fascinating and detailed account of Mora's heroic, but ultimately unsuccessful, efforts to restrain the Administration's detention policy, see Jane Mayer, "The Memo," *The New Yorker*, Feb. 27, 2006.

64. Secretary of Defense Donald Rumsfeld, "Memorandum for the General Counsel of the Department of Defense, re Detainee Interrogations," Jan. 15, 2003, reprinted in *Torture Papers*, 238; Working Group, "Report on Detainee Interrogations in the Global War on Terrorism: Assessment of Legal, Historical, Policy and Operational Considerations," April 4, 2003 ("Working Group Report"), reprinted in *Torture Papers*, 241.

65. "Working Group Report," reprinted in *Torture Papers*, 246, 247, 256.

66. 151 Cong. Rec. S1024, at 8794, July 25, 2005; see also Major General Thomas J. Romig, "Memorandum for General Counsel of the Department of the Air Force re Draft Report and Recommendations of the Working Group to Assess the Legal, Policy, and Operational Issues Related to Interrogation of Detainees Held by the U.S. Armed Forces in the War on Terrorism," March 3, 2003, reprinted in Karen J. Greenberg, ed., *The Torture Debate in America* (New York: Cambridge University Press, 2005), 387.

67. *Id.*, at 8796; see also Major General Jack Rives, "Memorandum for SAF/GC, re Final Report and Recommendations of the Working Group to Assess the Legal, Policy and Operational Issues Relating to Interrogations of Detainees Held by the U.S. Armed Forces in the War on Terror," Feb. 5, 2003, reprinted in *Torture Debate*, 378.

68. *Id.*, at 8794; see also Brigadier General Kevin M. Sandkuhler, "Memorandum for General Counsel of the Air Force, re Working Group Recommendations on Detainee Interrogations," Feb. 27, 2003, reprinted in *Torture Debate*, 383.

69. *Id.*, at 8795; see also Rear Admiral Michael F. Lohr, "Memorandum for General Counsel of the Air Force, re Working Group Recommendations Relating to Interrogation of Detainees," Feb. 6, 2003, reprinted in *Torture Debate*, 382; Rear Admiral Michael F. Lohr, "Memorandum for the Air Force General Counsel, re Comments on the 6 March 2003 Detainee Interrogation Working Group Report," March 13, 2003, reprinted in *Torture Debate*, 390.

70. "Working Group Report," 62–65.

71. Jess Bravin, "Pentagon Report Set Framework for Use of Torture," *Wall Street Journal*, June 7, 2004, A01.

72. "The State Department wasn't just on the back of the bus—it was left off the bus." Jane Mayer, "The Memo," *The New Yorker,* Feb. 27, 2006 (quoting Alberto Mora).

73. U.S. Department of State, Country Reports on Human Rights Practices—Turkey 2004, 2002, 2001, available at http://www.state.gov/g/drl/rls/hrrpt/2004/41713.htm; http://www.state.gov/g/drl/rls/hrrpt/2002/18396.htm; http://www.state.gov/g/drl/rls/ hrrpt/2001/eur/8358.htm.

74. U.S. Department of State, Country Reports on Human Rights Practices—China 2003, available at http://www.state.gov/g/drl/rls/hrrpt/2003/27768.htm.

75. U.S. Department of State, Country Reports on Human Rights Practices—Iran 2004, available at http://www.state.gov/g/drl/rls/hrrpt/2004/41721.htm.

76. U.S. Department of State, Country Reports on Human Rights Practices—Jordan 2003, available at http://www.state.gov/g/drl/rls/hrrpt/2003/27930.htm. See also 2002 Report, available at http://www.state.gov/g/drl/rls/hrrpt/2002/18279.htm; 2001 Report, available at http://www.state.gov/g/drl/rls/hrrpt/2001/nea/8266.htm.

77. U.S. Department of State, Country Reports on Human Rights Practices—Burma 2002, available at http://www.state.gov/g/drl/rls/hrrpt/2002/18237.htm; see also Country Reports on Human Rights Practices—Burma 2003, available at http://www.state.gov/g/ drl/rls/hrrpt/2003/27765.htm.

78. For a list of some of the other countries criticized by the State Department for engaging in practices authorized by the torture memo, see Human Rights Watch, "Descriptions of Techniques Allegedly Authorized by the CIA," available at http://hrw.org/english/ docs/2005/11/21/usdom12071_txt.htm.

79. Secretary of Defense Donald Rumsfeld, "Memorandum of the Commander, US Southern Command, re Counter-Resistance Techniques in the War on Terrorism," April 16, 2003, reprinted in *Torture Papers,* 360–62.

80. The rules governing interrogations in Afghanistan remain classified and have not been disclosed. On March 10, 2005, however, Vice Admiral Albert T. Church, the naval inspector general, completed a comprehensive review of interrogation operations in Afghanistan, Iraq, and Guantánamo. Only the Executive Summary has been made available to the public, but that summary describes the migration of interrogation practices from Cuba to Afghanistan, including the practices authorized in Secretary Rumsfeld's April 2003 order. See Naval Inspector General, Vice Admiral Albert T. Church, III, Report on Department of Defense Interrogation Operations, "Executive Summary," March 10, 2005, at 6–7, available at http://www.defenselink.mil/news/ Mar2005/d20050310exe.pdf.

81. Acting Assistant Attorney General Daniel Levin, "Memorandum for Deputy Attorney General James B. Comey, re Legal Standards Applicable Under 18 U.S.C. §§ 2340-2340A," Dec. 30, 2004, at 8, available at http://www.usdoj.gov/olc/dagmemo.pdf. For a discussion of the debate within the Administration over the creation of this memo, see Daniel Klaidman, "Palace Revolt."

82. *Id.,* at 16–17.

83. *Id.,* at 2 and n. 8.

Chapter Six: "The More Subtle Kind of Torment"

1. *Al Odah v. United States,* No. 02-5251, Transcript of Proceedings in the United States Court of Appeals for the District of Columbia Circuit, at 45 (Dec. 2, 2002).

2. President George W. Bush, remarks in Louisiana, Dec. 3, 2002, available at http://www.whitehouse.gov/news/releases/2002/12/20021203-4.html; Brian Ross and Richard Esposito, "Sources Tell ABC News Top Al Qaeda Figures Held in Secret Prisons," ABC News, Dec. 5, 2005, http://abcnews.go.com/WNT/Investigation/story?id= 1375123.

3. Bush, remarks in Louisiana.

4. Transcript of Deposition by Colonel Frank C. Schwable, reprinted in Appendix C, Raymond Lech, *Broken Soldiers* (Urbana: University of Illinois Press. 2000), 307.

5. Lech, *Broken Soldiers,* 177–78; "Red Germ Charges Cite 2 U.S. Marines," *New York Times,* Feb. 23, 1953, at 3.

6. Associated Press, "Clark Denounces Germ War Charges," *New York Times,* Feb. 24, 1953, at 2.

7. Document A/C.1/L.37 at 12, *United Nations Agenda Item 73: Question of Impartial Investigation of Charges of Use by United Nations Forces of Bacteriological Warfare,* reproduced in United Nations General Assembly Official Records, Seventh Session Annexes, vol. 2 (New York: Oct. 14, 1952–Aug. 28, 1953) (Agenda Item 73); Brody Greenwald, "False Confessions: The Past and Present of Coercive Interrogations," December 2005, 13 (unpublished manuscript on file with author).

8. A. M. Rosenthal, "Germ War Inquiry Demanded of Reds," *New York Times,* March 28, 1953, at 3.

9. Rosenthal, "Germ War."

10. Ambassador Henry Cabot Lodge, remarks at United Nations General Assembly, 462nd Plenary Meeting, 348, Nov. 30, 1953.

11. *Id.,* at 346; Philip Chinnery, *Korean Atrocity! Forgotten War Crimes* 1950–1953 (Shrewsbury, England: Airlife, 2000), 71.

12. A number of sources recount the horrors of this period. See, e.g., *id.* at 346–59; *Hearing Before the Subcommittee on Korean War Atrocities of the Permanent Subcommittee on Investigations of the Committee on Government Operations,* 83rd Cong., 1st Sess., Parts A-C (December 2–4, 1953); S. Rep. 848, 83rd Cong., 2d Sess. (subcommittee's report on Korean War atrocities); Lech, *Broken Soldiers.*

13. Chinnery, *Korean Atrocity!* at 349.

14. Document A/C.1/L.66 at 7–8, *United Nations Agenda Item 24: Question of Impartial Investigation of Charges by United Nations Forces of Bacterial Warfare,* reproduced in U.N. General Assembly Official Records, 8th Session Annex, New York, 1953 (Agenda Item 24); Greenwald, "False Confessions," 21.

15. Agenda Item 24, 7–9.

16. Lech, *Broken Soldiers,* 171.

17. Colonel Frank H. Schwable Case, Marine Corps Court of Inquiry, Findings Number 57, United States Marine Corps (April 27, 1954), reprinted in "Text of Inquiry Findings on

Marine Col. Schwable and Commentary by Defense Officials," *New York Times,* April 28, 1954, 16.

18. Agenda Item 24, 5–11; Greenwald, "False Confessions," 25.

19. Jane Mayer, "The Experiment," *New Yorker,* July 11 and 18, 2005, at 70–71 ("Sleep deprivation was such a common technique . . . that the interrogators called the process of moving detainees every hour or two from one cell to another 'the frequent-flier program.' ").

20. Agenda Item 24, at 9, 11; Greenwald, "False Confessions," 25–26.

21. Agenda Item 24, at 4–10; Greenwald, "False Confessions," 26–27.

22. Lech, *Broken Soldiers,* 171; Robert Alden, "Two Tried Suicide Under Red Torture," *New York Times,* Sept. 7, 1953, 2.

23. Agenda Item 24, at 4–11; Greenwald, "False Confessions," 23.

24. Agenda Item 24, at 4.

25. *Id.,* at 4–6; Lech, *Broken Soldiers,* 172.

26. Associated Press, "Ex-POW Describes Red Brainwashing," *New York Times,* Feb. 26, 1954, at 2.

27. Elie Abel, "3 Testify Germ War 'Confessor' Seemed to Be Not in Right Mind," *New York Times,* Feb. 20, 1954, at 1.

28. *Id.;* Lech, *Broken Soldiers,* 240.

29. Agenda Item 24, at 6, 8–9; "Freed Fliers Say Reds Sought Germ-War Confessions," *Washington Post,* Sept. 1, 1953, at 6; Greenwald, "False Confessions," 19–20.

30. Lech, *Broken Soldiers,* 170–71, 174.

31. Indeed, a number of airmen who were subjected to physical, rather than only psychological abuse, *did not* confess. Lieutenant Col. Thomas Harrison, for instance, was subjected to water-boarding, the same technique now authorized for use by the CIA. On one occasion, he collapsed during a water-boarding session and his captors revived him by searing his skin with a cigarette. Another airman was beaten repeatedly, dragged across the floor, and lifted by his head and ears. Another said the Koreans tied his feet to one end of a house and his arms to the other. They did not confess. See "Freed Fliers," *Washington Post;* Greenwald, "False Confessions," 18–19.

32. Michael Hirsh, John Barry, and Daniel Klaidman, "A Tortured Debate," *Newsweek,* June 21, 2004, at 52.

33. Human Rights Watch, "The United States' 'Disappeared': The CIA's Long-Term 'Ghost Detainees,' " "Annex VII Eleven Detainees in Undisclosed Locations," October 2004, available at http://www.hrw.org/backgrounder/usa/us1004/; Hirsh, Barry, and Klaidman, "Tortured Debate," 52; Stephen F. Hayes, "Case Closed: The U.S. Government's Secret Memo Detailing Cooperation Between Saddam Hussein and Osama bin Laden," *Weekly Standard,* Nov. 24, 2003, at 23 (reviewing an October 2003, sixteen-page government memo linking Iraq to al-Qaeda, though not mentioning al Libi by name).

34. Douglas Jehl, "High Qaeda Aide Retracted Claim of Link with Iraq," *New York Times,* July 31, 2004, at 1; President George W. Bush, Remarks on Iraq, Cincinnati, Ohio, Oct. 7, 2002, available online at http://www.whitehouse.gov/news/releases/2002/10/20021007-8.html.

35. Secretary of State Colin Powell, Address to the U.N. Security Council, Feb. 5, 2003, available at http://www.whitehouse.gov/news/releases/2003/02/20030205-1.html.

36. "We conclude that the Intelligence Community was dead wrong in almost all of its prewar judgments about Iraq's weapons of mass destruction. This was a major intelligence failure." See Commission on the Intelligence Capabilities of the United States Regarding Weapons of Mass Destruction, letter to President George W. Bush Transmitting the Commission's Final Report, March 31, 2005, available at http://www.wmd.gov/trans mittal_letter.pdf.

37. Human Rights Watch, "The United States 'Disappeared,' " quoting Michael Isikoff, "Iraq and Qaeda: Forget the 'Poisons and Deadly Gases,' " *Newsweek,* July 5, 2004, at 6. *Newsweek* reported that "[s]ome officials now suspect that al Libi, facing aggressive interrogation techniques, had previously said what U.S. officials wanted to hear."

38. See *Hearing Before the Subcommittee on Korean War Atrocities of the Permanent Subcommittee on Investigations of the Committee on Government Operations,* 83rd Cong. 1st Sess., Parts A-C (December 2–4, 1953); S. Rep. 848, 83rd Cong., 2d Sess.

39. Ambassador Henry Cabot Lodge, remarks at U.N. General Assembly, *supra.* Lodge read the following telegram from the North Korean foreign minister to the secretary-general, sent July 13, 1950: "In reply to your telegram of 12 July, I have the honour to inform you that the People's Army of the Democratic Republic of Korea is strictly abiding by the principles of the Geneva Convention in respect to prisoners of war." *Id.,* at 350.

40. *Id.,* at 350–51.

41. *Id.,* at 352.

42. See Alfred W. McCoy, "Cruel Science: CIA Torture and U.S. Foreign Policy," 19 *New England Journal of Public Policy* 209–217 (2004); Gayle Horn, *Torture in U.S. History* (unpublished manuscript on file with author, 2005), 1–24.

43. Executive Order 10631, 20 Fed. Reg. 6057 (Aug. 17, 1955). Eisenhower's order was amended by President Reagan to remove gender references. See Executive Order 12633, 53 Fed. Reg. 10355 March 28, 1988; see also United Press, "Red Tactics Spur Code for P.O.W.'s," *New York Times,* Aug. 14, 1955, at 1 (describing genesis of Code of Conduct and disagreement among service branches).

44. Greenwald, "False Confessions," 46–47.

45. Michael Durant, *In the Company of Heroes* (New York: G. P. Putnam's Sons, 2003), 104, 107; Greenwald, "False Confessions," 47–48.

46. Mayer, "The Experiment," 63; Department of the Army, *Army Regulation 350-30: Code of Conduct, Survival, Evasion, Resistance, and Escape Training* (Washington, D.C.: Department of the Army, 1985) ("SERE Training"), available at http://www.fas.org/irp/doddir/army/ar350-30.pdf.

47. "SERE Training," 2-7, Relationship of the Code of Conduct to the GPW. See also Mayer, "Experiment," 63–71; M. Gregg Bloche and Jonathan H. Marks, "Doing Unto Others as They Did Unto Us," *New York Times,* Nov. 14, 2005, A21. The Army modified the acronym to "Survive, Evade, Resist, Escape." See http://www.training.sfahq.com/sur vival_training.htm.

48. Mayer, "Experiment," 63–71; Greenwald, "False Confessions," 82.

49. Greenwald, "False Confessions," quoting Scott Shugar, "Hurt So Good," *Washington Monthly,* May 1988, at 11.

50. Greenwald, "False Confessions," 82–83.

51. See "Survival Training," available at http://www.training.sfahq.com/survival_train ing.htm; Mayer, "Experiment," 64.

52. "SERE Training," 9.

53. General James T. Hill, remarks at media availability, June 3, 2005, news transcript available at http://www.defense.gov/transcripts/2004/tr20040603-0810.html. ("The staff at Guantanamo, working with behavioral scientists, having gone up to our SERE school, developed a list of techniques which our lawyers decided and looked at, said were O.K. [and] I sent that list of techniques up to the Secretary . . .").

54. Vice Admiral Albert T. Church, Report on Department of Defense Interrogation Operations, "Executive Summary," available at www.defenselink.mil/news/Mar2005/d2005 0310exe.pdf, at 19; M. Gregg Bloche and Jonathan Marks, "Doctors and Interrogators at Guantanamo Bay," 353 *New England Journal of Medicine* 6, 7 (2005); Neil A. Lewis, "Red Cross Finds Detainee Abuse in Guantánamo," *New York Times,* Nov. 30, 2004, A1.

55. Mayer, "Experiment," 68; Bloche and Marks, "Doing Unto Others."

56. Mayer, "Experiment," 67; Bloche and Marks, "Doctors and Interrogators." There is some indication that interrogators at Guantánamo began to consult with Army BSCT teams early in 2002, long before their formal introduction at Camp Delta. The American Civil Liberties Union obtained a number of documents in their litigation written by BSCT team members regarding "interview strategies and training at GTMO." The text of the e-mails, however, has been redacted. See, e.g., Behavioral/Operational Consultation Team, "Memorandum to Criminal Investigation Task Force, re Assessment and Recommendations Regarding Interviewing, Debriefing, Interrogation of Al-Qaeda/ Taliban Detainees at Guantánamo Bay, Cuba (GITMO)," Feb. 13, 2002, available at https://www.aclu.org/torturefoia/released/FBI_4014_4020.pdf; Behavioral Science Consultation Team, "Memorandum to Criminal Investigation Task Force, re Behavioral Assessment of Security and Interview Strategies and Training at GTMO," March 11, 2002, available at https://www.aclu.org/torturefoia/released/FBI_4021_4030.pdf; Behavioral Consultation Team, "Memorandum to Criminal Investigation Task Force, re Behavioral Assessment of Security and Interview Strategies and Training at GTMO. Report on Consultation April 2–4, 2002," April 12, 2002, available at https://www .aclu.org/torturefoia/released/FBI_4031_4042.pdf; CITF-BSCT, "Memorandum to CITF Deputy Commander, re Consultation at GITMO July 9–11, 2002," available at https://www.aclu.org/torturefoia/released/FBI_4043_4047.pdf; BSCT, "Memorandum to CITF, re GTMO Interrogators Debrief, July 31, 2002," available at https://www .aclu.org/torturefoia/released/FBI_4048_4051.pdf.

57. Neil A. Lewis, "Interrogators Cite Doctors' Aid at Guantánamo," *New York Times,* June 24, 2005, A1.

58. Mayer, "Experiment," 69.

59. Josh White, "Documents Tell of Brutal Improvisation by GIs," *Washington Post,* Aug. 3, 2005, A1; Douglas Jehl and Tim Golden, "CIA Is Likely to Avoid Charges in Most Prisoner Deaths," *New York Times,* Oct. 23, 2005, A6.

60. Lewis Walshofer, Jr., an Army interrogator, was convicted of negligent homicide, with a maximum sentence of three years. Two other soldiers present during Mowhoush's fatal interrogation had murder charges dropped in exchange for their testimony against

Walshofer. Josh White, "U.S. Army Officer Convicted in Death of Iraqi Detainee," *Washington Post,* Jan. 23, 2006, A02.

61. Bloche and Marks, "Doing Unto Others" (quoting a memorandum from unnamed interrogator).

62. Mayer, "Experiment," 67.

63. Department of the Army, Army Field Manual 34–52, *Intelligence Interrogation* (Washington, D.C.: U.S. Government Printing Office, 1995), 1–8, available at http://www .fas.org/irp/doddir/army/fm34-52.pdf.

64. *Id.,* at 1–9.

65. Department of Defense News Release, "Guantanamo Provides Valuable Intelligence Information," June 12, 2005, available at http://www.dod.mil/releases/2005/nr20050612 -3661.html.

66. Colonel Frank H. Schwable Case, *supra;* Elie Abel, "Schwable Case Shows How Communist Torture Works," *New York Times,* March 14, 1954, E5.

67. Colonel Frank H. Schwable Case, Marine Corps Ct. of Inquiry, Statement of Gen. Lemuel C. Shepherd, Commandant, United States Marine Corps, April 27, 1954, reprinted in "Text of Inquiry Findings on Marine Col. Schwable," *New York Times,* April 28, 1954, at 16, emphasis added.

68. *Al Odah v. United States,* 321 F.3d 1134 (D.C. Cir. 2003).

69. *Gherebi v. Bush,* 374 F.3d 727, 738 (9th Cir. 2003).

70. Jess Bravin, "Pentagon Report Set Framework for Use of Torture," *Wall Street Journal,* June 7, 2004, A1.

PART THREE: OUR EXECUTIVE DOESN'T

Chapter Seven: "War Is Not a Blank Check"

1. Albert Camus, *The Plague* (New York: Modern Library, 1948), 66.

2. Quoted from an e-mail obtained by the ACLU in litigation against the Department of Defense and other government agencies under the Freedom of Information Act. E-mail (parties redacted) RE GTMO, available at http://www.aclu.org/torturefoia/ released/t3186_3187.pdf.

3. In June 2004, the FBI began an internal investigation into interrogation practices at Guantánamo. On July 9, 2004, the FBI Inspection Division sent an e-mail to all FBI personnel who had served, in any capacity, at the base. The e-mail asked agents to report whether they had seen "aggressive treatment which was not consistent with Bureau interview policy guidelines . . ." The mail was sent to 493 FBI employees, 434 of whom responded. It is not known what fraction of these agents were involved in interrogations or even in a position to observe mistreatment. Twenty-six agents said they had observed aggressive treatment of prisoners at the base. See Department of Defense, "Army Regulation 15-6: Investigation Into FBI Allegations of Detainee Abuse at Guantanamo Bay, Cuba Detention Facility," June 9, 2005 ("Schmidt Report"), available at http://www .globalsecurity.org/security/library/report/2005/d20050714report.pdf, at 1–2.

4. Quoted from two e-mails obtained by the ACLU in litigation against the Department of Defense and other government agencies under the Freedom of Information Act. E-mail

from Redacted to Redacted, August 2, 2004, available at http://www.aclu.org/torture foia/released/FBI.121504.5053.pdf; e-mail from Redacted to Redacted, July 12, 2004, available at http://www.aclu.org/torturefoia/released/FBI.121504.5054.pdf. There is no reason to believe Sergeant Lacey was involved in any of these abuses observed by the FBI at the base.

5. Quoted from an e-mail obtained by the ACLU in litigation against the Department of Defense and other government agencies under the Freedom of Information Act. E-mail from Redacted, INSD, FBI to Valerie Caproni, OGC, FBI re GTMO, August 2, 2004, available at http://www.aclu.org/torturefoia/released/FBI_4482_4483_4486.pdf.

6. Quoted from two e-mails obtained by the ACLU in litigation against the Department of Defense and other government agencies under the Freedom of Information Act. E-mail from Redacted to Redacted, Aug. 2, 2004, available at http://www.aclu.org/torturefoia/released/FBI.121504.5053.pdf.

7. Quoted from an e-mail obtained by the ACLU in litigation against the Department of Defense and other government agencies under the Freedom of Information Act. E-mail from Redacted, INSD, FBI to Valerie Caproni, OGC, FBI re GTMO, Aug. 2, 2004, available at http://www.aclu.org/torturefoia/released/FBI_4482_4483_4486.pdf.

8. Carol Leonnig and Dana Priest, "Detainees Accuse Female Interrogators," *Washington Post,* Feb. 10, 2005, A01. (Pentagon investigation confirms "numerous instances" of prisoners being smeared with fake menstrual blood.)

9. Quoted from a memorandum obtained by the ACLU in litigation against the Department of Defense and other government agencies under the Freedom of Information Act. Parties redacted, GTMO Issues for SAC Wiley, available at http://www.aclu.org/torturefoia/released/010505.html.

10. Quoted from a document obtained by the ACLU in litigation against the Department of Defense and other government agencies under the Freedom of Information Act. Hand-labeled "FBI Background," available at http://www.aclu.org/torturefoia/released/FBI_4585.pdf.

11. Quoted from an e-mail obtained by the ACLU in litigation against the Department of Defense and other government agencies under the Freedom of Information Act. E-mail from Redacted to Gary Bald, Frankie Battle, Arthur Cummings, re FWD: Impersonating FBI at GTMO, Dec. 5, 2003, available at http://www.aclu.org/torturefoia/released/FBI_3977.pdf.

12. *Id.*

13. Quoted from an e-mail obtained by the ACLU in litigation against the Department of Defense and other government agencies under the Freedom of Information Act. E-mail from Redacted to T. J. Harrington, copied to others at FBI, re instructions to GTMO interrogators, May 10, 2004, available at http://www.aclu.org/torturefoia/released/t3131_3133.pdf.

14. Neil A. Lewis, "Broad Use of Harsh Tactics Described at Cuba Base," *New York Times,* Oct. 17, 2004, A1.

15. *Id.;* Neil A. Lewis, "Guantánamo Tour Focuses on Medical Ethics," *New York Times,* Nov. 13, 2005; Mayer, "Experiment," *New Yorker,* 70–71.

16. Neil A. Lewis, "Red Cross Finds Detainee Abuse in Guantánamo," *New York Times,* Nov. 30, 2004, A1.

17. Tim Golden, "In U.S. Report, Brutal Details of 2 Afghan Inmates' Deaths," *New York Times,* May 20, 2005, A1 (quoting military police commander Captain Christopher Beiring).

18. Department of Defense, "Army Regulation 15-6: Investigation of the Abu Ghraib Detention Facility and 205th Military Intelligence Brigade," available at http://www.defenselink.mil/news/Aug2004/d20040825fay.pdf, at 63. While General Fay suggests these practices began only in December 2002, when Secretary Rumsfeld authorized their use at Camp Delta, available evidence indicates they were used in Afghanistan throughout 2002, just as they were used in Cuba long before they were officially approved. See Physicians for Human Rights, *Break Them Down: Systematic Use of Psychological Torture by U.S. Forces* (Cambridge, Mass.: Physicians for Human Rights, 2005), 21–23, 91–92.

19. Don Van Natta, Jr. and Ray Bonner, "Questioning Terror Suspects in a Dark and Surreal World," *New York Times,* March 9, 2003, A01 (quoting Colonel Roger King, spokesman for the U.S. military in Afghanistan).

20. See, e.g., Human Rights First, "Command's Responsibility: Deaths in U.S. Custody in Iraq and Afghanistan," Feb. 22, 2006, available at http://www.humanrightsfirst.info/pdf/06221-etn-hrf-dic-rep-web.pdf. As Dr. Steven Miles has shown, the failure to keep reliable records means this total almost certainly underreports the number of homicides in Iraq and Afghanistan. See Steven H. Miles, "Medical Investigations of Homicides of Prisoners of War in Iraq and Afghanistan," *MedScape General Medicine E-Journal,* July 5, 2005, available at http://www.medscape.com/viewarticle/507284.

21. Daniel Cooney, "U.N. Condemns Alleged Abuse of Afghans," Associated Press, May 22, 2005.

22. Dana Priest, "CIA Avoids Scrutiny of Detainee Treatment," *Washington Post,* March 3, 2005, A1; Douglas Jehl and Tim Golden, "CIA to Avoid Charges in Most Prisoner Deaths," *New York Times,* Oct. 23, 2005, A6. There is a slight difference between these two accounts of this incident. The *Post* reported the prisoner froze to death in his cell. The *Times,* reporting seven months later, said the CIA case officer ordered the guards to drag the prisoner outside, and that he froze to death outdoors. The quote by the unnamed government official, speculating about the prisoner's possible association with al-Qaeda, is from the *Post.* See also Dana Priest, "CIA Holds Terror Suspects in Secret Prisons," *Washington Post,* Nov. 2, 2005, A1.

23. Kate Clark, "Afghans Tell of U.S. Prison Ordeals," BBC News, July 21, 2005, available at http://news.bbc.co.uk/1/hi/world/south_asia/4648959.stm.

24. Douglas Jehl, "Army Details Scale of Abuse in Afghan Jail," *New York Times,* March 12, 2005, A1.

25. Tim Golden, "In U.S. Report, Brutal Details of 2 Afghan Inmates' Deaths," *New York Times,* May 20, 2005, A1.

26. Douglas Jehl, "Army Details Scale of Abuse in Afghan Jail," *New York Times,* Mar. 12, 2005, A01.

27. Douglas Jehl and Andrea Elliott, "Cuba Base Sent Its Interrogators to Iraqi Prison," *New York Times,* May 29, 2004, A1.

28. John Hendren and Mark Mazzetti, "Army Implicates 28 U.S. Troops in Deaths of 2 Afghan Detainees," *Los Angeles Times,* Oct. 15, 2004, A1.

29. *In Re Guantanamo Detainee Cases,* 355 F.Supp.2d 443, 465 (D.D.C. 2005) ("The government . . . has been unable to inform the Court how long it believes the war on terrorism will last. Indeed, the government cannot even articulate at this moment how it will determine when the war on terrorism has ended.")

30. Katharine Q. Seelye, "An Uneasy Routine at Cuba Prison Camp," *New York Times,* March 16, 2002, A8.

31. Katherine Q. Seelye, "Guantanamo Bay Faces Sentence of Life as Permanent U.S. Prison," *New York Times,* Sept. 16, 2002, A1, quoting prison hospital director Captain Albert Shimkus.

32. Quoted from a document obtained by the ACLU in litigation against the Department of Defense and other government agencies under the Freedom of Information Act. Summary of FBI Interview of Detainee at Guantanamo Bay (Detainee #3913–3914), Oct. 12, 2002, available at www.aclu.org/torturefoia/released/052505.

33. David Rose, "Operation Take Away My Freedom: Inside Guantanamo Bay on Trial," *Vanity Fair,* January 2004, 88.

34. James Yee, *For God and Country: Faith and Patriotism Under Fire* (New York: Public Affairs, 2005), 91.

35. Ted Conover, "In the Land of Guantanamo," *New York Times Magazine,* June 29, 2003, 40.

36. "Guantanamo Inmate Tries to Kill Himself," *St. Louis Post-Dispatch,* Jan. 7, 2004, A8; "Guantanamo Suicide Attempts Rise to 31," Associated Press, Aug. 21, 2003.

37. Yee, *For God and Country,* 101–02.

38. Rose, "My Freedom."

39. Lewis, "Red Cross Finds Detainee Abuse."

40. Physicians for Human Rights, "Break Them Down," 10.

41. Paisley Dodds, "3 Years in Operation, Guantanamo Remains," Associated Press, Jan. 10, 2005; Susan Okie, "Glimpses of Guantanamo—Medical Ethics and the War on Terror," 353 *New England Journal of Medicine* 2529, 2534 (2005).

42. Rose, "My Freedom" (quoting Captain Stephen Edmondson).

43. Rose, "My Freedom"; "Guantanamo Detainees Attempted Mass Suicide in 2003," *All Things Considered* (NPR radio broadcast, Jan. 24, 2005), available at http://www .npr.org/templates/story/story.php?storyId-4464452 (quoting statement from U.S. Southern Command).

44. "Detainees Sought Suicide En Masse," *Chicago Tribune,* Jan. 25, 2005, 1.

45. David R. Sands, "Global Support Swells for America," *Washington Times,* Sept. 14, 2001, A16.

46. Jean-Marie Colombani, "Nous Sommes Tous Americains," *Le Monde,* Sept. 12, 2001; "Chorus for Global Stand on Terrorism After US Attacks," Agence France-Presse, Sept. 12, 2001.

47. William Drozdiak, "Attack on U.S. Is Attack on All, NATO Agrees," *Washington Post,* Sept. 13, 2001, A25.

48. Clearly the war in Iraq represents another important wedge and my focus on Guantánamo is not meant to suggest otherwise. As we will see in Chapter 11, however, the prison at Guantánamo and the war in Iraq, and especially the abuses at Abu Ghraib prison, are increasingly linked in the Muslim world, becoming inseparable symbols of

American hubris. They act in tandem as powerful engines of animosity, combining to drive the U.S. ever further from the rest of the world.

49. Daniel McGrory and Martin Fletcher, "Suspects' Rights Rift," *The Times* (London), Nov. 28, 2001, 10.

50. "The Prisoner's Dilemma," *Economist*, Jan. 26, 2002.

51. Stephen Glover, "Even the SS Were Treated Better Than This," *Daily Mail*, Jan. 15, 2002, 13.

52. Ben Russell, "Straw Joins Row Over 'Torture' Pictures," *Independent*, Jan. 21, 2002, 1.

53. See U.N. High Commissioner for Human Rights, Statement on Detention of Taliban and Al Qaida Prisoners at US Base in Guantanamo Bay, Cuba, Jan. 16, 2002, available at http://www.unhchr.ch/huricane/huricane.nsf/0/C537C6D4657C7928C1256B43003E 7D0B?opendocument; Inter-American Commission on Human Rights, Decision on Request for Precautionary Measures (Detainees at Guantánamo Bay, Cuba), March 12, 2002, reprinted in 41 *International Legal Materials* 532, 533 (2002).

54. *R. v. Sec'y of State for Foreign and Commonwealth Affairs*, [2002] EWCA Civ 1598, at 107.

55. See U.N. Working Group on Arbitrary Detention, "Civil and Political Rights, Including the Question of Torture and Detention," U.N. Human Rights Commission, 59th Sess., Dec. 16, 2002, 19–21 (U.N. Doc. E/CN.4/2003/8); "US Court Decision on Guantanamo Detainees has Serious Implications for Rule of Law, Says UN Rights Expert," United Nations press release, March 12, 2003, available at http://www.unhchr.ch/huricane/ huricane.nsf/0/0C5F3E732DBFC069C1256CE8002D76C0?opendocument; European Parliament Resolution on the European Union's Rights, Priorities and Recommendations for the 59th Session of the U.N. Commission on Human Rights in Geneva (March 17 to April 25, 2003), available at http://europa.eu.int/abc/doc/off/bull/en/200301/ p102001.htm; Rights of Persons Held in the Custody of the United States in Afghanistan and Guantánamo Bay, Parliamentary Assembly Resolution No. 1340 (2003), adopted June 26, 2003.

56. Lord Johan Steyn, remarks to the British Institute of International and Comparative Law, Twenty-seventh F.A. Mann Lecture, Nov. 25, 2003, available at http://www.barhu manrights.org.uk/pdfs/FA_Mann_lecture1Dec03.pdf.

57. Lawyers Committee for Human Rights, *Assessing the New Normal* (Lawyers Committee for Human Rights, 2003), 77.

58. *Id.* at 77–78. In his address to the nation on Sept. 11, 2001, President Bush declared, "We will make no distinction between the terrorists who committed these acts and those who harbor them." Transcript available at http://www.whitehouse.gov/news/re leases/2001/09/20010911-16.html.

59. *Rasul v. Bush*, No. 03-334, Brief of the Center for Justice and Accountability *et al.* as *Amici Curiae* in Support of Petitioners, at 28 (citing BBC Monitoring, March 8, 2002, available at 2002 WL 15938703); see also Standard Bank, "Africa Newsbriefs," March 11, 2002, available at www.ed.standardbank.co.za/research/An020311.pdf.

60. Shehu Sani, "Inspiring Intolerance: U.S. Actions Send a Bad Signal to Africa," *International Herald Tribune*, Sept. 15, 2003.

61. Human Rights Watch, "In the Name of Security: Counterterrorism and Human Rights Abuses Under Malaysia's Internal Security Act," May 2004, available at

http://hrw.org/reports/2004/malaysia0504/malaysia0504.pdf (quoting "Malaysia Defends Detention Without Trial of Muslim Militants," Agence France-Presse, Sept. 9, 2003); Human Rights Watch, "Malaysia: P.M.'s Visit Puts Spotlight on Detainee Abuse," July 19, 2004, available at http://hrw.org/english/docs/2004/07/19/malays9097.htm; see also Human Rights Watch, "Detained Without Trial: Abuse of Internal Security Act Detainees in Malaysia," September 2005, available at http://hrw.org/reports/2005/malaysia0905/malaysia0905.pdf.

62. *Rasul v. Bush,* No. 03-334, Petitioners' Reply Brief, at 7, and Appendix, at 4a.

63. *Id.,* at 5a.

64. *Id.,* at 5–7, 4a–6a.

65. *Id.*

66. *Id.* at 6, 1a-6a, quoting Draft Memorandum regarding Administrative Review Procedures for Enemy Combatants in the Custody of the Department of Defense at Guantanamo Bay Naval Base, Cuba, available at http://www.defenselink.mil/news/Mar 2004/d20040303ar.pdf.

67. "Transfer of British Detainees Complete," Department of Defense news release, March 9, 2004, available at http://www.defenselink.mil/releases/2004/nr20040309-0443.html.

68. *Rasul v. Bush,* No. 03-334, *Al Odah v. United States,* No. 03-343, Brief of Hon. Nathaniel Jones *et al.* as *Amici Curiae* in Support of Petitioners, Jan. 14, 2004; see also *Rasul v. Bush,* No. 03-334, *Al Odah v. United States,* No. 03-343, Brief of Hon. John Gibbons *et al.* as *Amici Curiae* in Support of Petitioners, Oct. 3, 2003 (brief in support of petition for writ of certiorari).

69. *Rasul v. Bush,* No. 03-334, *Al Odah v. United States,* No. 03-343, Brief *Amicus Curiae* of Retired Military Officers in Support of Petitioners, Jan. 14, 2004, at 1–2, 4–30.

70. *Id.,* Brief of Former American Prisoners of War as *Amici Curiae* in Support of Petitioners, Jan. 14, 2004, at 1–3.

71. *Id.,* at 2.

72. *Id.,* at 2–3.

73. *Id.,* at 18–19.

74. *Id.,* Brief of 175 Members of Both Houses of the Parliament of the United Kingdom as *Amici Curiae* in Support of Petitioners, Jan. 14, 2004, at 2.

75. *Id.,* Diego C. Asencio, *et al.* as *Amici Curiae* in Support of Petitioners, Jan. 14, 2004, at 1–6, 13–14.

76. *Id.,* Brief of Fred Korematsu as *Amicus Curiae* in Support of Petitioners, Jan. 14, 2004, at 4. This is a history Stone was uniquely qualified to tell. See Geoffrey R. Stone, *Perilous Times: Free Speech in Wartime from the Sedition Act of 1798 to the War on Terrorism* (New York: Norton, 2004).

77. *Korematsu v. United States,* 323 U.S. 214 (1944).

78. Francis Biddle, *In Brief Authority* (Garden City, N.Y.: Doubleday, 1962), 212.

79. *Korematsu v. United States,* 584 F.Supp. 1406, 1420 (N.D. Cal. 1984).

80. *Id.,* at 1420.

81. Civil Liberties Act of 1988, Pub. L. No. 100-383, 102 Stat. 903 (1988).

82. Oral Argument for the Case of *Rasul v. Bush,* in the Supreme Court of the United States, April 20, 2004, at 3, available at http://www.supremecourtus.gov/oral_arguments/argument_transcripts/03-334.pdf.

83. *Id.,* at 26–30.

84. *Id.,* at 42–45.

85. Oral Argument for the Case of Rumsfeld v. Padilla, in the Supreme Court of the United States, April 28, 2004, at 22–23, available at http://www.supremecourtus.gov/oral_arguments/argument_transcripts/03-1027.pdf.

86. *Rasul v. Bush,* 542 U.S. 466, 487 (2004) (Kennedy, J., concurring).

87. *Id.,* at 467.

88. *Hamdi v. Rumsfeld,* 542 U.S. 507, 536 (2004).

89. *Id.,* at 541.

90. *Id.,* at 552.

91. *Id.,* at 545.

92. *Id.,* at 553.

93. *Id.,* at 544.

94. *Id.,* at 555, quoting 1 W. Blackstone, *Commentaries on the Laws of England,* 132–33 (1765).

95. "A Nation of Laws," *Buffalo News,* July 1, 2004, A10. "Justice Delivered," *Pittsburgh Post-Gazette,* July 2, 2004, A12; "Curbing Government," *Milwaukee Journal Sentinel,* June 29, 2004, A12; *Boston Globe,* June 29, 2004, A16 ("With two rulings that struck decisively at Bush Administration assertions of sweeping power over combat detainees, the Supreme Court yesterday kept the Bill of Rights from being a collateral victim of the war on terror.")

96. "Administration's Rogue Lawlessness Checked," *Ft. Lauderdale Sun-Sentinel,* July 2, A19. "High Court Upholds Basic U.S. Principles," *San Antonio Express-News,* July 3, 2004, B10; "No Blank Checks," *St. Louis Post-Dispatch,* June 29, 2004; "Rule of Law," *Houston Chronicle,* June 30, 2004, A26; "It's Called Democracy," *Los Angeles Times,* June 29, 2004, B12. See also "Justices Duly Uphold Due Process," *Atlanta Journal and Constitution,* June 29, 2004, A8 ("This is a major victory for those who believe the U.S. Constitution guarantee of due process applies all the time, during war and peace."); "Return to Balance," *Baltimore Sun,* June 29, 2004, A12 (" . . . the Supreme Court's decision provides much-needed reassurance—both at home and abroad."); "War No Excuse to Deny Suspects Their Due," *Chicago Sun-Times,* June 30, 2004, A39 ("[W]e believe, like the high court, that a state of war should never give a president a 'blank check' "); "The American Way," *Columbus Dispatch,* July 1, 2004, A6 ("Acting in Americans' best interests, the U.S. Supreme Court on Monday ruled that enemy combatants in U.S. custody have legal rights"); "The Right Decisions on Prisoners," *Rocky Mountain News,* June 29, 2004, A30 ("The two decisions leave much for the lower courts to sort out, but the high court made a welcome statement that the U.S. Constitution can't be waived"); "Detainees," *Minneapolis Star-Tribune,* June 30, 2004, A16 ("The decision is a triumph for a bedrock principle of American democracy—one that President Bush and his Administration should never have violated"); "Due Process Applies to All," *Newsday,* June 29, 2004, A32 ("Yesterday's historic Supreme Court decisions guaranteeing enemy combatants in United States custody their day in court are an important triumph for the rule of law"); "Reaffirming the Rule of Law," *New York Times,* June 29, 2004, A26 ("Fortunately, this court appears to be mindful of the mistakes of the past"); "Editorial: Court Says No, No and No," *The Oregonian,* June 29, 2004, B8 ("The justices had to push back and in-

sist on the rule of law—even when lawless enemies keep national security at risk");
"Rule of Law II," *San Diego Union-Tribune*, June 29, 2004, B6 ("In their rulings, the justices reaffirmed the most basic rights of Americans").

97. *See Hamdi v. Rumsfeld*, Civil Action No. 2:02cv439, Order (E. D. Va.) (Oct. 11, 2004); *Id.*,
Order (Oct. 5, 2004).

Chapter Eight: A Pattern of Deceit

1. As one government official put it shortly after the decision in *Rasul*, "We're not in a
good legal position. We have to minimize the heartburn." See Viveca Novak, "The
Guantanamo Detainees: Getting Heard," *Time*, July 12, 2004, 20.

2. See *Al Odah, et al. v. United States, et al.*, No. 02-CV-0828, Transcript of Telephone Conference, June 29, 2004; *id.*, Transcript of Telephone Conference, July 2, 2004.

3. *Rasul v. Bush*, 542 U.S. 466, 483 n.15 (2004).

4. See, e.g., *Al Odah, et al. v. United States, et al.*, No. 05-5064, 05-5095 through 05-5116,
Brief for the United States, et al., (D.C. Cir. Apr. 27, 2005), 11, 24.

5. Office of the Deputy Secretary of Defense, "Memorandum for the Secretary of the
Navy, re Order Establishing Combatant Status Review Tribunal," July 7, 2004
("Order"), available at http://www.defenselink.mil/news/Jul2004/d20040707review
.pdf.

6. *Enemy Prisoners of War, Detained Personnel, Civilian Internees, and Other Detainees*,
U.S. Army Regulation 190-8 (applicable to the Departments of the Army and Navy, the
Air Force, and the Marine Corps [Oct. 1, 1997]).

7. *Id.*

8. *Hamdi v. Rumsfeld*, 124 S. Ct. 2633, 2639 (internal quotations omitted; emphasis
added).

9. *Id.* at 2640–2641 ("A citizen, no less than an alien, can be part of or supporting forces
hostile to the United States or coalition partners and engaged in an armed conflict
against the United States.") (internal quotations omitted).

10. Deputy Secretary of Defense, "Order."

11. Stevenson Jacobs, "Prisoner Says Taliban Forced Him to Cook," Associated Press, Aug.
5, 2004.

12. Kathleen T. Rhem, "Reporters Offered Look Inside Combatant Status Review Tribunals," American Forces Press Service, Aug. 29, 2004, available at http://www.de
fenselink.mil/news/Aug2004/n08292004_2004082902.html.

13. *Id.*; Paisley Dodds, "Guantanamo Review Cases Pushed as Critics Attack Secretive Proceedings," Associated Press, Oct. 5, 2004.

14. *In Re Guantanamo Detainee Cases*, 355 F. Supp. 2d 443, 468–70 (D.D.C. 2005).

15. "Tunisian Tells Guantánamo Tribunal His Confession Forced by Torture," Armed
Forces Press, August 7, 2004; "Order," *supra*.

16. Corine Hegland, "Guantanamo's Grip," *National Journal*, February 3, 2006. The Defense Department says al Qahtani has implicated thirty prisoners at the base. "U.S.
Department of Defense, News Release," June 12, 2005, available at http://www
.defenselink.mil/releases/2005/nr20050612-3661.html.

17. Hegland, "Guantanamo's Grip."

18. Corine Hegland, "Empty Evidence," *National Journal,* February 3, 2006.

19. *Id.*

20. *Id.*

21. Carol D. Leonnig, "Panel Ignored Evidence on Detainee," *Washington Post,* March 27, 2005, A1.

22. *Id.*

23. Deputy Secretary of Defense, "Order," par. e: Composition of Tribunal; *id.* at par. a: Enemy Combatants; *id.* at par. g(12): Procedures.

24. Zachary Dowdy, "Debate Rages On, 'I Am a Civilian, So Why am I Being Tried in a Military Court?' " *Newsday,* Oct. 25, 2004.

25. Paisley Dodds, "Records Reveal Guantanamo Stories," Associated Press, May 23, 2005.

26. Deputy Secretary of Defense, "Order," at par. g(8): Procedures.

27. Department of Defense, "Secretary of Navy England Briefing on Combat Status Review Tribunal," July 9, 2004, press briefing transcript available at http://www.dod.mil/tran scripts/2004/tr20040709-0986.html (hereinafter "Briefing").

28. Deputy Secretary of Defense, "Order," par. g(8): Procedures.

29. Respondents' Factual Return to Petition for Writ of Habeas Corpus by Prisoner Mustafa Ait Idir, filed Oct. 27, 2004, at 13.

30. "Briefing"; Deputy Secretary of Defense, "Order," par. c: Personal Representative.

31. Corine Hegland, "Empty Evidence," *National Journal,* Feb. 3, 2006.

32. *Id.*

33. Mark Denbeaux, "Report on Guantanamo Detainees, A Profile of 517 Detainees through Analysis of Department of Defense Data," Feb. 6, 2006, available at http://law.shu.edu/news/guantanamo_report_final_2_08_06.pdf.

34. Statement of Defense Secretary Donald Rumsfeld, Jan. 27, 2002, available at http://www.dod.gov/transcripts/2002/t01282002_t0127cnr.html.

35. Denbeaux, "Report on Guantanamo Detainees," 6–7, 12.

36. *Id.,* at 17.

37. *Id.,* at 2.

38. *Id.,* at 16.

39. "U.S. Defends Guantánamo Tribunals," BBC News, Aug. 5, 2004.

40. Department of Defense Fact Sheet, "Guantánamo Detainees By The Numbers," Aug. 31, 2005, available at http://www.dod.mil/news/Aug2005/d20050831sheet.pdf; Robert Burns, "Pentagon Clears 38 Guantánamo Detainees," Associated Press, March 29, 2005.

41. James Yee, *For God and Country: Faith and Patriotism Under Fire* (New York: Public Affairs, 2005), 114.

42. Charles Savage, "Inside Guantánamo," *Miami Herald,* Aug. 24, 2003, L1 (describing the "tightly controlled media visits"). In an extended article, Jane Mayer, writing for the *New Yorker,* described the prison's reaction when an inmate tried to speak to her:

> As we reached the end of the cellblock, hysterical shouts, in broken English, erupted from a caged exercise area nearby. "Come here!" a man screamed. "See here! They are liars! . . . No sleep" he yelled. "No food! No medicine! No doctor! Everybody sick here!" A soldier near the detainee began ferociously signaling to the officials leading the tour to usher me out. As I was leaving, the detainee pointed

to his own cellblock, which was off limits to journalists, and screamed, "They are liars! Liars! Liars!"

"His English is pretty good," one official joked wanly.

Mayer, *The Experiment*, 60.

43. David Rose, *Guantánamo: The War on Human Rights* (New York: New Press, 2004), 4.
44. Adam Zagorin and Michael Duffy, "Detainee 063: Inside the Wire at GITMO," *Time,* June 20, 2005, 26.
45. Erik Saar and Viveca Novak, *Inside the Wire: A Military Intelligence Soldier's Eyewitness Account of Life at Guantánamo* (New York: Penguin, 2005), 153–54.
46. See "Inside the Wire: A Military Intelligence Soldier's Eyewitness Account of Life at Guantanamo," interview with Erik Saar by Democracy Now!, May 4, 2005, available at http://www.democracynow.org/article.pl?sid=05/05/04/1342253.
47. Steve Goldstein, "Specter Criticizes Defense After Rebuff at Guantanamo," *Philadelphia Inquirer,* Aug. 25, 2005. After the visit, Specter said that the military's position had moved him closer to joining the call for an independent commission into the Administration's detention practices.
48. *Baker v. United States of America,* First Amended Complaint, No. 05-221-JMH (E. D. Ky. 2005); "G.I. Attacked During Training," *60 Minutes II,* CBS television broadcast, Nov. 3, 2004, available at http://www.cbsnews.com/stories/2004/11/02/60II/main652953 .shtml.
49. "G.I. Attacked During Training."
50. *Baker,* 19-36; "G.I. Attacked During Training"; Associated Press, "Army Now Says G.I. Was Beaten in Role," *New York Times,* June 9, 2004, A8; Associated Press, "Soldier's Injuries Spur Criminal Probe; Army to Investigate Beating of Man Posing as a Detainee," *Washington Post,* June 15, 2004, A18.
51. Michael Hirsh, John Barry, and Daniel Klaidman, "A Tortured Debate," *Newsweek,* June 21, 2004, 50–53; Hayes, "Case Closed," *supra.*
52. Douglas Jehl, "Report Warned Bush Team About Intelligence Doubts," *New York Times,* Nov. 6, 2005, A1. As we will see in Chapter 9, the Defense Intelligence Agency had concluded as early as February 2002—more than a year before Powell's presentation to the U.N. and eight months before the president's speech in Cincinnati—that al Libi was not credible. In addition, though it relied on al Libi's confession in the run up to the Iraq war, the Administration did not reveal that his most specific assertions of a link between al-Qaeda and Iraq had been made during Egyptian interrogations. See Douglas Jehl, "Qaeda-Iraq Link U.S. Cited Is Tied to Coercion Claim," *New York Times,* Dec. 9, 2005, A01.
53. Similar deceptions have taken place in Iraq. In one case, the military reported that a prisoner at a forward operating base died of "natural causes . . . in his sleep." But at his funeral, a family member photographed injuries to his abdomen, arms, and wrists. Only after news agencies began to focus on the case did the public learn the prisoner had been beaten in U.S. custody and that he died after guards gagged him and tied him to the top of his cell door. A revised death certificate called the death a homicide caused by "blunt force injuries and asphyxia." Human Rights Watch, *The Road to Abu Ghraib,* June 2004 (available at http://hrw.org/reports/2004/usa0604/ (describing death of

Karim 'Abd al-Jalil). On another occasion, U.S. soldiers took an Iraqi man from his home. Months later, his family found him comatose in an Iraqi hospital. A U.S. medical report said that heat stroke had triggered a heart attack, which in turn caused the prisoner to lapse into a coma. How he got to the Iraqi hospital was not explained, nor was the prisoner's three skull fractures, his broken thumb, or the burns on the bottom of his feet. Ian Fisher, "Searing Uncertainty for Iraqi's Missing Loved Ones," *New York Times* (June 1, 2004). In still another case, a medic at Abu Ghraib prison inserted a catheter into the body of a prisoner who had been beaten to death in order to create the false impression that he had been alive when he left the prison. Jackie Spinner, "MP Captain Tells of Efforts to Hide Details of Detainee's Death," *Washington Post,* June 25, 2004, A18.

54. Kenneth Roth, Executive Director, Human Rights Watch, Letter to President George W. Bush, July 29, 2005, available at http://hrw.org/english/docs/2005/07/29/usdom11519.htm.

55. Bradley S. Klapper, "U.N.: U.S. Stalling on Guantanamo Request," Associated Press, June 23, 2005. The resistance to a visit by Manfred Nowak, the U.N. special rapporteur on torture, no doubt has something to do with his statement to the 61st U.N. Commission on Human Rights in Geneva, on April 4, 2005, where he repeated his request to visit Guantánamo Bay and made these pointed remarks:

> The absolute and non-derogable nature of the prohibition of torture and ill-treatment, which emerged after World War II in response to the Nazi Holocaust, unfortunately, did not lead to the universal eradication of torture. But Governments which practised, condoned or tolerated torture or ill-treatment, in fact have been well aware that they were violating a binding universal norm which has been firmly established in both treaty and customary law. For the first time since World War II, this important consensus of the international community seems to have been called into question by some Governments in the context of their counter-terrorism strategies. As my predecessor, I am deeply concerned about any attempts to circumvent the absolute nature of the prohibition of torture and other forms of ill-treatment in the name of countering terrorism. These attempts include, inter alia, narrow interpretations of the terms torture, cruel, inhuman or degrading treatment or punishment . . . attempts at evading the application of domestic or international human rights law by detaining and interrogating suspected terrorists abroad, by outsourcing interrogations with torture methods to private contractors or by returning suspected terrorists to countries which are well-known for their systematic torture practices; and attempts to admit confessions made under torture abroad as evidence in domestic judicial proceedings.

See Manfred Nowak, "Statement of the Special Rapporteur on Torture, Manfred Nowak to the 61st Session of the U.N. Commission on Human Rights," April 4, 2005, available at http://www.unchr.info/61st/docs/0404-Item11-SR%20Torture.pdf.

56. Richard Waddington, "U.N. Envoys Reject Guantanamo Visit," Reuters, Nov. 18, 2005, available at http://www.ezilon.com/information/article_13885.shtml.

57. Tim Golden & Eric Schmitt, "A Growing Afghan Prison Rivals Bleak Guantánamo," *New York Times,* Feb. 26, 2006, A01.

58. *Id.*

59. Carlotta Gall, "U.N. Monitor of Afghan Rights Accuses U.S. on Detentions," *New York Times,* April 23, 2005, A4; Warren Hoge, "Lawyer Who Told of U.S. Abuses at Afghan Bases Loses U.N. Post," *New York Times,* April 30, 2005, A7.

60. James Risen, *State of War: The Secret History of the CIA and the Bush Administration* (New York: Free Press, 2006), 21.

61. *Id.,* at 31.

62. Dana Priest, "CIA Holds Terror Suspects in Secret Prisons," *Washington Post,* Nov. 2, 2005, A1; Dana Priest and Scott Higham, "At Guantanamo, a Prison Within a Prison; CIA Has Run a Secret Facility for Some Al Qaeda Detainees, Officials Say," *Washington Post,* Dec. 17, 2004, A1.

63. Brian Ross and Richard Esposito, "Exclusive: Sources Tell ABC News Top Al Qaeda Figures Held in Secret Prisons," ABC News, Dec. 5, 2005, http://abcnews.go.com/WNT/Investigation/story?id=1375123.

64. Priest, "CIA Holds Terror Suspects"; "Profile: Al-Qaeda 'kingpin,'" BBC, March 5, 2003, available at http://news.bbc.co.uk/2/hi/south_asia/2811855.stm. Some published reports have indicated that Ibn Shaykh al Libi and Ramzi Binalshibh were at one time held at the CIA facility at Guantánamo Bay. See, e.g., Douglas Jehl, "Qaeda-Iraq Link U.S. Cited Is Tied to Coercion Claim," *New York Times,* Dec. 9, 2005, A1; Jane Mayer, "Outsourcing Torture," *New Yorker,* Feb. 14, 2005, 106 (both stating that al Libi was at Guantánamo); "Sept. 11 Alleged Coordinator Ramzi Binalshibh at Guantanamo," *Daily Times* (Pakistan), March 2, 2004, available at http://www.dailytimes.com.pk/default.asp?page-story_2-3-2004_pg7_53. The Administration refuses to confirm or deny these reports. Given the extraordinary efforts taken to shield CIA prisoners from judicial and public scrutiny, it is inconceivable that these prisoners remain at the base, if in fact they were once there.

65. Carlotta Gall, "Rights Group Reports Afghanistan Torture," *New York Times,* Dec. 19, 2005, A14.

66. Brian Ross and Richard Esposito, "CIA's Harsh Interrogation Techniques Described," ABC, Nov. 18, 2005, http://abcnews.go.com/WNT/Investigation/story?id=1322866.

67. Risen, *State of War,* 32.

68. Ross and Esposito, "Harsh Interrogation Techniques."

69. Dana Priest, "CIA Puts Harsh Tactics on Hold," *Washington Post,* June 27, 2004, A1; John F. Burns, "In Pakistan's Interior, A Troubling Victory In Hunt for Al Qaeda," *New York Times,* April 14, 2002, A20.

70. Risen, *State of War,* 32; Ross and Esposito, "Harsh Interrogation Techniques."

71. Douglas Jehl and Eric Lichtberg, "Shift on Suspect is Linked to Role of Qaeda Figures," *New York Times,* Nov. 24, 2005, A1; see also David Johnston and Don Van Natta, Jr., "Account of Plot Sets Off Debate Over Credibility," *New York Times,* June 17, 2004, A1.

72. Don Van Natta, Jr., "Questioning Terror Suspects In a Dark and Surreal World," *New York Times,* March 9, 2003, A1; Eric Schmitt and Douglas Jehl, "Qaeda Operative in Southeast Asia Has Fled U.S. Jail in Afghanistan," *New York Times,* Nov. 3, 2005, A12; Eric Schmitt and Tim Golden, "Details Emerge on a Brazen Escape in Afghanistan," *New York Times,* Dec. 4, 2005, A1.

73. See Letter of Abraham D. Sofaer to Hon. Patrick J. Leahy, Jan. 21, 2005, available at

http://www.humanrightsfirst.org/us_law/etn/pdf/sofaer-leahy-cat-art16-093005.pdf;
see also David Luban, "Torture, American-Style," *Washington Post,* Nov. 27, 2005,
B01.

74. Jane Mayer, "A Deadly Interrogation: Can the CIA Legally Kill a Prisoner?" *New Yorker,*
Nov. 14, 2005, 44.

75. Dana Priest, "At Guantanamo, a Prison Within a Prison."

76. Dana Priest, "Senate Urged to Probe CIA Practices; Intelligence Panel Should Examine
Use of Rendition, Rockefeller Says," *Washington Post,* April 22, 2005, A02.

Chapter Nine: "Finding Someone Else to Do Your Dirty Work"

1. *Habib, et al. v. Bush, et al.,* Respondents' Factual Return to Petition for Writ of Habeas
Corpus, No. 02-CV-1130 (D.D.C. October 4, 2004).

2. Megan K. Stack and Bob Drogin, "Detainee Says U.S. Handed Him Over for Torture,"
Los Angeles Times, Jan. 13, 2005, A1; Raymond Bonner, "Detainee Says He Was Tortured
in U.S. Custody," *New York Times,* Feb. 13, 2005, A1. The information regarding Mamdouh is also based on personal conversations he and I had after he left Guantánamo.

3. Stack and Drogin, "U.S. Handed Him Over"; Bonner, "He Was Tortured."

4. *Habib, et al. v. Bush, et al.,* No. 02-CV-1130, Declaration of Joseph Margulies in Support
of Application for Temporary Restraining Order (D.D.C. November 24, 2004), 3–4; *id.,*
Affidavit of Counsel Correcting Record (D.D.C. April 27, 2005), 1–2.

5. Declaration of Joseph Margulies, 2–3.

6. *Dateline: The Trials of Mamdouh Habib,* SBS television broadcast, July 7, 2004, transcript available at http://news.sbs.com.au/dateline/index.php?page=archive&daysum=
2004-07-07#.

7. Declaration of Joseph Margulies, 2–3.

8. *Id.,* at 3; see also Stack and Drogin, "U.S. Handed Him Over."

9. Declaration of Joseph Margulies, 3.

10. *Id.*

11. *Id.,* at 4.

12. *Id.,* at 4; see also Shafiq Rasul, Asif Iqbal, and Rhuhel Ahmed, "Composite Statement:
Detention in Afghanistan and Guantanamo Bay," July 26, 2004 ("Composite Statement"), available at http://www.ccr-ny.org/v2/reports/report.asp?ObjID=4bUT8
M23lk&Content=424; Jane Mayer, "Outsourcing Torture," *New Yorker,* Feb. 14, 2005,
118.

13. See U.S. Department of State, Country Reports on Human Rights Practices 2003:
Egypt, available at http://www.state.gov/g/drl/rls/hrrpt/2003/27926.htm (" . . . torture
and abuse . . . remained common and persistent"). Notably, the State Department has
repeatedly complained that the "International Committee of the Red Cross (ICRC) and
other domestic and international human rights monitors did not have access to prisons
or to other places of detention," and that the Egyptian government did not permit a
visit by the U.N. Special Rapporteur on Torture. *Id.* Yet for several years after September
11, the Administration refused to give the same U.N. official access to U.S. detention facilities, including Camp Delta. It has also periodically hidden some prisoners in De-

fense Department custody from the ICRC, and has flatly refused to give the ICRC access to any prisoners in CIA custody. See also, e.g., U.S. Department of State, Country Reports on Human Rights Practices 2004: Egypt ("According to the U.N. Committee Against Torture, a systematic pattern of torture by the security forces exists. . . .); U.S. Department of State, Country Reports on Human Rights Practices 2002: Egypt (" . . . numerous credible reports that security forces tortured and mistreated detainees"); U.S. Department of State, Country Reports on Human Rights Practices 2001: Egypt (" . . . numerous, credible reports that security forces tortured and mistreated citizens"); U.S. Department of State, Country Reports on Human Rights Practices 2000: Egypt (same). All of the State Department's country reports, from 1993 to 2004, are available at http://www.state.gov/g/drl/hr/c1470.htm.

14. *U.S. v. Alvarez-Machain,* 504 U.S. 655 (1992).

15. Steve Coll, *Ghost Wars* (New York: Penguin, 2005), 272–73, 377–78; Dana Priest and Barton Gellman, "U.S. Decries Abuse but Defends Interrogations," *Washington Post,* Dec. 26, 2002, A1; Douglas Jehl and Dennis Johnston, "Rule Change Lets CIA Freely Send Suspects Abroad to Jails," *New York Times,* March 6, 2005, A1; Shaun Waterman, "Ex-CIA Lawyer Calls for Law on Rendition," United Press International, March 8, 2005, available at http://www.washtimes.com/upi-breaking/20050307 -100706-9098r.htm; Shaun Waterman, "Rendition a Routine Practice," United Press International, March 8, 2005, available at http://www.washtimes.com/upi-breaking /20050307-071958-6783r.htm; Mayer, "Outsourcing Torture," 109–10; Katherine Rose Hawkins, *The Practice and Legality of Rendition* (unpublished manuscript on file with author), 24; *United States v. Alvarez-Machain,* 504 U.S. 655 (1992); see also *Alvarez-Machain,* 504 U.S. at 657 n.2 (" . . . DEA officials had attempted to gain respondent's presence in the United States through informal negotiations with Mexican officials, but were unsuccessful. DEA officials then, through a contact in Mexico, offered to pay a reward and expenses in return for the delivery of respondent to the United States.").

16. *Sosa v. Alvarez-Machain,* 542 U.S. 692 (2004).

17. Coll, *Ghost Wars,* 377; Priest and Gellman, "U.S. Decries Abuse"; Jehl and Johnston, "Rule Change"; Mayer, "Outsourcing Torture," 109–10.

18. Priest and Gellman, "U.S. Decries Abuse"; Jehl and Johnston, "Rule Change"; Waterman, "Ex-CIA Lawyer"; Waterman, "Routine Practice." See also Mayer, "Outsourcing Torture" ("Americans could give the Egyptian interrogators questions they wanted put to the detainees in the morning . . . and get answers by the evening").

19. Mayer, "Outsourcing Torture."

20. Jehl and Johnston, "Rule Change."

21. Dana Priest, "CIA's Assurances on Transferred Suspects Doubted," *Washington Post,* March 17, 2005, A1.

22. Priest and Gellman, "U.S. Decries Abuse."

23. President George W. Bush, remarks at press conference, March 16, 2005, transcript available at http://www.whitehouse.gov/news/releases/2005/03/20050316-2.html. In a press briefing nine days before the president's press conference, White House spokesman Scott McClellan was asked, "What is it that the Uzbekis can do in interrogations that the United States of America can't do?" McClellan answered, "It is important

that we gather intelligence to protect the American people." See Scott McClellan, remarks at press briefing, March 7, 2005, transcript available at http://www.whitehouse.gov/news/releases/2005/03/20050307-2.html.

24. One exception is the case of Ibn Shaykh al Libi, who was rendered to Egypt in January 2002. Al Libi is believed to be one of the masterminds of the 9/11 hijackings. While being tortured in Egypt, al Libi falsely confessed that he had received training in Iraq in explosives and chemical weapons. Since the debacle in al Libi's case, the Administration no longer renders senior members of al-Qaeda. Al Libi's false confession, however, has not convinced the Administration that it should discontinue the rendition program. See Douglas Jehl, "Qaeda-Iraq Link U.S. Cited Is Tied to Coercion Claim," *New York Times*, Dec. 9, 2005, A01.

25. Plaintiff's Complaint, *Arar v. Ashcroft*, No. CV-00249 (E.D.N.Y. filed Jan. 22, 2004); Ahmad Abou El-Maati & Barbara Jackman, *Ahmad Abou El Maati: Chronology*, available at http://www.amnesty.ca/english/main_article_home/elmaatichronology.pdf; Abdullah Almalki & Paul Copeland, *Abdullah Almalki: Chronology*, at 10–11, available at http://www.amnesty.ca/english/main_article_home/almalkichronology.pdf.

26. Plaintiff's Complaint, *Arar v. Ashcroft*, No. CV-00249 (E.D.N.Y. filed Jan. 22, 2004); Colin Freeze, "U.S. Cited Acquaintances in Deporting Arar," *Globe & Mail* (Toronto), Jan. 23, 2004, at A1; Stephen J. Toope, Commission of Inquiry into the Actions of Canadian Officials in Relation to Maher Arar: Report of Stephen J. Toope, Factfinder (Oct. 14, 2005), available at http://www.ararcommission.ca/eng/ToopeReport_final.pdf.

27. Clifford Krauss, "Qaeda Pawn, U.S. Calls Him. Victim, He Calls Himself," *New York Times*, Nov. 15, 2003, A4; *60 Minutes II: His Year in Hell* (CBS television broadcast, Mar. 30, 2004), transcript available at http://www.cbsnews.com/stories/2004/01/21/60II/main594974.shtml; Colin Freeze, "Arar Case Began Amid Fear of Attack on Ottawa," *Globe & Mail* (Toronto), Jan. 16, 2004, A1; "Canadian Returns After Long Ordeal in Syrian and Egyptian Jails," Canadian Press Newswire, Mar. 30, 2004; Jeff Sallott, "For the First Time, Abdullah Almalki Tells His Story," *Globe & Mail* (Toronto), Aug. 27, 2005, at A1.

28. Plaintiff's Complaint, *Arar v. Ashcroft*, No. CV-00249 (E.D.N.Y., filed Jan. 22, 2004); Declaration of James B. Comey, *Arar v. Ashcroft*, No. CV-00249 ¶ 3 (E.D.N.Y., Jan. 18, 2005); Memorandum in Support of the United States' Assertion of State Secrets Privilege 11, *Arar v. Ashcroft*, No. CV-00249 (E.D.N.Y., Jan. 18, 2005). The federal court dismissed the suit on other grounds. See *Arar v. Ashcroft*, No. CV-00249, Memorandum and Order (E.D.N.Y., filed Feb. 16, 2006).

29. Dana Priest, "Wrongful Imprisonment: Anatomy of a CIA Mistake," *Washington Post*, Dec. 4, 2005, A1.

30. *Id.* More recent reporting suggests that a German police officer may have been involved in Masri's interrogation, and that the German embassy in Skopje may have been informed about Masri's abduction days after it happened. See Don Van Natta, Jr., "Germany Weighs if It Played a Role in Seizure by U.S.," *New York Times*, Feb. 21, 2006.

31. See Priest and Gellman, "U.S. Decries Abuse."

32. Dana Priest and Dan Eggen, "Terror Suspect Alleges Torture," *Washington Post*, Jan. 6, 2005, A1.

33. *Confirmation Hearing on the Nomination of Alberto Gonzales to Be Attorney General of*

the United States: Hearing Before the Senate Comm. on the Judiciary, 109th Cong., 1st sess., Jan. 6, 2005, available at http://www.washingtonpost.com/wp-dyn/articles/A53883-2005Jan6.html.

34. Convention Against Torture and Other Cruel, Inhuman or Degrading Treatment or Punishment, Art. 3, Dec. 10, 1984, S. Treaty Doc. No. 100-20, 1465 U.N.T.S. 85, emphasis added.

35. United Nations Treaty Collection, available at http://www.unhchr.ch/html/menu 2/6/cat/treaties/convention-reserv.htm.

36. Dana Priest, "CIA's Assurances on Transferred Suspects Doubted," *Washington Post,* March 17, 2005, A1; Katherine Rose Hawkins, *The Practice and Legality of Rendition* (unpublished manuscript, on file with author), 16.

37. Priest, "CIA's Assurances"; Priest and Gellman, "U.S. Decries Abuse."

38. Shannon McCaffrey, "Canadian Sent to Syrian Prison Disputes U.S. Claims Against Torture," Knight-Ridder, July 29, 2004.

39. *60 Minutes: CIA Uses Rendering to Get Information from Suspects* (CBS television broadcast, Mar. 6, 2005).

40. Meaghan Shaw, "Emotional Reunion for the Prisoner of War on Terror," *Melbourne Age,* Jan. 29, 2005, 1; Dana Priest, "Detainee Sent Home to Australia," *Washington Post,* Jan. 29, 2005, A21.

41. Raymond Bonner, "Australia Uneasy About U.S. Detainee Case," *New York Times,* April 10, 2005, A10.

42. Priest, "Anatomy of a CIA Mistake."

43. Stephen Grey and Ian Cobain, "Suspect's Tale of Travel and Torture," *Guardian,* Aug. 2, 2005; Binyam Mohammed, " 'One of Them Made Cuts in My Penis. I Was in Agony,' " *Guardian,* Aug. 2, 2005. Mohammed's account became public after the Justice Department declassified interview notes taken by Clive Stafford Smith, one of his attorneys. See Kevin Sullivan, "Detainee Alleges Abuse En Route to Guantanamo," *Washington Post,* Aug. 3, 2005, A13.

PART FOUR: THE FUTURE OF CAMP DELTA

Chapter Ten: What If He's a Shepherd?

1. Christopher Cooper, "Detention Plan: In Guantanamo, Prisoners Languish in Sea of Red Tape," *Wall Street Journal,* Jan. 26, 2005 (citing Steven Rodriguez, head of interrogations at the base).

2. KUBARK manual at 48–49.

3. *Id.;* Human Resource Manual at F-20.

4. See, e.g., *Bacha v. Bush,* 05-cv-2349, Opposition to Respondents' Motion for an Order to Show Cause Why Case Should Not Be Dismissed for Lack of Proper Next Friend Standing, Declaration of Clive Stafford Smith at ¶¶103–106 (D.D.C. Jan. 17, 2006); *Al Razak v. Bush,* 05-CV-1601 (D.D.C. Aug. 10, 2005)(same); Hasim Kabir (Sadar and Arkeen Doe), No. 05-CV-1704 (D.D.C. Dec. 12, 2005)(same).

5. *Al Odah v. United States,* No. 02-CV-0828, Plaintiffs-Petitioners' Motion for Writ of Injunction, Affidavit of Tom Wilner, at 2–3 (D.D.C. April 20, 2005).

6. "The Ones Left Behind," *Guardian,* Feb. 19, 2005. *The Guardian* reports that the military delivered thirteen letters. Other reports indicate sixteen. See "An Interview with Brent Mickum," March 31, 2005, available at http://www.cageprisoners.com/arti cles.php?id=6130; E-mail from Brent Mickum to Author, re Redactions, Mar. 11, 2006, on file with author (confirming sixteen letters redacted and delivered by military).

7. *Rasul, et al. v. Bush, et al.,* No. 02-CV-0299 and others, Transcript of Oral Argument, Dec. 1, 2004, at 25–27.

8. *Id.,* at 27–30.

9. *Id.,* at 121–22.

10. *In Re Guantanamo Cases,* 355 F. Supp. 2d 443, 463 (D.D.C. 2005).

11. *Id.,* at 472–78.

12. *Id.,* at 464.

13. "Son of Al Qaeda," *Frontline,* PBS television broadcast, April 11, 2004, transcript available at http://www.pbs.org/wgbh/pages/frontline/shows/khadr/interviews/khadr .html.

14. David Rose, *Guantánamo: The War on Human Rights* (New York: New Press, 2004), 112.

15. *Id.,* at 118.

16. Martin Bright, "Guantanamo Has 'Failed to Prevent Terror Attacks,' " *Observer,* Oct. 3, 2004.

17. Samara Kalk Derby, "How Expert Gets Detainees to Talk," *Capital Times,* Aug. 16, 2004, A1.

18. John Mintz, "Most at Guantanamo to Be Freed or Sent Home, Officer Says," *Washington Post,* Oct. 6, 2004, A16; Georg Mascolo, " 'I Was Just A Nobody,' " *Der Spiegel,* Oct. 11, 2004.

19. Christopher Cooper, "Detention Plan: In Guantanamo, Prisoners Left to Languish in Sea of Red Tape," *Wall Street Journal,* Jan. 26, 2005, A1; Tim Golden and Don Van Natta, Jr., "U.S. Said to Overstate Value of Guantánamo Detainees," *New York Times,* June 21, 2004, A1.

20. Cooper, "Prisoners Left to Languish"; Paisley Dodds, "3 Years in Operation, Guantanamo Remains," Associated Press, Jan. 10, 2005.

21. Thomas Coghlan, "Writing Poetry Was the Balm That Kept Guantanamo Prisoners from Going Mad," *San Francisco Chronicle,* July 17, 2005; James Rupert, "Finally Freed," *Newsday,* Oct. 31, 2005, A27; N. C. Aizenmann, "In a Jail in Cuba Beat the Heart of a Poet," *Washington Post,* April 24, 2005, A19.

22. Coghlan, "Writing Poetry"; Rupert, "Finally Freed"; Aizenmann, "Heart of a Poet."

23. *60 Minutes,* "Inside the Wire," CBS television broadcast, May 1, 2005, available at http://www.cbsnews.com/stories/2005/04/28/60minutes/main691602.shtml.

24. *Id.*

25. Jane Mayer, "The Experiment," *New Yorker,* July 11, 2005, 60; see also Cooper, "Prisoners Left to Languish" (fewer than a third being interrogated).

26. Cooper, "Prisoners Left to Languish."

27. Audrey Gillar, "Hunger Strikers Pledge to Die in Guantánamo," *Guardian,* Sept. 9, 2005.

28. Center for Constitutional Rights, "The Guantánamo Prisoner Hunger Strikes & Protests: February 2002–August 2005," Sept. 8, 2005, available at http://www.ccr

-ny.org/v2/legal/september_11th/docs/Gitmo_Hunger_Strike_Report_Sept_2005 .pdf; Binyam Mohammed, Statement to Habeas Counsel, Aug. 11, 2005, available at http://www.ccr-ny.org/v2/reports/report.asp?ObjID=Dt1C09XkyL&Content=619; *Majid Ab-dullah Al Jouli, et al. v. George W. Bush, et al.*, No. 05-0301 (GK), Supplemental Declaration of Julia Tarver (D.D.C. Oct. 14, 2005), available at: http://www.ccr-ny.org/v2/legal/september_11th/docs/GTMOhearing_TarverSupplementalDeclaration1 01305.pdf; Will Dunham, "U.S. Says Fewer Hunger Strikers at Guantanamo Bay," Reuters, Jan. 7, 2006; Will Dunham, "U.S. Reports Surge in Guantanamo Hunger Strike," Reuters, Dec. 30, 2005.

29. Amnesty International, "Report of Hunger Strike at Guantánamo," July 2005, available at http://web.amnesty.org/pages/stoptorture-hungerstrike-eng.

30. Vanessa Blum, "U.S. Building New Prisons for Terrorists," *Legal Times*, Oct. 4, 2004; *Almurbati, et al. v. George W. Bush, et al.*, Civil No. 04-CV-1227, Declaration of Michael Bumgarner (D.D.C. Nov. 16, 2005), at 3 ("Camp 5 is a replica of an existing state prison facility in Indiana . . .").

31. *M.C. v. George W. Bush, et al.*, Civil No. 05-430, Motion for a Preliminary Injunction Concerning Conditions of Confinement, at 10, 19–21 (D.D.C.)

32. Josh White, "Guantanamo Desperation Seen in Suicide Attempts," *Washington Post*, Nov. 1, 2005, A1.

33. "Attorney Tells Why Guantanamo Detainee Attempted Suicide in Front of Him" *Democracy Now!*, radio broadcast, Nov. 2, 2005, transcript available at http://www .democracynow.org/article.pl?sid=05/11/02/1546249.

34. *Almurbati, et al. v. George W. Bush, et al.*, Civil No. 04-CV-1227, Memorandum of Law in Support of Motion for Temporary Restraining Order and Preliminary Injunction (D.D.C. Nov. 1, 2005); *Almurbati, et al. v. George W. Bush, et al.*, Civil No. 04-CV-1227, Declaration of Michael Bumgarner (D.D.C. Nov. 16, 2005); Edward H. White, Trial Attorney, U.S. Department of Justice, Letter to Joshua Colangelo-Bryan, re *Almurbati, et al. v. George W. Bush, et al.*, Dec. 15, 2005.

35. Susan Okie, "Glimpses of Guantanamo—Medical Ethics and the War on Terror," 353 *New England Journal of Medicine* 2529, 2534 (2005).

36. Department of Defense, "Army Regulation 15-6: Investigation Into FBI Allegations of Detainee Abuse at Guantanamo Bay, Cuba Detention Facility," June 9, 2005, 17–18 ("Schmidt Report"), available at http://www.globalsecurity.org/security/library/report/2005/d20050714report.pdf.

37. *Id.*, at 9–10.

38. *Id.*, at 6, 10, 22.

39. *Id.*, at 6–8.

40. *Id.*, at 11.

41. "Fact Sheet: Media Information, Guantanamo Bay, Cuba," JTF Public Affairs, May 2004, at 1, available at http://www.defenselink.mil/news/Aug2004/d20040818PK.pdf.

42. Schmidt Report, at 23.

43. *Id.*, at 24.

44. *Id.*, at 24–25.

45. *Id.*, at 25.

46. *Id.*, at 25.

47. *Id.,* at 25–26.

48. *Id.,* at 20.

49. Josh White, "Abu Ghraib Tactics Were First Used at Guantanamo," *Washington Post,* July 14, 2005, A1.

50. *Bourmediene, et al. v. Bush, et al.,* No. 05-5062; *Al Odah, et al. v. United States, et al.,* No. 05-5064, Transcript of Proceedings (D.C. Cir. Sept. 8, 2005), at 5, 17, 27.

51. *Id.,* at 36, 41.

Chapter Eleven: Asking Why

1. *Hirabayashi v. United States,* No. 870 (1942) (unpublished draft) (reprinted in Dennis J. Hutchinson, " 'The Achilles Heel' of The Constitution: Justice Jackson and The Japanese Exclusion Cases," 2002 *Supreme Court Review* 455, 468).

2. Jacobus tenBroek, Edward N. Barnhart, Floyd W. Matson, *Prejudice, War and the Constitution* (Berkeley: University of California Press, 1958), 83 (quoting *Monterey Press Herald,* Jan. 30, 1942). For a discussion of the same quote, see G. Edward White, *Earl Warren: A Public Life* (New York: Oxford University Press, 1982) (quoting Associated Press news release, Jan. 30, 1942).

3. tenBroek et al., *Prejudice,* 83–84 (quoting proceedings of a conference of sheriffs and district attorneys called by Attorney General Earl Warren on the subject of Alien Law Enforcement [Feb. 2, 1942, 3–7]). See also Ed Cray, *Chief Justice: A Biography of Earl Warren* (New York: Simon & Schuster, 1997), 115–23, 157–59. As late as June 1943— more than a year after the decisive victory at Midway Island—Warren continued to warn that allowing the Japanese to return to their homes "would be laying the groundwork for another Pearl Harbor." *Id.,* at 157.

4. Earl Warren, *The Memoirs of Earl Warren* (Garden City, N.Y.: Doubleday, 1977), 149. Others who had played pivotal roles in the internments expressed similar regrets. See "Summary of Report of the Commission on Wartime Relocation and Internment of Civilians," December 1982, reprinted in Peter Irons, ed., *Justice Delayed: The Record of the Japanese American Internment Cases* (Middletown, Conn.: Wesleyan University Press, 1989), 120; see also Geoffrey R. Stone, *Perilous Times: Free Speech In Wartime* (New York: Norton, 2004).

5. White, *Earl Warren,* 77.

6. For an account of the invective hurled at Warren, including the placards and billboards throughout the country calling for his impeachment, see Cray, *Chief Justice,* 387–92. In his memoirs, Warren claimed not to be overly bothered by the uproar (Warren, *Memoirs,* 303–6).

7. *United States v. Robel,* 389 U.S. 258, 263–64 (1967) (quoting *Home Building & Loan Ass'n. v. Blaisdell,* 290 U.S. 398, 426 [1934]).

8. *Hirabayashi v. United States,* 320 U.S. 81 (1943). By the time the Court decided *Korematsu,* Jackson had seen enough of wartime excess, and he dissented in *Korematsu.* See *Korematsu v. United States,* 323 U.S. 214, 242 (1944) (Jackson, J., dissenting); Hutchinson, *Achilles Heel,* 456.

9. Melvin I. Urofsky, "The Brandeis-Frankfurter Conversations," 1985 *Supreme Court Review* 299, 324. See also, e.g., *Schenck v. United States,* 249 U.S. 47, 52 (1919) ("We admit

that in many places and in ordinary times the defendants in saying all that was said in the circular would have been within their constitutional rights. . . . [But w]hen a nation is at war many things that might be said in time of peace are such a hindrance to its effort that their utterance will not be endured so long as men fight and that no Court could regard them as protected by any constitutional right.").

10. Spatial disorientation is a well-recognized phenomenon. Among others, the U.S. Air Force Research Lab maintains an elaborate Web site dedicated to providing information about SD. See http://www.spatiald.wpafb.af.mil/index.aspx. Michael Baker, technical editor of *Flying Safety,* authored a primer about SD: "In one of the most common—and dangerous—varieties of SD, the pilot doesn't know that he doesn't know which way is up. It is said there are two types of pilots: Those who have experienced SD and those who don't know they've experienced SD." See also Michael Baker, "A Primer on Spatial Disorientation," *Flying Safety,* July 1998, available at http://www .spatiald.wpafb.af.mil/There_Was.aspx?NID=1. The National Transportation Safety Board concluded that the "probable cause" of Kennedy's fatal accident was "[t]he pilot's failure to maintain control of the airplane during a descent over water at night, which was a result of spatial disorientation." "NTSB Releases Final Report on Investigation of Crash of Aircraft Piloted by John F. Kennedy, Jr.," *National Transportation Safety Board News,* July 6, 2000, available at http://www.ntsb.gov/pressrel/2000/000706.htm.

11. This is the thrust of Lincoln's famous speech to Congress, July 4, 1861, at which he defended his controversial decision to suspend the writ of habeas corpus with the rhetorical question, "Are all the laws, but one, to go unexecuted, and the government itself go to pieces, lest that one be violated?" See Message to Congress in Special Session, July 4, 1861, in Roy P. Basler, ed., *The Collected Works of Abraham Lincoln* (New Brunswick, N.J.: Rutgers University Press, 1953–55), 4:430. Notably, in his memo describing the breadth of the president's war power, John Yoo quoted another variant of this proposition: "Is it possible to lose the nation and yet preserve the Constitution?" See John Yoo, "Memorandum Opinion for Timothy Flanigan re The President's Constitutional Authority to Conduct Military Operations Against Terrorists and Nations Supporting Them," Sept. 25, 2001, reprinted in *The Torture Papers: The Road to Abu Ghraib,* ed. Karen J. Greenberg and Joshua L. Dratel (New York: Cambridge University Press, 2005), 4, n.1 (quoting *Youngstown Sheet & Tube Co. v. Sawyer,* 343 U.S. 579, 662 [1952] [Clark, J., concurring in judgment] [quoting Letter of April 4, 1864, to A. G. Hodges, in *The Complete Works of Abraham Lincoln* (Nicolay & Hay, ed. 1894), 66]).

12. For a discussion of the general phenomenon, see, e.g., William H. Rehnquist, *All The Laws But One* (New York: Knopf, 1998); Geoffrey R. Stone, *Perilous Times: Free Speech In Wartime* (New York: Norton, 2004), 540–50; David Cole, *Enemy Aliens* (New York: New Press, 2003). For a contrary view, see Richard A. Posner, *Law, Pragmatism, and Democracy* (Cambridge, Mass.: Harvard University Press, 2003), 296–304; Richard A. Posner, "The Truth About Our Liberties," 2002 *Responsive Community* 4, 4–5. Judge Posner notes that society has historically underestimated threats to national security. The conclusions he draws from this observation, however, have been criticized by a number of writers, who accuse him of giving the right answer to the wrong question. See, e.g., Mark Tushnet, "Defending *Korematsu?*: Reflections on Civil Liberties In Wartime," 2003 *Wisconsin Law Review* 273, 275–76 ("[M]any of [Judge Posner's] exam-

ples are quite removed from the question of domestic civil liberties in wartime. Perhaps U.S. officials did underestimate the risk that the Soviet Union would install missiles in Cuba . . . , but it is quite hard to identify domestic programs . . . that could have been undertaken to diminish the assertedly underestimated risks"); Jack M. Balkin, "The Truth About Our Institutions," 2002 *Responsive Community* 92, 94 ("Our lack of preparedness for Pearl Harbor resulted from failures of diplomatic and military intelligence overseas, not too many writs of habeas corpus or an overindulgent constabulary").

13. Of course, information may emerge in the fullness of time that casts doubt on the good faith of the participants in the current debate. That would hardly be unprecedented. We learned only in 1983, for instance, that many of the justifications given by the military for the Japanese internments had in fact been untrue, and that the Justice Department had deliberately misrepresented the facts in its briefs to the Supreme Court. See Peter Irons, *Justice at War* (New York: Oxford University Press, 1983). These disclosures led ultimately to the judicial decisions vacating the convictions of Fred Korematsu and Gordon Hirabayashi: *Korematsu v. United States,* 584 F. Supp. 1406 (N.D. Cal. 1984) (vacating conviction); *Hirabayashi v. United States,* 828 F.2d 591 (9th Cir. 1987) (vacating conviction for violating curfew); *Hirabayashi v. United States,* 627 F. Supp. 1445 (W.D. Wash. 1986) (vacating conviction for violating exclusion order).

Another episode, less widely known but equally unfortunate, involved the Roosevelt Administration's tenacious defense of martial law in Hawaii. Even in 1944, Admiral Chester Nimitz, commander of the Pacific Fleet, testified that "invasion by submarine commando raiders and espionage parties was imminent and constantly impending." Lieutenant General Robert Richardson, the top-ranking military official on the Islands, similarly testified that Hawaii remained critical to the defense of the entire West Coast, that the Islands remained in "imminent danger of invasion." For that reason, national security demanded that the Islands remain in the "immediate control and authority" of the military. Yet the military knew this was no longer the case. By the time Nimitz and Richardson testified, the military's own, internal, assessment was that the Islands were no longer at serious risk, and that the "national security" justification for martial law had passed. "Indeed, at the very time General Richardson and Admiral Nimitz were testifying . . . that the Hawaiian Islands remained in imminent danger of enemy attack, the War Department was preparing to reorganize its Central Pacific command, downgrading the Islands to a 'communication zone.' " As with internment, we learned of this deception only decades later, when Jane and Harry Scheiber uncovered a cache of previously undisclosed documents. See Harry Scheiber and Jane Scheiber, "Bayonets in Paradise: A Half-Century Retrospect on Martial Law in Hawai'i, 1941–1946," 19 *University of Hawaii Law Review* 477, 589 (1997).

14. Tim Golden, "After Terror, a Secret Rewriting of Military Law," *New York Times,* Oct. 24, 2004, A1.

15. Golden, "After Terror"; "Report of the Independent Panel to Review Department of Defense Detention Operations, August 2004," (Schlesinger Report), reprinted in *Torture Papers,* 923. The decision by the White House to reject the military's assessment that its troops should comply with the Geneva Conventions foreshadowed its decision several months later to reject the military's assessment of its troop needs during the war in Iraq.

See Bernard Weinraub with Thomas Shanker, "Rumsfeld's Design for War Criticized on Battlefield," *New York Times,* April 1, 2003, A1.

16. Golden, "After Terror."

17. *Id.* As we saw in Chapter 7, after he retired, Rear Admiral Guter supported our position in an important amicus brief to the Supreme Court.

18. Golden, "After Terror."

19. Cass R. Sunstein, *Why Societies Need Dissent* (Cambridge, Mass.: Harvard University Press, 2003), 145.

20. Tim Golden and Don Van Natta, Jr., "U.S. Said to Overstate Value of Guantánamo Detainees," *New York Times,* June 21, 2004, A1.

21. Quoted in Daniel Benjamin and Steve Simon, *The Next Attack: The Failure of the War on Terror and a Strategy for Getting It Right* (New York: Times Books, 2005), 60.

22. Secretary of Defense Donald Rumsfeld, "Memorandum for Gen. Dick Myers, Paul Wolfowitz, Gen. Pete Pace, Doug Feith Re: Global War on Terrorism," Oct. 16, 2003, available at http://www.usatoday.com/news/washington/executive/rumsfeld-memo .htm.

23. Jonathan S. Landay, "Bush Administration Eliminating 19-year-old International Terrorism Report," Knight Ridder Newspapers, April 16, 2005. The reports from 2000–2003 may be viewed at http://www.state.gov/s/ct/rls/pgtrpt/; the reports from prior years are available at http://www.state.gov/www/global/terrorism/annual_reports.html. A statistical compilation of the years 1982–2003 appears in the corrected version of Appendix G of the 2003 *Pattern of Global Terrorism Report,* June 22, 2004, available at http://www.state.gov/s/ct/rls/pgtrpt/2003/33777.htm.

24. Steven Komarow, "U.S. Chipping Away at Al-Qaeda Leadership, But Attacks Climbing," *USA Today,* Oct. 3, 2005, A12.

25. Carlotta Gall and Eric Schmitt, "Taliban Step Up Afghan Bombings and Suicide Attacks," *New York Times,* Oct. 21, 2005, A3; Gregg Zoroya, "Afghan Enemy Grows Fiercer," *USA Today,* Nov. 17, 2005, A1.

26. Benjamin and Simon, *The Next Attack,* 256.

27. "WMD May Never be Found—Blair," BBC News, July 6, 2004; Ed Johnson, "Blair: Guantanamo an Anomaly That Must End," Associated Press, July 6, 2004; "Blair: Guantánamo Is an Anomaly," *Guardian,* Feb. 17, 2006.

28. Benjamin and Simon, *The Next Attack,* 128; Somini Sengupta and Salman Masood, "Guantanamo Comes to Define U.S. to Muslims," *New York Times,* May 21, 2005, A1.

29. See, e.g., Pamela Hess, " 'Enemy Combatant' Added to DOD Doctrine," United Press International, April 8, 2005, available at http://washtimes.com/upi-breaking/ 20050408-043247-5208r.htm) ("For its part, the Pentagon maintains that though the Geneva Conventions do not apply to enemy combatants, the prisoners are treated humanely. It says any abuses of detainees that has occurred is the function of human failure rather than flawed policy.").

30. Stanley Milgram, *Obedience to Authority* (New York: Harper & Row, 1974), 3–4. In Milgram's experiment, "[e]ach switch was clearly labeled with a voltage designation that ranged from 15 to 450 volts . . . and verbal designations . . . Slight Shock, Moderate Shock, Strong Shock, Very Strong Shock, Intense Shock, Extreme Intensity Shock, Danger: Severe Shock." *Id.,* at 20–21, 170.

31. *Id.,* at 5, 14–16, 32–36, 59–62, 121–22. Subjects included "postal clerks, high school teachers, salesmen, engineers and laborers" of different educational backgrounds and ages. *Id.,* at 16.

32. See Craig Haney, Curtis Banks, Philip Zimbardo, "Interpersonal Dynamics in a Simulated Prison," 1973 *International Journal of Criminology and Penology* 1, 74–75; see also Philip Zimbardo, "Power Turns Good Soldiers into 'Bad Apples,' " *New York Times,* May 9, 2004, D11. The volunteers in the Stanford study were given a "background evaluation that consisted of a battery of five psychological tests, personal history and in-depth interviews." Philip G. Zimbardo, "A Situationist Perspective on the Psychology of Evil: Understanding How Good People Are Transformed into Perpetrators," in *The Social Psychology of Good and Evil,* ed. A. G. Miller (New York: Guilford Press, 2004), 39.

33. Haney, *Interpersonal Dynamics* at 74.

34. *Id.,* at 74, 80, 81; see also Zimbardo, "A Situationist Perspective," 32; Zimbardo, "Power Turns Good Soldiers into 'Bad Apples.' "

35. Zimbardo, "A Situationist Perspective on the Psychology of Evil: Understanding How Good People Are Transformed into Perpetrators," 34–35.

36. Milgram, *Obedience to Authority,* 9, 180–89.

37. David Rose, *Guantanamo: The War on Human Rights* (New York: New Press, 2004), 86.

38. William Howard Taft IV, remarks at American University, Washington College of Law, March 24, 2005, available at: http://www.humanrightsfirst.org/us_law/PDF/taft-amer -uni-32405.pdf.

Chapter Twelve: "Just Shut It Down and Then Plow It Under"

1. See, e.g., Carlotta Gall, "Protests Against United States Spread Across Afghanistan," *New York Times,* May 13, 2005, A1; Carol Leonnig, "Desecration of Koran Had Been Reported Before," *Washington Post,* May 18, 2005, A1 (correction printed May 21, 2005); Richard Serrano and John Daniszewski, "Dozens Have Alleged Koran's Mishandling," *Los Angeles Times,* May 22, 2005, A1; Eric Schmitt, "U.S. Tells How Quran Was Defiled," *San Francisco Chronicle,* June 4, 2005. The original article and the correction appear at Michael Isikoff and John Barry, "Gitmo: SouthCom Showdown," *Newsweek,* May 9, 2005, 10; Mark Whitaker, "The Editor's Desk," *Newsweek,* May 23, 2005, 6.

2. James Yee, *For God and Country: Faith and Patriotism Under Fire* (New York: Public Affairs, 2005), 110–22; Leonnig, "Desecration."

3. Serrano and Daniszewski, "Dozens Have Alleged."

4. Schmitt, "U.S. Tells How Quran Was Defiled." In 2003, the military issued orders requiring that the Koran be treated with respect.

5. Tim Golden, "In U.S. Report, Brutal Details of 2 Afghan Inmates' Deaths," *New York Times,* May 20, 2005, A1; Tim Golden, "Army Faltered in Investigating Detainee Abuse," *New York Times,* May 22, 2005, A1.

6. "Karzai Demands Custody of Detainees in Afghanistan," *New York Times,* May 22, 2005, A18; "Karzai Seeks More Control After Charges of U.S. Abuse," *Washington Post,* May 22, 2005, A20; David E. Sanger and Eric Schmitt, "Bush Deflects Afghan's Request for Return of Prisoners," *New York Times,* May 24, 2005, A12.

7. Irene Khan, Speech at Foreign Press Association, May 25, 2005, available at http://web.amnesty.org/library/Index/ENGPOL100142005.

8. See, e.g., E. J. Dionne, "Hyperbole and Human Rights," *Washington Post,* June 3, 2005, A23.

9. Thomas L. Friedman, "Just Shut It Down," *New York Times,* May 27, 2005, A23.

10. Bernard McGhee, "Carter Calls on U.S. to Shut Down Gitmo," Associated Press, June 7, 2005; The Carter Center and Human Rights First, "Promoting Human Rights and Human Security: Recommendations from The Carter Center and Human Rights First," June 7, 2005, available at http://www.cartercenter.org/doc2116.htm.

11. "Time Report Fuels Guantanamo Criticism," CNN.com, June 13, 2005.

12. *Meet The Press,* NBC television broadcast, June 12, 2005, transcript available at http://biden.senate.gov/newsroom/details.cfm?id=238924&&.

13. Transcript of Proceedings, United States Senate, Committee on the Judiciary, Detainees, June 15, 2005, 110–11.

14. "It's the Policies—Not Just the Place—That Matters," *USA Today,* June 16, 2005, A12; "Who We Are," *New York Times,* June 18, 2005, A12; "Congress Awakens," *Washington Post,* June 18, 2005, A18.

15. Christopher Cooper and Jess Bravin, "U.S. Studies How Detainees' Status Might Be Changed," *Wall Street Journal,* June 21, 2005, A6.

16. "Gitmo Debate," *Fox News Sunday,* Fox television broadcast, June 12, 2005, transcript available at http://www.foxnews.com/story/0,2933,159236,00.html.

17. Carl Hiaasen, "In Gitmo, Diet Rich in Carbs, Lean on Rights," *Miami Herald,* June 12, 2005.

18. Defense Secretary Donald Rumsfeld said, "arguably, no detention facility in the history of warfare has been more transparent or received more scrutiny than Guantanamo." See Secretary of Defense Donald Rumsfeld, remarks at Department of Defense news briefing, June 14, 2005, transcript available at http://www.defense.gov/transcripts/2005/tr20050614-secdef3042.html. Speaking in Denmark, President Bush said there was "total transparency" at the base. See President George W. Bush, remarks at press availability with Danish Prime Minister Rasmussen, July 6, 2005, transcript available at http://usinfo.state.gov/gi/Archive/2005/Jul/06-284553.html.

19. "Who We Are."

20. 151 Cong. Rec. S8836-8895, National Defense Authorization Act for Fiscal Year 2006 (daily ed., July 25, 2005).

21. *Id.,* at S8789–8790, Amendment 1557.

22. *Id.,* at S8798, Amendment 1556.

23. Eric Schmitt, "Cheney Working to Block Legislation on Detainees," *New York Times,* July 24, 2005, A23.

24. 151 Cong. Rec. S8790.

25. *Id.*

26. *Id.,* at S8798, Amendment 1556.

27. *Id.,* at S8791, Letter to Senator McCain from Fourteen Retired Military Officials.

28. *Id.*

29. Josh White and R. Jeffrey Smith, "White House Aims to Block Legislation on De-

tainees," *Washington Post,* July 23, 2005, A1 (recounting lobbying efforts by White House); Eric Schmitt, "Cheney Working to Block Legislation on Detainees," *New York Times,* July 24, 2005.

30. White and Smith, "White House"; Sheryl Gay Stolberg, "As August Recess Looms, Congress Finds High Gear," *New York Times,* July 27, 2005, A18 (Frist tries to cut off debate).

31. Neil A. Lewis, "Guantanamo Detention Site is Being Transformed, U.S. Says," *New York Times,* Aug. 5, 2005, A8; Josh White and Robin Wright, "Afghanistan Agrees to Accept Detainees," *Washington Post,* Aug. 5, 2005, A1; Matthew Waxman, "Beyond Guantanamo," *Washington Post,* Aug. 20, 2005, A17.

32. Lewis, "Transformed" (quoting Commander Anne Reese).

33. *Padilla v. Hanft,* No. 05-533, Petition for Certiorari (filed Oct. 25, 2005); *Padilla v. Hanft,* 423 F.3d 386 (4th Cir. 2005).

34. *Padilla v. Hanft,* 432 F.3d 582, 583–85 (4th Cir. 2005).

35. *Id.,* at 583; *Padilla v. Hanft,* 423 F.3d 582, 582, n.1.

36. Reuters, "Bush Threatens Defense Bill Veto, Warning on Prisoners," *Washington Post,* Sept. 30, 2005 (renewed threat of veto by White House); Liz Sidoti, "Senate to Engage in Debate Over Detainees," Associated Press, Oct. 5, 2005 (McCain vows to press forward). A copy of the October 3, 2005, letter to Senator McCain from 28 retired military officials is available at http://www.humanrightsfirst.org/us_law/etn/pdf/mccain-072205.pdf. More than thirty editorials supporting Senator McCain's proposed amendments are available at http://www.humanrightsfirst.org/us_law/etn/pdf/edit-mccain-amend-081805.pdf, including editorials from the *Tucson Citizen, Washington Post, Miami Herald, New York Times, Newsday, Atlanta Journal-Constitution, Kansas City Star, St. Louis Post-Dispatch, Baltimore Sun, Minneapolis Star-Tribune, Oregonian, State* (South Carolina), *Salt Lake City Tribune,* and *Houston Chronicle.* See also Charles Babington and Shailagh Murray, "Senate Supports Interrogation Limits," *Washington Post,* Oct. 6, 2005, A1.

37. 151 Cong. Rec. S11114, Oct. 5, 2005, available at: http://frwebgate.access.gpo.gov/cgi-bin/getpage.cgi?dbname=2005_record&page=S11114&position=all. When Senator McCain offered his proposal in October, he combined both sections into a single amendment to the National Defense Authorization Act for fiscal 2006. In November, he offered an identical amendment to the Department of Defense Appropriations Act 2006. The text finally approved by Congress is as follows:

> *SEC. 1002. UNIFORM STANDARDS FOR THE INTERROGATION OF PERSONS UNDER THE DETENTION OF THE DEPARTMENT OF DEFENSE.*
>
> *(a) IN GENERAL.—No person in the custody or under the effective control of the Department of Defense or under detention in a Department of Defense facility shall be subject to any treatment or technique of interrogation not authorized by and listed in the United States Army Field Manual on Intelligence Interrogation.*
>
> *(b) APPLICABILITY.—Subsection (a) shall not apply to with respect to any person in the custody or under the effective control of the Department of Defense pursuant to a criminal law or immigration law of the United States.*
>
> *(c) CONSTRUCTION.—Nothing in this section shall be construed to affect the*

rights under the United States Constitution of any person in the custody or under the physical jurisdiction of the United States.

SEC. 1003. PROHIBITION ON CRUEL, INHUMAN, OR DEGRADING TREAT-MENT OR PUNISHMENT OF PERSONS UNDER CUSTODY OR CONTROL OF THE UNITED STATES GOVERNMENT.

(a) *IN GENERAL.—No individual in the custody or under the physical control of the United States Government, regardless of nationality or physical location, shall be subject to cruel, inhuman, or degrading treatment or punishment.*

(b) *CONSTRUCTION.—Nothing in this section shall be construed to impose any geographical limitation on the applicability of the prohibition against cruel, inhuman, or degrading treatment or punishment under this section.*

(c) *LIMITATION OF SUPERSEDER.—The provisions of this section shall not be superseded, except by a provision of law enacted after the date of the enactment of this Act which specifically repeals, modifies, or supersedes the provisions of this section.*

(d) *CRUEL, INHUMAN, OR DEGRADING TREATMENT OR PUNISHMENT DEFINED.—In this section, the term "cruel, inhuman, or degrading treatment or punishment" means the cruel, unusual, and inhumane treatment or punishment prohibited by the Fifth, Eighth, and Fourteenth Amendments to the Constitution of the United States, as defined in the United States Reservations, Declarations and Understandings to the United Nations Convention Against Torture and Other Forms of Cruel, Inhuman or Degrading Treatment or Punishment done at New York, December 10, 1984.*

See Department of Defense Appropriations Act, 2006, H.R. 2863, 109th Cong., 1st sess. (2005).

38. "Binding the Hands of Torturers," *New York Times,* Oct. 8, 2005, A14; Babington and Murray, "Senate Supports Interrogation Limits"; see also Eric Schmitt, "Senate Moves to Protect Military Prisoners Despite Veto Threat," *New York Times,* Oct. 6, 2005, A22.

39. "End the Abuse," *Washington Post,* Oct. 7, 2005, A22.

40. See, e.g., Douglas Jehl, "Report Warned C.I.A. on Tactics in Interrogation," *New York Times,* Nov. 9, 2005, A1; "Vice President for Torture," *Washington Post,* Oct. 26, 2005, A18; "Legalized Torture, Reloaded," *New York Times,* Oct. 26, 2005, A26.

41. 151 Cong. Rec. S12,699 (daily ed. Nov. 10, 2005).

42. 151 Cong. Rec. S12,727–33 (daily ed. Nov. 14, 2005).

43. H.R. Conf. Rep. No. 109–360, printed in 151 Cong. Rec. H12,833–35 (daily ed. Dec. 18, 2005); H.R. Conf. Rep. No. 109–359, printed in 151 Cong. Rec. H12,309–11 (daily ed. Dec. 18, 2005).

44. Eric Schmitt, "New Army Rules May Snarl Talks with McCain on Detainee Issue," *New York Times,* Dec. 14, 2005, A1.

45. *Id.*

46. Jehl, "Report Warned C.I.A."

47. Schmidt Report, 20.

48. President George W. Bush, statement on the signing of H.R. 2863, the Department of

Defense, Emergency Supplemental Appropriations to Address Hurricanes in the Gulf of Mexico, and Pandemic Influenza Act, 2006, Dec. 30, 2005, available at http://www.whitehouse.gov/news/releases/2005/12/20051230-8.html.

49. Charlie Savage, "Bush Could Bypass New Torture Ban," *Boston Globe*, Jan. 4, 2006, A1.

50. On February 6, 2006, California Democratic Senator Dianne Feinstein asked Attorney General Gonzales whether the president has "ever invoked this [inherent] authority with respect to any activity other than the . . . NSA surveillance program?" Gonzales said he was "not comfortable going down the road of saying yes or no as to what the President has or has not authorized." See "U.S. Senate Judiciary Committee Holds a Hearing on Wartime Executive Power and the NSA's Surveillance Authority," *Washington Post*, Feb. 6, 2006, transcript available at http://www.washingtonpost.com/wp-dyn/content/article/2006/02/06/AR2006020600931.html.

51. *Id.*

52. Jane Mayer, "The Memo," *New Yorker*, Feb. 27, 2006.

53. *Id.*

54. U.N. Commission on Human Rights, "Situation of detainees at Guantánamo Bay: Report of the Chairperson of the Working Group on Arbitrary Detention, Ms. Leila Zerrougui; the Special Rapporteur on the independence of judges and lawyers, Mr. Leandro Despouy; the Special Rapporteur on torture and other cruel, inhuman or degrading treatment or punishment, Mr. Manfred Nowak; the Special Rapporteur on freedom of religion or belief, Ms. Asma Jahangir and the Special Rapporteur on the right of everyone to the enjoyment of the highest attainable standard of physical and mental health, Mr. Paul Hunt," Feb. 16, 2006, available at http://www.ohchr.org/english/bodies/chr/docs/62chr/E.CN.4.2006.120_.pdf.

55. CNN, "Annan: Shut Guantanamo prison camp," Feb. 17, 2006.

56. BBC, "Tutu calls for Guantanamo closure," Feb. 17, 2006.

57. "Press Briefing by Scott McClellan," February 16, 2006, transcript available at http://www.whitehouse.gov/news/releases/2006/02/20060216-1.html#e.

58. Tim Golden, "Tough U.S. Steps in Hunger Strikes at Camp in Cuba," *New York Times*, Feb. 9, 2006, A01; Josh White and Carol D. Leonnig, "U.S. Cites Exception in Torture Ban; McCain Law May Not Apply to Cuba Prison," *Washington Post*, Mar. 3, 2006, A04.

59. Josh White and Carol D. Leonnig, "McCain Law May Not Apply to Cuba Prison"; Neil Lewis, "Guantánamo Detainee Seeks Court Action," *New York Times*, Mar. 3, 2006.

INDEX